FROM NUCLEAR MILITARY
STRATEGY TO A
WORLD WITHOUT WAR

The Institute of War and Peace Studies
School of International and Public Affairs
Columbia University

This book was prepared under the sponsorship of the Institute of War and Peace Studies of Columbia University's School of International and Public Affairs.

In addition to *From Nuclear Military Strategy to a World Without War,* the Institute of War and Peace Studies has sponsored seven other books by Roger Hilsman: *To Move a Nation: The Politics of Foreign Policy in the Administration of John F. Kennedy,* 1967; *The Crouching Future: International Politics and U.S. Foreign Policy, a Forecast,* 1975; *The Politics of Governing America,* 1985; *The Politics of Policy Making in Defense and Foreign Affairs,* 1987, 1990, 1993; *American Guerrilla: My War Behind the Japanese Lines,* 1990; *George Bush Vs. Saddam Hussein, Military Success! Political Failure?* 1992; and *The Cuban Missile Crisis: The Struggle Over Policy,* 1996.

The Institute of War and Peace Studies sponsors the publication of works in international relations, international institutions, and American foreign and military policy. Among its studies of policy and the policy process by other authors are *The Common Defense* by Samuel P. Huntington; *Strategy, Politics, and Defense Budgets* by Warner R. Schilling, Paul Y. Hammond, and Glenn H. Snyder; *Planning, Prediction, and Policy-Making in Foreign Affairs* by Robert L. Rothstein; *The Illogic of American Nuclear Strategy* by Robert Jervis; *How Nations Behave* by Louis Henkin; and *Economic Statecraft* by David Baldwin.

FROM NUCLEAR MILITARY STRATEGY TO A WORLD WITHOUT WAR

A History and a Proposal

Roger Hilsman

PRAEGER

Westport, Connecticut
London

Library of Congress Cataloging-in-Publication Data

Hilsman, Roger.
    From nuclear military strategy to a world without war : a history
and a proposal / Roger Hilsman.
        p.   cm.
    Includes bibliographical references and index.
    ISBN 0–275–96242–3 (alk. paper)
    1. Nuclear warfare.   2. United States—Military policy.
3. International organization.   I. Title.
U263.H55   1999
355.02'17—dc21   98–46801

British Library Cataloguing in Publication Data is available.

Copyright ©1999 by Roger Hilsman

Library of Congress Catalog Card Number: 98–46801
ISBN: 0–275–96242–3

First published in 1999

Praeger Publishers, 88 Post Road West, Westport, CT 06881
An imprint of Greenwood Publishing Group, Inc.
www.praeger.com

Printed in the United States of America

The paper used in this book complies with the
Permanent Paper Standard issued by the National
Information Standards Organization (Z39.48–1984).

10   9   8   7   6   5   4   3   2   1

In the hope that it might in some way help to make their world a more peaceful one than that of either their grandparents or their parents, this book is dedicated to the children of Hoyt, Amy, Ashby, and Sarah— Eleanor's and my grandchildren—Michael Hilsman, Joseph and Christina Kastely, Patrick and William Hilsman, and Sophia Wakoff

Contents

Preface

The debate about how peace might be maintained in an age of missiles armed with nuclear warheads has revolved mainly around four approaches. All of these approaches will be analyzed in detail in the chapters that follow, but a brief description is necessary here.

One is the traditional military approach. Its emphasis is on deterrence—epitomized by the aphorism, "If you would maintain peace, prepare for war." But many of its advocates also believe that if deterrence fails, it will be possible to win a nuclear war. What is required, they argue, is a large stockpile of the very best weapons and a strategy that aims at destroying the enemy's capacity to inflict damage on one's own forces, economy, and people, or at least to minimize that damage.

Of recent presidents, the only one who came out strongly in public for the military approach was George Herbert Walker Bush, in a statement made when he was vice president. When he was asked, "How do you win in a nuclear exchange?" Bush's answer was, "You have a survivability of command and control, survivability of industrial potential, protection of a percentage of your citizens, and you have a capability that inflicts more damage on the opposition than it can inflict upon you. That's the way you can have a winner."[1]

A second approach is the Strategic Defense Initiative advocated by President Reagan and nicknamed "Star Wars." Reagan's hope was that Western technology could build a shield in outer space that would destroy incoming missiles in mid-flight.

A third approach is the so-called "no first use." In 1982, Robert McNamara, McGeorge Bundy, George Kennan, and Gerard Smith jointly proposed that the United States should deny itself the option of being the first to use nuclear weapons. However, this renunciation would be coupled with an increase in conventional forces, mainly in the NATO area, massive enough to match the much greater strength the Soviet Union then enjoyed in conventional forces. McNamara elaborated this view in a book, *Blundering Into Disaster*, published in 1986.[2]

Although McNamara favored negotiating with the Soviets on arms control, he did not believe that arms control agreements would ever succeed in eliminating nuclear weapons. This led him to two conclusions. The first was that nuclear weapons would continue to be a necessary part of the American defenses. The second was that the only rational purpose nuclear weapons could serve would be to deter the other side from using nuclear weapons.

In 1993, McGeorge Bundy, Admiral William J. Crowe, former chairman of the Joint Chiefs of Staff and later Ambassador to the Court of St. James, and Sidney D. Drell, a physicist and arms control specialist, proposed a variation on "no first use." The label they gave to this strategy was "defensive last resort." This was a public policy that would permit the United States to be the first to use nuclear weapons, but only when faced with defeat in a defensive war.[3]

A fourth approach is arms control. The history of the negotiations on arms control gives little encouragement. But when Reagan and Gorbachev signed the Intermediate Nuclear Forces treaty in 1988, many observers began to hope that it might be possible to negotiate a gradual reduction in nuclear forces on both sides until the possibility of nuclear war was reduced to a level very nearly approaching zero. When Bush and Yeltsin signed their 1992 agreement reducing both sides' stockpiles of intercontinental ballistic missiles, hopes rose once more.

But doubt quickly followed. The agreement between Bush and Yeltsin called for each side to reduce their stockpiles of long-range missile warheads from about 11,250 each to between 3,800 and 4,200 each. But, as argued in Chapter 14, it would take only about 200 warheads to destroy the seventy largest metropolitan areas in the United States, where over 50 percent of the American people live, and about 300 warheads to destroy the somewhat larger number of urban areas that is home to 50 percent of the Russian people. So what good does it do to reduce the stockpiles of nuclear warheads to 3,800 to 4,200 each? Both sides could still lose half their people and almost all their industry.

Some observers argued that the reduction agreed to by Bush and Yeltsin might easily turn out to be more dangerous than none at all. It might well give a false sense of security that would lead the participants to neglect their efforts to find a real solution to the problem of nuclear war. The argument was that it is not weapons that *cause* war, but political tensions.

For this very reason the reduction in political tensions between the United States and the Soviet Union, which began with Gorbachev's moves to withdraw from Eastern Europe, raised even more hope than the arms control agreements. For two generations the NATO and Warsaw pact countries had formidable forces armed with both conventional and battlefield nuclear weapons facing each other along what Winston Churchill called the "Iron Curtain." Almost any crisis could have escalated into conventional fighting. If one or the other side began to lose, the next step would have been an exchange of battlefield nuclear weapons. Within hours one side or the other would have then had to face a choice between disaster or going even more quickly to an attack on the other side's homeland. The result could easily have been an Armageddon of mutual annihilation.

So the series of agreements between the two sides, the mutual withdrawal of conventional forces, the unification of Germany, the increasing independence of the countries of Eastern Europe, and the ferment among the minority peoples of the Soviet Union and its subsequent breakup all significantly reduced the tension between the East and the West and thus the probability of war between the United States and Russia. The Cold War had come to an end.

Here at long last seemed to be an opportunity unparalleled in history. But again doubt quickly followed. Tensions had been reduced, but the reduction might be only temporary. Even worse, the reduction might be limited only to the tensions between the United States and Russia, the principal heir of the former Soviet Union.

Indeed, one result of the reduction of tensions between what used to be called the two superpowers seemed to be to unleash other tensions—in the Middle East, the Balkans, and Asia. And the ominous fact was that these tensions could lead not only to war but to nuclear war. The United States, Great Britain, France, China, and Russia all have nuclear weapons. So do India, Pakistan, and Israel. And the evidence is strong that several other states have made or are making an effort to build a nuclear stockpile—North Korea, Libya, Iran, and, until the Gulf War brought its effort to at least a temporary halt, Iraq.

Historically, war has served a central and essential function in human affairs. Wars and civil wars have been used to bring about—or to prevent—political and social change. War was the instrument for creating nation-states out of feudal principalities or by breaking up dynastic empires. War has been an instrument for spreading religion. It has been an instrument for spreading ideology, using the word in the sense of a systematic set of beliefs, such as capitalism, Nazism, or communism. War was the major vehicle for extending the dominance of Western civilization, for spreading its high valuation of modernization, its technology, and its mode of life. War has been the means for adding to the power of one state at the expense of another. Hitler and the Japanese militarists used war to try to create a new kind of empire, a new political and ideological dominance, and a new distribution of power. The Allies responded with war to prevent them from succeeding. War and civil war have replaced kings and emperors with parliaments and presidents. War and civil war have also replaced parliaments and presidents with storm troopers and dictators. War and civil war have shifted the locus of power within societies as well as between them. Warfare, in a word, has been the midwife of social and political change, for both good and evil. As a consequence, reducing the incidence of war depends upon finding a substitute for war that will perform the function of midwifing social and political change without violence.

In the history of humankind the only reliable instrument for reducing the incidence of war in any particular region has been government. Civil war may still occur in a territory with a single government, but throughout history, since the rise of the nation-state, the number of civil wars has been a small fraction of the number of wars between states. Since its inception, for example, the United States has fought seven major international wars and several minor ones, but only one civil war.

The reasons are two. First is the practical difficulty that rival groups inside a state have in acquiring the means for waging war. When labor and management quarrel, their quarrels are sometimes violent and sometimes people get killed. But it is difficult for either side to acquire warplanes, tanks, and artillery—the kind of weapons needed for the large-scale, organized violence that is war.

The second reason that wars have been less frequent within states than between them is that for most disagreements or grievances other arbiters exist within a state that are more or less satisfactory alternatives to the risk inherent in an attempt at large-scale violence. Principally, these alternatives are law and politics.

All states have legal systems that provide an opportunity to redress certain kinds of grievances and to settle certain kinds of disputes. The law may cover a wider range of disputes in one country than in another, and it may be more just and impartially enforced in one country than in another. But in even the most authoritarian of states, law provides an alternative to the use of force for certain kinds of disputes, depending on the particular state.

All states also have political systems, and no matter whether it is authoritarian or democratic, a political system serves as an alternative arbiter to war for most groups in the society that have the potential for organized violence. The point is that a political system provides the means by which one group or the other can acquire the power to get its way in a disagreement without the use of large-scale, organized violence. In one state the political system may involve elections and in another behind-the-scenes maneuvering for allies in the secret police and the army in preparation for a coup d'etat, but the social function is the same. In both the election and the coup there may also be violence—whether campus riots, street fighting, or the murder of a king in the palace corridor—but it is not the large-scale, organized violence of war.

The midwife of social and political change *between* states has been neither law nor politics, but war. What is ominous is that while some progress has been made in arms control agreements, very little has been made in building the kinds of international political institutions that would midwife social and political change between states as governments have done within states by legislation, the courts, and the political system.

The thesis of this book is that all four of the proposals that have been described here for maintaining peace in a nuclear age fail to grasp the significance of nuclear weapons and missiles. To be specific, they do not recognize and include in their analyses two fairly obvious points.

First, no matter which approach is pursued and no matter how vigorously, as long as both sides maintain nuclear arsenals and until worldwide political institutions are formed to midwife social and political change, nuclear war remains not just a possibility, but a probability. Indeed, if a long enough time span is taken, nuclear war is not only probable but actually inevitable. Sooner or later a crisis never intended to result in war, such as the Cuban missile crisis, will spiral out of control.

Second, war between nuclear powers can no longer serve the social and political functions that war has served in the past; war can no longer be, as Clausewitz maintained, merely a continuation of policy by other means. What the four approaches for maintaining peace just described have in common is that they are all attempts to return to a world in which war can still serve its former social and political functions at an acceptable cost in lives and treasure. Although each approach advocates a different route to reach it, their common—although unacknowledged—goal is, simply, to *rehabilitate* war.

Abolishing nuclear weapons while maintaining war as an institution is a will-o'-the-wisp. The United States succeeded in inventing nuclear weapons in the midst of a war. In fact, as Richard Rhodes, author of *The Making of the Atomic Bomb* and *Dark Sun* about the making of the hydrogen bomb, says, "every nation that has attempted to build an atomic weapon in the half-century since the discovery of nuclear fission has succeeded on the first try." In any war between major powers both sides would feel compelled to manufacture nuclear weapons as quickly as they possibly could, if only as a deterrent to the other side, and now that the know-how is so well known and so widespread they would both succeed. A panel on arms control convened in 1953 by Secretary of State Dean Acheson and chaired by J. Robert Oppenheimer with McGeorge Bundy as secretary reached this same conclusion: "Even if some reasonably complete international control of atomic energy should be established, knowledge would persist, and it is hard to see how there could be any major war in which one side or another would not eventually make and use atomic bombs."[4]

One or two wars between major powers might end without a resort to nuclear weapons, but sooner or later a war that began without nuclear weapons would spiral out of control and one side or the other would feel compelled to resort to its newly made nuclear weapons.

So it seems obvious that in an age of bombs and missiles and the knowledge to arm them with nuclear warheads a goal of merely rehabilitating war is not enough. As Albert Einstein is supposed to have said, the atomic bomb has changed everything except our way of thinking. But somehow humankind *must* learn to think beyond war.

This book is an attempt at that task. It gives a history of thinking about nuclear military strategy. Seeking lessons, it briefly examines the one occasion when the world came very close to nuclear war—the Cuban missile crisis. It looks at the social and political functions that war has performed in the past. It speculates about how those functions might be served without war. Finally, it suggests a series of steps, including an interim nuclear military strategy, that might make it easier for humankind to find a way to work toward a world without war of any kind.

These suggestions are not likely to provide any final answers. The hope is that they might at least help in pointing the way. If more people understand the impasse humankind has now reached, someone may think of something better than deterring war by preparing for it, by Star Wars, by "no first use" or "defensive last resort," or by arms control agreements taken alone—all of which are nothing more than attempts to turn back the clock to a less unforgiving time.

NOTES

1. Robert Scheer, *With Enough Shovels: Reagan, Bush and Nuclear War* (New York: Vintage Books, 1982, 1983), 261 ff.

2. McGeorge Bundy, George Kennan, Robert McNamara, and Gerard Smith, "Nuclear Weapons and the Atlantic Alliance," *Foreign Affairs*, Spring 1982; McNamara, *Blundering Into Disaster* (Pantheon Books, 1986).

3. McGeorge Bundy, William J. Crowe, and Sidney D. Drell, "Reducing Nuclear Danger," *Foreign Affairs*, Spring, 1993; McGeorge Bundy, William J. Crowe, and Sidney D. Drell, *Reducing the Nuclear Danger: The Road Away from the Brink* (New York: Council on Foreign Relations Press, 1993).

4. *The New York Times*, 17–18 April 1953.

Acknowledgments

I originally intended the title of this book to be *A Layman's Guide to Nuclear Military Strategy*. My idea was to honor the memory of Bernard Brodie, since the first of his many books on strategy, published in the early days of World War II, was entitled *A Layman's Guide to Naval Strategy*. Although Alfred T. Mahan was the first American to write extensively on strategy, it was Brodie who pioneered the subject as a legitimate concern of university research and teaching and thus a legitimate attempt by scholars to influence strategy. I studied under Brodie at Yale in the period immediately following World War II, and his guidance enabled me to continue an interest in strategy and defense policy originally awakened when I was a cadet at West Point.

That awakening happened on the opening day of a class in military history taught by Colonel Max S. Johnson, later a Major General and head of the Army War College. He was that rare creature, a military intellectual, and he thrilled and delighted me on the opening day by saying, "Gentlemen, welcome to Military History. Until today you have dealt with squads, platoons, and companies. Here you will deal with nothing smaller than a division!"

As it happened, however, as I began to understand what the consequences of the marriage of nuclear weapons and missiles would be, the purpose the book was intended to serve changed dramatically. The result was an entirely different book, requiring an entirely different title.

The book draws on several of my earlier books. It also draws on a number of my articles in periodicals such as *Foreign Affairs, World Politics*, the *Political Science Quarterly*, and others.

I am particularly grateful to Charles E. Lindblom, Robert A. Dahl, Alan Platt, Colonel William E. Naylor, Jr., Warner Schilling, Vladimir Shamberg, and Diane Bockar, all of whom read the manuscript and gave me extremely valuable suggestions. My thanks also go to David M. Burkoff, who helped enormously with library research at the last minute when the deadline was upon me.

Finally, I owe a very special thanks to Eleanor H. Hilsman, who not only read the manuscript at least three times and offered a host of invaluable suggestions, but also served as research assistant from start to finish and gave unstinting moral support.

PART I

THE FIRST ATTEMPTS AT NUCLEAR STRATEGY

Chapter 1

The Manhattan Project and
Early Strategic Thinking

In 1934, Emilio Segrè and Enrico Fermi, working in Rome, Italy, bombarded uranium with slow neutrons and reported that they had observed fission —that the uranium had broken apart.[1] But anything beyond this glimpse eluded them.

In 1938, Otto Hahn, a chemist at the Kaiser Wilhelm Institute in Berlin, wrote a letter to Lise Meitner, a noted physicist who was living in Sweden as a refugee from Nazi Germany, to tell her that he had repeated Fermi's experiment and had identified barium as one of the lighter elements in the residue. This clue enabled Meitner to work out and announce early in 1939 the theory of nuclear fission—that when an uranium atom was hit by a neutron it would split into atoms of lighter weight and that this would be accompanied by an enormous release of energy.

The implications were staggering. If enough neutrons were also released when the uranium atom split, they would in turn split other uranium atoms in the pile of uranium around it, and a chain reaction would ensue. The energy released could be used to run steam engines or it could be used to make an explosive of fantastic, almost unbelievable power.

These implications were obvious to any physicist anywhere in the world. Indeed, J. Robert Oppenheimer, who became the director of the Los Alamos laboratories that created the atomic bomb, was fond of telling a story that illustrates the point. He was discussing the news of Meitner's announcement with a faculty colleague in a bar in Berkeley, California, that was frequented by both faculty and students. Oppenheimer's colleague expressed some doubt that physicists everywhere would immediately deduce that an atomic bomb was possible. The two of them made a bet, called over a beginning student in the physics department, outlined Meitner's theory, and asked him what he thought it meant. "Why," the student replied after hesitating only a moment or two, "it means that a stupendous bomb can be made—an atomic bomb."

GETTING THE AMERICAN GOVERNMENT'S ATTENTION

In the next few months, physicists, and especially physicists who were refugees from Nazi Germany, were desperate to persuade the American government that it should try to build an atomic bomb before Hitler's Germany did. They asked Albert Einstein, the most prestigious scientist of them all, to write President Roosevelt a letter urging the attempt. One of Roosevelt's economic advisers who was also one of his personal friends, Alexander Sachs, was also a friend of the physicists, and they asked him to deliver the letter to the president in person.

Sachs took the letter to Roosevelt in October 1939. Sachs says that the letter alone did not seem to convince Roosevelt, who knew nothing of physics, but that he, Sachs, talked and talked, and Roosevelt's face finally "lit with comprehension." Sachs suggests that Roosevelt understood that the physicists might be wrong and that a bomb could not really be built. He also saw that they might succeed but too late to help in winning the war. But he understood that the United States could not take a chance that Hitler would be the first to get such a monstrously formidable weapon.

As McGeorge Bundy has pointed out, Sachs may be taking more credit than he deserved for getting Roosevelt to authorize the development of an atomic bomb.[2] The only action that Roosevelt took following his meeting with Sachs was to set up a committee under Lyman Briggs of the Bureau of Standards to keep in touch with the scientists and their work.

It was apparently Vannevar Bush who really got the U.S. government actively interested in developing the atomic bomb. Bush, formerly of the Massachusetts Institute of Technology, was president of the Carnegie Institute in Washington. A small group of scientists, including Bush, became convinced that several important scientific advances that could help with the war effort would come about only if the government took a more active part. Bush persuaded Harry Hopkins of this, and Hopkins arranged for Bush to talk to Roosevelt on June 12, 1940. Persuaded, Roosevelt created the National Defense Research Committee to study potential scientific advances that might contribute to the war effort and made Bush its chairman.

Bush's committee worked for a year. Its report, submitted on July 16, 1941, was devoted mainly to radar, which made a huge contribution to winning the war. But the report also mentioned a study, codenamed *Maud*, being made by a British committee of scientists on the possibility of making an extraordinary explosive by means of atomic fission. The report suggested that if the British study showed that making an atomic bomb was indeed feasible, the matter should be placed before the President. In the meantime, the British committee working on *Maud* had finished fifteen months of work. They had made a detailed, scientific study, and their report was persuasive—that a bomb could indeed be built in time to influence the outcome of the war. This report was made known to Bush and his committee, and they were completely convinced. Bush sought an appointment with Roosevelt on October 9, 1941, and Roosevelt made the decision to go ahead.

Although Roosevelt left no record of the reasons for his decision, it seems clear that the possibility that Hitler's Germany would make the bomb first was paramount. The irony is that the evidence now available is overwhelmingly persuasive that Nazi Germany never even considered trying to make a bomb.

The American physicists and intelligence experts concluded that if Germany did make an effort to build an atomic bomb, it would be centered around one man, Werner Heisenberg, a Nobel laureate in physics for his discovery of the principle of uncertainty. Accordingly, as described in a book by Thomas Powers published in 1993, the Office of Strategic Services (OSS), the U.S. wartime intelligence agency, first developed plans to kidnap Heisenberg, and later simply to kill him.[3] When Heisenberg delivered a lecture in Switzerland in December 1944, Moe Berg, who had been a major league catcher and was at the time a special agent of the OSS, was in the audience with a gun in his pocket. Berg, who had some knowledge of physics, was under instructions to make a judgment about whether or not Heisenberg was involved with a German attempt to make a bomb, and if the answer was yes, to kill him on the spot. Berg listened, but did nothing. A few days later Berg wangled an invitation to a dinner party for Heisenberg, engaged him in conversation, and then escorted him back to his hotel. Berg concluded that the prospects for Germany building a bomb were very dim and that in fact Heisenberg was ready to defect to the Allies. Whether Heisenberg was ready to defect is questionable, but Powers is convinced that he was in fact doing his best to divert the Nazis away from the idea of making a bomb and to delay any such effort.

Heisenberg himself, undoubtedly motivated at least in part by a desire to defend himself from criticism by other Germans, argued after the war that Germany made no attempt at all to build a bomb for several very practical reasons.[4] First, Germany did not have the resources that the United States did in terms of men, material, and industrial potential, and even with the advantage in all three the United States did not succeed in producing a bomb until after Germany had been defeated. Second, the German industrial machine was stretched to the limit in providing the conventional sinews of war. Third, the German homeland, unlike America, was under constant air attack, and the enormous industrial facilities necessary to build a bomb could not have been effectively protected. Finally, the men responsible for German war policy expected an early decision in the war and "any major project which did not promise quick returns was specifically forbidden." Accordingly, Heisenberg says, the experts made no attempt to persuade the supreme command that Germany should make the effort.

McGeorge Bundy finds Heisenberg's account completely persuasive and adds a persuasive argument of his own—the psychology of Adolf Hitler.[5] As Bundy says, although Hitler was capable of leaping on board fantastic projects—the V-2 rocket is an example—he felt most comfortable with the weapons he had known as a corporal in World War I. Hitler also called nuclear physics "Jewish physics," and his attitude toward it was "hopelessly confused by his pathological and murderous anti-Semitism."

THE MANHATTAN PROJECT

Roosevelt's decision resulted in the Manhattan Project, a broad-gauge attempt to build the bomb with secret funds. I. I. Rabi and Leo Szilard did much of the early theoretical work at Columbia University. Enrico Fermi, working under the old football stadium at the University of Chicago, built for the first time ever a uranium pile and achieved a chain reaction. Plants were built in Hanford, Washington, and Oak Ridge, Tennessee, each using a different method to try to separate the less stable uranium 235 isotope from the more common but stable uranium 238. The hope was that the less stable U-235 would provide the material to make a bomb.

J. Robert Oppenheimer was given the job of putting together all the pieces of the puzzle of how to make a bomb, and he assembled physicists and engineers from both the United States and Great Britain at Los Alamos, a remote and isolated mesa in New Mexico. An Army general, Leslie Groves, who knew nothing of physics but was a good organizer, was named to be the administrator.

Over the next few years, the physicists worked hard, and on July 16, 1945, they were ready to test a bomb at Alamogordo in the desert. As they were setting up the test, Enrico Fermi announced that he had been studying the possibility that the incredibly intense heat of the bomb might ignite the atmosphere and that he was prepared to handicap the odds on two bets. One bet was that the heat would spread to destroy all life on earth. The second bet was that it would dissipate and so destroy life only in the state of New Mexico.

General Groves had anticipated that the bomb might generate more energy than the physicists thought and that the test might kill the people observing it. So he had prepared a cover story for the press saying that Oppenheimer and the other physicists had been vacationing at Oppenheimer's ranch, which was not far away, and had been killed when an ammunition dump nearby had exploded accidentally. But Groves was not prepared for the total catastrophe that Fermi was suggesting. Finally, he decided that Fermi was indulging himself in some macabre joke. A number of senior physicists present did not agree—they understood that Fermi was *not* joking.

When all the preparations for the explosion had been made, the tension in the blockhouse where the scientists and technicians had gathered was excruciating. Different people reacted in different ways. George Kistiakowsky found his qualms about building a bomb becoming almost unbearable, and he went about pouring out his unhappiness to others.

The countdown began, and everyone fell silent. Suddenly a very, very bright light appeared at the test site. The bomb had worked.

Samuel Alison, whom Oppenheimer had appointed to ride herd on everyone else to make sure the test bomb was ready on time, remembers mumbling to himself, "Still alive. No atmospheric ignition." General Thomas Farrell, General Groves's deputy, was ecstatic, pounding on Alison's back and shouting congratulations. Alison began to share Kistiakowsky's doubts. "They're going to take this thing over," he wailed to James Conant, "and fry *hundreds* of Japanese!"

Oppenheimer's reaction, in keeping with his complex personality, was more convoluted. He had learned Sanskrit in order to read the Bhagavad-Gita in the original. In this holy book of Hinduism, two great armies are lined up for the final battle in a civil war. On the eve of the battle, the greatest warrior of one side, Prince Arjuna, shrinks from the thought that on the morrow he must kill his fellow humans, including relatives and friends. The Lord Krishna, disguised as Arjuna's chariot driver, explains why he must fight with all his strength—making the central point of Hinduism that what is evil depends upon one's caste and role in life, and since it is a warrior's role to fight, the act of killing is not an evil but a duty. Then Krishna suddenly reveals himself to Arjuna as a god in all his dazzling radiance, as both the creator and the destroyer of all things. Oppenheimer later said that when the bomb went off, he was in a dreamy reverie, induced in part by physical exhaustion. He remembered wondering if Krishna was in the center of the bomb's inferno. Later Oppenheimer said that as he became conscious of those around him again, "There floated through my mind a line from the Bhagavad-Gita 'I am become death, the shatterer of worlds.' I think we all had this feeling more or less."[6]

COMPOSITION OF THE BOMB

Since only one isotope of uranium—U-235—undergoes fission when it is hit by a neutron, the bomb had to be made of the U-235 isotope. However, this form of uranium is very rare; only one U-235 isotope occurs in nature in every 100 of the more plentiful U-238 isotope. Since the two are chemically identical, a nonchemical separation process is needed. Several different separation processes were launched, but the most successful was gaseous diffusion, done at the plant in Oak Ridge, Tennessee. However, the process was expensive and the yield was not great. By 1945, only enough of the uranium U-235 isotope had been produced for the test bomb at Alamogordo and one other bomb.

Matter in nature consists of ninety-two elements, of which uranium is the heaviest. For some time, physicists had speculated that other, even heavier elements were possible, and their speculations were verified during the research on the atomic bomb when two more, heavier elements were more or less by accident invented—element 93, named neptunium, and element 94, named plutonium.

Neptunium decayed too fast to be of practicable use in a bomb, but the plutonium isotope 239 turned out to be ideal. Moreover, plutonium 239 could be manufactured in quantity in chain reactors, such as the one Fermi had developed at Chicago, by bombarding the more plentiful uranium 238 with neutrons. When the test at Alamogordo was completed the United States had enough plutonium for a third bomb. However, the physicists could not be absolutely certain that something might not go wrong with the second uranium bomb, and the mechanism for exploding a plutonium bomb had not yet been tested.

The mechanism of the uranium bomb was a sort of cannon that fired one subcritical hunk of uranium into another, thus creating a critical mass under enough pressure to achieve a chain reaction and a nuclear explosion. The plutonium bomb, on the other hand, used the principle of "implosion." Conventional explosives were positioned around a sphere of plutonium which in turn surrounded a beryllium core. When triggered, the conventional explosives crushed the plutonium into a critical mass, again under enough pressure to create a chain reaction and a nuclear explosion.

However, the uranium bomb had worked—and it had not ignited the atmosphere. What next?

THE "DECISION" TO DROP THE BOMB

Much later, Oppenheimer said, "We always assumed that if bombs were needed they would be used." Bureaucratic momentum took over. President Truman had been informed of the progress on the bomb. In May, a committee had been set up to consider atomic policy—the "Interim Committee," since a more permanent body would have to be created by legislation. The chairman was Henry L. Stimson, secretary of war, former secretary of state, and undoubtedly the most prestigious member of Truman's administration. About one hour of a six-hour session of the committee was devoted to the question of dropping bombs on Japan. Germany had already been defeated.

The committee discussed the question of whether the Japanese should be given prior warning. Oppenheimer played the role of the pure scientist (Nuell Pharr Davis, in his book *Lawrence and Oppenheimer*, describes the part that Oppenheimer played less charitably as the role of the "idiot savant").[7] Oppenheimer testified that either or both of the two bombs that the scientists expected to be ready if the test worked might actually turn out to be a dud. In any case, even if the bombs worked, the scientists could not guarantee the force of the explosion. The committee agreed that if warning was given and the bombs failed, the Japanese would probably fight even harder.

Other possibilities were that if warned the Japanese might go to extraordinary lengths to shoot down the delivery plane or even bring American prisoners into the target area. On the other hand, surprise would maximize the psychological effect and increase the possibility that the Japanese would surrender. However, it should be noted that a very short warning that named not just Hiroshima but, say, several cities as possible targets would have considerably lessened the possibility of countermoves, and a warning would have certainly improved the American political position for building a stable peace. But no one thought of this possibility.

In any case, the loss of life would probably be no greater than in the incendiary bombing of Tokyo. That raid had created a fire storm whose terrible winds sucking air into the conflagration knocked down buildings over a huge area, hurling debris—and people—into the inferno to feed the flames.

The conclusion of the committee was not only that the two bombs should be dropped without warning, but also that they should not be used on purely military targets. To achieve the greatest possible psychological impact each bomb should be dropped on a "vital war plant employing a large number of workers and closely surrounded by workers' houses."

General Marshall seems not to have taken a large role in the decision to drop the bomb. At first he thought the bomb should be used against a purely military target, such as a naval installation. Then he thought it might be used against a large war industry. In either case, Marshall believed a warning of some kind should be given in advance that would permit the workers to be evacuated. But he apparently did not push hard for either of these alternatives, and acquiesced in the decision to attack Hiroshima and Nagasaki without warning.[8]

In fact, only two people made a serious effort during the various deliberations in Washington to argue the case for warning. One was Ralph Bard, undersecretary of the Navy and a member of the committee. Although he had agreed to the original recommendation that the bombs should be dropped without warning, he changed his mind a few days later and suggested that the Japanese be given some general information about the bomb two or three days in advance. The other person was John J. McCloy, then assistant secretary of the Army. He not only argued that the Japanese should be warned but that an attempt should be made to try to induce them to surrender so that the bomb would not have to be used at all.[9]

McCloy says that he had several long talks with Joseph Grew, the undersecretary of state who had been ambassador to Japan, and that Grew's appraisal of the attitudes of the Japanese made a deep impression on him: "In short, Grew persuaded me that we would have nothing to lose by warning the Japanese of the cataclysmic consequences of the weapon we possessed and indicating that we would be prepared to allow Japan to continue as a constitutional monarchy with reasonable access to raw materials so that the Japanese could achieve a viable economy, provided they surrendered their armed forces."

The decision to drop the atomic bomb on Japan was made at a White House meeting called for June 18, 1945, at which the president, the secretary of war, and the joint chiefs of staff were to be present. The subject of the meeting was not whether to use the atomic bomb, but when and where an invasion of the main Japanese islands should take place.

The night before the meeting, Henry Stimson, the secretary of war, told John J. McCloy, the assistant secretary, that he was not feeling well and asked McCloy to attend in his place. They discussed at length not only the problem of an invasion, but whether the atomic bomb should be used. As it turned out, at the last minute Stimson decided to attend the meeting, but with the president's permission he asked McCloy to remain.

At the meeting there was a discussion of a blockade and a continuation of the bombing as alternatives to an invasion. General Marshall, with the support of Admiral King, argued that neither would be effective and recommended an invasion of the southern island of Kyushu as a preliminary to an attack on the main island of Honshu. No mention was made of the atomic bomb—probably because a number of people were present who did not have the necessary security clearance for such a discussion.

President Truman gave his permission for an attack on Kyushu, and as people were packing up to leave, he noticed McCloy and said, "McCloy, you didn't express yourself, and nobody gets out of this room without standing up and being counted. Do you think I have any reasonable alternative to the decision that has just been made?"

McCloy said that he *did* think that there was an alternative and that they all ought to have their heads examined if they did not seek some way of ending the war other than by a conventional attack and landing. McCloy said that he thought a political solution would not only be honorable but highly desirable in view of the expected casualties. The American superiority, both physically and morally, was fantastic—particularly because we had the atomic bomb. In his account of the meeting, McCloy said that his mention of the bomb, even in that high circle, was "like mentioning Skull and Bones in good Yale society."

The president asked McCloy to spell out what he meant. McCloy said that the president should send a strong communication to the Emperor describing our overwhelming military superiority and demanding a full surrender. The communication should say that the United States would recognize Japan's right to continue as a nation after ridding itself of the elements that had brought the country such destruction. It should also (as Grew had suggested) say that the Mikado could continue but only as a constitutional monarch, and that the country would continue to have access to raw materials. If no offer of surrender was forthcoming, McCloy continued, the United States should notify the Japanese that we had a weapon that could destroy an entire city in one blow, and we would be compelled to employ it. McCloy said he was prepared to use the term "atom bomb," but if the prevailing air of secrecy prevented using that term, then other words could be used, provided they were "graphic enough to be more compelling than the threat of Hitler's secret weapons had been."

President Truman said that what McCloy had said was in the nature of what he was seeking and that McCloy should take up the matter with James F. Byrnes, who at that time was assistant to the president. McCloy did so immediately, but found that Byrnes opposed the proposal because it "might be considered a weakness on our part." Byrnes said that he might not insist on treating the Emperor as a war criminal but he would oppose any "deal" as a concomitant of a demand for surrender. Accordingly, as McCloy says, the communication sent from Potsdam did not mention the bomb or the status of the Emperor.[10]

McCloy did not attend the Potsdam meetings, but he was told that when Stalin was informed about the bomb he said, "Well, that's fine. Let's use it. What's the next item on the agenda?"[11]

In the meantime, a number of physicists were becoming uneasy about the morality of using the bomb. Several working in Chicago signed a petition suggesting that the bomb be dropped in the presence of a group of international observers on a desert island or some other place that would minimize the casualties. They sent the petition to Groves and Stimson. Groves's reaction was to bury it. He was convinced, as he said, that if the bomb was not used Congress would launch an investigation that would blame them all "for the blood of our boys shed uselessly." I have found no record of what Stimson thought. In any case, no one could think of a demonstration that they were sure would be convincing to the Japanese.

Truman was in the midst of preparations to meet with Churchill and Stalin at Potsdam, and the record *is* clear that Stimson hesitated to fire up the government for a full-scale, top-level meeting to address the question unless he could be given firmer assurances that the bomb would actually work. So he sent the petition to Oppenheimer and Fermi at Los Alamos asking, again, whether they were sure that the bomb would work before he raised the issue with Truman.

Oppenheimer and Fermi had no knowledge of the military situation and thus no reason to challenge the need for an invasion. In their response they said that the physicists were divided and that, in any case, physicists had no special competence on the moral question. They then reaffirmed their judgment that on technical grounds the bombs could not be guaranteed to work and that if they were used there should therefore be no warning.

Bureaucratic momentum continued. Stimson informed Truman of the committee's actions and also told him that if the test bomb worked an invasion of Japan might not be necessary. Although no one knows where he got his figures, Stimson also told Truman that an invasion, which was scheduled for November, would cost a million American casualties, not to mention Japanese casualties. Truman raised no objections to the committee's recommendations.

The target-selection people in intelligence were given the guidelines, and among the cities they recommended was Kyoto. Kyoto did fit the guidelines, since it contained vital war plants surrounded by workers' houses. But Kyoto was also the ancient capital of Japan and the site of many of Japan's oldest and most revered religious and historical monuments.

Ordinarily, once the guidelines had been laid down, selecting the targets would be a military matter. But Henry L. Stimson, as secretary of the army, intervened. He raised the subject of targets with Groves, and, over Groves's objections, insisted on seeing the list. When he saw that Kyoto had been selected, Stimson vehemently objected. He had visited the city when he was governor general of the Philippines and felt that he understood its enormous significance to the Japanese.

Stimson insisted that Groves and he discuss the matter with General Marshall. Stimson took the position that using the atomic bomb on Kyoto would damage the "historical position" that the United States would occupy after the war. Groves kept repeating that for a variety of technical reasons Kyoto was an ideal target. Stimson was adamant. Even after the meeting with Marshall, Groves continued to raise the question until Stimson took the matter up with Truman during the

Potsdam talks and got his concurrence that Kyoto would not be a target.[12] Finally, the two targets chosen were Hiroshima and Nagasaki. Two bombers were readied and their crews briefed.

If the effort had been made to get all the top officials together to address the question—to make a truly "national decision" similar to the one that was made years later in the Cuban missile crisis (as described in Part II)—it would have revealed that General George C. Marshall, chief of staff of the Army, estimated the cost of an invasion not at one million casualties but at forty thousand and that General "Hap" Arnold of the Army Air Corps and Admiral William Leahy, who was President Truman's personal military adviser, both believed that an invasion would not be needed, even if the bomb was not used. The debate involved in making such a national decision would also have highlighted the fact that Japan had already approached both Switzerland and Russia about negotiating a peace.

But the debate would also have revealed that the American soldiers in the field and probably most of the civilians at home would have applauded any decision, including a decision to drop the bomb, that promised to end the war quickly and stop the terrible and continually growing casualties.

Also, Magic intercepts of Japanese diplomatic communications in July 1945, showed that advocates of continuing the war were winning in the debate with those who wanted to surrender. Magic intercepts also showed that Japanese intelligence had either discovered or deduced that the first Allied invasion of the home islands would be on Kyushu, and that it was being heavily reinforced.[13] British Ultra intercepts of German diplomatic messages indicated that the Japanese reinforcements of Kyushu had reached 900 thousand men. The Japanese navy could no longer offer any resistance, but its place would be taken by swarms of suicide boats, manned torpedoes, one-man submarines, and about 5 thousand aircraft. The Japanese had demonstrated their ability to extract fearsome casualties in their defense of the Philippines, Iwo Jima, and Okinawa. Their plans for the defense of Kyushu called for volunteer pilots to fly *kamikase* planes, to ride and steer rocket bombs twenty feet long, and to ride and steer torpedoes called *kaiten* and speedboats filled with explosives—all of which would be steered into American ships.

Also, Kyushu is more rugged than Okinawa, much bigger, and just as riddled with caves. Okinawa was a foot-by-foot, yard-by-yard fight to root out the Japanese holed up in caves that cost the Americans 40 thousand Army and Marine Corps casualties and 10 thousand Navy casualties. The battle for Kyushu promised to be worse. Instead of a total of 50 thousand casualties that Okinawa had cost, the invasion of Kyushu alone could easily cost 100 thousand.

It must also be remembered that the firestorms that had followed the conventional bombing of Dresden, Hamburg, and Tokyo had caused at least as many casualties as those expected at Hiroshima and Nagasaki. The great heat rising from a firestorm sucks debris of all kinds, including people, into the central maelstrom. The casualties were enormous in the three cities and so was the horror. In

Hamburg, for example, both the bellies and heads of the people near the center of the firestorm burst, their intestines and brains tumbled out, and they were quickly charred to ashes along with the bodies from which they came. People crossing a road got their feet stuck in the melted asphalt and when they reached down to try to push themselves out, their hands stuck as well. Those who did not die immediately did so in agony, screaming for help.

Historians later established that the goal of the Japanese military was to impose such severe casualties on the Americans that they would lose their will to go on fighting and settle for a peace without the disarmament and occupation of Japan. It was not an unreasonable expectation. One American general who commanded a division that had fought in Europe reported that when his troops were told that they were scheduled to be sent on to fight in the Pacific their opposition approached "open sedition and mutiny."

In fact, the prospects for the Kyushu invasion were so awesome that General George C. Marshall was considering using a total of six atomic bombs on the beachheads in preparation for landing.

But Stimson did not fire up the government for a national decision, and bureaucratic momentum continued to rule. In reality, Roosevelt's original decision to try to make the bomb was the only one approaching a national decision that was ever made. From that time on, the only decisions were *not* to undertake the effort to make a national decision, and *not* to disturb the inevitable, massive, irresistible juggernaut of bureaucratic momentum.[14]

Some who have written on the subject believe that a warning would not have weakened the bomb's contribution to ending the war and might have enhanced it. The argument is persuasive, and if this view had prevailed, and if the results were as these critics assume, the United States would have been in a better political position after the war for the task of building a stable peace.[15]

Shortly after the two atomic bombs were dropped, Japan surrendered. There seems to be no question that the shock of the bombs, along with the Soviet Union entering the war, hastened the Japanese decision. But some scholars later came to believe that General "Hap" Arnold and Admiral Leahy were right that the Japanese would have surrendered even if the bombs had not been dropped, that Japan had already been defeated, and that dropping the bombs on Hiroshima and Nagasaki was "like giving a dying man poison." Their judgment was that what defeated the Japanese was a combination of three factors: first, attrition on the battlefields of the Pacific, China, and Burma; second, the steady erosion of Japanese shipping by the submarine war against Japanese supply lines; and, third, the conventional bombing of Japan, with bombing playing the least important role of the three.

On the other hand, studies of the struggles in Tokyo between the peace faction and the hard-line military and of the crucial role played by the Emperor when he intervened on the side of the peace faction suggest that if the bomb had not been dropped a full-scale invasion might well have been required to bring about the surrender.[16]

NOTES

1. The major sources for this account are Nuell Pharr Davis, *Lawrence and Oppenheimer* (New York: Simon and Schuster, 1968); McGeorge Bundy, *Danger and Survival: Choices About the Bomb in the First Fifty Years* (New York: Random House, 1988); and Richard Rhodes, *The Making of the Atomic Bomb* (New York: Simon and Schuster, 1987). Others are Fletcher Knebel and Charles W. Bailey, *No High Ground* (New York: Harper, 1960); Alice Smith, "Behind the Decision to Use the Atomic Bomb: Chicago, 1944–45," *Bulletin of the Atomic Scientists* (September 1958); and Michael Amrine, *The Great Decision: The Secret History of the Atomic Bomb* (New York: G. P. Putnam's Sons, 1959).

2. Bundy, *Danger and Survival*, 36. See also Rhodes, *Making of the Atomic Bomb*.

3. Thomas Powers, *Heisenberg's War: The Secret History of the German Bomb* (New York: Alfred A. Knopf, 1993).

4. Werner Heisenberg, "Research in Germany on the Technical Application of Atomic Energy," *Nature*, 16 August 1947, pp. 211–215.

5. Bundy, *Danger and Survival*, 20–23.

6. Davis, *Lawrence and Oppenheimer*, 240. I have looked at half a dozen or more translations of the *Bhagavad-Gita* and found that none of them give this exact wording of the line. Most render it in some variation of either, "I am death, the destroyer of worlds," or "I have become death, the destroyer of worlds." On one occasion, a taping for a TV documentary, Oppenheimer also used this more conventional translation. All this leads me to believe that "the shatterer of worlds" was Oppenheimer's own translation.

7. Davis, *Lawrence and Oppenheimer*, 247.

8. Ed Cray, *General of the Army George C. Marshall, Soldier and Statesman* (New York: W. W. Norton, 1990). See also John J. McCloy's account of the decision to drop the bomb, which is contained in a portion of his unpublished memoirs that was published as an appendix in James Reston, *Deadline: A Memoir* (New York: Random House, 1991).

9. The following is drawn from John J. McCloy's account of the decision to drop the bomb in Reston, *Deadline*.

10. In 1993, a number of documents were made public under the Freedom of Information Act dealing with the interception and decoding of wartime messages—"Magic" was the American system for decoding Japanese messages and "Ultra" was the British system for decoding German messages. One of the decoded messages was from a German diplomat stationed in Tokyo describing a conversation he had with a high-ranking Japanese Naval officer on May 5, 1945, just three days before Germany surrendered. The message said, "Since the situation is clearly recognized to be hopeless, large sections of the Japanese armed forces would not regard with disfavor an American request for capitulation even if the terms were hard." Although intelligence analysts flagged this piece of information when it was distributed, it was not mentioned in any of the discussions on whether or not to drop the bomb.

When the report became public in 1993, General Andrew Goodpaster, who had been in the Pentagon office responsible for strategic planning during the war, was asked why the message had not had more influence on the American decision to drop the bomb. His answer implied that dropping the bomb seemed to be the only viable alternative to an invasion that would have been extremely costly in terms of American lives and even more costly than dropping the bomb in terms of Japanese lives: "We anticipated that we would have losses of 500,000 killed or wounded and the Japanese perhaps 10 times that many" (*The New York Times*, 11 August 1993, p. A9).

Although a number of revisionist historians are inclined to regard the fact that this intercepted German report did not have more influence on the decision to drop the bomb as significant, it is not really surprising that it did not. The report is one man's opinion, and being the representative of a country that he knew was about to surrender he could have had a number of motives for exaggerating Japanese thinking.

11. In his account, McCloy goes on to say that he believes that if the American ultimatum had described the atomic bomb, the retention of the Emperor, and continued access to raw materials, the Japanese would have surrendered without the United States having to drop the bombs.

McCloy argues that, in any case, the matter was "not given the thoroughness of consideration and the depth of thought that the president of the United States was entitled to have before a decision of this importance was taken." He specifically deplores the fact that no one from the Department of State was present. On matters as important as this, the president should be presented with a full consideration of all the plausible alternatives and options. "This," McCloy writes, "is what I was told he asked for and what I believe he did not get."

12. Leslie R. Groves, *Now It Can Be Told: The Story of the Manhattan Project* (New York: Harper & Row, 1962), 273–275.

13. What follows was drawn from James MacGregor Burns, "Kyushu, the War-Ending Invasion That Wasn't," *The New York Times*, 13 August 1995, p. E6.

14. Some revisionist historians have argued that the motive for dropping the bombs on Japan was to impress the Soviet Union. I cannot improve on McGeorge Bundy's refutation of this canard: "This assertion is false, and the evidence to support it rests on inferences so stretched as to be a discredit both to the judgment of those who have argued in this fashion and the credulity of those who have accepted such arguments. There is literally no evidence whatever that the timetable for the attack was ever affected by anything except technical and military considerations; there is no evidence that anyone in the direct chain of command from Truman to Stimson to Marshall to Groves ever heard or made any suggestion that either the decision itself or the time of its execution should be governed by any consideration of its effect on the Soviet Union" (Bundy, *Danger and Survival*, 88).

15. See, for example, the people listed in ibid., 75.

16. See, for example, Robert J. C. Butow, *Japan's Decision to Surrender* (Stanford: Stanford University Press, 1954).

Chapter 2

Nuclear Strategy and the Attack on Korea

Immediately after Japan surrendered, President Truman, the scientists, and Congress all turned to the question of what to do with this nuclear genie that had been loosed on the world. In November 1945, the United States proposed that the United Nations should supervise the production of all nuclear energy, and the U.N. General Assembly created an Atomic Energy Commission to consider the question.

THE BARUCH PLAN

In June 1946, the United States proposed the Baruch plan (which took its name from Bernard Baruch, chairman of the committee that developed the plan), under which atomic weapons would be outlawed and U.N. inspectors would have the authority to operate freely in any country. The idea was that once the system was in place, the United States would destroy all the nuclear bombs in its stockpile.

Many Americans were fearful of the Baruch plan, so many that the Senate may never have ratified it. However, the question became moot when the Soviets rejected the scheme out of hand. They were well on their way to developing their own bomb, and their political system could not easily accommodate U.N. inspectors poking around. If nuclear weapons could not be abolished under the supervision of the United Nations, they would soon be included in the world's arsenals. Strategists had to assume that they would be used in future wars. But how?

THE STRATEGY OF AIR POWER

The answer seemed to lie in the strategy of air power. After World War I, the carnage of warfare in the trenches was more than anyone could bear to think of repeating, so in the period following World War I both military strategists and politicians sought desperately for an alternative. One approach was political—resulting in the League of Nations and disarmament treaties. Another, which took two forms, was to try to develop a new military strategy that would avoid the stalemate of the trenches.

One form of a new military strategy was to try to restore mobility to the battlefield by the use of tanks and close-support aircraft. In England, both Basil Liddell Hart and Major General J.F.C. Fuller wrote a great deal on the subject, while in Germany the same effort was going on inside the German military establishment under the leadership of General Heinz Guderian.

The other form of a new strategy was the theory of *strategic* air power. In Italy, Brigadier General Giulio Douhet wrote extensively on the theme, arguing that bombers alone could win wars—perhaps even make war obsolete. In many other countries, the advocates of air power were serving airmen, such as Colonel William "Billy" Mitchell in the United States. While Douhet wrote books about air power, Mitchell drew attention to it by denouncing the views of his superiors and provoking a court-martial.

The strategy of air power called for first attaining mastery of the air by massive strikes on enemy air bases, presumably in an attack that achieved surprise. Once air superiority was won, bombers would turn to the enemy's industry and cities. Most air power theorists believed that civilian morale would quickly collapse under the bombers' pounding. But even if it did not, the destruction of the enemy's factories, railroads, and other lines of communication would soon bring his whole war effort to a halt—or so the advocates of air power believed.

In World War II, neither side put all of their military eggs into the basket of strategic air power, but the resources that both did put into strategic air power were very substantial. In 1940, when the Germans reached the channel after defeating the British and French armies, they immediately launched bombing attacks against British air bases. Their purpose was not to destroy British morale nor to pave the way for an attack on British industry, but to achieve command of the air for their planned invasion of Britain itself.

The first Nazi attacks on London and other cities were in response to a token British raid on Berlin. However, even after the Germans gave up their plans for an invasion, their air attacks on British cities continued. Gradually, the attacks turned into the "blitz"—massive bombing attacks on British cities in an attempt to break morale and destroy the factories producing war materiel. The blitz was what the British people called the air campaign, mistaking it for the *blitzkrieg* or "lightning war" doctrine the Germans had developed to break the stalemate of World War I by integrating infantry, armor, and air power to puncture trench defenses and exploit the resulting breakthrough.

Ironically, by turning their attention to the cities, the Germans gave the Royal Air Force a respite in which to recover from the heavy damage it had suffered in the initial German attempt to gain mastery of the air by concentrating their attacks on the British air bases.[1] Later in the war, the Germans continued to try to affect civilian morale by attacking population centers with their V-1 and V-2 rockets.

As soon as the British were able, they in turn began to bomb cities. Air defenses inflicted awesome losses on incoming bombers in daylight hours, when the bombing was more accurate, so the British adopted a strategy of "area" bombing and made their raids at night. When the Americans entered the war, they decided on daytime raids, in spite of the losses. By the end of the war, German cities had been reduced to rubble, and civilian casualties had been high.

THE STRATEGIC BOMBING SURVEY

Immediately after the war, the United States undertook a major study of what the bombing had accomplished in both Germany and Japan—the Strategic Bombing Survey. For air power enthusiasts, the results were disappointing. Most observers had assumed that in a dictatorship, such as Nazi Germany, war production would have peaked before the war even began—in, say, 1938—and that it would have declined under the relentless pounding of the bombers. But it turned out that both assumptions were wrong.

In the first place, dictatorships contain powerful groups, such as the secret police and industrialists, that make nonmilitary claims on resources and so prevent all-out military production even after a war begins. In the second place, bombing with conventional warheads was not as effective against industry as the air power enthusiasts had thought it would be. As the Allies learned from the Strategic Bombing Survey, German war production actually reached its greatest output in 1944, the fourth year of the bombing and also the year of maximum bombing.

The bombing clearly hurt the German war effort and slowed the movement of supplies to the front. But the evidence suggested that the results would have been better if the Allies had put more of the resources used for strategic bombing into other forces, including close-in air support.

The survey also confirmed that Japan was defeated more by attrition on the battlefields and by submarine warfare than by bombing. As already mentioned, the atomic bombs on Hiroshima and Nagasaki, as well as the Soviets entering the war, made it easier for the Emperor and the peace faction in the Japanese government to force a decision to surrender, but the result was only to hasten the end of the war by a few weeks or, at the most, months.

But nuclear weapons seemed to have made the Strategic Bombing Survey irrelevant. No one doubted that when nuclear weapons became plentiful they would give new life to the theory of air power.

THE THEORY OF NUCLEAR AIR POWER

The new theory of nuclear air power was based on three assumptions: (1) Nuclear bombs would continue to be scarce and expensive, suggesting that the targets would have to be the enemy's cities; (2) the American monopoly would continue for many years; and (3) since the range of the existing bomber (the World War II B-29) was only 4 thousand miles, overseas bases would be essential.

The third point implied not only that the United States would need allies, but that it would have a strong reason for using nuclear weapons to protect those allies. The enemy was taken to be the Soviet Union, and the strategy required seemed simple and straightforward—attain air superiority by demolishing the enemy's air forces and then destroy his war-making capacity and break the morale of his civilian population by bombing his industry and cities. All that was needed to carry out the strategy was a stockpile of nuclear bombs, airplanes to deliver them, and bases within range of the Soviet Union.

THE ATLANTIC TREATY

This was the military side of the equation. On the political side, the Berlin blockade and events in Eastern Europe and Greece escalated into the Cold War and were interpreted in the West as evidence of Soviet aggressiveness. Arguing that Hitler would have been effectively deterred and World War II prevented if it had been clear that the United States would eventually enter the war, the Allies responded with the Atlantic Pact. They believed that this statement of intentions added to the military facts of nuclear bombs and the airplanes and bases necessary to deliver them would make a fully adequate deterrent.

But both the military and political assumptions were rather quickly eroded. On the military side, improvements in the technology of nuclear bombs tested in 1948 indicated that bombs would soon be more plentiful. The Soviet nuclear test in 1949 showed that the American monopoly would not last for long. The introduction of the longer-range B-36 in 1948 lessened the need for overseas bases, and the introduction of the B-52 in 1955 lessened it even more. In the meantime, the U.S. Navy successfully argued that "super-carriers" would also lessen the need for overseas bases.

On the political side, even though the threat of being bombed with nuclear weapons might deter the Soviets from an all-out assault on Europe, such a threat was clearly not deterring them from doing things that were very unpleasant. Probably the most vivid example was the Soviet blockade of Berlin, begun in the middle of 1948. Blocked from sending food, coal, and other supplies by road, the Allies instituted an airlift, a steady shuttle of planes from the Western zones into Tempelhof airport. Tensions were high and the possibility of war seemed uncomfortably close.

It was the Berlin crisis that inspired James V. Forrestal, Truman's secretary of defense, to raise the issue in the National Security Council of whether nuclear weapons would be used if it came to war. A decision was made that the Soviets should not be given the "slightest reason" to believe that the United States would not use nuclear weapons in war. This decision apparently stilled the doubts, and from that time (1948) on nuclear weapons were the central feature in American war plans.

Many people in both Europe and America and both inside and outside government believed that it was only the threat of the American stockpile of nuclear weapons that held the Soviets back from seizing Berlin by force. Indeed, many believed that the threat might in fact have held the Soviets back from something even more dramatic, such as an attempt by Eastern Germany to unify Germany by force. In March 1949, Winston Churchill put this conclusion in the most emphatic terms: "It is certain that Europe would have been communized and London under bombardment some time ago but for the deterrent of the atomic bomb in the hands of the United States."

THE EARLY DEBATE ON THE STRATEGY OF NUCLEAR AIR POWER

At the same time, the Western Allies began to debate about how they should defend Europe and the strategy that they should follow. The Soviets had 22 divisions stationed in Eastern Germany and another 60 divisions in the Eastern European area. Intelligence credited the Soviets with having another 93 divisions stationed in the Soviet Union itself—a total of 175 divisions. Although a number of these were second-line troops manned by reservists and some of the first-line divisions were stationed in Asia too far away to be a threat to Europe, all of the American armed services shared an interest in highlighting the threat rather than trying to treat it realistically. So nothing much was said to put the figure of 175 divisions in perspective until Robert McNamara's time as secretary of defense.

But in 1948 the fact that the actual Soviet strength was considerably less than 175 divisions did not really matter very much. At that time the Allies had available in Europe—even if some reservist divisions were counted—no more than twelve divisions, of which two were American. All were poorly equipped and trained. There were no plans for fighting them as a unified force, no command structure, and no communications network linking them together. They were not deployed for defense but for occupation duty—in penny packets all over the German landscape. They lacked both armor and airfields, and some of the airfields they did have were actually in front of the troops they were supposed to support. Supply lines for both the British and the American forces ran not perpendicular to the front, but parallel to it, from Hamburg and Bremerhaven on the extreme left, and often less than fifty miles from Soviet armor. There were few prepared defense positions, and probably not enough ammunition in all of Europe to last more than a couple of weeks.

Allied planners recognized that if a Soviet attack came, it would be without warning. The twenty-two Soviet divisions could be secretly increased to thirty without violating secrecy and without much difficulty. These could then hold maneuvers in Eastern Germany and suddenly change direction and drive for the bridges over the Rhine. NATO intelligence estimated that if the Soviets did attack, they could reach the Pyrenees in six to eight weeks, just about the time it would take an army to march the distance without having to fight at all. A joke that was passed around among staff officers at the time started with a question: "What equipment will the Soviets need to reach the Pyrenees?" The answer was, "Shoes."

But what was most frightening to these staff officers, all of whom had served one way or another in World War II, was not just the overwhelming numbers of the Soviet divisions and the probability that if war came the Soviets would quickly occupy all of Europe. The Nazis had conquered Europe at the beginning of World War II, but the Allies had eventually triumphed. The more important danger was revealed to many newly arrived officers in a briefing in a large, two-story room in which one huge wall was a display area for maps. At one point the briefing officer drew back a curtain to reveal a gigantic blow-up of an air photo of the 1944 beachhead at Normandy. The picture had been taken just a day or two before the Allied breakout from an altitude of about 10 thousand feet on a cloudless day, and the soldiers in their foxholes on both sides were clearly visible.

Suddenly the briefing officer pulled a cord and an overlay dropped down over the air photo. It was a transparency showing the area of destruction wrought by the atomic bomb that had been exploded over Hiroshima. Every foxhole was obliterated. Invariably, the response in the audience of World War II veterans was a sharp intake of breath. "Gentlemen," the briefing officer said, "there will be no more Normandies. If we ever get kicked off the continent, we will never, ever get back."

But things were actually even worse than the briefing indicated. The Hiroshima bomb had the explosive power of between 12 and 14 thousand tons of TNT, but much more powerful bombs were already in the stockpile, and President Truman had already announced the decision to try to develop the H-bomb, which promised to have explosive power not of 12 to 14 *thousand* tons of TNT but as much as 10 or 20 *million* tons of TNT!

So it was obvious that the theory of nuclear air power had to be amended. If the Soviet armies occupied Europe in a lightning blow, what good would it do to bomb Soviet cities and factories with nuclear bombs? The Soviet armies would continue to occupy Europe, and their war supplies could be produced by the European factories. If the United States then bombed the Soviet occupying armies and the European factories supplying them, enormous numbers of people who were America's allies would be killed. Obviously, an effective deterrent would have to include ground forces large enough to prevent the Soviet forces from occupying Europe while the nuclear bombs did their work on the Soviet homeland.

An effort to establish such allied ground forces had begun under the aegis of the Brussels Pact, the alliance of Western European states that preceded the Atlantic Treaty. The analysis of what would be needed for an effective defense of Western Europe started with the assumption that for some years nuclear weapons would continue to be too scarce to be used for anything but attacking cities or a beachhead like Normandy. The analysis then applied to the terrain of Europe the hoary principles of United States Army Field Manual 100-5, the "General's Handbook."

The North German plain, the Belfort gap, and the Fulda gap, which were the traditional invasion routes, would have to be fully defended in accordance to FM 100-5's rules of thumb about divisional fronts. The mountainous terrain between these routes could be covered more lightly, by screening forces. Finally, following the principle of two on the front and one in reserve, a force of one-third the total would have to be provided to serve as the reserve. For the old Western Front—the line between Basel in Switzerland and the mouth of the Rhine-Ijssel in the Netherlands—the total came to between eighty and eighty-five divisions. To this had to be added ten more divisions for the Brenner Pass and Trieste area and about five for the Scandinavian area, making a grand total of about one-hundred divisions.

An attacker needs at least a three-to-one superiority to dislodge a force that is adequate to the terrain it is defending with its flanks anchored on natural obstacles and a reserve to seal off a penetration or stop a turning movement. And even if the attacker has an even greater superiority, of five-to-one or more, the battle may still go to the defender, depending on skill, morale, luck, and the other intangibles of war.

But it would take more than either skill or luck to save an outnumbered force that is also inadequate to its terrain. In the kind of war the planners visualized, similar to that of World War II, an allied force of only sixty or seventy divisions would have had to choose between cutting the defenses in the major approaches or scaling down the reserves to a force too small to make its intervention decisive. In a battle against 175 Soviet divisions, which is what allied intelligence thought the Soviets had, disaster would have been inevitable. But with a force of about 100 divisions, the Allies could hope to hold, not only against 175 divisions but with luck against even twice that many. In the end, ninety-six divisions became the preferred "requirements" figure, and it was finally enshrined in 1952 as the "Lisbon Force Goals," a term that was almost always capitalized.

THE "CLOSING-THE-GAP EXERCISE"

For three years prior to the attack on Korea, military representatives of the Brussels Pact countries had been engaged in what was called the "Closing-the-Gap Exercise." The gap was the difference between ninety-six divisions and the few that were actually on station plus the divisions of reservists, mainly French, that could be mobilized and transported to the front within the first forty-eight hours. Some of the debate was about whether the reservist divisions were well enough trained and equipped to qualify as part of the ninety-six needed, but even if the worst of them were counted, the gap was still very large.

The Brussels Pact was intended to be only a regional arrangement, so the U.S. representatives were only observers. But every few months these observers would suggest that perhaps the solution was to rearm Germany—and the French would vehemently object. The argument had gone around and around for three years, but no progress had been made. No one had any sense of urgency.

THE H-BOMB DECISION

Some feeling of urgency did flurry briefly when the Soviets exploded an atomic weapon in August 1949. The reaction in the Pentagon and elsewhere inside the U.S. government was that the United States had better begin to develop the "super," the hydrogen or H-bomb. It also seemed prudent to build small, tactical, "battlefield" nuclear weapons, both bombs and artillery shells, in large quantities. A few people, however, notably Paul Nitze, head of the Policy Planning Staff at the State Department, felt that building an H-bomb was not enough, and that the United States should rebuild its military forces across the board. In the end, President Truman approved the recommendation to proceed with the H-bomb and to build tactical nuclear weapons. But he refused to increase the defense budget beyond the $15 billion ceiling he had committed himself to in the presidential campaign of 1948.

NSC-68

However, as a sop to people who wanted to do more than build the H-bomb and tactical weapons, President Truman instructed the secretaries of state and defense to undertake a broad study of strategic plans in light of the fact that the Soviets had developed an atomic weapon. This led to NSC-68, which was shepherded through the government decision-making process by Nitze. The document pictured the Soviet Union as expansionist and aggressive, and it recommended that in addition to building the H-bomb and tactical weapons the United States should embark upon a broad-based and very rapid military buildup—in effect, rearmament to wartime readiness.

When NSC-68 and its recommendation for rearmament came before the NSC in April 1950, President Truman still wanted to keep to the budget ceiling of $15 billion (it ended up being $17.7 billion), and his reaction to the recommendation for a broad-based rearmament was to stall. He appointed a subcommittee to look into details on programs and costs.

THE KOREAN WAR AND
THE ESTABLISHMENT OF NATO

Then, on June 24, 1950, North Korea attacked South Korea. Within twenty-four hours the South Korean forces were in retreat. On Monday, June 26, President Truman authorized U.S. air and naval forces to attack any North Korean forces south of the 38th parallel. On June 27, the North Koreans captured Seoul. That same day the U.N. Security Council, which the Soviets were boycotting at the time, passed a resolution calling on U.N. members to assist the South Korean government in resisting the North Korean aggression. On June 29, Truman authorized the bombing of military targets in North Korea and the limited use of American ground troops to secure the airfield and port areas of Pusan at the southern tip of the Korean peninsula. On June 30 he authorized General MacArthur, who commanded the American forces occupying Japan, to use all of the ground forces under his command in any way he saw fit. Three American divisions were ordered to Korea from Japan, but it was not until late July that they were ready. By this time South Korean forces held only a small perimeter around the southern port of Pusan.

In both the Brussels Pact countries and the United States it was the attack on Korea that provided the sense of urgency. When that attack came, everyone's attitude quickly changed. All over the West, people assumed that the Soviets had ordered the North Koreans to attack. The opinion was unanimous that the Soviets, having broken the West's monopoly of atomic bombs, had decided that the time had come to test both its defenses and its will.

This is not to say that very many Western observers thought that the Soviets wanted a full-scale war or that they were readying themselves for an immediate attack. But since they had ordered the attack on South Korea, the reasoning went, the Soviets were obviously willing to take higher risks of war than anyone had thought. The conclusion was that unless the West quickly built up its defenses in Europe, the Soviets might well order the East Germans to attack West Germany.

In any case, there was little debate and remarkable unanimity. Everyone agreed that the Soviets had shifted from political means for achieving their ambitions to military ones.

People began to talk in Washington, in the capitals of the European Allies, and in the Brussels Pact meetings, about 1954 being the "year of maximum danger." Just how that particular date was chosen is shrouded in mystery. It may have been chosen because the atomic physicists thought it would take the Soviets five years to go from their 1949 test to an adequate stockpile of bombs. More probably, 1954 was chosen because that was the earliest date that the United States and the Allies could get their own defenses in order—airfields built, pipelines in place, and the supply lines reoriented from Hamburg and Bremerhaven and thence parallel to the front to a new route from Bordeaux and across France perpendicular to the front.

Following the attack on Korea, Truman promptly gave up trying to keep the defense budget low and agreed to a rearmament program. The defense budget went from $17.7 billion in fiscal year 1950 to $53.4 billion in fiscal year 1951, and Congress passed the necessary legislation. The U.S. Senate also passed a resolution early in 1951 approving a troop buildup in Europe, and additional American divisions began to arrive shortly thereafter. The other Allies followed with increases of their own.

The Allies also agreed that Germany should be rearmed, though it was not until 1955 that the first German soldiers took to the field. And all the Allies agreed to form the North Atlantic Treaty Organization (NATO). It was the first international force with a unified command ever established in the absence of actual war. Also in early 1951, Dwight D. Eisenhower, whose wartime reputation for getting along with difficult personalities among the Allies was unsurpassed, became the Supreme Allied Command, Europe (SACEUR).

At the time people everywhere assumed that NSC-68 was the blueprint for the American rearmament effort and that the United States was fortunate that a plan had already been prepared and was ready to be implemented. Years later, when the document itself became available to the public, it turned out to be not a solid piece of policy analysis as everyone had thought, but a rhetorical trumpet call to action, describing the Soviet threat in overblown and simplistic terms. And even as a call to action, the document is, in the words of one scholar, "an amazingly incomplete and amateurish study."[2]

SOVIET INTENTIONS

But if the writers of NSC-68 do not look very astute in hindsight, neither does anyone else. In fact, years later many people came to doubt the underlying assumption shared at the time by everyone concerned—the writers of NSC-68, the American staff officers in Europe, the Allies, and academics—that it was the Soviets who ordered the North Koreans to attack South Korea.

The most convincing piece of evidence that this basic assumption was wrong came in 1969–1970, when Khrushchev's memoirs were smuggled out of the Soviet Union and published in the West. At first some Sovietologists thought the memoirs might be a KGB forgery. However, a few months later copies of the tapes onto which the memoirs had been dictated were also smuggled out, and when the "voice prints" were compared with those in tapes of Khrushchev's public speeches any doubt that the memoirs were genuine disappeared.

Of course, Khrushchev painted himself in the best possible light, and he was also dictating from memory—he was "retired," living under house arrest with no access to documents. But the story he tells about how North Korea's invasion of the South came about is very convincing, partly because it has been confirmed by other evidence, but partly because it makes no effort to conceal how naïve Khrushchev himself still was even after his years at the top.

According to Khrushchev, the idea of the invasion came not from Stalin, but from Kim Il-Sung, the leader of Communist North Korea. As Khrushchev tells the story, Stalin hesitated to give his blessing to Kim's proposal to attack South Korea because he was worried that the Americans might jump in to help the South Koreans unless the conquest was very swift, and he urged Kim to think it over. Kim went home, and returned to Moscow after he had "worked everything out."

Stalin was still reluctant and decided to ask Mao Zedong's opinion.[3] Mao thought the North Koreans should be permitted to go ahead and that the United States would not intervene.

Even in hindsight, Khrushchev thought that "no real Communist would have tried to dissuade Kim Il-Sung from his compelling desire to liberate South Korea from Syngman Rhee and from reactionary American influence," especially since it would be an "internal" matter which the Koreans would be settling among themselves. To have turned Kim down "would have contradicted the Communist view of the world." So Khrushchev, far from condemning Stalin for agreeing to Kim's plan to attack the South, applauds him, saying that he, Khrushchev, would have done the same if he had been in Stalin's place.

Khrushchev's criticism of Stalin is not for approving the invasion, but just the opposite—for not doing more to make sure that the North Koreans would be able to win and win quickly. Khrushchev relates that the invasion did not go as swiftly as planned. They had expected a pro-Communist insurrection in the South, but it did not materialize. The Communist Party's organizational work to prepare for the invasion had been inadequate. Syngman Rhee's forces, bolstered by some Americans, held on at Pusan. A large American force then landed at Inchon, cutting off the entire North Korean army. Khrushchev then says that Stalin was partly to blame for this precarious situation: "It's absolutely incomprehensible to me why he did it, but when Kim Il-sung was preparing for his march, Stalin called back all our advisors who were with the North Korean divisions and regiments, as well as all the advisors who were serving as consultants and helping to build up the army. I asked Stalin about this, and he snapped back at me, 'It's too dangerous to keep our advisors there. They might be taken prisoner. We don't want there to be evidence for accusing us of taking part in this business. It's Kim Il-sung's affair.'"[4]

Khrushchev even suggested that the Soviets send General Malinovsky, who later became Khrushchev's defense minister, to Korea as an advisor. But Stalin reacted with "extreme hostility." Even in retirement, Khrushchev regrets that the Soviets had not at the very beginning sent in one or two tank corps to help the North Koreans. If they had done so, he believed, Pusan would have fallen quickly, and the Americans would not have intervened.

So the fundamental allied and American decisions to create NATO, to rearm Germany, to increase the American troop strength in Europe, and to rebuild their military strength all turned out to be based on a basic premise that was false—that Stalin had ordered North Korea to attack South Korea as a test of the American will.

But then, one wonders. Even if Stalin and the Soviet Union did not order the attack, what would have happened if the U.S. government had not sent Americans to fight in Korea? Would the East Germans have decided that the failure to intervene in Korea showed a lack of will even though it had not been designed as a test? Would they then have pressed Stalin to authorize a similar attack on West Germany? It is a question to which there is no definitive answer.

But all the second thoughts came later. The Allies established NATO in June of 1949, and in 1950 General Eisenhower took leave from the presidency of Columbia University to take command. Each of the Allies increased the number of troops stationed along the Western front, and the rearmament of Germany was begun.

NOTES

1. Lawrence Freedman, *The Evolution of Nuclear Strategy* (New York: St. Martin's Press, 1981, 1983), 11.

2. Samuel F. Wells, Jr., "Sounding the Tocsin: NSC-68 and the Soviet Threat," *International Security* 4, no. 2 (1979).

3. The spelling used here is Pin Yin, which is preferred by the current Chinese regime. Until recently, in the West Mao's name was spelled in the Wade-Giles system (i.e., Mao Tse-tung).

4. Nikita Khrushchev, *Khrushchev Remembers*, trans. and ed. Strobe Talbott (Boston: Little, Brown, 1970), 370.

Chapter 3

New Look, Massive Retaliation, and Flexible Response

To sum up, the U.S. response to the successful Soviet test of an atomic weapon in 1949 was not a change in strategy but an attempt to build an H-bomb, a subject to which we will return in the next chapter. The response to the attack on South Korea, however, *was* a change in strategy. Nuclear weapons meant that if the Allied forces were pushed off the European continent they would never be able to get back. The threat to bomb Soviet cities with nuclear weapons was a powerful deterrent to a direct Soviet attack on Europe, but suppose the Soviet armies occupied Europe in a lightning blow and simultaneously evacuated their cities? They could get their supplies from the farms and factories of occupied Europe, holding the Allied population hostage to American restraint. The Allied strategic planners concluded, to repeat, that an effective deterrent would have to include ground forces stationed in Europe that were large enough to hold back the Soviet forces until the nuclear bombs had done their work.

ENDING THE WAR IN KOREA

Meanwhile, the war in Korea dragged on and on. Casualties mounted. The economic drain on the United States, and in turn on America's allies, was enormous. The Truman administration gave at least some thought to using nuclear weapons to bring the war to a rapid conclusion. But such thoughts were quickly dismissed.

The stockpile of nuclear weapons at that time was about 200. The military argued a twofold position. They argued, first, that the stockpile was not yet sufficient to provide an effective deterrent to the Soviets and should not be drawn down for use in Korea. Second, they argued that in any case there were no suitable targets for nuclear weapons in Korea—that is, no targets that would bring a quick and decisive end to the war.

The only possible exception was to target the entire North Korean civilian population and annihilate it, which would of course create a storm of disgust from the world and the American people. The enemy troops were not jammed together on a beachhead, as in Normandy, and the bulk of the enemy's supplies came not from their own factories but from China and the Soviet Union. Only a fraction of the North Korean population was concentrated in cities and, quite apart from the moral question of massacring innocent civilians, the effect on the fighting forces of attacking the civilian population with nuclear weapons might only be to make them fight harder.

As it happened, President Truman made a slip in a press conference that ended up demonstrating that the administration had not come even close to using nuclear weapons in Korea. In November 1950, after the Chinese had intervened and were advancing rapidly, anxiety in the United States was high. In answer to a question in a press conference, Truman said that the United States would take whatever steps were necessary to meet the military situation. A follow-up question was whether those steps included using the atomic bomb. Truman said that the government was always considering every weapon it had. Pushed to say whether consideration meant "active consideration," he said that there is always active consideration. But he went on to say that he did not want to see the atomic bomb used, and that it was a terrible weapon that should not be used against innocent men, women, and children who had nothing to do with the aggression in Korea.

These last caveats should have shown that the Truman administration had no plans to use the bomb, but even so, there was a worldwide hullabaloo, fanned by the press. Clement Attlee, then prime minister of Great Britain, flew to Washington to obtain Truman's personal and direct assurances that the bomb would not be used. However, the episode did make the point for everyone in the world to see that the bomb was not a cure-all, that in some kinds of military and political situations the bomb had no practical utility at all.

But the American people clearly wanted an end to the war in Korea. During his 1952 campaign for the presidency, Eisenhower dramatically announced that he would "go to Korea." Immediately after the election, and before his inauguration, he did make the trip. On his return, he said to the press that what was needed was not talk but deeds—deeds in "circumstances of our own choosing." Eisenhower's statement was in a sense itself a threatening "deed," in that it indicated he might not be bound by Truman's assurances to Attlee that the bomb would not be used in Korea.

Another threat, rather than a deed, was made on February 2, 1953, when Eisenhower, in his State of the Union speech, said that the Seventh Fleet patrols in the Taiwan straits would no longer be charged with screening the mainland from attacks by the Chinese Nationalists. However, the threat was rather hollow, since the Chinese Nationalists had never actually mounted even a raid and so the patrols had never actually stopped anything.

Later that spring came a true deed, though it was also a threat. Bombers that could deliver nuclear bombs and presumably the bombs themselves were moved to Okinawa. Then, in May 1953, John Foster Dulles, Eisenhower's secretary of state and principal adviser in these matters, visited India and issued still another threatening warning to high officials there, certain that it would be passed on to the Chinese.

Both Eisenhower and Dulles later made it clear that they believed that these threats to use nuclear weapons were what brought about the end to the Korean War. Others, however, doubted their conclusion. One doubter was McGeorge Bundy. In his book *Danger and Survival*, Bundy pointed out that, except for Eisenhower's vague statement on returning from his visit to Korea and the rather empty announcement about the Seventh Fleet, the Chinese concession that broke the logjam on negotiating the end of the war came before the Chinese could have known of any of the other threatening words or deeds. What brought about the change in the Chinese attitude, Bundy believed, was the death of Stalin.

Continued stalemate in Korea had cost Stalin nothing, but it kept the level of tension high, and for Stalin this had some utility. But Stalin died on March 5, 1953. Later that month, the Communist negotiators in Korea accepted a proposal by the Americans and South Koreans for an exchange of sick and wounded prisoners that had been made six weeks earlier. Negotiations, which had been suspended since October, were renewed. Then, on March 30, when Zhou Enlai returned from Stalin's funeral, he announced that the Chinese and North Koreans would no longer insist, as they had up until that time, that all prisoners should be repatriated, even those who resisted and would have to be repatriated by force.[1] Bundy says that in the 1980s, during the thaw in relations before the repression of the students in Tiananmen Square in 1989, this interpretation was confirmed by Chinese officials. They quoted Zhou Enlai himself as saying that what had made it possible to end the war was Stalin's death.[2]

However, the Joint Chiefs of Staff recommended that if the war in Korea started up again, the United States should make "extensive strategical and tactical use of atomic bombs." Eisenhower approved the recommendation as the one "most likely to achieve the objective we sought."

At various stages in the presidential campaign of 1952 and in the early months of the Eisenhower administration, some Republicans talked of provoking disputes that would force the Communists to give up their gains in Eastern Europe. But this notion of "roll back" never amounted to anything more than rhetoric. What some people saw as an opportunity to push the Communists back arose with the Hungarian revolt in 1956. The revolt was ruthlessly put down by invading Soviet troops, but the Eisenhower administration decided not to take any action. After that nothing more was heard about "roll back."

But the search for a new strategy continued. Partly the search was motivated by revulsion at the losses and frustrations of the Korean War. It was disturbing to think that the Soviet Union might bleed the United States at different places all over the globe with this kind of "war by proxy."

Partly, however, the motive was economic. Eisenhower was convinced that economic strength was the highest priority and that military budgets that were out of line with the economy would create weakness, not strength. In 1948, long before he became president, he had advised Secretary of Defense Forrestal that a military budget of $15 billion was all that the United States could support. But the budget he inherited from the Truman administration was $45 billion, with recommendations for increasing it even further.

Eisenhower found a powerful ally for his view that the health of the economy would be jeopardized by higher defense budgets in Secretary of the Treasury George Humphrey. Another ally was Admiral Radford, the chairman of the Joint Chiefs of Staff. But Radford's motivation was his faith in nuclear weapons rather than fears for the economy.

The answer to both the economic and military fears seemed to be nuclear weapons. Only nuclear weapons seemed to promise adequate defense at affordable cost. What also made the Eisenhower administration turn to nuclear weapons was that by 1954 nuclear weapons were no longer either very scarce or very costly. The era of nuclear plenty had arrived. This made it possible, as the newspaper wags put it, to get "a bigger bang for a buck." Eisenhower personally insisted that the Strategic Air Command would be *the* major deterrent to Soviet aggression. In his memoirs, he said that he intended "to launch the Strategic Air Command [against the Soviet homeland] immediately upon trustworthy evidence of a general attack against the West."[3]

Eisenhower also approved, in a formal decision of the National Security Council on October 30, 1953 (NSC 162/2), a policy statement that, in the event of hostilities, "the United States will consider nuclear weapons to be as available for use as other munitions." However, he also specified that this decision should not be made public without further consideration by the NSC. He also commented that, although the Joint Chiefs of Staff could count on using nuclear weapons in "the event of general war," they should not plan to use them in "minor affairs."[4]

It should also be noted that this was a contingency plan. Contingency plans do not always turn out to be what is actually done if the contingency arises. In the Truman administration, for example, Secretary of State Acheson, in a speech at the National Press Club, drew the defense perimeter against Communism between Japan and Korea—excluding Korea. But in the actual event of the North Korean attack, the United States decided to fight.

Eisenhower approved the use of nuclear weapons in the event of general hostilities, but he retained in his own hands the power to decide to use the bombs rather than delegate it to the military commanders. In the case of an all-out attack on the West by the Soviets, he probably would have had no choice but to order the Strategic Air Command (SAC) to retaliate with nuclear bombs. But if fighting had resumed in Korea, he might well have decided not to use them, for he expressed "great anxiety" that if the United States used nuclear weapons in Korea, the Soviets might use them against the "almost defenseless" population of Japan.[5]

Still on January 8, 1954, the NSC formally approved the policy of using nuclear weapons if the Communists renewed the fighting in Korea. Eisenhower also approved removing two army divisions from Korea, and he explained to Congressional leaders that this was because of the government's confidence in air power and the new weapons. The story leaked, but there was no public reaction, suggesting that both the press and public accepted the idea that if the fighting resumed, using nuclear weapons would be an acceptable response.

A year later, the Joint Chiefs of Staff (JCS)—the military heads of the Army, Navy, Air Force, and Marine Corps—proposed that NSC 162/2 be revised because the policy it laid down was one of "defensiveness," emphasizing "reactive" rather than more "positive" measures. In the internal debate that followed, it was clear that what the JCS meant by a more "positive" policy was preventive war. Eisenhower firmly rejected the idea, and his decision was supported by all his principal advisers.

Eisenhower also had strong opinions about the risk in the future of large-scale conventional war. Whereas the staff officers of NATO were agreed that nuclear weapons meant that "there would be no more Normandies," Eisenhower believed that nuclear weapons also meant that there would be no more large-scale, conventional wars such as World War II. To clinch his argument, he pointed to what two Hiroshima-type atomic bombs would have done to the two artificial harbors on which the Allied forces were dependent for the buildup and breakout following the Normandy landing.

In 1959, in keeping with his view that if deterrence ever failed the war with the Soviet Union would be nuclear and that it would be over very quickly, Eisenhower killed the mobilization plans for a four-year war. He once remarked that in a nuclear age the Army would be useful only for enforcing martial law.[6]

But while Eisenhower felt that nuclear weapons ensured that there was no risk in pulling two American divisions out of Korea, he agreed with his secretary of state, John Foster Dulles, that withdrawing American divisions from Europe posed a delicate political problem. So the decision was that withdrawing American troops from Europe would have to wait until a full "retaliatory capability" was in place and until the NATO Allies caught up to the American government in understanding the implications of nuclear weapons.

THE "NEW LOOK"

Thus, the resolution of what the Eisenhower administration saw as the problem of providing adequate defense without doing irreparable damage to the American economy was a radically different force posture, nicknamed the "New Look."

Prior to the Eisenhower administration the budgets of the Army, Navy, and Air Force were roughly equal. Under the New Look, the budgets of both the Army and the Navy, but especially the Army, were to be cut severely and their forces reduced, while the budget of the Air Force would be greatly increased.

The strategy for employing this New Look force was twofold. The answer to the threat of direct Soviet aggression was to build on the base provided by the Truman administration: the establishment of NATO, the buildup of allied ground forces (which had reached about thirty divisions of the ninety-six called for by the Lisbon force goals), and vastly improved infrastructure. To this the Eisenhower administration added a larger Air Force, an increasing stockpile of nuclear bombs, and a determination by the commander in chief to launch SAC immediately against the Soviet homeland if the Soviets attacked the West.

THE SINGLE INTEGRATED OPERATIONAL PLAN

If there was any doubt that Eisenhower meant what he said about his determination to launch SAC in the event of a Soviet attack on the West, it was dispelled by his decision in the last year of his administration, 1960, to establish the Single Integrated Operational Plan (SIOP).

When the Polaris submarine began to come on line, General Curtis LeMay, commander of SAC, proposed a single unified planning command to select the targets in case of war. The purpose was to avoid duplication and to maximize the effect so that the attack would utterly paralyze the Soviet Union. The Navy, on the other hand, wanted to make its own list of targets. Eisenhower in no uncertain terms said that in the event of a Soviet attack the U.S. response must be massive, its nuclear forces should be used to the hilt, those forces should be fully coordinated, and the resulting plan must be obeyed to the letter. He gave responsibility for developing the SIOP to a newly organized Joint Strategic Target Planning Staff (JSTPS) at SAC headquarters.

TACTICAL NUCLEAR WEAPONS

In the meantime, the small, tactical, or battlefield nuclear weapons that the Truman administration had ordered to be developed began to enter the stockpile. By the end of the Eisenhower administration the total number of tactical nuclear weapons available to all three services was probably about 10 thousand. In 1954, Field Marshal Montgomery, then deputy Supreme Allied Commander, Europe, said publicly, "I want to make it absolutely clear that we at SHAPE [Supreme Headquarters, Allied Powers Europe] are basing all our planning on using atomic and thermonuclear weapons in our defence. With us it is no longer: 'They may possibly be used.' It is very definitely: 'They will be used, if we are attacked.'"[7]

President Eisenhower seemed to confirm Montgomery's statement in a press conference in March 1955: "Where these things are used on strictly military targets and for strictly military purposes, I see no reason why they shouldn't be used just exactly as you would use a bullet or anything else."

But at the same time, Eisenhower had his doubts about the increasing reliance on nuclear weapons. In 1960, he puzzled that "if we use thousands of small weapons we would be in a general war situation, in which the hydrogen weapon would be used, making the smaller ones insignificant." Later that same year, he said that the more the armed services depended on nuclear weapons the dimmer his hopes were for containing a limited war or for keeping it from spreading to general war. Later still, he said that we were unfortunately so committed to nuclear weapons that "the only practical move would be to start using them from the beginning without any distinction between them and conventional weapons and also, assuming there was direct Russian involvement, mount an all-out strike on the Soviet Union." As McGeorge Bundy writes, "The logical consequences of the New Look might nag him, but he continued to accept them, at least in theory. Even a small war would be nuclear, and to limit even a small nuclear war would be hard—impossible if it involved the Russians."[8]

THE "STABILITY/INSTABILITY" DILEMMA

For the Eisenhower administration, these policies settled the problem of deterring the Soviet Union from direct aggression—that is, for deterring the big war. For lesser wars, the problem was more complicated. Academics came to call this difference between the big war and little wars the "stability/instability" dilemma.

If the Eisenhower policies and force structure were an effective deterrent to the Soviets, the top of the strategic spectrum was stabilized. But the very fact of stability at the top seemed to be a temptation for lesser aggressions. The Communist world, the stability/instability argument ran, could encourage limited wars by proxy, such as the attack by North Korea on South Korea, with a high level of confidence that the risks of escalation into a larger war would be small. The stability at the level of nuclear war and war between the superpowers made for instability at the level of lesser wars.

MASSIVE RETALIATION

The Eisenhower administration's solution for dealing with this lower-level but worldwide threat was "massive retaliation." Just one year after President Eisenhower was inaugurated, in January 1954, his secretary of state, John Foster Dulles, described the policy in a speech. Dulles said that the United States would no longer meet aggression on the same terms that the aggression had been made. The United States, for example, had responded to the attack by North Korea with exactly the same weapons used by the Communist side in making the attack—infantry, armored divisions, and aircraft using conventional (nonnuclear) bombs. Henceforth, Dulles declared, the United States would depend "primarily upon a great capacity to retaliate instantly by means and at places of our own choosing."

Everyone took Dulles's statement to mean that any attack made with conventional forces, such as that in Korea, would be met with air power armed with nuclear weapons and that the response might be on Moscow or Peking rather than at the point of attack. This interpretation was reinforced by a statement by Vice President Richard M. Nixon reported in *The New York Times* of March 14, 1954. "Rather than let the Communists nibble us to death all over the world in little wars," Nixon said, "we would rely in the future primarily on our massive mobile retaliatory power which we could use in our discretion against the major source of aggression at times and places that we choose."

"BRINKMANSHIP"

Dulles also reinforced this interpretation by both talk and action that came to be known as "brinkmanship." During the Quemoy–Matsu crisis, Dulles hinted that his tactic was to go quickly to the "brink" of war so that an opponent had to be the one to choose between backing down or himself taking the decision to go to war.

However, the basic policy document, NSC 162/2, had not been so stark as Dulles made it out to be, and he attempted to clarify the policy in an article in the magazine *Foreign Affairs* of April 1954. What was intended, Dulles explained, was not "massive retaliation," but "flexible retaliation." The secret to effective deterrence was that the aggressor should be made certain that he would suffer costs that would outweigh any potential gains. An all-out attack on Europe would indeed call for massive retaliation. But lesser aggressions would be met with something less—though still large enough to outweigh any possible gains. But the impression remained, reinforced by the New Look force posture, that the lesser, more appropriate response would still be nuclear.

THE CRISIS OF DIENBIENPHU

If the basic policy document was more cautious than Dulles's public statements, in actual practice the Eisenhower administration was even more cautious than the policy document suggested it would be. Both the crisis of Dienbienphu and the Quemoy–Matsu crisis illustrate.

In the wake of World War II, European colonies in Asia began demanding independence. The French were stubbornly determined to maintain their colony in Indochina; and the Viet Minh independence movement, which came to be dominated by the Communists, turned to the tactics of guerrilla warfare. The crisis in this First Indochina War came in early 1954, when the Viet Minh guerrilla forces surrounded the French at Dienbienphu in a mountain valley at the junction of roads leading to China, Laos, and Vietnam (the latter two were at that time still parts of Indochina).

It was at this time that President Eisenhower, in a press conference, laid out the "falling domino" theory. He warned that if Indochina fell to the Communists, the other states of Southeast Asia would also fall, like a row of dominoes. But in spite of these fears, President Eisenhower made it vehemently clear that he was opposed to sending American ground forces to relieve the French.

But his reservations apparently did not include air forces. On a visit to Washington the French general Paul Ély stressed the need for air support, and Eisenhower seemed interested. A few days later Admiral Radford proposed an American bombing raid on the Viet Minh surrounding Dienbienphu. He and General Nathan Twining, chief of staff of the Air Force, developed a plan to drop three small tactical nuclear weapons on the forces surrounding the French. There were no towns anywhere near Dienbienphu and so no risk of civilian casualties. There was no air opposition, so the bombs could be placed very carefully and accurately to avoid damage to the French defenders.

Years later, General Twining still believed that the plan would have worked, that it would have taught the Chinese a good lesson, and that it might well have avoided the later difficulties the United States got into in Vietnam. There is also convincing evidence that Dulles suggested to Georges Bidault, the French Foreign Minister, that atomic bombs might be made available to the French for use at Dienbienphu.[9]

Vice President Richard M. Nixon, Secretary of State John Foster Dulles, and Admiral Arthur W. Radford, chairman of the Joint Chiefs of Staff, all favored some sort of air strike, although it is not clear that they all thought the strike should be nuclear. The only one of the top Eisenhower officials who was strongly opposed to an air strike of any kind was General Matthew B. Ridgway, chief of staff of the Army. Ridgway proceeded to fight the proposal in every way he could.

First, Ridgway piled up memo after memo citing his reasons.[10] He argued that air power alone would not be decisive and that if the United States became involved by bombing it would have to take the further step of introducing ground forces to complete the job. Ridgway assembled a team of military experts of all kinds and sent them to Vietnam with instructions to investigate all aspects of the terrain, port facilities, and road and rail networks and report back in a matter of days on whether an American intervention would be feasible and its prospects for success.

The team's report stated that bombing alone would not work, that more ground troops would be needed than the United States currently had (with the strong implication that the reason the United States did not have enough ground troops was because of the New Look decisions), and that the terrain and logistics backup was so unfavorable that even if the United States did have the requisite number of troops it still might not be able to win.

Even though Eisenhower had been interested in a quick air strike in support of the French at Dienbienphu, he had insisted all along that no action would be taken without the full participation of Congress. However, Ridgway had not only submitted his memos to the president and members of the National Security Council, he had also taken care to make his views known to key leaders in Congress. As a result, when Congressional leaders were consulted, they were skeptical. It is an irony of history that one of the most vociferous objectors to intervention was Lyndon B. Johnson, who was then majority leader of the Senate. Congressional leaders insisted that allies such as Great Britain be a part of the intervention. When consulted, the British government would have none of it, and the proposal for an air strike was dropped.

The French forces at Dienbienphu surrendered, and the result was a negotiated settlement at Geneva making Laos and Cambodia independent countries and "temporarily" dividing Vietnam along the 17th parallel.

THE CRISIS OF QUEMOY AND MATSU

The next crisis was over Quemoy and Matsu, two small islands just off the mainland of China that the Nationalists continued to occupy when they retreated to Taiwan. In 1954 and 1955, the Chinese Communists began to build up their forces facing the islands, and the Nationalists in turn built up their forces on the islands.

In February 1955, Dulles took a trip to the Pacific area, and on his return he said that he felt it was essential that Quemoy and Matsu be held, and that the only way to hold them in case of an all-out attack was with nuclear weapons. Eisenhower sent a trusted military aide, Colonel (later General) Andrew J. Goodpaster, to consult with Admiral Felix Stump, the senior American commander in the Pacific, and Goodpaster reported back on March 15 that within two weeks the defenses on Quemoy and Matsu would be so strong that the Communists could take the islands only by launching a full-scale amphibious attack. As Eisenhower knew better than almost anyone else, an amphibious assault is the most difficult and dangerous kind of military operation. He believed that the Chinese would not be willing to pay such a high price for these two small islands. So he concluded that the next ten days were the time of greatest danger.

The next day, on March 16, Eisenhower was asked at a press conference if the United States would use tactical atomic weapons in a general war in Asia. Eisenhower answered that against a strictly military target the answer would be "yes." Writing later in his memoirs, Eisenhower said that he "hoped this answer would have some effect in persuading the Chinese Communists of the strength of our determination."[11]

THE SOVIET *SPUTNIK*

The Eisenhower administration recognized that eventually the Soviet Union would draw even with the United States in nuclear weapons, and NSC 162/2 explicitly said so. The administration also realized that technology would move ahead too. Eisenhower, in fact, approved the development of the Polaris submarine and four missile systems, the Atlas and Titan intercontinental ballistic missiles (ICBMs) and the Thor and Jupiter intermediate-range ballistic missiles (IRBMs).

But the administration was surprised, American scientists dismayed, and the general public shocked when the Soviets launched the first man-made satellite, *Sputnik*, on October 4, 1957. It had been understood that both the United States and the Soviets had been working on ballistic missiles, following the lead of the Germans with their V-2 rocket that had been used against Great Britain just before the end of World War II. But the Soviets had come in first. If the Soviets had a missile that could launch a satellite, it would not be long before it had one that could launch a nuclear warhead.

THE GAITHER REPORT

A few weeks later, the contents of the top-secret Gaither report were leaked to the *Washington Post*. In the previous year, the point had been made inside the administration that sooner or later the Soviets would develop a capacity to bomb U.S. territory, and that the opposite side of the coin of massive retaliation had to be a civil defense program to protect the American people from a Soviet counterretaliation. The logic was sound, but Eisenhower found the preliminary estimates of the cost—$20 billion—appalling. So he appointed the blue-ribbon Gaither committee to study the problem. The committee sought and obtained permission to broaden their mandate to include the whole range of strategy.

The final report, drafted mainly by Paul Nitze, the hard-line author of NSC-68, said that the Soviet Union had probably surpassed the United States in ICBMs and that SAC was threatened "by the prospects of an early Russian ICBM capability." In the press reports, at least, the Gaither Report was also described as an attack on the New Look and massive retaliation and as a recommendation for rebuilding the Army and Navy back to their former strength, for measures to protect SAC bases from surprise attack, and for a crash program to catch up with the Soviets on ICBMs as well as for providing for civil defense.

THE "MISSILE GAP"

At the same time, the CIA was estimating that Soviet missile production was moving forward and that the Soviets would draw decisively ahead of the United States in no more than two or three years (i.e., by 1962 or 1963). Air Force estimates of Soviet missile production were even higher. Both the CIA and the Air Force leaked their estimates to sympathetic members of Congress and the press. It was widely believed that if the Soviet Union was not already ahead of the United States in missiles, it soon would be. In the election campaign of 1960, John F. Kennedy and the Democrats made much of this upcoming so-called "missile gap."

Over the remaining years of the Eisenhower administration criticism of massive retaliation and the New Look military policy was intense—in Congress, among academic foreign policy and defense specialists, in the press, and among what academics call the "attentive publics." Opponents of massive retaliation and the New Look argued that such policies limited the United States to only one response—nuclear war. An accidental outbreak of violence, for example, could be met only with nuclear weapons. Such a response would obviously increase the risk of World War III, and a nuclear World War III at that.

What is more, the critics argued, such a policy lacked credibility. It was simply not believable that the United States would launch a nuclear war in response to another attack on South Korea by North Korea if this meant that the Soviets then had the option of striking the American homeland. If a threat is to be an effective deterrent it has to threaten to do something that the potential aggressor believes will actually be done. The threat has to be "credible."[12]

FLEXIBLE RESPONSE

By the election of 1960 the Democrats in Congress, their supporters in the Army and Navy, and academic specialists in defense policy had developed a rival doctrine, that of "flexible response." The theory here was that the United States should have balanced military forces consisting of land-based intercontinental missiles, missile-carrying submarines, land-based bombers, carrier-based bombers, both nuclear and conventional ground forces, and both nuclear and conventional naval forces. In this way the United States could respond to threats of any kind and at any level in precisely the same terms on which the threats were posed.

Pointing to the Korean War, the advocates of flexible response argued that the United States should be able to meet any level of threat without raising the level of the fighting and that this would ensure that a limited war would remain limited. Only in this way could accidental or limited aggression be met while minimizing the risk that violence might escalate into a much larger war, a nuclear World War III.

The key to deterrence, again, was the credibility of the threatened retaliation. Potential aggressors would be more effectively deterred if the United States had a wide variety of forces from nuclear to conventional at its disposal and, consequently, a range of responses corresponding to the range of threats.

NOTES

1. Zhou Enlai is here spelled in Pin Yin, rather than Wade-Giles, which would be Chou En-lai.

2. McGeorge Bundy, *Danger and Survival: Choices About the Bomb in the First Fifty Years* (New York: Random House, 1988), 240–241.

3. Dwight D. Eisenhower, *The White House Years: Mandate for Change* (Garden City, N.Y.: Doubleday, 1963), 453.

4. *Foreign Relations of the United States, 1952–54*, vol. 2 (Washington, D.C.: U.S. Government Printing Office), 532, 533, 593.

5. *Foreign Relations of the United States*, vol. 15 (Washington, D.C.: U.S. Government Printing Office, 1952–1954), 1062 ff.

6. David Rosenberg, personal communication with author.

7. Field Marshal Bernard Law Montgomery, "A Look Through a Window at World War III," *Journal of the Royal United Services Institute* (November 1954), 508.

8. Bundy, *Danger and Survival*, 323. The quotes from Eisenhower also appear in Bundy, where their sources are given.

9. The views of General Twining and the reports of Dulles's offer to Bidault are as cited in ibid., 266–267.

10. This account draws on Melvin Gurtov, *The First Vietnam Crisis* (New York: Columbia University Press, 1967).

11. *White House Years*, 477.

12. The concept of "credibility" was developed by William W. Kaufmann. See his "The Requirements of Deterrence" in W. W. Kaufmann, ed., *Military Policy and National Security* (Princeton, N.J.: Princeton University Press, 1956).

Chapter 4

The H-Bomb and the
Balance of Terror

The Korean War stimulated the West to form NATO and to rearm, but it did little to push forward the debate on nuclear strategy. Nor was the debate pushed forward by the argument on massive retaliation versus flexible response. Neither did the cogitations of strategists add very much—except to make the point that massive retaliation lacked credibility and that flexible response would be enormously expensive. The engine that really drove the debate on nuclear strategy was technological development.

THE SOVIETS TEST AN ATOMIC BOMB

The Soviets' first atomic test was in late August 1949. American air-sampling flights picked up evidence of the explosion, and on September 23, President Truman announced the Soviet achievement to the world.

Truman's response was to authorize the development of the "Super," the hydrogen or H-bomb. He announced the decision on January 31, 1950. But between the announcement of the Soviet test and the announcement of the decision to develop the Super, the officials concerned went through a bitter, wrenching debate.

THE H-BOMB

The atomic bomb, to repeat, is based on the principle of fission, in which very heavy elements like uranium or the man-made plutonium break into several lighter elements and in the process release fantastic amounts of energy. The H-bomb is based on fusion. Two hydrogen atoms are fused into one atom of helium, and in the process release even more fantastic amounts of energy.

Hydrogen is more plentiful and cheaper than U-235 or plutonium. But of even greater practical consequence is the fact that there is no theoretical limit to the size of a fusion bomb, while there are very definite limits to the size of a fission bomb. In a fission bomb, once a critical mass of U-235 or plutonium is brought together and held for an instant, it explodes. Practical engineering difficulties set a top limit on the amount of fissionable material that can be safely and effectively brought together. In fact, the limit is not much larger than the critical mass itself (about 2 kilograms). The rest is simply blown away unexploded. There is no such limit to the amount of hydrogen that can be brought together and exploded.

The theoretical possibility of an H-bomb had been recognized early. At Los Alamos, Edward Teller had specialized on the Super. At first the key seemed to be deuterium. The nucleus of most hydrogen atoms has one proton. However, the nucleus of one in about five thousand hydrogen atoms has both a proton and a neutron, hence the name deuterium (in heavy water the H of the H_2O is almost all deuterium). If two deuterium nuclei collide, the result should be fusion, the creation of an atom of helium.

But the forces holding the two deuterium nuclei apart are stupendous, and to overcome those forces the deuterium nuclei have to be very hot. Teller and the others thought that by using a fission bomb as a trigger, the temperature of deuterium could be raised high enough and quickly enough to ignite a thermonuclear reaction. In the early days at Los Alamos, hopes for a hydrogen bomb ran high. But then it became clear that the fission trigger would not raise the temperature of the deuterium fast enough to achieve fusion before the trigger's own force blew the whole thing apart.

Teller's next idea was to use both deuterium and tritium as the hydrogen fuel, the latter being an unstable isotope of hydrogen with two protons as well as a neutron. A large amount of tritium would be needed. Since tritium has a half-life of only 12.26 years, it does not occur in nature. It would have to be manufactured by bombarding an isotope of lithium, Li-6, with neutrons inside an uranium reactor such as Fermi's at the University of Chicago. The process is similar to the way plutonium 239 is produced by bombarding uranium 238 with neutrons. Teller designed a Super that would use both deuterium and tritium, but it was simply not possible to produce enough tritium in time to affect the outcome of the war.

With the war won, most of the scientists wanted to go home, back to basic research and teaching and away from weapons. Those scientists who did remain at Los Alamos worked mainly on improving the fission bomb. But just as soon as the Trinity test at Alamogordo proved the fission bomb, Teller, with the help of Fermi, again took up the theoretical work on the Super.

Teller was driven not only by the scientist's search for ultimate truths, but by a passionate hatred of both Communism and Russia. After a while, Teller accepted a position at the University of Chicago, where he could work with Fermi. For several years, Teller had a happy and scientifically productive life at Chicago. But the relentless march of the Cold War aroused his fundamental fears of Communism and Russia—the Communist coup in Czechoslovakia in 1948, the block-ade of Berlin, and the Chinese Communist victory in 1949.

For Teller there was also a personal element. His parents and sister in Hungary had survived the Nazi slaughter of Jews, but by 1949 the Communists had taken over full power in Hungary, and what Churchill called the Iron Curtain had clanged down. In the summer of 1949, Teller requested leave from the University of Chicago to work full time on weapons at Los Alamos. So when President Truman announced that the Soviets had exploded a fission weapon on September 23, 1949, Teller was in place and eager to go full speed ahead on the Super.

A secret debate began immediately on whether the United States really should go all-out to develop such a weapon. The fact that there were so few participants in the debate—less than one hundred—probably made it more bitter. The people involved were the members and some staff of the Atomic Energy Commission (AEC); the members of the General Advisory Committee of the AEC, whose chairman was J. Robert Oppenheimer; the members of the Joint Committee on Atomic Energy of Congress and a few of the staff; the Joint Chiefs of Staff and a few of their "Indians" (Pentagon slang for the staff working for the "Chiefs"); Louis Johnson, the secretary of defense, and a few other top civilians in the Pentagon; Dean Acheson, the secretary of state, and some of the top State Department officials; and a handful of scientists with the necessary security clearances. One of the latter was Teller, who went to Washington on his own to lobby for the Super.

The General Advisory Committee chaired by Oppenheimer recommended increasing the production of fissionable materials, boosting the power of fission bombs with the addition of tritium, and exerting greater efforts to make "tactical" nuclear weapons—small bombs and artillery shells for use on the battlefield. But they recommended against developing the Super.

Their reasoning was, first, that the Super would be a weapon of mass destruction with no other military use. Second, the Super would require large amounts of tritium, since the only design for an H-bomb so far conceived was Teller's, which called for both deuterium and tritium. No one could be certain that Teller's design would work, and making the amounts of tritium needed for the H-bomb would slow down the production of fission bombs, which had been proven beyond any doubts at Alamogordo, Hiroshima, and Nagasaki. Since the stockpile at that time—1949—consisted of only about 200 bombs, national security would be better served, they argued, by continuing to add fission bombs to the stockpile.

All the members of the General Advisory Committee signed the report, but majority and minority annexes were added. The majority annex argued that the Super should *never* be produced. If the United States succeeded in building the Super, the majority argued, it would not deter the Soviets from making one too. On the other hand, if the Soviets were successful in building a Super and used it against the United States in some future war, reprisals with our large stock of fission bombs would be just as effective as a Super. The minority annex—signed by Rabi and Fermi—agreed that the Super was a weapon of genocide and "an evil thing considered in any light." But they argued that the promise not to develop a Super should be conditional on the Soviets making the same commitment. In this way the *question* of a Super might be used to launch a new effort in arms control.[1]

The five members of the Atomic Energy Commission were divided. Lewis Strauss was determined that the United States should go full speed on the Super. He quickly found out that Teller and Lawrence agreed, and he then enlisted Sidney Souers as an ally. Souers was a banker from Missouri who was a Reserve Corps Admiral and a very, very close friend and adviser to President Truman. David Lilienthal, the chairman of the Commission, decided that the decision on the Super was a foreign policy question and therefore more a matter for the State Department and the White House than the Commission, and he told Acheson that this is what he thought. The Commission then submitted a divided report.

General Omar Bradley, chairman of the Joint Chiefs of Staff, testified before the Joint Committee on Atomic energy, chaired by Senator Brien McMahon, that the Chiefs believed that if it was possible to build a Super, it would be "intolerable" if the Soviets got one first. Influenced by this testimony, Senator McMahon and the Joint Atomic Energy Committee strongly favored going full speed ahead.

Faced with these differing views, President Truman appointed the secretary of state, the secretary of defense, and the chairman of the Atomic Energy Commission as a special committee of the NSC to advise him on the problem. Acheson was chairman, and he quickly decided that Lilienthal and Johnson were so far apart in their views that he, Acheson, had to serve as an intermediary in working out their recommendation. In the end they recommended that the United States go ahead with the Super. But they also called for a "reexamination of our objectives in peace and war," which was the genesis of what became NSC 68.

What really persuaded Truman, however, was apparently a paper from the Joint Chiefs of Staff.[2] Truman, who had been an artillery captain in World War I, had a high respect for the military and even higher respect for General Omar Bradley, the JCS chairman. First, the JCS paper argued, as Bradley had done before the Joint Committee, that it would be intolerable for the Soviets to have the Super and the United States not to have it. Second, the paper argued that a decision by the United States not to build the Super would not prevent it from being developed elsewhere.

When the special committee of Acheson, Johnson, and Lilienthal met with President Truman, the meeting took seven minutes. Truman asked whether the Soviets could build such a bomb. Everyone agreed that they could. Truman's response was that, in that case, the United States had no choice but to go ahead.

"TELLER'S GIMMICK"

When Truman made the decision to go ahead, the scientists at Los Alamos believed a Super was theoretically possible, but they still had no concrete idea of how to make one. All they had was Teller's notion of a bomb based on both deuterium and tritium. A mathematical simulation of a thermonuclear explosion had to be done, which would require calculations of enormous complexity, by far the most complicated that humankind had ever undertaken. As a practical matter, such calculations would not have been possible until the invention of electronic computers. The first primitive electronic computer, the ENIAC, was put to work on the problem during the summer of 1950. In the end the calculations showed that Teller's design for the Super simply would not work.

As it turned out, the riddle of how to make an H-bomb was solved by an entirely new concept. For years it was known to outsiders as "Teller's gimmick," but it was Stanislaw Ulam who had the original idea, and Teller who perfected and added to it, so it is now called the "Teller–Ulam configuration."[3] So even though Teller is often called the "father of the H-bomb," it really had two fathers. However, it was Hans Bethe who had the last word on the bomb's parentage: "I used to say that Ulam was the father of the hydrogen bomb and Edward was the mother, because he carried the baby for quite a while."[4]

The problem, to repeat, was that the fission trigger would blow the whole thing apart before the hydrogen fuel reached the temperature necessary for fusion. But a fission bomb produces a large amount of x-rays as well as shock waves. X-rays travel at the speed of light while shock waves travel at the speed of sound. Ulam's idea was that if the fission trigger was physically separated from the hydrogen fuel the x-rays would reach the fuel a fraction of a second before the shock waves, which might be time enough to raise the temperatures to the proper level before the shock waves blew the whole thing to smithereens.

But even though the x-rays would raise the temperature, they would not provide the pressure that was also needed. The solution was ordinary plastic. If the hydrogen fuel was encased in plastic, the x-rays from the trigger exploded a certain distance away would instantly turn the plastic into a very hot ionized gas— a plasma—which expands at extreme speed to generate pressures much greater than ordinary explosives would. Moreover, since the x-rays travel at the speed of light, the plastic would all be transformed into a plasma simultaneously. The result would be an almost perfectly symmetrical implosion of great force. At the same time, the x-rays would continue to the hydrogen fuel, raising it to the required temperature. In this way both the temperature and the pressure required for fusion would be reached *before* the shock waves from the fission trigger arrived to blow everything apart.

However, still one more innovation was needed to get the fusion reaction well started. Although not all the information has been declassified, the key was apparently threefold.

The first was to put a casing of U-238 around both the trigger and the hydrogen fuel. The U-238 casing served to concentrate the x-rays on the plastic.

The second was to put another casing of U-238 *inside* the plastic and around the hydrogen fuel. When this second blanket of U-238 was bombarded by the flow of neutrons at the beginning stages of the thermonuclear reaction, it would fission and supply still more neutrons to continue the thermonuclear burning.

The third key was a central core of plutonium. The plastic implosion would crush the plutonium into a critical mass, triggering fission. This would in turn add to the temperature and pressure on the thermonuclear materials, squeezing them from the inside as well as the outside.

When Oppenheimer was told of the new design, even though he dreaded the thought of an H-bomb, he could not help being impressed. He called the design "technically sweet."

On November 1, 1952, a device based on the Teller–Ulam configuration, codenamed "Mike," was tested at Eniwetok atoll in the South Pacific, from which the natives had been evacuated. It exploded with the power of over 10 million tons of TNT. The fireball had a diameter of three miles. Most of the water in the atoll's lagoon was turned to steam. Where the island that housed the device had been there was a crater half a mile deep and two miles wide.

The hydrogen fuel used in the Mike device was liquid deuterium and tritium. This made the scientific measurements simpler, but it also made the device too bulky and heavy (65 tons) for a deliverable bomb. But turning the device into a deliverable bomb posed no great problems. The hydrogen fuel for a true bomb would be a dry powder, lithium deuteride, in which the lithium was the isotope Li-6. The neutrons from the fission trigger and boosters would convert the Li-6 to tritium, which, under the enormous temperature and pressure developed by the Teller–Ulam configuration, would then fuse with the deuteride, producing a true thermonuclear explosion.

Early in 1954, a "dry," deliverable bomb was tested. Its yield was 15 megatons.

THE SOVIET H-BOMB

As for the Soviets, the evidence, including the testimony of Andrei Sakharov, the "father of the Soviet bomb," is that they decided to develop an H-bomb several months earlier than the Americans did. That is, the Soviets made their decision immediately following the success of their first atomic test in August 1949. They tested a device with a "hydrogen component" in August of 1953, and on November 23, 1955, they tested a true H-bomb, dropped from an aircraft. In later tests, the Soviets exploded the largest bomb that has ever been fired—before or since—an H-bomb with a yield of about 60 megatons.

RADIOACTIVE FALLOUT

In the course of testing the H-bomb an unexpected lethal effect was discovered—radioactive fallout.

Before the tests it was well understood that both fission and fusion bombs destroy life by blast and fire, as conventional explosives do. The force of the blast and fire was fully expected, and it was awesome. The Nagasaki bomb, with an estimated yield of 22 kilotons, was exploded at an altitude of 1,850 feet. The blast knocked down buildings, which requires 5 psi (pounds per square inch) of overpressure, at a distance of 7,500 feet or 1.4 miles from ground zero. A 3-megaton H-bomb exploded on the surface will topple brick structures at a distance of 4 miles from ground zero, giving a total area of such destruction of 50 square miles. For a 10-megaton bomb, the radius is 6.5 miles, and the area is 133 square miles.

The urban area of greater Moscow is 1,035 square miles; the urban area of greater New York City (including Nassau, Rockland, Suffolk, and Westchester counties) is 2,136 square miles. Thus, greater Moscow could be totally destroyed by twenty-one missile warheads of 3 megatons each, if they were perfectly targeted, and greater New York by forty-three. Warplanes carrying 10-megaton bombs could wreak the same damage on Moscow with nine bombs and on New York with sixteen bombs.

These figures are for blast alone. The thermal effects from nuclear weapons can be even more devastating. Heat from the Hiroshima bomb boiled away the internal organs of people in the open within one-half mile of the hypocenter and reduced their bodies to piles of black char an instant later. Almost everyone in the open within a mile of the hypocenter suffered fatal burns. People as far away as two to two and one-half miles suffered lesser, though often fatal burns.

The heat from a fission bomb also starts innumerable fires, sometimes at considerable distances, depending on the weather. As a rule of thumb, the distance can be assumed to be three times that of the blast effect and nine times the area. With a large number of fires starting simultaneously at many different points in a city under attack, a firestorm will often develop.

To enlarge on what was said about firestorms in Chapter 2, what happens is that the large amount of heat rising from so many fires draws strong winds in from the surrounding areas. These fan the flames even higher into one great conflagration. The winds suck in debris, which feed the flames of the central inferno even higher. The winds also suck in people. The casualties from burning and suffocation in the areas on fire will be as great as the casualties in the blast zone. Because of firestorms, probably all that would be needed to destroy Moscow would be three 3-megaton missile warheads or one 10-megaton bomb, and to destroy New York five 3-megaton missile warheads or two 10-megaton bombs.

The Los Alamos scientists also knew that some people would be killed by direct radiation from the fireball. However, at Hiroshima the deaths and maiming from radiation were much greater than had been expected. Robert Jay Lifton, a psychiatrist who interviewed many of the survivors, describes the effects:

Soon after the bomb fell—sometimes within hours or even minutes, often during the first twenty-four hours or the following days and weeks—survivors began to notice in themselves and others a strange form of illness. It consisted of nausea, vomiting, and loss of appetite; diarrhea with large amounts of blood in the stools; fever and weakness; purple spots on various parts of the body from bleeding into the skin (purpura); inflammation and ulceration of the mouth, throat, and gums (oropharyngeal lesions and gingivitis); bleeding from the mouth, gums, throat, rectum, and urinary tract (hemorrhagic manifestations;) loss of hair from the scalp and other parts of the body (epilation); extremely low white blood cell counts when those were taken (leukopenia); and in many cases a progressive course until death.[5]

A fission bomb exploded high in the air, such as the Hiroshima and Nagasaki bombs, blasts out the radioactive products that result from fission itself. The area covered by these radioactive products will depend on wind and weather conditions at the particular altitude of the explosion. Although an H-bomb exploded high in the air produces tritium, carbon 14, and certain other radioactive products, it is no more "dirty" with radioactivity than its fission trigger.

The surprise—the unanticipated lethal effects—came when the United States tested an H-bomb at Bikini atoll on March 1, 1954, the *Bravo* test in the *Castle* series in a surface explosion. It turned out that both fission and fusion bombs exploded at the surface pick up debris from the surface and make it radioactive. So bombs exploded at the surface will deposit both the products of fission *and* surface debris made radioactive by the explosion downwind of the explosion in a cigar-shaped pattern. The *Bravo* bomb had a yield of 15 megatons. Over one-hundred miles downwind from the explosion radioactive "fallout" sickened the crew of a Japanese fishing boat, the *Lucky Dragon*, and one of the crewmen eventually died. The fallout from the *Bravo* explosion covered 7 thousand square miles in which "survival might have depended upon prompt evacuation of the area or upon taking shelter and other protective measures."[6]

It was quickly realized that bombs could be deliberately made that were much, much "dirtier" than even this. Any U-238 that is present in a fission bomb does not split. But in the environment of an H-bomb, with its much higher temperatures and faster moving neutrons, U-238 does fission. It releases still more energy, and many more radioactive byproducts. So surrounding an H-bomb with a thick jacket of U-238 will not only contribute to the total energy released, but it will also vastly increase the radioactive fallout.

Areas dusted with radioactive fallout will be highly dangerous to all forms of life. Many people in such an area will die within several days. Others will develop cancers that kill them later. Still others will survive, but with genetic damage that will affect future generations. As Bernard Brodie, one of the very first academic strategists of the nuclear age remarked, "The Hiroshima and Nagasaki bombs each destroyed a whole city. Now a bomb can be made that will destroy two cities—one by heat and blast and the other, downwind, by radioactive fallout."[7]

NOTES

1. The report and the annexes are reproduced in Herbert York, *The Advisors: Oppenheimer, Teller, and the Superbomb* (San Francisco: W. H. Freeman, 1976), 150 ff.

2. McGeorge Bundy, *Danger and Survival: Choices About the Bomb in the First Fifty Years* (New York: Random House, 1988), 213.

3. This account of the Teller–Ulam gimmick draws mainly on Richard Rhodes, *The Making of the Atomic Bomb* (New York: Simon and Schuster, 1987), 772 ff.

4. Jeremy Bernstein, *Hans Bethe: Prophet of Energy* (New York: Basic Books, 1980), 95.

5. Robert Jay Lifton, *Death in Life* (New York: Random House, 1967), 57.

6. "The Effects of High-Yield Nuclear Explosions," Atomic Energy Commission release, Washington, D.C., 15 February 1955.

7. Bernard Brodie, personal communication with the author shortly after the Bravo test.

Chapter 5

The Debate on Nuclear Strategy

The H-bomb and the lethal potentialities of fallout sparked a new debate on nuclear strategy, and Winston Churchill was among the first to be heard. In a speech in Parliament on March 1, 1955, he argued that there was "an immense gulf between the atomic and the hydrogen bomb."

What inspired Churchill was probably the work of P. M. S. Blackett, who had been a pioneer in "operations research" that had led to the successful convoy system of World War II. Suppose, Blackett reasoned, a defending country put substantial resources into antiaircraft equipment, such as jet fighters, antiaircraft missiles, and so on (this was before the development of ICBMs and other long-range missiles). If so, the attacking force would have to be a fleet of bombers, along the lines of those in World War II. To equal the damage done to Germany by air attack in World War II, Blackett estimated that 400 Hiroshima-type bombs would be needed, and to make sure that 400 bombs arrived on target the attacking fleet would have to start out with 1 thousand.[1]

Vannevar Bush seemed to agree; he argued that at least for the immediate future the atomic bomb was not an absolute weapon, in the sense that it was not "so overpowering as to make all other methods of waging war obsolete."[2]

The atomic bomb, Churchill went on to say, "with all its terrors," did not carry us beyond the scope of human control. But the H-bomb, he argued, had revolutionized the entire foundation of human affairs and placed mankind "in a situation both measureless and laden with doom."[3]

The point was that the same destruction wrought by 400 atomic bombs could be accomplished by about forty H-bombs. And even in the face of an air defense system, rather than 1 thousand bombers, only one hundred would be needed.

However, Churchill then went on to suggest that, paradoxically, peace might become the "sturdy child of terror" and "survival the twin brother of annihilation." There would be no "winners" in a war fought with such horrifying weapons, so humankind might be too frightened of the consequences to fight at all.

Others quickly picked up this notion of a "balance of terror." In a nuclear age, the argument went, the United States and the Soviet Union are like two scorpions in a bottle. If either strikes, the other will still have enough strength to strike back, and both will die. Thus peace will be preserved, the argument continued, through mutual terror. What is more, the argument went on, this peace born of terror was likely to be stable and long-lasting, simply because both sides understood the consequences and would act with the utmost caution.

For a brief time, strategists—thinking that nuclear stockpiles would continue to be very limited—talked of "broken-back" war. The notion was that both sides would use up their stockpile of nuclear weapons but that enough troops and industrial potential would survive to permit the two cripples to continue fighting, although at a much reduced level of violence. But it soon became clear that the stockpiles would not be limited, and no more was heard of the idea of "broken-back" war.

The strategic situation resulting from unlimited stockpiles of nuclear weapons came to be known as Mutual Assured Destruction, and with gallows humor it was quickly dubbed MAD, suggesting that we live in a mad, mad world. The point of MAD is that defense is simply impossible. The only protection is through deterrence, arms control, or a combination of the two.

DETERRENCE THEORY

Strategists quickly came to understand that this situation posed a most peculiar problem for the theory of deterrence, vividly described by a parable concocted by Professor Warner R. Schilling of Columbia University.

Visualize a sort of fortress-like squash court with ceilings fourteen feet high and divided down the middle by a heavy concrete wall ten feet high. On one side of the wall is a totally evil person who is armed with a single hand grenade. With him are ten innocent babies. On the other side of the wall is a person who is totally good. He also has a grenade, and on his side of the wall are another ten innocent babies. If either one throws his grenade, the other will have just enough strength before dying to pull the pin and throw his grenade too.

Both the good guy and the bad guy will soon realize that their strategic situation is highly unstable. If the bad guy throws his grenade, the good guy and his ten babies will die. But if the good guy retaliates by throwing his grenade, the only result would be the death of the bad guy at the cost of the lives of ten more innocents. The point is that if deterrence fails, the only motive for retaliating is revenge. Revenge is not a moral motive, so if deterrence fails, a truly good person would not retaliate. So the bad guy has no reason to be deterred.

In strategic parlance this situation is known as the problem of credibility. Unless both sides are totally convinced that the other side will retaliate even if retaliation accomplishes nothing, deterrence is ineffective. How do you make the other side believe that you will launch a second strike no matter what?

What can the good guy do? The only effective strategy is for him to build a "doomsday machine." In the parable, a feasible doomsday machine would be a catapult held down by a string. If the bad guy throws his grenade, the explosion will sever the string holding the catapult, which is rigged to pull the pin and launch the good guy's grenade automatically.

With a doomsday machine like this catapult, the good guy can say to the bad guy well in advance of a crisis, "I no longer have any control. Retaliation will be automatic. The immoral decision to kill us all is solely yours." Deterrence is once again established, and the strategic situation is stabilized.

Again with gallows humor, analysts at the RAND corporation, the think tank for strategy in Santa Monica, California, proceeded to figure out a way of making a real-world doomsday machine. This was in the days before missiles when the manned bomber was king, and what they proposed was appointing General Curtis L. LeMay to the lifetime job of commander of the Strategic Air Command. "Curt" LeMay was a hardline Air Force general who wanted to end the Vietnam war by bombing North Vietnam "back to the stone age." The United States, he argued, was "swatting flies in South Vietnam." What it should do was to destroy "the manure pile in North Vietnam" where the flies were breeding. No one in the world would doubt that LeMay would retaliate, even if he had to fly the last surviving bomber himself.

For the second half of the problem—the point that if deterrence failed a second strike was meaningless—the RAND analysts suggested a second lifetime job. This would be LeMay's deputy, and he would have secret orders that if, in spite of everything, deterrence failed, then he was to shoot LeMay!

But except for RAND's macabre joke, none of the strategists seemed to have an answer to the problem.

SIOP-62

It was not until September 13, 1961, that President Kennedy and his secretaries of state and defense, Dean Rusk and Robert S. McNamara, were briefed by the chairman of the Joint Chiefs of Staff, General Lyman L. Lemnitzer, on the Single Integrated Operational Plan for Fiscal Year 1962—SIOP-62.

As the Air Force, Navy, and Army had acquired nuclear bombs and missiles, they had made plans to use them in case of war on targets that were important to that service's particular mission. The results were not only that the different services would hit some of the same targets, but they would interfere with each other as they were flying over those targets—indeed, they might destroy each other. As already described, in the last years of the Eisenhower administration the SIOP was developed to eliminate this duplication. The first SIOP was approved in December of 1960 and went into effect in April of 1961, just after Kennedy took office.

General Lemnitzer's briefing was on SIOP-62. In accordance with this plan, approximately one half of the bombers of the Strategic Air Command were kept on a fifteen-minute alert on the runways, and a small number of B-52s were kept on continuous airborne alert. About one-third of the ICBM force of seventy-eight missiles were always on alert, and so were two of the Navy's five Polaris submarines (each carrying sixteen missiles).

General Lemnitzer also discussed a strategy of preemption. The consequences of a Soviet first strike with nuclear weapons on the United States would be so horrendous that one of SIOP's options was for a preemptive attack. If intelligence showed that the Soviets were preparing to attack by fitting warheads to missiles, fueling missiles, moving bombers to advance bases in the Arctic, and so on, SIOP-62 provided the president with the option of ordering the United States to strike first—to "launch on warning."

The United States Air Force Bombing Encyclopedia at the time listed 80 thousand targets. Of these, 3,729 had been placed on the National Strategic Target List as essential to the Soviet bloc if it decided to attack. These targets included missile sites, airfields and other military facilities, military and government command and control sites, and major urban and industrial centers in the Soviet Union, China, and countries in Eastern Europe and elsewhere that were Soviet allies. These 3,729 targets were so situated that nuclear warheads exploded at 1,060 Designated Ground Zero (DGZ) points would destroy them all.

If the alert option was executed—that is, if the United States decided to preempt in a crisis in order to get in the first blow—1,685 nuclear warheads would be launched against these 1,060 DGZs, thus increasing the probability that each DGZ would be hit at least once.

However, General Lemnitzer warned that "under any circumstances—even a preemptive attack by the United States—it would be expected that some portion of the Soviet long-range nuclear force would strike the United States." Also, any attempt to increase the forces on alert in a time of tension would run the risk of triggering a Soviet preemptive attack of its own.

SIOP-62 was clearly a war plan to implement a strategy of massive retaliation. It was also politically unsophisticated, taking no account of the growing evidence of a Sino–Soviet split and of the stirrings in Eastern Europe. It was a knee-jerk, spasm sort of strategy, and Kennedy, Rusk, and McNamara were appalled. As they were leaving the briefing, Kennedy remarked in aside to Rusk, "And we call ourselves the human race!"[4]

Disgusted with SIOP-62 and armed with the knowledge that the missile gap favored the United States rather than the Soviet Union, the Kennedy administration set about to develop a different strategy and a different SIOP.

FLEXIBLE RESPONSE EXTENDED

The strategy of flexible response was initially concerned with how to deal with lesser aggressions, such as the 1950 attack on South Korea, rather than an all-out assault on the United States or on Europe. The idea, to repeat, was that the

United States and its allies should have the capacity to meet any aggression, at whatever force level, on the same level as it was made. Accordingly, an all-out nuclear assault should be met by an all-out nuclear response. But a large-scale assault with conventional weapons, such as infantry, tanks, and close-in air support, and that was geographically limited, should be met with exactly the same weapons and confined to the same limited geographic area.

McNamara now began to try to apply this notion of flexibility to the strategy to be used in a war with the Soviet Union itself, including a nuclear war. What McNamara wanted was a range of options in case of a Soviet attack that would permit the president a greater choice than that between surrender and suicide.

CITY AVOIDANCE AND DAMAGE LIMITATION

McNamara's first innovation in strategy was "city avoidance"—the targets would be military forces and installations, not cities and population. But even though cities would not be targeted as such, everyone soon realized that in an attack on the enemy's military his cities would inevitably suffer substantial damage.

McNamara entertained no hope that an attack on the Soviet Union's forces could be successful enough to disarm it. An effective counterforce strategy would have to provide at least two very accurate missiles to attack each of the enemy's missiles. Even so, some Soviet forces—whether missed missiles, bombers in the air, or submarines at sea—would undoubtedly survive and be able to counterattack. Even if more than two missiles were provided for each Soviet missile, the Soviets could just build more missiles. And the Soviets would have to build only one new missile for each two or more that the United States built.

For all these reasons, it was important that the United States not be seen to harbor any thoughts of a first strike. The purpose of targeting the enemy's military forces was, first, to deny him the possibility of victory and, second, to limit the damage he could inflict on the United States and its allies. The United States would invite the Soviets to join it in avoiding cities, but it would also adopt measures for "damage limitation," measures that would result in as little damage as possible to the United States.

To some extent, the notion of damage limitation was an answer to the question, "What does the United States do if deterrence fails?" When Kennedy came to office, relations between the Soviet Union and the United States were tense. As already described, at the very beginning of the Kennedy administration, Khrushchev had threatened "wars of national liberation," he had blustered about Berlin in the Vienna meeting, and the Berlin wall had been erected shortly afterwards. In the summer of 1961, the possibility that deterrence might fail seemed very real.

Part of the new McNamara strategy was to hold back some forces from the initial assault—unlike SIOP-62's preemptive option which from the very outset of the war threw everything in the U.S. stockpile at the enemy. A certain proportion would be kept as a reserve. These weapons could be used to meet unforeseen contingencies. Or, after the bulk of the enemy military was destroyed, these reserve weapons could be used to force him to surrender by threatening his economic base and, if necessary, even his cities.

Another part of the strategy was an effort to protect the American command and control centers, putting some deep inside of mountains and others in airplanes on continuous airborne alert.

The final part of the strategy was what seemed at first a rather bizarre notion that the enemy's command and control system should *not* be attacked. But the argument made sense: The enemy must be left with the means both to make a decision to surrender and to communicate that decision to any of his forces that survived. Otherwise those remnants might use their remaining strength to attack American cities.

In June 1962, McNamara announced the new strategy in a speech at Ann Arbor, Michigan. If the Soviet Union attacked the United States or its allies, the United States would respond by attacking not the enemy's cities and civilian population, but his military forces. The military forces of the United States and its allies, McNamara said, would be able to survive a massive surprise attack and still be able to destroy the enemy's society if driven to it. "In other words," he said, "we are giving a possible opponent the strongest possible incentive to refrain from striking our own cities."

CRITICISMS

The major criticism of McNamara's strategy of "city avoidance and damage limitation" was that the forces required for such a strategy were pretty much the same as those required for a first-strike force. The Soviets, and many critics in the West, said a counterforce strategy and a first-strike strategy were identical. Nuclear war, said the Soviets, could not be conducted with "Marquis of Queensbury rules." In nuclear war, they argued, mass destruction was inevitable.

Furthermore, even if McNamara's intentions were good, a damage-limitation strategy would require an attack on certain "rear-echelon" targets deep in enemy territory. Some of these targets would inevitably be near or even in cities. In practice, it would be difficult if not impossible for the enemy being attacked to tell the difference between the two strategies.

To McNamara's dismay, America's European allies welcomed the counterforce doctrine as an excuse not to make too great an effort in building up their conventional defenses as McNamara had been urging them to do. They saw the strategy as adding to the credibility of the threat to retaliate on the Soviet homeland in response to an attack on Europe and therefore as lessening the need for them to make defense preparations of their own.

Even more distressing to McNamara was the U.S. Air Force interpretation of his city-avoidance and damage-limitation strategy. People in the Air Force concluded that the strategy would work only if the United States got in the first blow. So they treated McNamara's strategy as if it were a preemptive, counterforce strategy aimed at destroying the enemy's forces and so compelling the enemy to accept peace on American terms. No one suggested openly that the United States should launch a surprise first strike along the lines of the Japanese attack on Pearl Harbor. But they did argue that the United States should launch a preemptive attack as soon as intelligence indicated that the Soviets were making preparations for an attack. Many strategists doubted that there was any difference between a preemptive strike and an American Pearl Harbor, but their doubts were conveniently ignored.

NOTES

1. P.M.S. Blackett, *The Military and Political Consequences of Atomic Energy* (London: Turnstile Press, 1948), 54.

2. Vannevar Bush, *Modern Arms and Free Men* (London: Heinemann, 1950), 100.

3. Blackett, *The Military and Political Consequences of Atomic Energy*, 54.

4. Richard Reeves, *President Kennedy: Profile of Power* (New York: Simon and Schuster, 1993), 230.

Part II

THE CUBAN MISSILE CRISIS:
A CASE STUDY
OF NUCLEAR STRATEGY

Chapter 6

The Crisis

Again it was events that drove the debate on nuclear strategy forward—at this point, the Cuban missile crisis.[1]

In their rocket program, the Soviets decided on a bold move—to skip the logical next step, rockets of 350 thousand pounds of thrust like the American Atlas, and go straight to giants of 800 thousand pounds thrust. The missile was to be not only the behemoth that launched Yuri Gagarin as the first man in space, but also the workhorse of their long-range missile force—ICBMs.

THE MISSILE GAP

In 1960, American intelligence picked up rumors that the Soviets were beginning to deploy these ICBMs at Plesetsk near the Arctic circle. Gary Powers was dispatched in a U-2 to take pictures of the area, but he was shot down en route. In the brouhaha that followed, President Eisenhower was forced to promise not to fly the U-2 over the Soviet Union again, and American intelligence was blinded. But the evidence already available showed that there was a "missile gap" in the Soviets' favor.

Fearing the effects on the economy of increased military spending, the Eisenhower administration argued that America's advantage in manned bombers made a crash ICBM program unnecessary. But the Pentagon leaked its unhappiness with this decision to Congress and the press, and Senator John F. Kennedy made the missile gap a central feature in his successful 1960 campaign for the White House.

But when the Soviets began to deploy their giant rockets at Plesetsk, they discovered immediately—and the Americans only much later—that they were just too big and bulky for operational weapons. The Soviets had to start all over again to design a smaller version, and the Soviet missile program was set back many months.

But so long as the United States did not know the true situation, the Soviets could continue to act as if they were ahead, and they did just that. Shortly after Kennedy's inauguration, Khrushchev made a belligerent speech announcing Soviet support for "wars of national liberation." Later that year, in his meeting with Kennedy, Khrushchev blustered that "Berlin belongs to us." When the flow of refugees through Berlin to the West became a flood, the Communist side built the Berlin wall to keep them in.

THE MISSILE GAP IN REVERSE

Then, during the summer of 1961, the United States flew its first successful picture-taking satellites and discovered the true situation. Rather than a missile gap in favor of the Soviet Union, there was one in favor of the United States.

As it turned out, during the Cuban missile crisis the United States had 140 ICBMs on alert and ready to fire, while the Soviets had 44. In addition, the United States had a handful of manned bombers on airborne alert capable of reaching the Soviet Union, a somewhat larger number on fifteen-minute ground alert, and approximately 200 more in various states of readiness. The Soviets also had a small number of bombers capable of bombing the American homeland, although for most of them it would have been a one-way trip.

The Soviets continued to threaten Berlin, and President Kennedy decided that they had to be told that the United States knew the true situation. An announcement by the president, secretary of state, or secretary of defense might appear threatening, but one at too low a level might not be credible. So the decision was to have the deputy secretary of defense, Roswell Gilpatric, make it in a low-key, numbers-laden, unprovocative speech. The message was reinforced by a round of briefings of the NATO Allies, with U-2 pictures. And to make sure that the Gilpatric speech would be reinforced and confirmed through Soviet intelligence channels, the briefings deliberately included some allies whom the United States knew were penetrated by KGB agents.

For their part, the Soviets quickly realized that to reach the conclusion that the missile gap was in their favor, the Americans must have made an intelligence breakthrough. The implications were horrendous. It was not so much that the Americans had military superiority—the Soviets were already well aware of that. What was bound to alarm them much more was that the Americans now *knew* they had military superiority. Even worse, the Soviet leaders quickly realized that the Americans could not have calculated the total number of missiles unless they had found a way to pinpoint where those missiles were located. If the location of the Soviet ICBMs were secret, they would be effective for both a first, surprise strike and a second, retaliatory strike. But if the United States had a map with all the pads plotted, the system would retain some of its utility as a first-strike weapon, but almost none as a second-strike weapon. The whole Soviet ICBM system was suddenly obsolescent.

While the Soviets fretted over these intractable problems, Castro clamored more and more insistently for military protection, couching his pleas so as to magnify the threat of an American invasion. But it is doubtful that the Soviet Union believed that the United States would invade Cuba with American troops. Khrushchev in his memoirs says that the idea of putting missiles in Cuba was his own. He writes that it came to him while he was pacing up and down in his hotel room during a visit to Bulgaria worrying about the fact that the Americans were not only ahead in ICBMs but knew that they were ahead.

Khrushchev writes that he was concerned that the United States might launch another Bay of Pigs invasion. But this is obviously a rationalization. Khrushchev knew all about the pressure the CIA had put on Kennedy to intervene with American forces at the time of the Bay of Pigs and the fact that Kennedy adamantly refused. He knew how much criticism Kennedy had taken for that refusal and that in spite of that criticism Kennedy had not ordered any military preparations whatsoever for another attempt, as he was being urged to do. The truth of the matter is that there were no conceivable circumstances in which the Soviet Union would have taken even the tiniest risk of war with the United States to save Castro and a Communist Cuba. What was really agitating Khrushchev as he paced up and down his hotel room in Bulgaria, and what loomed over everything else, was, as Khrushchev wrote in his memoirs, "what the West likes to call the 'balance of power.'"

As Khrushchev says, it suddenly came to him that since the Soviet Union had a huge supply of MRBMs and IRBMs, the solution was to deploy them to Cuba. For their part, the president and his advisers realized that the Soviets would find a missile gap against them intolerable, and they anticipated that the Soviet response would be a crash ICBM program. The Americans knew that the Soviets had a huge oversupply of medium-range and intermediate-range missiles, but they had never deployed missiles outside their own borders and no one expected that they would do so now.

THE SOVIET PLAN

The Soviet plan was in two phases. In the first phase, Cuba was to be ringed with defenses—twenty-four batteries of surface-to-air antiaircraft missiles with a slant range of twenty-five miles; over one hundred MIG fighter planes; short-range harbor defense missiles (with a range of thirty-five to forty miles); coastal patrol boats armed with ship-to-ship missiles; and IL-28 light bombers.

The second phase was to deploy to Cuba six battalions of the MRBMs and four battalions of the IRBMs. In Western Cuba, three battalions of the MRBMs were to be at San Cristóbal and three at Sagua La Grande. In central Cuba, two battalions of the IRBMs were to be at Guanajay and two more battalions at Remedios. Thus, San Cristóbal and Sagua La Grande would each have twelve launching pads and Guanajay and Remedios would each have eight, for a total of forty pads. Each pad was to be equipped with two missiles, so forty missiles could be fired in an initial salvo and forty more could be launched in a follow-on.

The warheads for the MRBMs and IRBMs had the explosive force of one megaton; that is, the equivalent of one million tons of TNT. By comparison, the bomb that destroyed Hiroshima had an explosive force of only 14 kilotons; that is, only 14 thousand pounds of TNT.

During the crisis, over twenty Soviet cruise missile installations were also identified. Such missiles normally carry nuclear warheads and have a range of several hundred miles, but it is not clear just what their targets were to be. However, the most likely possibility would be troop concentrations in Florida if the United States started preparing for an invasion.

It was to be a major military deployment, in some ways as complicated to plan and carry out as a landing on a hostile shore, such as the Normandy landing in World War II and the Inchon landing in the Korean war. Each of the twenty-four antiaircraft sites was to have twenty-four missiles thirty feet long—a total of 576 missiles—and a variety of special trailers, fueling trucks, and radar vans. Each of the ten IRBM and MRBM missile battalions was to have eight missiles sixty feet long, and dozens of special vehicles, missile erectors, and personnel carriers.[2]

The missile forces were to be accompanied by four battle groups of special ground troops, a total of about 42 thousand men. Armed with tactical nuclear weapons with a range of 40 kilometers, these troops were to protect the missiles from ground attack, either by invasion or from the American base at Guantánamo. They would be a formidable force of infantry, artillery, and battlefield nuclear weapons. It is probably no accident that if Castro ever took a notion to try to take over the missiles for himself, this force could have defeated the whole Cuban army in very short order.[3]

The grand total of men, weapons, and materiel was staggering. A measure of its magnitude is the fact that a ship can carry twenty to thirty railroad train loads of materiel and that the deployment required more than one hundred ships to carry it all, making a total of 2 to 3 thousand train loads of war materiel.

The first Soviet arms shipment to Cuba was in the summer of 1960. In November, the Eisenhower administration announced that at least twelve Soviet shiploads of arms had been delivered. This was followed by a lull. The shipments started again in July 1962. By late August, about twenty shiploads had arrived. On September 13, 1962, President Kennedy issued a warning. Denying that the United States had any intention of invading Cuba, he went on to say that if the Soviet buildup threatened American security or the security of other American states, the United States would "do whatever must be done to protect its own security and that of its allies."

On Sunday, October 14, a U-2 made a routine flight to photograph an area that had not been covered since September 5. Routinely, the package of films was flown to the processing laboratories that night. Routinely, the processed film was flown to the photo-interpretation center in Washington, D.C., on Monday morning, October 15. Routinely, the photo-interpreters began going over the pictures, frame by frame.

Then, suddenly, routine stopped. At San Cristóbal in Western Cuba the photographs clearly showed the erector launchers, missile-carrying trailers, fueling trucks, and radar vans of a battalion of Soviet medium-range ballistic missiles. President Kennedy immediately put Cuba under virtually continuous air surveillance. From that time on, there was hardly an hour of daylight that did not see a U-2 over some part of Cuba.

At one stage, the Soviets and others proposed that the Soviet missiles in Cuba be traded for the American missiles in Turkey. But the two were entirely different. The American missiles in Turkey had been deployed at the request of the NATO Allies in response to the Soviet deployment of MRBMs and IRBMs aimed at Europe. It was a joint decision by NATO, and a decision to remove them would also have to be a joint decision. Finally, the decision to deploy missiles to Turkey had been made only after an open and long public debate, while the Soviet decision to send missiles to Cuba had been taken and carried out in the utmost secrecy.

At the same time, Kennedy recognized that trading the missiles in Turkey for those in Cuba was better than a war, and he took steps to make such a trade less harmful politically if such a "deal" turned out to be the only way to avoid war. So he arranged for the secretary general of the United Nations, at an appropriate time during the negotiations to be determined later, to "request" both the United States and the Soviet Union to withdraw all their missiles stationed abroad.

In international law a blockade is technically an act of war. Kennedy, remembering Franklin D. Roosevelt's "quarantining the aggressors" speech in support of the Allies in the early days of World War II, chose to call it a quarantine rather than a blockade. Both the Pentagon and the CIA agreed that a blockade might keep the Soviets from increasing the missiles in Cuba, but they argued that it would do nothing to remove those that were already there. The climax came at a meeting of the Executive Committee of the National Security Council, an ad hoc group nicknamed ExCom, that President Kennedy did not attend, and it fell to his brother, Robert Kennedy, to present the case not so much for a blockade as against an attack without warning, and he did so with dramatic force. "For the United States to attack a small country without warning," he said, "would irreparably hurt our reputation in the world—and our own conscience." A sudden, surprise attack would be morally reprehensible, in violation of American traditions and ideals. In wrenching words that moved everyone present, Robert Kennedy said that he did not want America to commit the "infamy" of a Pearl Harbor. He did not want his brother "to be the Tojo of American history."

The president made the announcement on television on Monday, October 22. He opened by saying that this "urgent transformation of Cuba into an important strategic base—by the presence of these long-range and clearly offensive weapons of sudden mass destruction—constitutes a threat to the peace and security of all the Americas." He made what Abram Chayes, the legal adviser to the State Department, called "a little international law for the nuclear age."

He said that if the Soviet Union launched a nuclear missile from Cuba against any nation in the Western Hemisphere the United States would regard it as an attack "on the United States, requiring a full retaliatory response upon the Soviet Union." He then called for an immediate meeting of the Organization of American States (OAS) to consider a naval blockade of Cuba, and a meeting of the U.N. Security Council to take action against this latest Soviet threat to world peace.

THE RESOLUTION

To avoid forcing the Soviet Union into a corner that might lead to what Kennedy called a "spasm reaction," he and his advisers had crafted a gradual, step-by-step policy that would give the Soviets plenty of time to ponder the consequences of their response to each move by the United States.

Twenty-four hours passed before the OAS could meet and approve the proposal for a quarantine, a delay that Kennedy wanted and planned for. Having obtained the OAS approval, Kennedy then announced that the quarantine would go into effect on Wednesday, October 24 at 10:00 A.M.—providing still another twenty-four-hour pause. He then instructed the Navy to wait another twenty-four hours before stopping a Soviet ship—still another pause. Then Kennedy deliberately chose as the first ship to be stopped a Soviet oil tanker, the *Bucharest*, precisely because it could not possibly carry any arms. The *Bucharest* was hailed on Thursday, October 25, but not boarded. Still another twenty-four hours passed. The first boarding did not occur until Friday, October 26 at 8:00 A.M., and Kennedy had ordered that the ship to be boarded should *not* be a Soviet ship. So the ship chosen was a Lebanese freighter on Soviet charter, since it would clearly not be carrying any sensitive armaments.

Two days earlier, on Wednesday, October 24, the president had authorized the Navy to fly low-level reconnaissance flights over the missile sites, and the pictures revealed that work was proceeding at a frantic speed. The pictures also revealed for the first time the presence of Soviet ground forces. They also revealed the presence of the battlefield nuclear weapons. A total of fourteen such weapons were eventually identified.

Also on Wednesday, the Soviets rejected the U.S. quarantine proclamation. Ominously, the Soviet ships heading for Cuba were joined by six Soviet submarines.

Then, late on Wednesday, October 24, came the first hint of a break: Some of the Soviet ships heading toward Cuba altered course. These included two ships with extra-large hatches that the United States suspected were the ones that were used to carry the sixty-foot-long missiles. The rest of the ships stopped dead in the water, wallowing while they waited for orders. The president was determined to pace events, and issued orders that there was to be no shooting. The Soviet ships were to be kept in view but none were to be boarded until he issued the instructions.

Low-level reconnaissance flights on Friday, October 26, showed that work on the missile sites was still proceeding at a furious pace. A White House announcement describing these activities concluded that the Soviets were trying to achieve "full operational capability as soon as possible."

But this was the day of the first real break. In the Cuban missile crisis, the decisive channels of communication were letters between Kennedy and Khrushchev, exchanges between Robert Kennedy and Ambassador Dobrynin, and one very unusual, completely unofficial channel. Aleksander Fomin, whom the Americans knew to be head of the Washington office of the KGB, sought out John Scali, an ABC correspondent. The Soviets knew that Scali and I were friends, and since I was head of the State Department's Bureau of Intelligence and Research, Fomin asked Scali if he could find out from me if the highest levels of the U.S. government would be interested in the following solution to the crisis:

1. The Soviets would withdraw the missiles in Cuba.
2. U.N. inspectors would be allowed to supervise and verify the removal.
3. The Soviet Union would promise not to reintroduce missiles to Cuba—ever.
4. The United States would publicly pledge not to invade Cuba.

Scali told Fomin that if the message was genuine and had indeed originated at the highest levels of the Soviet government, then he believed that I, as the head of the State Department's intelligence bureau, would be willing to convey it to the secretary of state and the president. Fomin repeatedly assured Scali that the message came from Khrushchev himself. Scali took it to me, and after hearing of Fomin's assurances that the message came from Khrushchev himself, I took it to Rusk and Kennedy. They decided to have me bring Scali to Rusk's office by way of the secretary's private elevator. In his office, Rusk asked Scali to go back to Fomin and tell him the United States was interested, but that time was very, very short—no more than two days. Rusk had written what Scali was to say on a piece of yellow paper in his own handwriting: "I have reason to believe that the USG [United States Government] sees real possibilities and supposes that the representatives of the two governments in New York could work this matter out with U Thant and with each other. My impression is, however, that time is very urgent."

THE CABLE FROM KHRUSHCHEV

That evening a long, rambling "four-part" cable—a letter from Khrushchev to Kennedy—began to come in. The message was conciliatory, but it contained nothing specific. One key passage, for example, likened the crisis to two men pulling on each end of a rope with a knot in the middle: "Mr. President, we ought not to pull on the ends of the rope in which you have tied the knot of war because the more the two of us pull, the tighter that knot will be tied, and the moment may come when it will be tied so tight that we will not have the strength to untie it and then it will be necessary to cut the knot, to doom the world to the catastrophe of nuclear war."

The Soviets had on earlier occasions used this technique of sending a vague message through official channels and a very specific message through unofficial, easily deniable channels. The combination of the approach through Fomin and the long cable from Khrushchev convinced most of us in the Intelligence Bureau that this was the break that we had all been hoping for. The cable communicated a general willingness to negotiate. The Fomin message gave the specifics.

It was apparently Fomin's assignment to stimulate the U.S. government's interest in Khrushchev's imprecise formulations by adding specifics—especially on the question of inspection, which Moscow knew was central for the United States. There were hints of other important points scattered through the Khrushchev cable like "raisins in a cake," as George Ball aptly put it, but the all-important offer of inspection had not appeared at all.

When the ExCom met at ten o'clock on Saturday morning, hopes were running high. Then, at 10:17 A.M., the news tickers cleared the first bulletin of a new statement being broadcast by Radio Moscow. As the details came in it seemed clear that the Soviets had reversed their position. What they offered now was to trade their missiles in Cuba for American missiles in Turkey.

News also came in that a single Soviet ship had detached itself from the others outside the quarantine line and was steaming straight for Cuba. It looked very much as if the Soviets had decided to test our determination in a confrontation at sea after all, or even to provoke an incident.

Worse news quickly followed. The SAM (Surface-to-Air Missile) network of antiaircraft missiles had become operational. An American U-2 had been shot down, and the pilot, Major Rudolf Anderson, Jr., had been killed.

The ExCom was also informed that the CIA had concluded that twenty-four of the MRBMs were fully operational.[4] It also had to be assumed that the forty-four operational Soviet ICBMs based inside the Soviet Union had been placed on alert.

It was the blackest hour of the crisis. The Soviets must have realized that shooting down U-2s would force the United States to take direct action against the SAMs, so the shoot down seemed to mean that they had decided on a showdown. There was speculation that the hardliners in the Kremlin might be taking over, possibly backed by the military.

THE "STRANGELOVE" INCIDENT

Then it was the American's turn to make a slip.[5] Early that afternoon, as a small meeting in his office with Ambassador Thompson was breaking up, Rusk drafted me to carry a proposed response to the Moscow broadcast over to the White House, where I was going for another purpose anyway. When I arrived, the president and McGeorge Bundy were talking in the little office occupied by Mrs. Lincoln, the president's secretary, and after a short discussion about the proposed message during which the president indicated that he preferred to wait until the ExCom met that afternoon, I left to return to the State Department.

As I passed the ground floor entrance by McGeorge Bundy's office, one of Bundy's aides grabbed me to say that my office was calling me—urgently. The caller was Joseph Scott, a deputy director of the Intelligence Bureau whose responsibilities included coordinating U-2 operations worldwide. He said that in his other hand he had a phone connected to the War Room of the Pentagon. Another U-2, totally unrelated to the missile crisis, on a routine air-sampling mission from Alaska to the North Pole had picked the wrong star for its return flight and was at that moment over the Soviet Union. Soviet fighter planes had scrambled. The U-2 pilot had gone on the air—in the clear—calling frantically for help. American fighters in Alaska had also scrambled and were attempting to rendezvous with the U-2 to escort it home.

I ran upstairs and found the president and Bundy still in Mrs. Lincoln's office. At a glance the president knew that something was terribly wrong. Out of breath from running upstairs and pale and shaky from over thirty hours without sleep, I told my story.

The implications were as obvious as they were horrendous. The Soviets might well regard this U-2 flight as a last-minute intelligence reconnaissance in preparation for nuclear war. It was just this sort of invitation to miscalculation that Kennedy's detailed instructions had been designed to prevent. "One of your planes," Khrushchev himself later wrote, "violates our frontier during this anxious time we are both experiencing, when everything has been put into combat readiness. Is it not a fact that an intruding American plane could easily be taken for a nuclear bomber, which might push us to a fateful step . . . ?"

Ernest Hemingway once described true courage as "grace under pressure." The president was the first to break the awestruck silence. He gave a short, ironic laugh. "There is always some son of a bitch," he said, "who doesn't get the word."

The president told me to get on top of the situation immediately, to ensure that the Soviets were informed that the U-2 intrusion was an accident totally unrelated to the crisis, and to make certain that our planes took care to avoid any provocations of any kind. I turned to carry out the instructions, but dizzy from lack of sleep I would have fallen if McGeorge Bundy had not steadied me. He told the president that I had not been to bed for a couple of days and asked if someone else might not take care of the problem. The president looked at me keenly, ordered me to go home and get some sleep, and told Bundy to find someone else to handle the problem. The plane returned safely. The Soviets made no follow-up move, and the president decided to ignore the incident. Later, when Khrushchev made his protest, Kennedy apologized.[6]

Removing the missiles from Turkey would require approval of both Turkey and of NATO, since the deployment had been a multilateral decision. NATO would not be a problem, but Turkey was. Getting the original approval from the parliament had been bruising for the Turkish government, and it was reluctant to go back to it until the scheduled deployment of American missile-carrying submarines in the Mediterranean provided an excuse. Although Kennedy was well aware of all this, he was annoyed to think that despite his earlier instructions to remove them, the missiles were still there, political albatrosses around his neck. Since the missiles in Turkey were obsolete, removing them should not be a great problem in subsequent negotiations. But that did not help now. The Soviets were continuing construction of their missile bases in Cuba at a rapid pace and negotiations were politically impossible while that work continued. A statement to this effect was drafted as a response to the Soviet proposal and released to the press.

At about this time, the Navy reported that the Soviet ship headed toward Cuba was an oil tanker, and so could not be carrying any war materiel. President Kennedy ordered the Navy to let it pass. Kennedy also decided to postpone for at least a day or two the retaliatory bombing of the SAM site that the ExCom had previously concluded was the appropriate response if a U-2 was shot down. He wanted first to craft a message to Khrushchev and, second, to wait for Khrushchev's reply before retaliating.

THE "TROLLOPE PLOY"

With all the evidence on the table, the ExCom met to consider what to do next. And it was Robert Kennedy who conceived a brilliant diplomatic maneuver, later dubbed the "Trollope ploy" after the recurrent scene in Anthony Trollope's novels in which the girl interprets a squeeze of her hand as a proposal of marriage.

His suggestion was to deal only with Friday's package of signals—Khrushchev's cable and the Fomin approach—as if the conflicting Moscow broadcast on Saturday linking the missiles in Cuba with those in Turkey simply did not exist. The Moscow broadcast, as already mentioned, had in fact already been rejected in a public announcement. The thing to do now, Robert Kennedy suggested, was to answer the Friday package of approaches and make the answer public, which would add a certain political pressure as well as increase the speed.

Khrushchev's Friday-night cable had not mentioned or even hinted at inspection, but inspection had been a key element in the proposal put forward by Fomin. Selecting such welcome points from the Fomin approach and others from the Khrushchev cable, and simply ignoring the Moscow broadcast of Saturday morning, the ExCom drafted a statement for the president's signature:

I have read your letter of October 26th with great care and welcome the statement of your desire to seek a prompt solution to the problem. The first thing that needs to be done, however, is for work to cease on offensive missile bases in Cuba. . . . Assuming this is done promptly, I have given my representatives in New York instructions that will permit them to work out this weekend—in cooperation with the Acting Secretary General and your representative—an arrangement for the permanent solution to the Cuban problem.

Then came the "Trollope ploy":

As I read your letter, the key elements of your proposals—which seem generally acceptable as I understand them—are as follows: (1) You would agree to remove the weapons systems from Cuba under appropriate UN observation and supervision [which had been mentioned only by Fomin]; and undertake, with suitable safeguards, to halt the further introduction of such weapons systems into Cuba. (2) We, on our part, would agree—upon establishment of adequate arrangements through the United Nations to ensure the carrying out and continuation of these commitments—(a) to remove promptly the quarantine measures now in effect and (b) to give assurances against an invasion of Cuba.

This message was released for broadcast to Moscow and the public. The president then personally dispatched Robert Kennedy to explain the American position in detail to Dobrynin.

In addition to the military consequences of permitting the missiles to remain in Cuba, President Kennedy was also sensitive to the political consequences. The political damage to the United States of permitting even one Soviet missile to remain in Cuba would have been severe—as Kennedy said, "It would have politically changed the balance of power." He was convinced that if the missiles did not come out, "no one would be able to conduct a sensible American foreign policy for years to come."[7] Later, Robert Kennedy said to the president, "If you hadn't acted, you would have been impeached." The president agreed: "That's what I think—I would have been impeached."[8]

Now there was nothing to do but wait for Khrushchev's response. As the meeting broke up, President Kennedy remarked that it could "go either way."

Just before nine o'clock Sunday morning, October 28, Moscow radio announced that it would have an important statement to broadcast at nine sharp. It was a letter from Chairman Khrushchev: "In order to eliminate as rapidly as possible the conflict which endangers the cause of peace . . . the Soviet Government . . . has given a new order to dismantle the arms which you described as offensive, and to crate and return them to the Soviet Union."

To tie the final strings, a White House statement was quickly drafted confirming the agreement and just as quickly broadcast over the Voice of America. A fuller reply to the chairman's letter was then prepared and this, too, was released for publication and broadcast. The crisis was over. The two greatest military powers in the world had avoided war—a nuclear war—and the tension subsided.

No one knows for sure what Khrushchev felt, but there are a few clues. In a speech in December reporting on the crisis, he spoke of a "smell of burning" in the air, indicating that he felt the world had come close indeed to a nuclear holocaust and that his own personal feeling was a sense of relief.

Another hint of how Khrushchev felt came the same Sunday that the crisis ended. Late that day, October 28, Scali met with Fomin for the last time. "I have been instructed," Fomin said in the classic language of diplomacy, "to thank you and to tell you that the information you supplied was very valuable to the Chairman in helping him make up his mind quickly."

As for Kennedy, he was naturally elated. But he permitted himself to express it only privately, to his brother Robert, and he did so with his typical wryness: "Maybe this is the night I should go to the theater," he said—thinking of Abraham Lincoln and Ford's.

NOTES

1. For a full account of the Cuban missile crisis, see Roger Hilsman, *The Cuban Missile Crisis: The Struggle Over Policy* (Westport, Conn.: Praeger, 1996), from which this chapter was drawn.

2. What is referred to here as an MRBM was designated by American intelligence as the SS-4 (the SS stands for surface-to-surface), a single-stage rocket. Without the nose cone, which is how it was normally transported, it was fifty-nine feet long. What is referred to here as an IRBM was designated by American intelligence as the SS-5, also a single-stage rocket. Without its nose cone it was eighty-two feet long and eight feet in diameter.

3. The United States believed at the time that the Soviet ground forces in Cuba numbered only about 20 thousand men and did not learn the true total was about 42 thousand until years after the crisis had been resolved. But low-level reconnaissance flights instituted on October 23, just after the crisis became public, over the next two or three days identified fourteen of the battlefield nuclear missile launchers, the weapon that the Soviets called the *Luna* and American intelligence called the *Frog*.

4. In the conference between Americans, Soviets, and Cubans on the crisis held in Havana in 1992, a Soviet general said that at this time some of the MRBM warheads were still en route, but that thirty-six had already arrived in Cuba (i.e., that thirty-six MRBMs were ready to fire, not twenty-four).

5. "Strangelove" was the name given by the American participants in the crisis after the movie, *Dr. Strangelove or How I Learned to Stop Worrying and Love the Bomb*. In this movie, the world is destroyed in a nuclear war caused when a single plane, whose radio had been knocked out by antiaircraft fire, did not get the message to turn back and dropped a nuclear bomb on the Soviet Union, which in turn set off an American "doomsday" machine of nuclear missiles that were triggered automatically by a nuclear explosion anywhere in the world.

6. This U-2 incident was important in bringing about the establishment of the so-called "hot line," providing a round-the-clock communications link between Moscow and Washington, that was established after the crisis.

7. McGeorge Bundy, *Danger and Survival: Choices About the Bomb in the First Fifty Years* (New York: Random House, 1988), 412.

8. Robert F. Kennedy, *Thirteen Days: A Memoir of the Cuban Missile Crisis* (New York: W. W. Norton, 1971), 45.

Chapter 7

The Significance

Why did the Soviets back down in Cuba? Was the crisis a turning point in history? Did the crisis have anything to suggest about the role of war in a nuclear age?

The risks to both sides in the Cuban missile crisis were real, direct, and very high. As Dean Rusk said, a misstep might have meant the "incineration" of the entire Northern Hemisphere, including the North American continent. Even so, it is not possible to say that it was the nuclear threat, as such, that caused the Soviets to back down. The Soviet leaders seem to have had considerable confidence in the judgment, restraint, and sense of responsibility of the American leaders, and they undoubtedly assumed the American response would begin with conventional means and would continue to be restricted to conventional means unless the Soviets themselves did something that raised the ante.

On the other hand, it is also not possible to say that the Soviets backed down solely in the face of a threat to invade Cuba with conventional, nonnuclear forces, even though they knew that the troops they had in Cuba could not stand up to such an invasion—or, to be completely accurate, even though they knew that the troops they had in Cuba could not stand up to such an invasion without using nuclear weapons. The Soviet leadership often repeated, and only partly for self-serving motives, that limited war would always carry a risk of escalation to nuclear war. And certainly in the Cuban missile crisis there were a number of ways that events could have gotten out of hand.

If the crisis had not been resolved when it was, for example, events could easily have escalated until the United States launched an invasion. The Soviet troops were armed with battlefield nuclear weapons, and the commander had advance permission to use them against an invading force. The preliminary American plans provided tactical nuclear weapons for the invasion force, and even if the president had decided that they should not actually accompany the troops, they could have been brought forward very quickly. In circumstances such as these, the crisis could easily have spiraled out of control. But Khrushchev and the top Soviet leadership were as sensitive to the risks as Kennedy and the ExCom were, and also just as sensitive to the fact that sooner or later one side or the other would lose control and that there was therefore an urgent need to resolve the crisis quickly before that happened.

On balance, in other words, the best judgment seems to be that the Soviets backed down in the face of a threat that combined both conventional and nuclear power. Cuba was close to the sources of American strength and distant from the sources of Soviet strength. With vastly shorter lines of communication, the United States could apply overwhelming conventional power at the point of contact—Cuba—and do so under an umbrella of nuclear power that foreclosed any possibility of the Soviets trying to use nuclear weapons to redress the imbalance at the contact point. It was this combination of overwhelming conventional power on the spot and adequate nuclear power overall that proved irresistible.

Let it also be said that the decision to withdraw the missiles required courage on the Soviet side and that, although putting the missiles in Cuba was threatening and irresponsible, the Soviets handled the ensuing crisis with wisdom and restraint. As it worked out, none of the IRBMs actually arrived in Cuba, but all of the MRBMs were operational by October 28. Many of the participants, myself included, felt that if the Soviets had not agreed to withdraw their missiles, the United States would have no choice but to invade. What might have happened as American ground and air forces attacked Soviet nuclear missiles poised on their pads and defended by Soviet ground forces equipped with tactical nuclear weapons is simply mind-boggling.

In any case, the first and most obvious lesson of the Cuban missile crisis is that of power. The United States decided to accept the Soviet challenge and American strength and determination were sufficient to meet the challenge. The United States had both the power and the will, and the Soviet Union backed down.

But it would be a mistake to conclude that this same formula of will and power can be translated into success in every kind of confrontation—that it would necessarily have worked in Laos, for example, or Vietnam. The arena in the Cuba case was close to the sources of American power, as we have said, and far from the sources of Soviet power. But, more important, there was no doubt at all about the stakes: The threat from Cuba in October 1962 was nuclear, and it was directed at the American heartland.

It would also be a mistake to think that the formula of will and power is appropriate to all political objectives. The issue here is the relationship of means to ends, the appropriateness and acceptability both to world opinion and to the conscience of the American people of using military force to accomplish particular objectives. It is acceptable and fitting that the United States use the full panoply of its military power to meet a threat to its survival. But at some point, as one moves down the scale from national survival to progressively lesser objectives, the political cost of using raw military force begins to exceed the potential gain. When that point is reached, wise leaders shift away from military force as the means to achieve their nation's goals and adopt other instrumentalities.

Reasonable people may quarrel about the wisdom of the exact point at which President Kennedy chose to make this shift in the Cuban missile crisis. He chose to shift just after the removal of the missiles but before the withdrawal of Soviet advisers and the elimination of the Castro regime. Reasonable people might argue for making the shift at some different point, but they would not question the principle itself.

Because we still live in a nuclear world, we cannot see the final meaning of the Cuban missile crisis or measure the full dimensions of its place in the history of humankind. But surely any assessment of its significance must begin with the fact that it was the first nuclear crisis the world has ever seen and that what President Kennedy and the United States did in meeting the crisis set precedents applicable to all the subsequent international crises of our time.

The keynote of the U.S. response was flexibility and self-disciplined restraint— a graduated effort that avoided trying to achieve too much and that stopped short of confronting an adversary with stark and imperative choices. Out of that basic policy flowed the precedents: restraint in the use of power; flexibility in developing a solution; the pacing of events to give the other side time to think and so obviating "spasm reactions"; the "making of a little international law" outlawing the secret and rapid deployment of nuclear weapons, as Abram Chayes said; the deliberate regard for precedent and the effect of present actions on the longer-range future; and, finally, the relevancy of moral integrity to that longer-range future, a point on which both President Kennedy and Robert Kennedy so strongly insisted.

Whether the Cuban missile crisis marked a turning point in world history is as yet impossible to say. The Soviets put missiles into Cuba in an attempt to solve a particular set of problems: a strategic imbalance, the exigencies of the Sino–Soviet dispute, and the impossible combination of demands on their limited resources made by defense, their space program, their people's appetite for consumer goods, and the drain of foreign aid needed to support their foreign policy. When the crisis was over and the missiles withdrawn, the same set of problems remained.

One irony is that these same problems, which brought the world so near to nuclear war, later brought about the so-called détente, a relaxation of Cold War tensions. For it was the same pressures that led the Soviets to put missiles in Cuba that later led them to take up Kennedy's proposal in his American University speech for a treaty banning nuclear testing.

The nuclear test ban treaty that Kennedy had in mind included on-site inspections. The Soviets had flatly rejected inspection on all the previous occasions on which it had been raised. The reason was simple. A police state simply cannot tolerate international inspectors wandering around. The only way that a police state can remain a police state is to keep its people ignorant of the outside world.

This time, however, Khrushchev was willing to permit three U.N. inspections a year. The Pentagon insisted that there be a minimum of five, and nothing the president said or did could shake their determination. He met just as solid a stone wall when he tried to get the Soviets to agree to five.

Kennedy felt certain that if he agreed to three inspections rather than five the hard-liners in the Pentagon lobbying the hard-liners in Congress would defeat the treaty. But Kennedy felt that half a loaf now would permit him to come back in a year or two and get the other half, so he agreed to a treaty with no inspections at all as a first step. He did not calculate on being assassinated.

Following the crisis, the Soviets had only two alternatives. One was a crash ICBM program to redress the strategic imbalance. This would mean austerity at home, and a return to the coldest kind of Cold War abroad. The Communist world would have to close ranks, and so, as a most unpalatable corollary, the Sino–Soviet dispute would need to be healed if at all possible, even if the Chinese demanded that it be on their terms.

The other alternative was the one the Soviets actually chose: easing the tensions of the Cold War with the limited test ban treaty as the first concrete step. The Soviet ICBM program could then be stretched out, and the burdens lightened of competing so aggressively in the underdeveloped world. And this course of action also had a corollary for the Sino–Soviet dispute—a sharpening of the tension between Communist China and the Soviet Union.

THE LONG-RANGE SIGNIFICANCE

But the Cuban missile crisis quite clearly had deeper, more profound, and longer-range effects. One of the longer-range effects was to change attitudes toward nuclear weapons. Before the Cuban missile crisis, most of the American officials who later participated in the crisis deliberations believed in Churchill's balance of terror. They assumed that to keep the peace all that the United States needed to do was to make certain that its nuclear forces were adequate, that the country maintained the will and determination to use those weapons if the worst came to the worst, and that appropriate steps were taken to ensure that the other side understood all this. Presumably, the Soviet leaders had reached a similar set of conclusions.

But during the Cuban missile crisis the leaders of both sides probed the awesome dimensions of what they faced and drew back. In the Cuban missile crisis both the American and the Soviet leaders gazed down the gun barrel of nuclear war and shrank from the holocaust they saw there.

But in spite of all the precautions on both sides, it proved impossible to avoid dangerous missteps, misunderstandings, slips, and unauthorized actions by subordinates. The number of these potential disasters and the extreme risk they posed is startling.

The greatest miscalculation, of course, was Khrushchev's original decision to send missiles to Cuba. On the other hand, the United States also made an early miscalculation that was extremely serious. The Americans realized that the Soviets would be alarmed by the news in Gilpatric's speech and the NATO briefings that the United States had learned that the missile gap was in their favor. Yet American intelligence failed to see that one possible Soviet response would be to send missiles to Cuba. As a result, as already discussed, President Kennedy's various speeches and messages warning against putting offensive weapons in Cuba came not in the winter and early spring of 1962, when they might have convinced the Soviets that sending missiles to Cuba would be a mistake, but in September, long after the decision had been made and its implementation begun.

[The United States also came very near making a tragic miscalculation on another occasion. When the crisis was in full swing a very large jet aircraft, equipped with extra fuel tanks for long flights, departed from Moscow and headed for Cuba. An emergency meeting at the White House speculated that this airplane might be carrying the warheads we had not yet seen. Robert Kennedy and others thought that the United States had no choice but to shoot the plane down over the Atlantic. Finally, however, it was decided to let the plane land, but to keep it under air surveillance with fighter-bombers standing by, and if warheads started coming out of the airplane's hold to attack immediately and destroy them on the ground. As it turned out, the plane was inaugurating a new Aeroflot route to Cuba, and its cargo consisted of about 200 journalists!] *example of poss. mishaps = disaster*

Another miscalculation was the shooting down of Major Anderson's U-2. The ExCom had decided that if a U-2 was shot down, the SAM responsible would be immediately destroyed. If a second U-2 was attacked, then all the SAMs would be taken out. But President Kennedy decided to hold off the retaliation until the American response to the package of Khrushchev's cable and the approach through Fomin could be sent and a reply received. If he had not held back, the Soviets might have decided that they, too, must retaliate against the retaliation—and the situation could have quickly escalated.

In 1987, a conference to discuss the crisis was held between some American scholars and three Soviet officials who had knowledge of the crisis although they occupied lower-level positions at the time. The Soviet representatives at the conference asserted that the decision to shoot down the U-2 was made without consulting Moscow by a Soviet one-star general, Igor D. Statsenko.[1]

It is awesome to think about how an American reprisal might have sparked a Soviet counter and so on, spiraling into war if Kennedy had not held off bombing the SAM site. But it is even more frightening that the Kremlin had such little control over the troops in the field that a local commander could order the U-2 to be shot down without authority from Moscow. Yet the Soviets' very admission that they had so little control lends the assertion credibility.

The violation of Soviet airspace by the American U-2 on an air-sampling mission to the North Pole in the midst of the crisis was equally frightening. As Khrushchev said, it could easily have been misinterpreted as a reconnaissance in advance of a preemptive nuclear attack. Humankind is fortunate that Khrushchev, like Kennedy, held back.

Another major slip was the harsh Moscow Radio broadcast on Saturday morning that seemed to reverse the proposals contained in Khrushchev's cable and the Fomin approach the night before. If the analysts in the State Departments's Bureau of Intelligence and Research had failed to notice the language differences that indicated that the Moscow broadcast clearly predated the Khrushchev–Fomin approach or if Robert Kennedy had not come up with the Trollope ploy that was designed as a way of getting around the Saturday broadcast, the crisis might have escalated very rapidly.

The Americans made equally dangerous mistakes. In a decision that was both irresponsible and insubordinate, General Thomas S. Power, without consulting higher authority, deliberately sent the message putting the Strategic Air Command on alert in the clear, presumably to frighten the Soviets. It was not only unauthorized but provocative and dangerous.

The Soviet decision to test the blockade by sending one of the ships that had been halted at sea speeding toward Cuba was equally provocative and dangerous, even though the ship was a tanker and could not carry missiles—especially since this move was obviously fully authorized by Moscow. What if Kennedy had not decided to let it go without challenge? The Soviet submarines escorting it would probably have attacked the challenging American vessel. If so, they would have undoubtedly sunk it. What would have happened then?

The Americans made equally provocative and dangerous moves. To give the Soviets time to think about their countermoves, Kennedy ordered the Navy to put the blockade line well out to sea rather than following traditional practice in putting it close in to shore. The Navy disobeyed. Still another dangerous American move was the Navy's forcing the Soviet submarines to surface in their presence to recharge their batteries. Even more alarming is the evidence that the American Navy used practice depth charges to drive some of the Soviets submarines to the surface.

Many of the American participants in the policy decisions during the crisis were shocked and troubled by these various missteps and unauthorized actions. Their faith in both deterrence and Churchill's balance of terror was deeply shaken.

The threat of a nuclear holocaust would clearly make all nations more careful, and this caution might well preserve the peace for years and even decades. But after the Cuban missile crisis the danger of a world in which nuclear weapons remained in national arsenals seemed painfully clear. One, two, or even three more such crises might be handled with equal success. But sooner or later a crisis would occur in which the leaders on both sides were not so prudent as Kennedy and Khrushchev had been. In one crisis or another even greater slips and miscalculations would be inevitable. The conclusion seemed inescapable that so long as nuclear weapons and the missiles to deliver them remained in the world's arsenals, sooner or later there would be a nuclear holocaust.

It also suddenly seemed clear that the old verities must be reexamined. Germany, for example, seemed less a threat in a nuclear age. In fact, as we will examine in Chapter 10, the entire political landscape of Eastern Europe looked startlingly different.

But by far the most important verity that demands reexamining is the institution of war itself. As described in the preface to this book, the four major approaches for maintaining peace in this now-nuclear world are all attempts to rehabilitate war, to turn back the clock to a world in which war can still serve its former social and political functions at an acceptable cost in lives and treasure. What the Cuban missile crisis suggests is that humankind's only hope is to find a way to abolish war itself.

NOTE

1. Raymond L. Garthoff, "Cuban Missile Crisis: The Soviet Story," *Foreign Policy* (Fall 1988). The Soviet ambassador to Cuba, Aleksandr Alekseyev, said that the order was the result of a "trigger-happy Soviet air defense commander." However, Sergo Mikoyan said that General Statsenko did command the Soviet forces in Cuba, in spite of his relatively low rank. Mikoyan also said that just before his death in October 1987, Statsenko confided that he was the one who had made the decision to fire.

PART III

POST-CRISIS ATTEMPTS AT A NUCLEAR STRATEGY

Chapter 8

McNamara II, the Schlesinger Doctrine, and Star Wars

For many people, in and out of government, the Cuban missile crisis exposed most of the debate on nuclear military strategy as irrelevant. When confronted by missiles in Cuba, Kennedy and the ExCom became convinced they had no alternative to threatening a full nuclear retaliation—junking the notion of city avoidance and the rest. What is more, they also became convinced it was imperative to disperse the B-47s to civilian airfields. Since most of these airfields were right next to cities, the action denied the Soviets a counterforce option, as Kennedy and his advisers well understood.

For many people, in and out of government, the crisis also marked the end of the "foreign policy consensus" in the United States. It has often been said that the Vietnam War was responsible for the breakdown of the consensus on foreign policy. But it was the Cuban missile crisis that was at least the beginning of the end. For many of us who were involved in the deliberations, the crisis destroyed Churchill's assumption that the balance of terror would bring a stable peace, or at least it destroyed any hope that the stable peace could be expected to last forever.

The crisis also raised with exquisite poignancy and urgency a question that remains unanswered to this day: What strategy should be followed if deterrence fails? The Cuban missile crisis demonstrated to many of those involved that, balance of terror or not, sooner or later another nuclear crisis would occur. It did not really help that the crisis would most likely be precipitated by some action that was never intended as a move toward war. Sooner or later one side or the other would handle a crisis with less skill than Kennedy and Khrushchev had handled the Cuban missile crisis, and the result would be war (the compliment does not apply to Khrushchev's decision to deploy missiles to Cuba in the first place). One, two, or three such crises might be settled without war or kept within nonnuclear bounds. But as the missile crisis demonstrated, slips would occur, and sooner or later one or another would trigger a spiral into nuclear war.

ASSURED DESTRUCTION AS A STRATEGY

Recognizing from the experience of the Cuban missile crisis that his strategy of city avoidance, damage limitation, and counterforce was a failure, McNamara turned to a strategy designed not to fight a war but to deter it. The idea was to make it absolutely inevitable that the Soviet Union would be totally destroyed no matter which side got in the first blow. Faced with "assured destruction," the Soviets would be deterred from launching a deliberate attack. To assure that destruction, the United States needed a force that the Soviets knew could absorb a first strike and still be able to launch a second-strike, retaliatory blow that would cause a level of destruction that the Soviets would find "unacceptable."

It was a matter for debate, of course, just what level of destruction the Soviets would find "unacceptable." More or less arbitrarily, McNamara and his staff set it at between one-third and one-fifth of the Soviet population and between three-fourths and one-half of the Soviet industrial capacity.

These figures were not the result of some sort of "scientific" study of the Soviet tolerance for destruction. Nor were they some sort of goal. In fact, in 1968 the Pentagon estimate was that the weapons the United States had on hand could have killed about 50 percent of the Soviet people and destroyed about 80 percent of Soviet industry. Apparently McNamara chose the figures he did on the basis of diminishing marginal returns—doubling the stockpile would lead to less than a 10-percent increase in the number of Soviet casualties and only a 1-percent increase in the amount of industry destroyed.[1]

If McNamara and the defense analysts he had recruited from the RAND corporation and academia could not figure out what to do if deterrence failed, they could at least make sure that deterrence was powerful. They clearly realized that, following the Cuban missile crisis, the Soviet Union had embarked on a large-scale military buildup all across the board—in missiles, conventional forces, and naval forces. But, as mentioned earlier, McNamara and the defense analysts seem to have assumed that there was nothing the United States could do about that except launch a preventive war, and nobody was prepared to advocate an American Pearl Harbor.

Essentially, McNamara and his colleagues were starting all over again with Churchill's notion of a balance of terror, except that they called the situation "Mutual Assured Destruction" or MAD. But where MAD was a *situation* brought about by the nature of the technology, McNamara and his colleagues were going to try to turn it into a *strategy*. The idea was to make the destruction one-sided, rather than mutual; that is, try to find a way that would continue to assure that the bulk of the Soviet population and industry would be destroyed and yet at the same time preserve a significant proportion of the American and allied population and industry.

On the question of force structure, part of having a true second-strike force was making sure that it could survive a first strike and still be able to strike back. So hardening missile silos and providing mobility in the form of missile-launching submarines was an essential part of a strategy of assured destruction.

As for defending the population rather than just missile sites, the Kennedy administration had started a civil defense program in 1961. The hope was that it would at least offer protection from radioactive fallout. But by 1965 it was clear that no matter how much money the United States put into civil defense, the Soviets could very cheaply nullify the effort by simply building a few more missiles. So the hope of finding a way of protecting the population was abandoned.

On the question of an antimissile defense to protect either the retaliatory forces or the population, McNamara took the position during the Johnson administration that the technology available was simply not up to the task of shooting down incoming missiles. The pressure from the JCS and Congress finally grew too strong to resist, and McNamara reluctantly agreed to an anti-ballistic missile (ABM) system. But he did so on the grounds that even though it would not be effective against Soviet missiles, it might well be effective against the less sophisticated system that the Chinese were assumed to be about to build (in fact, the Chinese have yet to produce a missile force that would be a threat to the U.S. homeland).

THE DEFENSE OF NATO

During McNamara's tenure as secretary of defense, the question of how to defend Europe became a problem that seemed separate from the problem of overall deterrence, and a puzzling, convoluted problem at that.

As described earlier, American strategy following World War II was based on the old theory of air power, but with nuclear bombs. Then, as battlefield nuclear weapons began to come into the stockpile, the generals and staff officers in NATO assumed that once these weapons became plentiful they would be used to make up the difference between the ninety-six divisions of the Lisbon Force Goals and what their governments were actually willing to provide.

What might happen to civilians if battlefield nuclear weapons were used in a war in Europe was turned into a blazing headline in 1955 because of a set of NATO maneuvers—codenamed, in a morbid twist, *Exercise Carte Blanche*. In this exercise, the opposing players ended up dropping 335 simulated atomic bombs on Germany within forty-eight hours. The umpires concluded that over 5 million German civilians would have been casualties, of whom 1.5 million would have been killed. In a similar exercise held the same year in Louisiana, *Operation Sage Brush*, the umpires ruled that all forms of life in the state would have "ceased to exist." To no one's surprise, the Europeans thereafter resisted the idea of basing NATO defenses on "battlefield" nuclear weapons.

To resolve the conflict between their fear of becoming a nuclear battlefield and their fear of being conquered by the Soviets, the Europeans put their hopes mainly on deterrence—on avoiding war entirely. The way to make sure that the Soviets were effectively deterred, the argument ran, was to leave no doubt in their minds that an attack on Europe would bring an immediate retaliation on the Soviet homeland with the full nuclear power of the United States.

As a result, the Europeans' greatest fear was of what came to be called "decoupling." Suppose the Soviets launched an attack on Europe using only conventional forces; that is, an attack with their overwhelming manpower and frightening superiority in tanks. And suppose they refrained from attacking the American homeland. The Americans would surely be tempted to hold back their nuclear retaliation on the Soviet homeland in the hope of saving American cities and civilian population. If so, an attack on Europe and the American nuclear response would be "decoupled." Faced with this possibility, the Europeans favored any move that seemed to promise greater coupling of nuclear retaliation to the security of Europe and opposed any move that seemed to suggest decoupling.

An example is the idea that the United States and its allies should adopt a policy of not being the first to use nuclear weapons. Most of the European governments saw "no first use" as decoupling. They had pressed both Truman and Eisenhower to refuse to consider any policy but one of a massive attack on the Soviet homeland with nuclear weapons at the very outset of any Soviet invasion of Europe, including an invasion that used only conventional forces.

At the beginning of the Kennedy administration, there were hints that Kennedy might publicly adopt a policy of "no first use," but the Berlin crisis turned him away from the idea. Not only did the Allies oppose it, but Berlin was well inside Eastern Germany and surrounded by Soviet and Warsaw Pact forces. Giving up the first use of nuclear weapons seemed to be the equivalent of giving up Berlin.

Intermediate-range missiles, on the other hand, in the European view tended to couple. It was in fact under European pressure that the decision was made in the Nixon administration and confirmed in the Carter administration to deploy the intermediate-range Pershing II missiles to Europe in response to the Soviet deployment of the 2-thousand-mile, intermediate-range SS-20 that threatened Europe.

In the first place, the argument went, just as ground forces deter ground forces and ICBMs deter ICBMs, IRBMs were needed to deter IRBMs. If the Soviets used SS-20s against Europe, the United States might hesitate to use ICBMs to retaliate, since doing so would be likely to bring down a Soviet counterretaliation with ICBMs against the American homeland. But Pershing IIs stationed in Europe would be under fire themselves if the Soviets attacked and so there would be a strong incentive for them to fire back.

In the second place, the European idea was that deterrence would be enhanced if the Soviets believed that *any* attack on Europe would immediately spiral into a nuclear war. If Pershing IIs were in the path of a Soviet advance, the Americans would have to make a conscious and wrenching decision not to use them. On the other hand, in the case of ICBMs stationed in the continental United States it would be the other way around—the United States would have to make a conscious and wrenching decision *to* use them. So the Soviets would be more likely to believe that the Americans would retaliate if American nuclear missiles were in the line of fire as well as American ground forces.

DEPLOYING BATTLEFIELD NUCLEAR WEAPONS TO NATO

As to the question of deploying battlefield nuclear weapons to NATO immediately, before hostilities began, the story is more complicated. The original strategy of flexible response, developed in criticism of massive retaliation, held that any aggression should be met with the same kind of forces and in the same geographic area in which the threat was made. Over the next few years, however, flexible response took on still another meaning, at least as far as the defense of Europe was concerned. The new meaning was that NATO's defense strategy should be flexible in the sense of being able to fight either a conventional war or a war that included small, battlefield nuclear weapons.

Following the Cuban missile crisis, a decision was made at McNamara's urging to preposition a huge stockpile of these battlefield nuclear weapons in Europe—6 thousand of them. What struck students of military strategy inside and outside the services was that this massive deployment was made before anyone had yet figured out just how to use battlefield nuclear weapons without destroying the defenders as well as the attackers.

It is true that throughout history almost all new weapons have been deployed before anyone knew just how they would be used—before, to use the military jargon, a *doctrine* had been developed for their use. To illustrate this point and to show what the military mean by doctrine, consider the history of the machine gun as an example.

THE DEVELOPMENT OF THE MACHINE GUN

The first crude machine gun was invented in the United States just prior to the Civil War, and the Gatling gun came into service just after it. New and improved versions of the machine gun came on the scene every few years, until by 1912 it was essentially the gun we know today, in spite of vast improvements in the interim.

During the fifty years between the gun's invention and World War I, the machine gun had been used frequently by European powers in their colonial wars. But the various general staffs paid little attention to it, and it played no significant role in the Franco–Prussian War, the Spanish–American War, or the Russo–Japanese War.

As late as the beginning of World War I, no specific doctrine for using the machine gun had been developed. The assumption was that it was just a specialized type of artillery. So the doctrine used for the procurement, training, and deployment of the machine gun was artillery doctrine. Just before the war, a British division was equipped with only twenty-four machine guns. The gun was deployed well behind the front lines so that, like artillery, it could fire over the heads of the infantry.

Both sides began World War I with similar doctrines for defense. When an attack began, the artillery would engage the advancing enemy infantry; the main line of defense would be the defender's infantry in trenches. A second line of defense would be behind the first, also consisting of infantry in trenches. The reserves would be used to counterattack at the critical moment when the attackers had lost their momentum.

However, in the crucible of battle when the attacking infantry succeeded in overcoming the trench lines and came upon a machine gun that had by chance been sited on the military crest of a hill and sweeping a good field of fire, the corpses of the attacking infantry were left in windrows as each wave came into the gun's range. Everyone suddenly realized that the machine gun was the most formidable defensive weapon since the introduction of the armored knight.

Both sides rushed to manufacture and deploy more machine guns, and the battlefield quickly stalemated. The doctrine for the use of machine guns and the whole concept of defense developed in the hothouse of battle was radically different from what was accepted at the war's beginning. Now the main line of resistance was a series of machine-gun strong points whose fire interlocked, and the role of the rifleman was not to meet the attacking infantry head-on, but to protect the machine gun from any individual enemy soldiers who by some miracle got close enough to the gun to throw a hand grenade.

As for a doctrine that would integrate the machine gun into the attack, neither side made any headway until Ludendorff's 1918 offensive. In this offensive, the infantry moved forward by infiltrating under the protection of the machine gun (and fighter–bomber aircraft), rather than the orthodox advance in a line, and the gun then leapfrogged forward to protect still another infiltration.

No one has yet offered a doctrine for using battlefield nuclear weapons in a way that would not destroy the defenders as well as the attackers. So the conclusion seems inescapable that just as the generals of World War I assumed that machine guns were just another form of artillery, the generals of today are assuming that battlefield nuclear weapons are also just another, although vastly more powerful, form of artillery.

So it must be presumed that McNamara urged the deployment of so many battlefield nuclear weapons to Europe not because he had some new doctrine for using battlefield nuclear weapons, but because if war came he did not want to have to clog the supply lines with anything that could be sent to Europe beforehand.[2]

In any case, after much debate, NATO gradually adopted the policy of flexible response—meaning the use of battlefield nuclear weapons—in an informal way, with formal adoption not coming until 1967. NATO ended up with about half the divisions called for by the Lisbon Force Goals, and everyone assumed that the difference would be made up by relying heavily on battlefield nuclear weapons.

What made the Europeans agree to this in spite of the fears of becoming a nuclear battlefield with all the civilian casualties foretold by *Exercise Carte Blanche* was the idea that battlefield nuclear weapons would tend to couple. If so, the Soviets would be deterred by the fear that any war at all in Europe would instantly bring down a massive nuclear attack on the Russian homeland by ICBMs based in the United States.

So it was very clear that the Europeans hoped that nuclear weapons would never be used at all. Hence, their policy was to try to create circumstances that would ensure two things. The first was that any war at all between the NATO and the Warsaw Pact forces would be nuclear from the outset and not just on the battlefield but on the Soviet homeland as well. The second was that any war at all would therefore be so horrible that no sane Soviet leader would do anything that entailed any risk of any kind of war at all.

THE NEUTRON BOMB

Consider, for example, the attitude of the European governments toward the neutron bomb. Nuclear scientists conceived an idea for a bomb in which the amount of radiation emitted would be greatly stepped up but the blast greatly reduced. The Americans hailed this idea for a neutron bomb as a weapon that could be used by NATO forces against tanks, which the Soviets had built in overwhelming numbers, but without damaging nearby villages and towns and the people who lived in them. But the Europeans feared that the result would be to make war less terribly destructive and hence more feasible. Their only hope, to repeat, was to make sure that any war in Europe would be so horrible for everyone concerned that no nation would dare do anything that might bring it about. So pressure from America's European allies forced the Carter administration to decide against going ahead with the idea of the neutron bomb. For the Europeans, deterrence was everything, and they did not really want to think about what to do if deterrence failed.

THE NIXON ADMINISTRATION AND THE
SCHLESINGER DOCTRINE

During the first years of the Nixon administration, Henry Kissinger, Nixon's national security adviser, talked about "sufficiency" in strategic forces, since "superiority" was no longer realistically obtainable. Melvin Laird, Nixon's first secretary of defense put his emphasis on the "triad": ICBMs, submarine-launched ballistic missiles (SLBMs), and manned bombers. His idea was that each leg of this triad should strive to be by itself a secure second-strike force.

But these were not really changes in strategic thinking. The Nixon administration's new ideas on strategy did not come until 1974, with the doctrine named for Nixon's then secretary of defense, James Schlesinger, the "Schlesinger doctrine" of "limited nuclear options."

Schlesinger had spent a number of years as a defense analyst at the RAND corporation, and he relied on many of the same RAND specialists that McNamara had used. So his new strategy was in many ways an extension of McNamara's attempt to increase the number of strategic options. The key to Schlesinger's strategy was not only to avoid attacking Soviet cities at the outset, but also to hold back a portion of the American forces as a reserve to threaten the cities if the Soviets did not in turn avoid American cities. The idea was that this would create an incentive for the Soviets to follow suit in avoiding cities.

The strategy would be counterforce, as in McNamara's original strategy. McNamara had eventually turned against a counterforce strategy because the collateral damage on cities of attacking military installations would be so great. But Schlesinger believed that the development of smaller warheads with much greater accuracy would make it possible to hold down collateral damage to a point where a counterforce strategy really did make sense.

As time went on it seemed clear that the Schlesinger doctrine was intended to serve three different purposes. One would be to help the NATO ground forces if the Soviets attacked in Europe. Another would be "damage limitation" after a nuclear war had begun—to destroy the remaining Soviet missiles and bombers before they had a chance to attack American cities. The third would be to establish what had come to be known as "escalation dominance." The idea here was that at any given level on the escalation ladder the American forces should be stronger than the Soviet forces. The Soviets would have to be the ones to make the decision to go up another rung on the escalation ladder. And not only would the Soviets have to make the decision, they would have to make it in the face of a balance in the United States's favor at the next rung as well.

All three of these purposes were already part of Pentagon plans. So in a sense the Schlesinger doctrine—or at least going public with it—was to provide a rationale to win budgetary support for what the military were already doing.

CRITICISMS OF THE SCHLESINGER DOCTRINE

Although the criticism of the Schlesinger doctrine was less strident than it had been of McNamara's city-avoidance, damage-limitation, and counterforce strategy, it focused on essentially the same points. The critics, who were mainly interested in arms control and were pushing the Strategic Arms Limitation Treaty (SALT), thought it was unrealistic to believe that a nuclear war could be controlled. If governments deluded themselves into thinking so, the chance of a crisis turning into a nuclear war would, in their view, be much greater.

Another criticism was that emphasizing counterforce again would lead to just another arms race. What was worse than these flaws, the critics argued, was that the only conditions in which the Schlesinger doctrine made any sense was if the Soviets began a war with a limited number of selected nuclear strikes. But from the information available in the West, the Soviets continued to base their strategy on an all-out attack at the very outset of a war. And if the United States followed the Schlesinger doctrine in a preemptive strike, it would only lead to a massive Soviet attack on American cities.

STRATEGY IN THE CARTER ADMINISTRATION

The Carter administration, for its part, adopted still another variation of McNamara's city-avoidance, damage-limitation, counterforce strategy—the "countervailing strategy," approved in a presidential directive in July 1980.

In the countervailing strategy, the enemy's military forces remained the principal target. But the strategy also targeted the enemy leadership as well. This was a drastic departure from the previous idea that both the leadership and communications system of the enemy country should be avoided so that it would have the means of making a decision to surrender and communicating it to its surviving forces. Presumably the change was made on the grounds that while a threat to the population might not always deter the Soviet leadership, a threat to their own lives would. At the same time, the strategy called for a variety of options that would include targeting industry and cities. The goal, again, was to give the president a range of options, thus deterring the Soviets at all possible levels.

In effect, the countervailing strategy was one of providing a second-strike force but at several different levels and with a certain number of both counterforce and countervalue options, "countervalue" meaning attacks on cities, the civilian population, and other things that did not contribute to a country's military strength but that it might value. No one seemed to have any hope that the United States could destroy the Soviet capacity to retaliate, which seemed impossible, nor even to limit the damage of a Soviet retaliation very much, which seemed equally elusive. The goal seems to have been to enhance deterrence across the full range of conceivable scenarios.

Critics argued that, in spite of its name, countervailing strategy was just McNamara's assured destruction in a new garb. They also argued that providing so many options required such huge missile forces that the expense would be astronomical. Also, the critics argued, it was difficult to believe that a president could discriminate so precisely among a large range of options in the midst of a nuclear war or that the enemy would be able to distinguish among the different kinds of attack and so understand the purpose behind the strategy chosen. In any case, the critics argued, such a countervailing strategy would spur the Soviets on to even greater efforts, thereby fueling the arms race.

An even greater flaw in the countervailing strategy, the critics argued, was that it would be destabilizing rather than stabilizing. As the United States developed more options with more precise weapons, it would convey to the Soviets a growing potentiality of being able to launch a successful first strike. Faced with even a remote possibility that its capacity to retaliate would be destroyed, the Soviet Union would be forced to consider a policy of launch on warning, and the warning might be false.

PRESIDENT REAGAN AND STAR WARS

When Reagan took office, he was appalled to find that the strategic choices were limited to deterrence, arms control, or a combination of the two. Apparently influenced by the urging of Edward Teller, in March 1983, Reagan proposed a massive research effort to restore the possibility of true defense: the Strategic Defense Initiative (SDI), which the press promptly nicknamed "Star Wars" after the science fiction movie.

The idea was to develop a defense system based largely in space that would prevent missiles from reaching the U.S. homeland. Soviet launching sites would be monitored by spy satellites, and the instant they started to count down for a launch they would be attacked by lasers from other satellites or by other weapons based in space. A second line of defense would attack in mid-flight any missiles that got through the first line of defense. Satellites would carry nonnuclear weapons such as chemical lasers or particle beams. To this defense would be added x-ray lasers, launched from either submarines or bases on the ground and triggered by nuclear explosions in space. A final defense would be ground-based lasers attacking incoming missiles during the last stages of their flight, as they descended to their targets.

CRITICISMS OF STAR WARS

The first criticism of Reagan's Star Wars defense was that it would violate the 1972 ABM treaty, which limited each side to one ABM shield each with no more than one-hundred interceptor missiles. In addition, the treaty banned testing in space, which the development of Star Wars would require.

Another criticism was that some of the components of the system had yet to be invented and might not even be possible. Even those parts of Star Wars that were theoretically possible might be unworkable in practice, particularly the parts of the system that depend on laser or particle-beam weapons. In addition, according to newspaper reports in April 1988, a study by the Office of Technology Assessment, a Congressional research agency, concluded that even the orthodox parts of the system, those that used rockets, would be vulnerable to equipment and computer software failures that would make them unworkable in the stress of war.

Another objection along the same lines pointed to the fact that nuclear explosions create an electromagnetic pulse that can blind radar, disrupt communications, and disable computers and other electronic equipment. The point is that the high-altitude nuclear explosions called for by the Star Wars defense system might bathe the entire United States in an electronic pulse that would paralyze the rest of the defense.

Another objection to Star Wars was that even if the weapons could be invented, a wide variety of countermeasures would be open to the Soviets. Satellites are very vulnerable, so they would be the Soviets' primary target. Without the satellites the system simply could not work. The Soviets could also improve their missiles, by making them faster, by equipping them with defensive devices, and by giving their warheads a very small radar cross-section. The United States, for example, had developed a technology for a very low radar profile for the Stealth bomber and was applying that technology to missile warheads. The Soviets would undoubtedly do the same. The Soviets could also develop their own missile defense system, which would frustrate those parts of the Star Wars strategy that called for attacking the pads from which the Soviet attacking missiles were being launched.

Still another objection to Star Wars was that the expense would be almost incomprehensible, with a figure of over a trillion dollars mentioned as a starter.

Paul Nitze, in a public statement, set two conditions that would have to be met if Star Wars was to be an acceptable system. The fact that Nitze was one of the Reagan administration's top arms-control negotiators made the "conditions" seem more like doubts.

The first condition was that the system, especially the parts based in space, would have to be able to survive a first strike; the second condition was that the system would have to be "cost effective at the margin." What Nitze meant by "cost effective at the margin" was that if additional Star Wars defenses were more expensive than additional Soviet attacking missiles, the Soviets could double or triple the number of incoming missiles and overwhelm whatever defense system was built. The result would be a new arms race. So a Star Wars defense system would be feasible only if the additional Star Wars weapons were much cheaper for the United States than additional offensive missiles for the Soviet Union.

Still another objection to Star Wars was that even if a reasonably reliable and effective system could be invented, it would still not accomplish the purpose of making the world no longer MAD; that is, it would not eliminate mutual assured destruction. To do that, a system would have to be 100-percent effective, for if only 1 percent of the attacking missiles got through, the casualties would still be in the millions.

A final objection was that the Star Wars defense would not protect against manned bombers and cruise missiles—the air-breathing, low-flying, robot-piloted drones that can deliver nuclear warheads with great accuracy. Most defense specialists believed that cruise missiles would become more important as time went on, and protection against them would require an entirely different system, more like the old air-defense systems against manned bombers. Neither would Star Wars defend against germ or chemical warfare. Nor would it protect against "suitcase" bombs, planted in strategic places by enemy agents, which might in the future turn out to be as serious a threat as ICBMs.

Finally, the critics argued, even if a Star Wars system could eventually be developed that was 100-percent effective, the interim period in which it was less than fully effective would be very long indeed and such an interim period would be highly unstable.

Suppose, for example, that the interim U.S. Star Wars system could knock out 20 or 30 percent of incoming missiles. If the United States retained its current counterforce capabilities, it would have the capability to launch a surprise attack that would reduce the Soviet retaliatory strike substantially. Even though the Star Wars defense force could not provide 100-percent protection, it would reduce the Soviet retaliatory strike still more, and the force remaining might be small enough to limit American casualties to 20 or 30 million. If so and if the Soviets also concluded that the United States might find that level of casualties tolerable under certain conditions, then the Soviets would have to consider launch on warning. As mentioned before, the warning might be false.

The fears of the critics that the Soviets would see Star Wars as part of a strike-first strategy seemed to be confirmed when some Star Wars advocates themselves pointed out in private that Star Wars would be best used as part of a preemptive strike. Their argument began by admitting that the best that Star Wars could hope to achieve would be a partial defense—a shield, but a leaky one. A leaky shield would not do much good defending against an enemy's first strike. But it might be very useful defending against the ragged retaliation that an enemy could launch after a preemptive first strike by the United States had destroyed the bulk of his forces.

Similarly, the critics' fears of a long period in which the Star Wars system would be used to protect only missile forces and not population also seemed to be confirmed when one of Reagan's high-level defense department officials testified before Congress that, although the aim was to provide a defense for cities eventually, the program would begin some time in the 1990s with a partial defense to protect missile launching sites in the hope of having it grow into a defense for cities in the next century.[3]

Another confirmation of the critics' fears came in 1988, when it was reported that the JCS had decided that the best an initial Star Wars system could do would be to blunt an attack by destroying 50 percent of the Soviet SS-18 missiles and 30 percent of the entire Soviet missile force. This would mean that 3,500 missiles would get through. A Princeton University study published in 1988 estimated that if these 3,500 were directed only at American military targets, they would still kill 13 to 34 million people and seriously injure another 64 million.

Hans Bethe, a Nobel prize–winning physicist, summed up the objections to Star Wars in a sentence: "It is difficult to imagine a system more likely to induce catastrophe than one that requires critical decisions by the second [i.e., each second of time], is itself untested and fragile, and yet is threatening to the other side's retaliatory capability."[4]

Bethe's point about making "critical decisions by the second" brings up a criticism of almost all strategies, such as Star Wars, that depend on "high-tech" weapons systems. This criticism is that the advocates do not consider the implications for their strategies of what the military for generations have called the "fog of war" and the G.I.s of World War II turned into a gallows-humor joke by coining the word SNAFU—"situation normal, all fucked up."

An example of the fog of war used in training U.S. infantry in the years before World War II was an incident in the Meuse–Argonne offensive of World War I. An American company was given the mission of taking a hill several hundred yards to its direct front. In the confusion of bullets flying, artillery shells exploding, smoke, and all the rest, the company changed direction shortly after it had penetrated the first line of German trenches without anyone realizing that it had changed direction. From that time on, the company was attacking parallel to the front rather than perpendicular to it toward its objective. So the company's attack cut the German line of communications. By doing so, the company's action was the key to winning the entire engagement, and it was given credit for doing so, even though its commander had been completely unwitting.

This example of the fog of war has a happy ending. But most do not. An example was the shooting down of Iranian flight 655, a civilian airliner on a routine flight, over the Persian Gulf by the American cruiser *Vincennes*. When the *Vincennes* sent electronic beams and messages trying to identify the approaching aircraft, the *Vincennes*'s crew—who were in the middle of a firefight with some Iranian gunboats and very tense—misinterpreted the electronic responses and thought they were being attacked by an Iranian F-14. The captain of the *Vincennes* decided that he should not take a chance with his ship and the lives of his crew. He fired and the airliner was shot down with the loss of 290 civilian lives.

Undoubtedly in the captain's mind was what had happened to the American frigate *Stark* several months earlier, also in the Persian Gulf. The *Stark*'s radar picked up an incoming plane. As with the *Vincennes*, electronic beams and messages were sent, and the responses were confusing. The *Stark*'s captain did not fire, and his ship was hit by an Exocet missile fired by an Iraqi plane by mistake. Thirty-seven of the *Stark*'s crew were killed.

History abounds with examples of the fog of war and the confusion when radios, weapons, and the other machines of war do not work the way they ought to: the Soviet's shooting down the Korean Airlines 007; the M-16 rifle in Vietnam that jammed so often in combat that many American soldiers threw it away and got themselves something else; the World War II assault on Arnheim, when the radios of some units were not compatible with the radios of other units; and so on throughout the history of humankind and war.

History is also full of examples of nations that tested a weapon in peace and assumed that it would work just as well in war. The Germans, for example, tested their air defense systems before World War II with a single, incoming aircraft—and assumed that because the air defenses worked perfectly in the test they would work perfectly when a thousand planes were coming in and the antiaircraft crews were being bombed and strafed.

A wise government must assume that when the bullets start flying things will go wrong. And when the system is as highly complicated as Star Wars and the consequence of even the most minor failure is nuclear holocaust, it is simpleminded to assume that everything will work as planned. The Pentagon officially abandoned Star Wars as hopeless, but it continued to work on a system that might intercept a few missiles launched by accident or by a rogue country, such as North Korea, Iran, or Iraq. Then, sixteen years after President Reagan proposed the Star Wars system, President Clinton, as described in Chapter 14, proposed building such a limited missile defense system, depending on the outcome of a series of four tests to begin in June 1999.

NOTES

1. Alain C. Enthoven and K. Wayne Smith, *How Much is Enough? Shaping the Defense Program, 1961–1969* (New York: Harper & Row, 1971), 177–178, 207–208.

2. See Diana Bockar, "Battlefield Nuclear Weapons," 1985, Ph.D. diss., Columbia University.

3. *The New York Times*, 22 February 1985, p. A13.

4. Senator Sam Nunn, Democrat of Georgia and chairman of the Senate Armed Services Committee, who had been a strong critic of Reagan's Star Wars idea, in January 1988, proposed a limited anti-ballistic missile shield based solely on land, rather than space. The system, which Nunn called the "Accidental Launch Protection System," would be designed to protect cities from a single Soviet missile fired by accident or one or two missiles fired deliberately by some terrorist state, such as Qaddafi's Libya. Since Nunn's limited system would be based on land, it would not violate the 1972 treaty and it would be comparatively cheap—about $5 billion. One criticism of Nunn's proposal was that it might be an insurance policy—a very expensive insurance policy—but it seemed clear that the major objection was that Nunn's limited shield might be the first step leading to a full Star Wars defense system.

Chapter 9

No First Use, Counterforce, and MAD as a Strategy

So the debate on strategy continued. There were arguments for and against not only the strategies laid out in the Truman, Eisenhower, Kennedy, Johnson, Nixon, Carter, Reagan, and Clinton administrations, but also on what constituted an effective deterrent.[1] The debate also included proposals for at least three nuclear strategies that have not been adopted by any of these administrations. The first of these was a strategy that combined a declaration that the United States had adopted the policy of no first use of nuclear weapons with a buildup of conventional forces large enough to meet the Soviets without having to rely on nuclear weapons, especially in Europe. The second was a counterforce strategy designed to fight and win a nuclear war. And the third was to give up the idea in McNamara's second strategy that the destruction of the Soviet Union could be "assured" in some way that would permit the United States to escape destruction, to accept the certainty that the "assured destruction" would be *mutual*, and to concentrate on making certain that the United States could *guarantee* the destruction of the Soviet Union. Mutual assured destruction had been a condition or situation imposed by the nature of the weapons. The idea here was to make MAD a strategy. We will examine each of these three strategies in turn.

NO FIRST USE

In 1982, Robert McNamara, McGeorge Bundy, George Kennan, and Gerard Smith jointly proposed that the United States should deny itself the option of being the first to use nuclear weapons and couple this renunciation with an increase in conventional forces, mainly in the NATO area, massive enough to match the much greater strength the Soviet Union then enjoyed in conventional forces.

McNamara later acknowledged that NATO's threat to use battlefield nuclear weapons did serve to deter the Soviets from a conventional attack on Europe. But he argued that it was inherently not credible that NATO would actually resort to nuclear weapons when it was inevitable that the Soviets would respond in kind in Europe (if not against the United States as well), an action that would inflict greater damage on Europe than any conventional war could do.

McNamara went on to argue that the reality was that nuclear warheads of any kind could really not be used in a war: Using even small, battlefield warheads would escalate rapidly into a Soviet–American holocaust that would destroy the Soviet Union, the United States, Europe, and much of the rest of the Northern Hemisphere as well. Using battlefield nuclear weapons to defend against a Soviet conventional attack, in other words, would bring down a Soviet nuclear response that would wreak vastly more damage over a much wider part of the globe than would a conventional war fought mainly in Europe.

Presumably McNamara would also acknowledge that the U.S. threat to retaliate with a nuclear attack on the Soviet homeland did serve to deter the Soviets from a conventional attack on Europe. But presumably he would also argue that if this deterrent failed and the Soviets did attack Europe with conventional forces, the United States would hesitate to retaliate on the Soviet homeland with nuclear missiles since this would inevitably bring down Soviet nuclear missiles on the American homeland.

McNamara elaborated his view in a book, *Blundering Into Disaster*, that was published in 1986. His position, in a nutshell, was that he could discover no strategy, if deterrence failed, for using any kind of nuclear weapon that would give the United States an advantage, much less win a war. He believed that both Reagan's Star Wars and a scaled-down version designed to protect American retaliatory forces rather than the whole population were not technologically feasible and that to try to develop them would be highly destabilizing.

Although McNamara favored negotiating with the Soviets on arms control, he did not believe that arms control agreements would ever succeed in eliminating nuclear weapons. Hence, he concluded that nuclear weapons would continue to be a necessary part of the American defenses, but that the only purpose nuclear weapons serve is to deter the other side from using nuclear weapons.

Thus, to deter the Soviets from attacking Europe with conventional forces, McNamara argued, the NATO Allies needed to build up their own conventional forces to a level that would convince the Soviets that they could not gain anything by such an attack. If this was done, it should then be possible for both sides to agree to reduce their stockpiles of nuclear weapons to the "lowest force level consistent with stability" (i.e., the minimum number necessary to deter the other side from an attack). This number McNamara estimated to be about 500 each.

CRITICISMS OF NO FIRST USE

Two major criticisms were made of this proposal. The first, made mainly by Europeans, was that it was decoupling. In an interview after his book was published, McNamara said that a leading European security expert had come up to him at a meeting to say that McNamara, Bundy, Kennan, and Smith "had done more to weaken NATO than any other human beings in the postwar period."

The second criticism was that the proposal was unrealistic in the sense that none of the Allies, the United States as well as the Europeans, would be willing to spend the vast sums needed to match the Soviet conventional strength. They would rather put their hopes in deterrence, in avoiding war entirely by threatening the Soviet troops with battlefield nuclear weapons and the Soviet homeland with ICBMs launched from submarines and from the United States. Indeed, even if the Europeans had doubts that deterrence was permanent, they would rather put their hopes in deterrence. And they preferred to do so even if they were not able to answer the question of what to do if deterrence failed.

One other criticism needs to be made of this strategy of no first use combined with a conventional buildup. Like Reagan's Star Wars, the strategy is an attempt to rehabilitate war. But conventional wars have been lost before in history, and the consequences for the defeated have been bad enough for nations to suffer extraordinary casualties and destruction before surrendering. Nations in the past, to put the point another way, have agreed with Ernest Hemingway when he said that many things are worse than war and that all of them come with defeat.

Suppose the Allies did build up NATO's conventional strength to the Soviet level, no matter what the cost. But suppose then that through a series of miscalculations, errors, and accidents the NATO Allies and the Soviets found themselves at war. Conventional war or not, within a few days or at most weeks, one side or the other would begin to lose a little. The losing side would then be confronted with the choice: Negotiate or stem the enemy's advance with battlefield nuclear weapons. The criticism is that if war came in Europe it seems likely that within a few days or weeks the Soviets and the NATO countries would find themselves either at the negotiating table or using battlefield nuclear weapons.

And if the decision was to use battlefield nuclear weapons, within a few days, if not hours, one side or the other would again begin to lose a little. And again the losing side would have to face another choice: Negotiate or go to the next level of nuclear weapons—ICBMs against the enemy's homeland.

The point that no one was willing to face, neither the advocates of Star Wars nor the advocates of no first use, is that nuclear weapons have made war obsolete. The point, to repeat, is not that nuclear weapons have abolished war. Nuclear war is not only possible but if a fairly long time frame is taken, it is actually probable, even inevitable. The point is that nuclear war, even a very small nuclear war, will be so destructive that it cannot possibly serve any rational social or political purpose.

THE COUNTERFORCE STRATEGY

A number of people, inside and outside the government but especially in the Air Force, continued to believe that the only truly effective deterrent would be the ability to fight, survive, and win a nuclear war. For these people, the preferred strategy was counterforce—to attack Soviet military forces of all kinds and to destroy them before they could do decisive damage to our own forces, population, or homeland.

Against the objections that technology will not support a truly effective counterforce strategy, the Air Force and their supporters argued that technology always improves and never goes backward. So, they argued, the United States should continue to try to develop a technology that will support a counterforce strategy and in the meantime continue to upgrade its counterforce capability as each new development becomes practicable.

The information available on the various Single Integrated Operational Plans indicates that the nuclear war planners in the Pentagon have quietly pursued this general policy of striving toward a counterforce posture no matter what new doctrine each passing president and secretary of defense adopted as the declaratory policy of the United States.

A counterforce strategy would essentially continue along the lines laid down in the early part of the first Reagan administration; that is, a defense buildup of all categories of weapons and a countervailing strategy transformed into a counterforce strategy as rapidly as developments in weapons technology permitted.

The advocates of a counterforce strategy would not devote much effort to negotiating arms control agreements, since they regard these as useless or even detrimental. Negotiations would continue mainly out of the political necessity of giving the appearance of an effort, and agreements would be made only on measures that clearly added to the American strategic posture, detracted from the Soviet Union's, or eliminated weapons that both sides regarded as expensive but not really very effective.

CRITICISMS OF THE COUNTERFORCE STRATEGY

The major criticisms of the counterforce strategy were threefold. The first was that it was hopelessly optimistic to believe that future technologies would benefit only counterforce. If future technology can produce effective counterforce weapons system, how long will it be until technology produces an effective defense against such a weapons system? Another objection was the same as for both Star Wars and no first use: the cost. All three—Star Wars, no first use, and counterforce—would mean astronomical expense but no real guarantee of security. The third criticism was also the same as the one applied to Star Wars and no first use—that the counterforce strategy was an attempt to rehabilitate war and shied away from facing the probability that nuclear weapons have made war obsolete, that nuclear war, even a very small nuclear war, would be so destructive that it could not possibly serve any rational social or political purpose.

MAD AS A STRATEGY

MAD so far has been a situation that the nuclear powers find themselves in, rather than a strategy that they have deliberately adopted. McNamara's strategy of assured destruction was to try to make sure that the Soviet Union was destroyed while at the same time attempting to protect as much of the American and allied population and industry as possible. To the extent that it has been a MAD world so far, it is not because MAD has been adopted as a strategy, but because technology and the astronomical cost of protecting populations by civil defense measures have made it a MAD world—a world of mutual assured destruction.

MAD as a strategy begins with the proposition that no one can "win" a nuclear war, no matter what. Because of this, the argument goes, a relatively small force would be an adequate deterrent. The idea of adopting MAD as a strategy was to adopt not a policy of the assured destruction of the other side, as McNamara sought, but a policy of *mutual* assured destruction.

In a MAD strategy, nuclear forces would be designed not for counterforce but solely for a second strike against population centers. The forces would be mobile, including submarine-launched missiles and small, single-warhead missiles, such as the proposed Midgetman, that could be put on trucks that would be constantly on the move around large military reservations. Deliberately, none of the missiles would be very accurate, so as to avoid any suspicion that they could be turned into first-strike weapons against the enemy's retaliatory forces. None of the missiles would be equipped with multiple independently targetable reentry vehicles (MIRVs); that is, each missile would have only one warhead. And, finally, the total number of missiles would be modest. Since the purpose of a MAD force would be purely to deter an enemy by the threat of destroying his population in a retaliatory strike, a rather small force would be sufficient.

A second element in a MAD strategy would be to make no effort whatsoever to defend, protect, or evacuate the civilian population—in effect, to let the population and the cities serve as hostages to the other side and so to convince them that the United States would not attempt a first strike.

In fact, none of the nuclear powers have done very much in the way of civil defense. Although the Star Wars program was aimed at finding an active defense against missiles, no one claimed to have succeeded as yet in developing a technology for shooting down missiles with 100-percent success. But if only a single warhead aimed at a city got through the Star Wars defenses, millions of people would be killed. So until an antimissile system that is 100-percent effective is perfected, it makes no sense to spend money on civil defense. Even a miserably ineffective program to protect the civilian population is inconceivably expensive. As a result, as soon as the consequences of ICBMs with multimegaton warheads became well understood, neither side did very much for civil defense. In the MAD strategy, however, populations would be left unprotected as a matter of deliberate policy, rather than because of lack of technology or cost.

A third element in a MAD strategy would be a renewed effort to reach an agreement on arms control. Because the strategy is not provocative, the argument goes, adopting it should make negotiating an effective agreement easier.

Adopting MAD as a strategy, to sum up the argument, would produce a stable deterrent because the main emphasis would be on weapons that could survive a first strike, mainly through mobility, and still be able to strike back against population centers. At the same time, lacking accuracy and being small, the force would not put any pressure on the other side either to embark on an arms race or to consider a strategy of launch on warning.

And such a force would be very inexpensive compared to the cost of any other strategy, since it would require only a minimum second-strike force and no civil defense at all. Building a force designed solely to survive a first strike and still be able to strike back at population centers and combining that force with a policy of leaving the American population unprotected would in effect guarantee not only that the destruction would be assured but that it would be mutual.

Finally, because MAD as a strategy would not threaten the other side's retaliatory force and so would not be provocative, it would provide a strong incentive for the other side, first, to follow suit by adopting a MAD strategy and reducing their forces to the same level and, second, to negotiate effective arms control agreements.

CRITICISMS OF MAD AS A STRATEGY

The objections to MAD as a strategy were twofold. The first objection was that it might be difficult to maintain its credibility. Adopting MAD as a strategy would announce to the world that the United States had given up hope of fighting and winning nuclear wars. If this admission raised a suspicion in the mind of an aggressive enemy that the United States would lack the will and determination to launch a retaliatory strike if deterrence failed, then deterrence *would* fail. It is the dilemma described in the parable of the good guy and the bad guy and their babies.

The second objection, also described in the parable, is the mirror image of the first: If deterrence failed, retaliation against populations would be neither a moral course of action nor a rational one in the sense of bringing any benefits to the side striking back. If deterrence fails, a truly moral people—or perhaps only a people who were sickened by the sheer horror of it all—would *not* retaliate.

Another possible objection relates to how many casualties the other side would find tolerable. Although a majority of the Soviet population was urban, it was not as high a proportion as the American population. So casualties of 30 percent might be the maximum that a MAD strategy could achieve. In certain circumstances and with a set of Soviet leaders like Stalin, the argument went, the certainty of losing 30 percent might not be an adequate deterrent.

NUCLEAR WINTER

A new factor was introduced into the debate on strategy by research that raised the possibility of a "nuclear winter."[2] This work suggested that even a rather small nuclear war would create such dense clouds of dust and soot that the sun would be obscured. Photosynthesis could be blocked, and a nuclear winter might set in that would threaten all life on the planet.

Historical evidence to support the possibility of a nuclear winter actually exists. In 1815, a volcanic island, Tambora, in what is now Indonesia, blew itself to smithereens and spewed its several cubic miles of rock and earth into the upper atmosphere in the form of dust and ash. This cloud so obscured the sun that the following year, 1816, brought a killing frost every month of the year throughout the Northern Hemisphere. People living at the time called 1816 the "year without a summer." In New England the lack of winter fodder meant that the animals had to be slaughtered, and the shortage of food sparked a migration to the more promising lands in the Middle West. In Rome, it snowed in August, a miracle that was commemorated by building still another church, Our Lady of the Snows.

At first glance, nuclear winter appeared to be in effect a doomsday machine, as in the parable of the good guy and the bad guy and their babies. But although everyone recognized that the effects of a nuclear war on the environment would be severe, more recent research suggested that the result could not be rightly called a nuclear winter in the sense that it might bring the end of life on earth or in the Northern Hemisphere.

It is also far from clear just what the effect that nuclear winter, if it turns out that there is such a thing, would have on strategic thinking. If it turns out that some precise level of nuclear explosions forms a threshold to nuclear winter, it is possible that the effect would be not to inhibit an aggressor, but to give him an incentive to launch a first strike with just under the number of warheads that would create a nuclear winter, leaving the victim country only the suicidal choice of surrendering or destroying most life on earth, including its own people.

NEW PROBLEMS IN MAINTAINING A STABLE PEACE

Quite apart from the possibility of nuclear winter, technology has created new problems in maintaining a stable peace. A first-strike weapon is defined as one that is capable of attacking an enemy's weapons, is accurate enough to hit very close to an enemy missile, and is powerful enough to destroy it. Improvements in accuracy can turn an ordinary missile into a first-strike weapon. So can increases in the size of the warhead. Thus, the very heavy Soviet missiles, like the SS-18, were regarded as at least potentially first-strike weapons.

A first-strike force would be one designed to take out the entire enemy retaliatory force. Such a force is obviously destabilizing—its threat to disarm an enemy and remove the deterrent of his threat to strike back tempts that enemy to launch a preemptive attack, either on warning or whenever an opportunity presents itself.

A second-strike weapon by definition is one that has some capability for surviving a first strike and striking back. Thus, hardening a missile's silo—by encasing it, say, in very thick concrete—increases the missile's second-strike capability. So does making it mobile, by putting it on an aircraft, a railroad car, a truck, or a submarine. A second-strike force contributes to deterrence and hence to stability by denying an enemy any possibility of profiting from a surprise attack and so removes both temptation and provocation.

As long as one missile could carry only one warhead and as long as missiles were not very accurate, deterrence was relatively easy to maintain, and the peace was rather stable, as Churchill foresaw in his notion of a balance of terror. But this stability was eroded by two developments.

The first was the multiple, independently targetable reentry vehicle. The Minuteman missile could carry three warheads, each of which could be directed to different targets several hundred miles apart. The MX and the Soviet SS-18 could carry ten such warheads. The D-5, the missile carried by the Trident submarine, could carry eight, and the Navy wanted to build a newer version that would carry twelve. The Soviet SS-24, deployed in 1988 on railway cars, could carry ten warheads.

The second development was the improvement in the accuracy of missiles, which was simply awesome. The Soviet SS-20 at a range of 3 thousand miles had a 1,200 foot CEP (circular error probable), which means that half of the warheads launched by SS-20s would fall within a circle 1,200 feet in diameter. The MX had a CEP of less than 750 feet at a range of 6 or 7 thousand miles. The D-5 had a CEP of 400 feet at a range of 4 thousand miles. With this kind of accuracy a nuclear warhead would destroy a missile inside a silo no matter how much that silo had been hardened. Thus a hardened missile could no longer be considered a second-strike missile.

The problem with the MX was how to base it. If it was based in fixed silos, like the Minuteman, the MX would be very vulnerable. So based, the MX would be destabilizing. Since each MX missile could attack five enemy missiles on their pads with two warheads to each and do so with extremely high accuracy, it could be a formidable first-strike weapon. On the other hand, when the threat the MX missile force posed was combined with a high vulnerability (as MX missiles deployed in fixed bases certainly would be), then in a time of crisis the temptation for an enemy to launch a preemptive first strike would become overwhelming.

Obviously what was needed was a way to make the MX mobile. The first idea for basing the MX so that it would be at least partly mobile was offered during the Carter administration. The MX was too big and bulky to be carried in an airplane or on a truck, so the idea was to base it on railway cars. The proposal called for a special railroad to be built in a remote, unpopulated area in the form of a giant racecourse. Every few miles a siding would be built surrounded by a revetment. Around this racecourse, railway cars carrying MX missiles would be shuttled, and also a number of railroad cars containing dummies of the MX. Instead of being put in a fixed silo, the MX would be at least partially mobile, and it would also take advantage of a certain amount of deception. Basing the MX on such a railway racecourse would be extremely expensive, but the main flaw was that it would be relatively cheap for the Soviets simply to provide enough missiles to destroy *all* the revetments, the dummies along with the real missiles.

The Carter administration asked Congress to fund 200 MXs, but the request bogged down in the debate about basing. When the Reagan administration came to power, it agreed with Congress about basing and explored some thirty different basing modes. One, to give an example, was nicknamed "Densepack." The idea was to base the MX in silos very close together in a remote area. If the Soviets attacked, the first of their own missiles to arrive would blow up or deflect the rest of those coming in, and so enough MX missiles would presumably survive to be able to launch a devastating retaliatory blow. But this idea, too, seemed flawed. Without a test, no one could be sure whether or not enough MXs would survive to constitute an adequate deterrent.

In the end, the Reagan administration asked Congress for one hundred MX missiles to be based in refurbished Minuteman silos. In 1982, Congress finally authorized only fifty, and specifically said that the reason for cutting the request in half was the MX's vulnerability in fixed silos.

The first ten MX missiles were deployed in refurbished Minuteman silos at Warren Air Force Base in Wyoming and became operational in December 1986. The rest were to be deployed by the end of 1988. Thus, by 1988 Warren Air Force Base had fifty MX missiles each with ten warheads, and 160 of the old Minuteman missiles, each with three warheads.

At the same time that the first MX missiles were deployed, the Reagan administration asked Congress for another fifty, to be based on railroad cars, but not in the "racecourse" design. Two of the MX missiles would be placed on each of twenty-five trains. The trains would be shuttled around inside military reservations until time of crisis, when they would be deployed over the entire United States railway system.

With the MX and the Soviet equivalent deployed, the world entered a period when one missile launched in a surprise first strike could aim two warheads at each of five land-based missiles in fixed silos of the victim's retaliatory, second-strike force so accurately that little hope remained that any of the missiles being attacked could survive no matter how much they were hardened. If the only effective deterrent was a secure, second-strike force, then that force would have to consist of submarine-based missiles, airborne missiles, mobile land-based missiles, or bombers with very advanced technology for getting through the enemy's radar and air defenses.

Suppose the United States came to rely not on submarine-based and mobile land missiles like Midgetman but mainly on the MX based in the old Minuteman silos, where they were both very vulnerable and very tempting, even provocative targets. Suppose also that the Soviets continued to rely for their main missile force on land-based missiles in fixed silos. The result would be that both sides would have to consider a strategy of launch on warning. If so, the United States and the Soviet Union would be like two old-time Western gunfighters in a saloon—each eyeing the other suspiciously and tensed to draw the instant the other showed any sign of making a move, even to scratch his nose.

NOTES

1. See the various works on the subject by Bernard Brodie, Thomas Schelling, George Kennan, Henry Kissinger, William Kaufmann, Warner Schilling, Herman Kahn, George

Quester, Glenn Snyder, Robert Jervis, James King, Colin Grey, Patrick Morgan, Hans Morgenthau, Michael Howard, McGeorge Bundy, Alexander George, Richard Smoke, and Robert McNamara, among others. For an overview, see the collection of articles on the subject from *Foreign Affairs*, in William P. Bundy, ed., *The Nuclear Controversy: A Foreign Affairs Reader* (New York: New American Library/Meridian for the Council on Foreign Relations, 1985).

   2. R. P. Turco, O. B. Toon, T. P. Ackerman, J. B. Pollack, and Carl Sagan, "Nuclear Winter—Global Consequences of Multiple Nuclear Explosions," *Science* 222, no. 4630 (1983): 1283–1292; Carl Sagan and Richard Turco, *A Path No Man Thought: Nuclear Winter and the End of the Arms Race* (New York: Random House, 1990).

Chapter 10

The Breakup of the Soviet Union and the Bush–Yeltsin Agreement

Then, after all its decades of struggle with the United States, the Soviet Union ceased to exist. The landscape of the nuclear age was transformed overnight.

The Soviet Union consisted of fifteen republics: Armenia, Azerbaijan, Belarus, Estonia, Georgia, Kazakhstan, Kyrgyzstan, Latvia, Lithuania, Moldova, Russia, Tajikistan, Turkmenistan, Ukraine, and Uzbekistan. Of these fifteen republics, nine signed a treaty forming the Commonwealth of Independent States in December 1991 when the Soviet Union broke up. Georgia, Estonia, Latvia, and Lithuania did not sign, and Azerbaijan and Moldova failed to ratify the treaty. However, in the fall of 1993, both Georgia and Azerbaijan joined.

Shortly after the breakup of the Soviet Union, the Chechen–Ingush Autonomous Soviet Socialist Republic of the Russian Federation declared its independence. The republic occupied what was regarded as a strategic position, and in the months that followed Yeltsin intervened in Chechnya, first in a covert operation and then with Russian troops. After many months of struggle, Russia finally agreed to Chechen independence. So, at the present time, the Commonwealth consists of Russia, Kazakhstan, Ukraine, Belarus, Armenia, Uzbekistan, Turkmenistan, Kyrgyzstan, Tajikistan, Georgia, and Azerbaijan.

It is important to understand that the Commonwealth is not a unitary state. It is, in fact, a confederation of independent states. Although its permanent shape and division of responsibilities are far from being final, the Commonwealth will presumably end up being responsible for defense and foreign affairs and possibly some aspects of trade and commerce, while the members will retain sovereignty over all other matters.

The first question is why. What were the fundamental causes of the Soviet breakup? The second question is how this new line up will affect the problem that nuclear weapons pose.

CAUSES OF THE SOVIET BREAKUP

In one of the more overblown claims to which politicians are partial, George Bush claimed that the cause of the Soviet breakup was the policy the Reagan and Bush administrations had followed toward the Soviet Union. In fact, the policies of *all* the American administrations since World War II deserve some of the credit. But one could also argue very persuasively that the breakup would have occurred even sooner if a number of those policies had been different, including those of the Reagan and Bush administrations!

Many Americans watching the tumultuous events in the former Soviet Union assumed that the basic cause was that the Soviet peoples were fed up with Communism and were yearning for democracy. But this is much too simple. Many of these people did idealize democracy and frequently the American form of democracy as well. But it is also clear that many others thought the American system of government was undignified, noisy, and too much influenced by lobbyists, big business, the newspapers, and television. Too often these peoples read about bribery and sex scandals in the American government and Congress and were shocked. Corrupt officials in the American government are exceptions, and the very publicity inherent in the American system tends to keep its officials more honest than in some countries. But this did not alter the perception among the peoples of the former Soviet Union.

In fact, the evidence is that most of these people thought the ideal system of government would include the full employment and low prices for food and housing that the Soviet system provided in the past but with a wider choice of consumer goods and a larger supply of them. The Soviet peoples also wanted free and fair elections. They were determined to see the power of the KGB reduced and an end to the domination of the Communist Party and its *apparatchiks*. However, as elections in Lithuania in 1992 and Russia in 1993 demonstrated, they often preferred experienced former communist officials to life-long advocates of democracy who had no government experience.

The people of the former Soviet Union clearly wanted more human rights and human freedom, including freedom to travel abroad, freedom to complain about government policies and officials, and freedom from the government's smothering oversight that blanketed all aspects of their lives. Notice, however, that they wanted only a *little* more freedom to complain. They would not be comfortable having a newsman call Yeltsin both a wimp and a twit, as the columnist Russell Baker once called President Bush. What most Russians wanted to criticize were those of Yeltsin's policies with which they disagreed. But if the taste for democracy grows, so does a taste for its nastier side. In the fall of 1993, Yeltsin was subject to severe—even indecent—public criticism, something that was unthinkable under the Soviet system.

The successor states to the Soviet Union are clearly going to try a free-enterprise system. But just as the so-called capitalist countries are to some extent hybrids that regulate industry and trade more or less strictly, these successor states will also likely come to a hybrid system. In their case it will probably have more regulation than the capitalist countries do, rather than less. The upheaval in the former Soviet Union, in other words, was not so much a rebellion against the *ideal* of communist ideology as a rebellion against the way that Communism had been implemented.

THE INEFFICIENT ECONOMY

But there were also other causes of the upheaval. The first was frustration with the inefficiency of the Soviet economy: the shortage of consumer goods, housing, and food supplies. The Soviet economy was inefficient partly because it was a highly centralized "planned economy." This stifled both competition and market stimuli. Centralization also put many economic decisions into the hands of a Moscow bureaucracy far removed from the farms and factories, a bureaucracy whose traditions and inefficiency went back to Czarist times. The one economic failing that was peculiar to Communism was agriculture. Farmers worldwide just do not respond to collectivism. Most have a deep-seated desire to own the land they work.

The Soviet economy was also distorted by the fear of a revival of German militarism in the early days and, later, by fear of the military threat posed by the United States and the West in general. This fear led Stalin and his successors to give extremely high priority to defense and capital goods, and a very low priority to consumer goods.

The fact is that the Soviet economy simply could not compete with the economy of the United States. The American gross national product (GNP) at the end of the Cold War was about $4.5 trillion. For years about 6 to 7 percent of this was spent on defense—between $270 billion and $315 billion a year.

Western economists estimate that the Soviet GNP at that time was about $2 trillion. Soviet economists think it was much lower, perhaps only about $1.5 trillion or even as low as $1 trillion. On Soviet defense spending, exact figures are impossible to discover, but estimates range from 15 percent to 25 and even 30 percent of GNP. So the Soviet defense budget cost the Soviet people somewhere between a low of $150 billion and a high that could have been as much as $400 billion.

THE ROLE OF NATIONALISM

However, an even more basic and fundamental cause of the turmoil that led to the breakup of the Soviet Union than the inefficient economy was frustrated nationalism—a longing among the different peoples in the Soviet Union who thought of themselves as nations to go their own way.

Less than half of the people of the Soviet Union were Great Russians, only about 48 percent. Eighteen percent were Ukrainian. Uzbeks were about 5 percent. Byelorussians and Kazakhs were each about 3 percent. All the rest of the population, totaling 23 percent, were made up of peoples each of whom numbered less than 2 percent of the total population of the Soviet Union. Most of these people had some nationalistic feelings—not for the Russian empire of the Czars or for the

Soviet Union of the Communists, but for their own peculiar nationalism—and some of these nationalistic feelings were enormously powerful.[1]

The Czars tried to keep their empire together by the sword—the image of Cossacks charging an unarmed crowd leaps to mind—and by alliances with local nobles, princes, khans, and the like. The Soviet leaders tried desperately to tame the different nationalisms, using both the carrot and the stick. With one hand they gave as many of them as they thought safe the trappings of "independent" identities as republics within a federal structure. With the other hand they brutally suppressed any nationalist feelings that seemed to go too far.

So if one of the fundamental causes of the breakup of the Soviet Union was the dreadfully inefficient economy brought about by arbitrary and heavy-handed centralization, the second was nationalism, because it is nationalism that gives a sense of "we-ness" that makes people demand the right to go their own way.

Whether most of the minority people of the former Soviet Union will eventually demand independence is questionable. The fact that the Chechens are landlocked and have no common border with any other country made the Chechens an unlikely candidate to demand independence. But their fierce nationalism gave them the strength and determination to fight and win a very bloody war against enormous odds. But the nationalisms that the central Soviet government took most seriously were those sharing a border with other countries, such as the Ukrainians, Georgians, Azerbaijani, and the Armenians, or that bordered on a sea leading to the outside world, such as the Latvians, Lithuanians, and Estonians.

Of all of these, the most important was the Ukrainians, because the Ukraine had a population of 50 million; because it had a territory the size of France; because it had outside borders with Poland, Romania, and the Black Sea; because it was highly industrialized; and because it was also one of the most important of the Soviet Union's bread baskets.

Troubles with the economy, shortage of consumer goods, poor housing, frustration with bureaucracy, and nationalism—these factors have ebbed and flowed since the Soviet empire first came into being. And to these was recently added worldwide economic interdependence. Brute force, exercised by the party and the KGB, helped keep the lid on all these frustrations, but even more important was fear of Germany. The military threat from Germany and later from the United States and the West kept the lid on nationalist demands, but changes in military technology eventually lessened the threat of Germany and caused Gorbachev and the other Soviet leaders to do things that in effect lifted the lid on all the other frustrations and desires.

THE ROLE OF MILITARY TECHNOLOGY

In World War II the Germans killed 20 million Soviet citizens. Another 5 to 15 million died of hunger or disease in the territories occupied by the Germans or in places under siege, such as Leningrad. In the rest of Eastern Europe, casualties were not so appalling, but they were high. And all of Eastern Europe suffered the trauma of the German occupation. Understandably, in the post–World War II era, the Soviet Union and its people were driven by fear of Germany.

But developments in military technology made even a united Germany a third-rate power in military terms, of the same order as Sweden, Switzerland, and the Netherlands. Sitting as it does in the middle of Europe within ten to fifteen minutes of Soviet missiles armed with nuclear warheads, Germany could no longer be a threat. Technology had decreed that only a country of continental size can play the nuclear game. Japan came to understand this, and so did Germany. Japan with its mountainous homeland and large population densely packed in the lowlands was too vulnerable to try to continue to be a great power in a military sense. Neither could Germany, with its own densely packed population living within fifteen minutes of Soviet nuclear missiles. As for the United Kingdom, it saw early on that its influence had to be exercised through its allies, principally the United States.

Although neither Gorbachev nor anyone else foresaw the roller coaster of events that lay ahead, it may well be that Gorbachev did begin to understand that in an age of nuclear missiles Germany could no longer be a threat to the Soviet Union. If so, this explains why he decided that the gigantic effort to chain Eastern Europe to the Soviet empire was no longer worth the trouble and expense. Or it may be that he did not really reach firm conclusions on these points and that circumstances and events forced him to abandon the effort. In either case, what Gorbachev did not foresee was the turmoil inside the Soviet Union that led to its breakup, to his personal loss of power, and to the rise of Yeltsin.

NEGOTIATING WITH THE NEW RUSSIA

On June 17, 1992, Presidents Bush and Yeltsin agreed to reduce the American and former Soviet stockpiles of long-range missile warheads, from the then current level of about 11,250, in two steps. The first step would reduce each side's warheads to a total of between 3,800 to 4,200. The second would reduce them to a total of between 3,000 to 3,500 each. This second step would be completed no later than the year 2003 or, if the United States helped Russia with the cost of destroying its missiles, by the year 2000. However, the agreement did not deal with short-range or battlefield nuclear weapons, of which each side still had about 15 thousand.

To keep within the ceiling, Russia was required to give up all of its land-based SS-18 and SS-24 missiles, leaving Russia with the nuclear bombs carried by its long-range aircraft and with a handful of submarine-based missiles. For its part, the United States was required to give up its fifty land-based MX missiles and to replace the three independently targeted warheads on the Minuteman missiles with only one warhead each. The United States was permitted to keep its Trident submarines, provided that the total number of warheads carried by the submarine force was reduced to 1,750, a 50-percent cut. Bombers would not be counted as carrying the number of bombs they were *capable* of carrying, but the number they were *equipped* to carry.

THE UNITED STATES

When the agreements were fully implemented, the United States would have 500 Minuteman missiles with 500 warheads and eighteen missile-carrying Trident submarines with 1,728 warheads. This is a total of 2,228 warheads. The remaining 1,272 warheads would be allocated to bombers, although it was not clear just how these would be portioned out among the 950 B-52 H, the 95 B-1B, and the 20 B-2 bombers. The result of the agreements, as speculated by the International Institute of Strategic Studies (IISS), is shown in the following:[2]

	Delivery weapons	Warheads
ICBM:		
Minuteman II & III	500	500[3]
SLBM:		
Trident	432	1,728
(8 I/C-4 & 10 II/D-5)		
Bombers:		
B-52H Air-Launched Cruise Missile (ALCM)	950	—
B-1B	95	1,272
B-2	20	—
Totals	1,997	3,500

RUSSIA

When the agreements were fully implemented, that is, after the Strategic Arms Reduction Treaty II (START II), Russia's SS-18, SS-19, and SS-24 missiles would be eliminated. The older SS-11, SS-13, and SS-17 were already being retired. So for land-based missiles, Russia would have its road-mobile SS-25s. It would also have its force of bombers and its missile-launching submarines, the total number of which would have to be reduced by either retiring older submarines or by downloading multiple-warhead missiles. The International Institute of Strategic Studies speculated that one possible Russian force posture would be as follows:

	Launchers deployed	Warheads/ launchers	Total warheads	Warhead limit
Mobile ICBM SS-25	700[4]	1	700	
Other ICBM SS-19	105[5]	1	105	
SLBM SS-N-20	120	10	1,200	
SS-N-23	112	4	448	
Total Ballistic Missiles	1,037		2,453	

	Launchers deployed	Warheads/ launchers	Total warheads	Warhead limit
Bombers				
ACLM-equipped				
Tu-95H16	40	16	640	
Tu-95H6	20	6	120	
Tu-160	20	12	240	
Total Bombers	80		1,000	
Grand Total	1,117		3,453	3,500

Eliminating the SS-18 and SS-24 on the Russian side and the MX on the American side as agreed to in the Bush–Yeltsin agreements were clearly steps in the right direction. All these systems that were to be eliminated had the accuracy, range, and explosive power to threaten the other side's missiles based on land in fixed silos. All were MIRVed (equipped with multiple independently targetable reentry vehicles), which is to say that each missile carried several warheads, each of which could be aimed at widely separated targets. A multiwarhead missile is a mortal threat to the other side's retaliatory force. But it is also provocative. For the fact is that a country needs to launch only one missile in a preemptive strike to take out a MIRVed missile that threatens as many as ten of that country's missiles. MIRVed missiles, in other words, tempt the other side to preempt.

In the second place, while all these missiles threatened the other side's retaliatory force, they were themselves extremely vulnerable. Thus, with these missiles in the stockpiles in a time of international crisis, both sides would have to consider a decision to preempt—that is, to launch on warning. The SS-18, SS-24, and the MX are, in a word, destabilizing.

The Bush–Yeltsin agreement was an important step in the right direction. But the agreement also raised two doubts. The first doubt came from the fact that the agreement was so one-sided. The agreement required Russia to give up *all* of its land-based SS-18 and SS-24 missiles, each of which carried ten warheads that could be directed to targets hundreds of miles apart. This would leave the Russians with the SS-25 missiles, the nuclear weapons carried by their long-range bombers, which are limited in both numbers and effectiveness, and with its submarine-based missiles, which are also limited in both numbers and effectiveness.

The agreement required the United States, on the other hand, to give up, first, its fifty land-based MX missiles, each of which carried ten warheads that could also be directed at widely separated targets. Second, the agreement required the United States to replace the three independently targeted warheads on the Minuteman III missiles with only one warhead. But the United States could keep its most-advanced missiles based on the Trident submarines, provided it reduced the eight MIRV warheads on each missile to four.

As one American official crowed, the Russians were required to give up the "backbone" of their force, the land-based, multiple-warhead ICBMs, while the

United States got to keep the missiles that were its greatest strength, those based on submarines. Right up to the last minute, Yeltsin had argued vehemently that he would never agree to anything but parity. What apparently made him change his mind was Bush's threat that otherwise Russia would get none of the aid its people needed so desperately.

Many Americans were obviously pleased to see the United States beat its old enemy so badly at the bargaining table, but other Americans felt that taking advantage of the Russians' grim plight might turn out to be shortsighted. Yeltsin's position continued to be vulnerable, and it seemed likely that powerful elements in Russia who still occupied most positions of influence—the military, the KGB, and former members of the Communist Party—would find this agreement too demeaning to tolerate. So by taking advantage, the United States put at risk not only the arms reduction treaty itself but Yeltsin and the Russian leaders who seemed to be trying to transform the country into a democracy.

An even more serious doubt was how much a reduction of nuclear weapons would accomplish, even a substantial reduction, as long as the stockpiles on both sides continued to contain 3,000 to 3,500 warheads. As calculated in Chapter 4, it would take three American warheads arriving on target to kill most of the inhabitants of greater Moscow, and five Russian warheads to kill most of the inhabitants of greater New York. Since about 75 percent of both the American and Russian population is urban, a quick calculation suggests that it would take about 200 warheads to destroy the seventy metropolitan areas containing over 50 percent of the American population and about 300 warheads to destroy the much larger number of urban areas containing 50 percent of the Russian population.

The point is simply that a nuclear war fought with each side having 3,000 to 3,500 warheads that could be used on the other side's homeland is not much of an improvement over a nuclear war fought with each side having 12,500 warheads. Either way both sides could easily lose half their people and almost all of their industry. So nuclear war will continue to be a sword of Damocles hanging over the heads of all humankind. A sudden turn of events that puts the United States and the new Russia into tension could bring the world back to the Cold War, or to the kind of nuclear missile crisis that we saw in Cuba in 1962.

One element, however, is crucially different. The Soviet Union had a "nationalities problem," but dealing with rival nationalities *within* a unitary state is easier than dealing with rival nationalities that are states themselves. First, as we saw, the fear of Germany and then of the United States among the rival Soviet nationalities helped to keep them quiet. Second, a rival nationality that is itself a state can raise troops and equip them with arms with vastly greater ease than can a rival nationality that is a minority within a larger state. The conclusion seems inescapable that the new Russia will have more reasons than fear of the West to want to maintain a certain level of arms and armies. Before Russia can safely agree to any particular arms control proposal, it will have to be certain that the newly independent states of the former Soviet Union, and particularly Ukraine, will be part of the same agreement.

The conclusion is obvious and was foreshadowed when Russia announced that it would not carry out the provisions of the Bush–Yeltsin accord until it had reached an agreement with Ukraine, Belarus, and Kazakhstan about the fate of the Soviet ICBMs still in their hands.

NOTES

1. As is well known, in World War II, in spite of the fact that Germany followed policies in the Ukraine that exploited the peasants as badly as Stalin had done, the Germans succeeded in recruiting quite a number of Ukrainians to fight on the German side against the Soviet Army. What is less well known is that about one-fourth of the fortress troops manning the German defenses at Normandy and up and down the coast of Europe were actually Soviet citizens, minority nationalities who were captured and then volunteered or who were recruited in German-occupied territories, such as the Ukraine.

2. *The Military Balance, 1992–1993* (London: Brassey's for International Institute of Strategic Studies, 1992), 224 ff.

3. Minuteman III downloaded from three to one warhead per missile.

4. Not all SS-25 would be mobile, maybe 50 percent in silos.

5. Downloaded to single warhead.

Part IV

THE WORLD TURNED UPSIDE DOWN

Chapter 11

Developments in Weapons

In the meantime, technology continued apace. By the late 1990s, the weapons already in the stockpile and planned for the future were as follows.

THE MIDGETMAN MISSILE

The Midgetman was designed but never produced. It was to be a small missile weighing 37 thousand pounds as opposed to 190 thousand pounds for the MX. It would have only one warhead, as opposed to the ten carried by the MX. Being so much lighter, Midgetman could be mobile, mounted on trucks that were armored to withstand blast from explosions further away than a near-miss as well as fallout. The idea was to provide a missile that everyone would understand was a second-strike weapon, because it would carry only one warhead and would be less accurate than the MX.

The main objection to Midgetman was the cost to develop and deploy it, estimated at $40 to $50 billion for 500 Midgetman missiles as compared to only $15 billion to build fifty MX with ten warheads each, since the development costs of MX had already been spent and since the MX required only one missile for ten warheads.

THE B-1B BOMBER

The Air Force goal was to have its own "triad": the B-1B bomber armed with cruise missiles, the Stealth bomber, and the MX missile. The B-1B bomber was designed to penetrate Soviet defenses at high speeds and very low altitude, below

Soviet radar. It was canceled by President Carter, revived by President Reagan, and began to become operational in 1986. The last of the one-hundred-plane fleet (one crashed, leaving ninety-nine operational) was delivered in 1987.

The B-1B was designed to have counterforce capabilities—it was intended to seek out and destroy mobile missiles inside the Soviet Union. However, troubles with electronic gear relegated the B-1B to a lesser role. In 1994, a ten-year program costing $3 billion was launched to convert the B-1B fleet to serve as missile launching platforms. The planes would stand off 1,000 to 1,500 miles outside the Soviet Union and launch cruise missiles to penetrate Soviet air space. This change in role was made inevitable when the Stealth bomber became operational.

By 1997, six squadrons of B-1B bombers were operational with total strength of ninety-five aircraft. However, the B-1B continued to suffer from severe maintenance problems. Although the Air Force standard for mission capability is 75 percent, the average rate had been only 55 percent from 1993 to 1997.

THE STEALTH BOMBER

As mentioned, the Stealth or B-2 bomber was designed to have a very small radar profile. It was built mainly of an epoxy composite with metal parts shielded or placed so as to scatter radar waves. The Air Force visualized a nuclear war lasting days or even weeks. The idea was that cruise missiles and B-1B bombers would together clear a path through Soviet defenses. The Stealth bomber's mission would be to go through that path, destroy Soviet command posts, and hunt down and destroy mobile Soviet missiles mounted on trucks and trains.

The first criticism of the Stealth bomber was cost—$500 million per plane for an estimated total of $50 billion over a ten-year period. Another objection was that the Soviets were undoubtedly developing ways to get around the Stealth bomber's low radar profile. Stealth technology was designed to scatter the radar waves rather than bounce them back to the transmitter, so one method to foil Stealth technology, at least partially, would be to put the radar transmitter in one place and the receiver in another so the receiver could pick up the scattered waves. Stealth technology was also designed to lessen its visibility from ground-based radar, so another method to foil Stealth technology would be to put the radar on high-flying airplanes or satellites so as to look down on the Stealth bomber from above.

In 1998, two squadrons with a total of twelve B-2A aircraft were operational. Five more B-2As are used for experiments at the Air Force Flight Test Center. The last two of an initial twenty-plane production run were delivered in fiscal year 1997. The aircraft are undergoing an upgrade program at a so-far unspecified cost so that by the year 2000 all will be capable of both conventional and nuclear operations. However, rumors persist that the stealthiness of the aircraft is limited. Although the Air Force has denied the reports, it is alleged that during exercises in 1995 the radar of F-16 aircraft succeeded in detecting the B-2A.

CRUISE MISSILES

Cruise missiles are air-breathing, pilotless drones, which began life flying at 550 miles per hour—a modern version of the German V-1 rockets. By the 1980s they had advanced guidance systems. In effect, a cruise missile had in its computer memory a map of the terrain over which it was intended to fly and a TV camera that took pictures of the ground. The computers compared what the TV camera saw with the memory map and made course adjustments accordingly. A cruise missile could be programmed with a complicated flight path to avoid obstacles and elude the enemy's defenses. It had a range of 1,500 miles, was accurate within twenty to thirty feet, and carried one warhead, either nuclear or conventional.

By 1988, Boeing had made and delivered to the Air Force 1,715 cruise missiles that could be launched from aircraft. The Air Force plan was to convert the old B-52s to serve as airborne launchers for cruise missiles, both with and without nuclear warheads. At the beginning of 1997, the ninety-four B-52s of all classes were on hand and, of these, sixty-six were serving in operational roles. The newest cruise missiles, named Bloc III, employ the Global Positioning System (GPS) for navigation rather than the TERCOM guidance system of earlier models.

In September 1996, in retaliation for an alleged Iraqi effort to assassinate former President George Bush during a visit to Kuwait, the Navy fired thirty-one Bloc III Tomahawk missiles and the Air Force fired thirteen Bloc III Aircraft Launched Cruises Missiles (ALCM) from B-52H aircraft at targets in Iraq. The Navy reported that 80 percent of its missiles hit within 12 meters of their targets and the Air Force reported a figure of 70 percent.

The next step is a cruise missile that can fly at supersonic speeds and has the Stealth technology to give it a low radar profile. The Air Force intends to buy 1,400 of these. Also under development is a guidance system using laser technology that will make a cruise missile accurate within a few inches. Such accuracy would be redundant for a cruise missile armed with a nuclear warhead, but it would make a cruise missile with a conventional warhead a formidable weapon.

In the 1980s, Tomahawk cruise missiles costing $1.5 million each were carried aboard most U.S. warships. Later, the Navy acquired a newer version equipped with conventional warheads that was more accurate than the 1980s version. If such cruise missiles had been available for the 1986 raid on Libya, the Navy argued, the United States could have avoided the loss of a plane and its two-man crew.

In 1987, the United States had bases for ground-launched cruise missiles armed with nuclear warheads in Great Britain, West Germany, Italy, and Belgium. Another base was under construction in Great Britain and still another was scheduled for the Netherlands. American plans called for a total of 464 land-based cruise missiles to be deployed in these six bases by early 1989. However, in accordance with the Intermediate Nuclear Forces (INF) Treaty that Gorbachev and Reagan signed in December 1987, all land-based cruise missiles stationed in Europe were dismantled.

However, cruise missiles have become so popular that no definitive count of their numbers seems to exist. Air Force procurement alone routinely averages in excess of 1,200 missiles per year. For example, in 1994 it purchased 1,666 missiles, and, in 1997, 1,215.

TRIDENT SUBMARINES AND THE D-5 MISSILE

The eighteenth and last Ohio-class Trident submarine was commissioned in the late summer of 1997. By the end of 1989, the Trident was carrying the D-5 (Trident II) missile, with eight very accurate, independently targeted warheads, for a total of 192 warheads per submarine. A program to give the Tridents the ability to launch cruise missiles was in progress, but had not been completed by 1997.

The Trident force was projected to decline to fourteen submarines in the year 2000; however, the Navy reportedly does not have the funds to convert four of the older craft in the series from the C-5 to the larger D-5 missile. This may result in the fleet declining to twelve or even ten submarines by the year 2001.

A Trident submarine patrols for seventy days. It is then reprovisioned and the second of its two crews takes it out. A Trident spends two-thirds of its time on patrol, as opposed to one-half for other submarines and one-third for most surface ships. It takes eighteen days to repair and replenish a Trident between patrols.

The last of the Navy's Poseidon submarines was retired in 1994. At least two of these were converted for special operations, which involved converting the missile bays to carry SEAL and Marine special forces teams and equipment.

The fleet of attack submarines, designed to seek out and destroy both the enemy's missile-carrying and attack submarines, declined from one hundred in 1988 to seventy-eight in 1997. These included twenty-seven Los Angeles class SSNs (nuclear-fueled submarines), thirty-one improved Los Angeles class SSGN boats, eighteen Sturgeon class SSN boats, the USS Narwhal (the only SSN of its class), and one Seawolf SSGN. The force is projected to decline to fifty-five boats in the year 2001. The first of two Seawolf submarines was commissioned in 1996. The second is due to enter service in 1998. A third Seawolf was funded in the Navy's 1997 budget.

ARMY WEAPONS

For some time the Army has been equipped with short-range battlefield nuclear weapons. In 1997 it also had under development the Line of Sight Antitank missile (LOSAT) mounted on a HUMVEE all-terrain vehicle.

The Army's tank armor is now made from a steel-encased mesh of depleted uranium (i.e., uranium that is no longer radioactive or with so little radioactivity left that it is judged harmless). Uranium is two and one-half times as dense as steel and cannot be penetrated by antitank artillery shells except those also made from depleted uranium.

The Army's new light division has 10 thousand men instead of 17 thousand. It is also light in terms of artillery, antitank, and support units. A light division with its armored personnel carriers, tanks, and artillery can be moved in 516 flights of C-141 transport planes as against 2,852 flights needed for a mechanized division. Light divisions are designed as part of the Rapid Deployment Force, and they are also trained to fight guerrillas. In 1997, elements of three light divisions were in service. One was the 10th Mountain Division, stationed at Fort Drum, New York, consisting of two brigades and the division headquarters. The second was the 25th Infantry Division, with two brigades and the division headquarters stationed at Schofield Barracks, Hawaii, and a third brigade stationed at Fort Lewis, Washington. The third is the 6th Independent Infantry Brigade, consisting of one brigade and brigade headquarters stationed at Fort Richardson, Alaska.

WEAPONS IN THE GULF WAR

Although debate has been hot on what may or may not have been accomplished by the Gulf War, everyone agrees that it provided a test for the American military equipment used.[1]

The tanks and other mechanized equipment worked better in the harsh desert environment than anyone had dared to hope. The laser-guided precision bombs were a fantastic success. During World War II, Korea, and Vietnam, bombers sometimes made over one hundred sorties before scoring a direct hit on a pinpoint target such as a bridge. Although the laser bombs made up barely 7 percent of the bombs dropped—6,520 tons out of 88,500 tons—they hit their targets 80 percent of the time. Unlike the laser bombs, conventional bombs were not very accurate. According to official Air Force figures, 74 percent of the conventional bombs missed their targets.

For the B-52s, the percentage of misses must have been much, much higher. B-52s flying at high altitude are effective against area targets, such as cities, but hardly effective at all against pinpoint targets such as bridges or dug-in troops. In the Gulf War the B-52s were used mainly against dug-in troops, tanks, and other equipment, and they seemed to have had very little effect, except perhaps on enemy morale.

As for the Patriot missile, scientists testified to Congress after the war that the Patriot missile was very successful against aircraft, for which it was designed, but that employing it against incoming Iraqi Scud missiles did more harm than good. The scientists asserted that more damage was done by debris caused by the Patriots than would have been done by the Scud missiles alone.

Casualties from "Friendly Fire"

The Pentagon reported to Congress that 35 of the 148 Americans killed in the Gulf War were actually killed by "friendly fire"; that is, by fire from other Americans. Of the 467 wounded, friendly fire was responsible for 72. Among the Allies, nine British soldiers were killed by American A-10 warplanes. On another occasion, two more British soldiers were also killed by friendly fire. There is no information on casualties among the other Allies from friendly fire.

A 1986 Army study of earlier wars concluded that in all the wars from World War I through Vietnam the casualties from friendly fire were less than 2 percent. In the Gulf War, friendly fire was responsible for 23 percent of those killed and 15 percent of the wounded.

All the M1A1 tank casualties were caused by friendly fire. The American forces used armor-piercing ammunition made of depleted uranium. These shells leave a small but detectable trace of radioactivity, and all the U.S. tanks knocked out showed this tell-tale trace. Actually, probably none of the conventional, armor-piercing ammunition used by the Iraqi forces would have been capable of piercing the extremely thick and hard, depleted uranium armor on the M1A1s.

There were a total of twenty-eight friendly fire incidents. U.S. ground forces attacked other U.S. ground forces sixteen times, killing 24 Americans and wounding 57. American airplanes attacked American ground forces nine times, with 11 killed and 154 wounded. One American warship attacked another American warship, but there were no casualties. One American ground force unit attacked an American Navy jet, but again there were no casualties.

One explanation for the high casualties from friendly fire is that the technology for killing at a distance has outdistanced the technology for distinguishing between friend and foe. Another reason was offered by Colonel Roy Alcala, an aide to General Carl Vuono, at that time chief of staff of the Army. Colonel Alcala pointed out that the percentages in the Gulf War were skewed because "in previous wars a lot of people died from things that didn't happen in this war—the other side fighting back."[2] If the other side does not fight back, the only casualties tend to be those inflicted by your own forces, so the percentage of total casualties caused by friendly fire is much higher.

NOTES

1. This section draws on Chapter 12, "Postmortem on the War," of Roger Hilsman, *George Bush vs. Saddam Hussein: Military Success! Political Failure?* (Novato, Calif.: Presidio Press, 1992).

2. Barton Gellman, "Gulf War's Friendly Fire Tally Triples," *Washington Post*, 14 August 1991, pp. 1, 26.

Chapter 12

The Members of the Nuclear Club and Their Arms

To recapitulate, when the Bush–Yeltsin agreements are fully implemented, the American long-range nuclear warheads will total 3,500. The 500 Minuteman missiles will carry 500 warheads. The eighteen Trident submarines will carry 432 missiles with four warheads each, for a total of 1,728 warheads. The B-52H bombers will carry 950 cruise missiles with 950 warheads. The B-1B bombers will carry ninety-five nuclear bombs, and the B-2 bombers will carry twenty nuclear bombs.

The United States plans to keep twelve Trident submarines at sea at all times. To maintain this schedule, each submarine will have two crews, one at sea on patrol and one on shore training for its turn. Each submarine will carry twenty-four D-5 missiles with four warheads each. So the United States will keep on full alert a Trident force of twelve submarines armed with 1,152 missiles.

In 1993, the Congressional Budget Office published a study asserting that even if none of the eighteen submarines in the current fleet are replaced, the Navy plan would cost $46.6 billion. The study made two major suggestions. The first was to retire the six oldest submarines instead of refitting them with new missiles. The second suggestion was to keep only six submarines at sea at all times, thereby reducing the crews needed from two to one per vessel. The study argued that these changes would not significantly lower the level of security provided, but would save $17.5 billion. However, neither Congress nor the Clinton administration expressed an interest in making the suggested changes.

NONNUCLEAR CONVENTIONAL FORCES

Following the breakup of the Soviet Union, the Bush administration conducted a so-called "bottom-up" review of American nonnuclear, conventional military needs in the immediate future, a future in which Russia and a number of lesser powers had replaced the Soviet super-state. The decision was to provide the forces to fight and win two regional, nonnuclear, conventional wars at the same time. Dubbed the "win–win" strategy, the argument was that if the United States was fighting a war in the Middle East, for example, North Korea would be tempted to attack South Korea unless the United States had the strength to fight in both places at the same time. The only concession the Bush administration made was to assume that the two wars would not begin at exactly the same time, thus permitting substantial savings on transport ships and cargo planes.

An important assumption behind the Bush proposals was that the United States would not be able to count on substantial help from its allies, but would have to fight alone. Critics were quick to point out the substantial contribution that the Allies had made to the Gulf War and to ask what had changed.

When the Bush administration began its review, the Army had fourteen active and six reserve divisions, each consisting of 18,300 men and 324 tanks organized into three brigades. The Bush administration proposed remaking the force into twelve active and eight reserve divisions, keeping the total number of divisions the same.

The Navy had thirteen carrier battlegroups and one training battlegroup, each consisting of one aircraft carrier with cruiser and destroyer escorts. The Navy argued

1. That a permanent naval presence is needed in the Mediterranean, in the Persian Gulf, and in the far Pacific.

2. That that naval presence should consist of a carrier battle group with a full complement of escort vessels (usually 12 ships).

3. That these battle groups must be continuously modernized just as they were during the height of the Cold War. For each carrier on station, another would be undergoing overhaul, and two more would either be in transit, on home leave, or in training, making a total of twelve if the three different areas were to be covered at all times.

The Bush administration accepted the argument, settling on a total of twelve carrier battlegroups.

The Air Force had sixteen active and twelve reserve fighter wings, each wing consisting of three squadrons of eighteen to twenty-four aircraft each. The Bush administration proposed reducing this to fourteen active and ten reserve fighter wings.

When the Clinton administration came into office, they conducted a similar bottom-up review. At first the Clinton administration looked at a strategy of fighting and winning one war only, and merely holding the line in any second war— dubbed the "win–hold–win" strategy. The idea caused much uneasiness among a number of Congressmen and among such allies as South Korea, and in the end the Clinton administration adopted the Bush win–win formula. It also adopted the assumption that the United States would have to fight alone, without any help from its allies. It also adopted the idea that savings could be made on sea and air transport because the two wars were not likely to start at exactly the same time.

One important difference was that the Clinton administration plan called for pre-positioning the weapons and equipment for several Army brigades overseas, some for use in a Middle East war and others for a war in Korea. Other differences were that the Clinton plan would spend more on precision-guided missiles and bombs and on additional transport ships. It also emphasized ground-based defenses against such surface-to-surface missiles as the Scud, rather than antimissile defenses based in space that were emphasized by the Bush administration.

Like the Bush proposals, the Clinton plan accepted the idea that an American military presence should be maintained in various trouble spots around the world. Accordingly, the Clinton plan called for very modest cuts in the Navy and actually proposed to maintain the Marine Corps at greater strength than the Bush proposal would have done. The Bush plan would have cut the Marine Corps from 180 thousand to 159 thousand, while the Clinton plan called for a cut from 180 thousand to 174 thousand. Under the Clinton plan, the overall military manpower would be cut from 1.7 million to 1.4 million over a five-year period.

Only two weapons programs would be eliminated in the Clinton plan: the Navy's AFX bomber designed to avoid radar and the Air Force's fighter designed to fulfill several different roles. And even though the Air Force gave up 200 of these fighters, it gained an equal number of bombers for tactical use. On the other hand, the Clinton administration planned to go ahead with the planes that the Navy and the Air Force had put at the top of their priority list: the Navy's new version of the FA-18 and the Air Force's new F-22 fighter.

The total cost of the Clinton plan was $13 billion more than its five-year budget projection of $1.2 trillion for the military. The hope was that ways could be found to make additional cuts to make up the difference.

Behind both the Bush and the Clinton proposals were motives that went beyond defense. One motive was to preserve production lines and technological skills that would otherwise be lost. For example, the Navy already had in service two of the very advanced Seawolf attack submarines, and it admitted that two were all that were needed for the present. But both the Bush and Clinton proposals called for building a third Seawolf at a cost of $2.4 billion. Similarly, plans called for still another nuclear-powered aircraft carrier to be built, at a cost of $3.6 billion.

The military rationale for building a third Seawolf and still another nuclear-powered carrier was twofold. First, it assumes that the world situation will continue much the same as it has been in the past and that the United States should maintain into the long-term future a military presence in the three major trouble spots—the Mediterranean, the Persian Gulf, and the far Pacific. The second assumption was that if the world situation continues much the same as it has been in the past, the United States will sooner or later have to replace the present submarines and aircraft carriers with more advanced versions. Referring to the decision to build a third Seawolf, Secretary of Defense Les Aspin said that it would be too costly to close down the production line and then restart it when the new submarines are actually needed. The same rationale was obviously behind the decision to build another carrier.

Also behind these decisions were some purely economic and political motives. The third Seawolf submarine will be built in Groton, Connecticut, by the Electric Boat Division of the General Dynamics Corporation. Electric Boat is the largest private employer in both Connecticut and Rhode Island, second only to the two state governments. Even with the contract for the third Seawolf, Electric Boat's payroll will drop from 17,500 to 7,500. The additional aircraft carrier will be built in Newport News, Virginia, by Newport News Shipbuilding, a division of Tenneco, Inc. It, too, is a large employer, and it, too, will undergo substantial payroll cuts in spite of the contract for another carrier. But the carrier contract still preserves from 5,000 to 7,500 jobs. Both Connecticut and Virginia have serious economic and unemployment problems, and they would be even worse without the third Seawolf and the additional carrier.

THE UNITED KINGDOM

The United Kingdom has three nuclear-fueled ballistic-missile submarines of the Resolution class, each of which carries sixteen Polaris A-3TK missiles for a total of forty-eight missiles.

The British Army totals 234,600 men and women. These are organized as one armored division, one mechanized division (with two mechanized and one airborne brigade), and a variety of independent battalions. The reserves include some thirty-six infantry battalions as well as a number of battalions of specialized troops.

The British Navy consists of 59,300 men and women, including 6,500 in the Air Force and 7,250 Marines. The fleet includes fifteen tactical submarines; two Invincible carriers, eight Sea Harrier carriers, and twelve Sea King carriers; twelve destroyers; twenty-six frigates; and various support vessels.

The British Air Force consists of 80,900 men and women organized as eight squadrons of fighter-bombers that can carry nuclear weapons, five squadrons of ground attack fighters, seven squadrons of fighters, and a variety of reconnaissance, transport, tankers, and so on.

The United Kingdom wants to follow policies that contribute to the worldwide reduction of nuclear weapons, but it also wants to maintain a credible deterrent. In July 1998, it announced plans for restructuring for a world in which United Nations and NATO challenges are replacing those of the Cold War. Britain will maintain a fleet of four nuclear-fueled, ballistic-missile submarines of the Vanguard class, equipped with Trident II (D5) missiles armed with British-designed warheads. An announcement in the summer of 1998 said that the number of operationally available nuclear warheads will be reduced to 200.

The $36 billion defense budget will be trimmed by $1.1 billion and the number of reserve troops, tanks, and warplanes reduced. However, it will strengthen its rapid reaction forces with two new super-carriers, attack helicopters, amphibious machinery, and Harrier jump jets. The military will also buy four long-range transport planes and four roll-on, roll-off container ships to move personnel and equipment. The army is to be restructured to sustain distant military operations with two deployable divisions, one in Britain and one in Germany, where Britain has 22 thousand troops.

FRANCE

France has five nuclear-fueled ballistic-missile submarines armed with a total of eighty missiles, eighteen land-based IRBMs, and sixty bombers that can carry nuclear bombs.

The French Army consists of 241,400 men and women organized as four armored divisions and one infantry division and a variety of specialized regiments and battalions.

The French Navy consists of 65,400 men and women, including 11 thousand naval air and 6 thousand Marines. France maintains fourteen tactical submarines, two carriers, one cruiser, four destroyers, thirty-five frigates, and a variety of specialized vessels.

The French Air Force consists of 90,600 men and women organized in eleven squadrons of fighters, eleven squadrons of ground attack fighters, and a variety of reconnaissance, transport, and other specialized aircraft.

CHINA

The International Institute of Strategic Studies estimates that China has some fourteen ICBMs, some of which are MIRVed, some ninety IRBMs, and one nuclear-fueled ballistic-missile submarine equipped with twelve missiles.

The Chinese Army consists of some 2,300,000 men and women organized into seventy-six infantry divisions, two mechanized divisions, ten armored divisions, and a variety of specialized troops.

The Chinese Navy consists of 260 thousand men and women. It maintains, in addition to its one ballistic-missile submarine, forty-six submarines, eighteen destroyers, thirty-eight frigates, and a variety of specialized ships.

The Chinese Air Force consists of 470 thousand men and women. It has 120 medium-range bombers, some probably capable of carrying nuclear weapons, 350 light bombers, 500 ground attack fighters, about 4 thousand fighters, and a variety of specialized aircraft.

SOUTH AFRICA'S NUCLEAR WEAPONS

In March 1993, President F. W. De Klerk made public the fact that South Africa had begun a nuclear weapons program in 1974 and had succeeded in building six atomic bombs with about the same power as the bomb dropped on Hiroshima. South Africa was at work on a seventh atomic bomb when his administration decided in 1989 to stop the program, dismantle the weapons, and downgrade the enriched uranium to make it unsuitable for weapons. Although South Africa did not conduct any tests, nuclear weapons experts said there was no reason to believe that the bombs would not have worked.

For several years after South Africa refused to sign the nuclear nonproliferation treaty, there was speculation that it was working on a bomb. The most general suspicion was that Israel was helping South Africa build a bomb in exchange for supplies of South African uranium. In 1977, both American and Soviet satellites photographed two 500-foot-deep concrete holes in the Kalahari desert designed as underground test sites for nuclear weapons. But they were never actually used.

South Africa finally signed the nonproliferation treaty in July 1991. De Klerk said that the decision to destroy the South African nuclear stockpile was made because the Cold War was waning and because Cuba was withdrawing its troops from nearby Angola. However, many observers in both South Africa and abroad speculated that another reason was fear that the weapons might fall into the hands of a successor government of South Africa controlled by militant blacks.

INDIA AND PAKISTAN

In 1974, India tested a single nuclear device, but there was no follow-up. In March 1998, the Bharatiya Janata Party (BJP), a militant nationalist party with extremist Hindu, anti-Muslim religious views, after many, many years in the political wilderness, finally won enough seats to form a coalition government. A short time later, on May 11 and 13, 1998, India conducted five underground tests of nuclear weapons, to the complete surprise of the CIA and the American government. Hindus literally danced in the streets, newsmen reported, since "India had now assumed its rightful place as one of the world's great powers." In reaction, Pakistan, on May 28 and 30, conducted two nuclear tests of its own. It also publicly threatened to deploy nuclear-tipped missiles that could reach a number of major Indian cities. The United States imposed economic sanctions on both India and Pakistan, but no other major powers joined in the action.

There are many points of tension between India and Pakistan that could lead to war, of which the most obvious is Kashmir, now divided between the two. Prime Minister Atal Bihari Vajpayee and Home Minister L. K. Advani, the leaders of the BJP, are not in any sense warmongers, but they feel deeply that India must someday retake all of Kashmir. The subcontinent seemed to be entering its most dangerous phase since the India–Pakistan war of 1971 and possibly since the bloodshed that accompanied the partition of British India in 1947.

Then, in late September 1998, Pakistan announced that it was prepared to sign the international treaty banning nuclear testing within a year, and three days later India followed suit—a remarkable change in policy for both countries. Using the authority newly granted by Congress, Presiden Clinton lifted the sanctions on both countries.

THE SUCCESSOR STATES TO THE SOVIET UNION

Russia ratified the Strategic Arms Reduction Treaty on November 4, 1992, but announced that it would not carry out the provisions until it had reached an agreement with Ukraine, Belarus, and Kazakhstan, the three other former states of the Soviet Union on whose territory Soviet ICBMs had been stationed. All three states had committed themselves to nuclear-free status, promised to sign the 1968 nuclear nonproliferation treaty, and agreed that Russia was to become the sole successor to Soviet obligations under the START agreements and the nuclear nonproliferation treaty.

There was some resistance among the top officials of Ukraine to giving up the nuclear weapons stationed on its soil. Then Yeltsin met with Leonid M. Kravchuk, president of Ukraine, and after the meeting the two of them announced that Russia was willing to give Ukraine the security guarantees it sought, contingent on Ukraine signing START I and the nuclear nonproliferation treaty.

In 1993, Ukraine, faced with a deepening economic crisis and a heavy debt for oil and gas to Russia, announced that it would dismantle the 175 weapons with nuclear warheads remaining in Ukraine but specified that Ukraine would keep the uranium extracted from their warheads to be used in nuclear power plants and that Ukraine would sell its share of the Black Sea Fleet to Russia.

When President Clinton visited Ukraine in January 1994, he succeeded in confirming the plan. Ukraine agreed to dismantle all the nuclear weapons on its soil—1,240 warheads mounted on SS-19 and SS-24 missiles and 564 warheads on cruise missiles carried by bombers. The warheads would be shipped to Russia, dismantled, and the uranium extracted and sold as fuel for nuclear reactors around the world, with Ukraine sharing in the proceeds. For its part, the United States promised Ukraine $176 million in aid to help pay the cost of dismantling the weapons and an additional $155 million in general financial aid.[1]

As for Belarus, by June 1993, it had ratified the START I treaty and pledged to adhere to the nuclear nonproliferation treaty, although it had not yet signed it. Belarus had also signed an agreement with Moscow to ship all eighty-one of the SS-25 mobile missiles stationed on its soil to Russia for dismantling by the end of 1994. When President Clinton stopped in Belarus in January 1994, he pledged $50 million in American aid, including $25 million to help Belarus carry out the agreement. For their part, Belarus officials repeated their promise to ship the missiles to Russia for dismantling.

Kazakhstan ratified START I, and there seemed to be no obstacle to its also adhering to the nuclear nonproliferation treaty.

ISRAEL'S NUCLEAR ARSENAL

It had been generally believed for many years—and confirmed by CIA documents released to the newspapers on January 27, 1978—that Israel had long since completed all the component parts for a nuclear weapon. The familiar joke was that the answer to the question, "What does Israel need to build a nuclear bomb?" was "A wrench, a screwdriver, and ten minutes to put it together."

In 1991, Seymour Hersh, a well-known newspaper correspondent, came out with a book describing a much larger Israeli nuclear weapons program producing a wider variety of weapons than had been suspected by anyone. The title of the book was *The Samson Option*, referring to the bible story of Samson's act of desperation in pulling down the temple, killing both his enemies and himself.[2]

Hersh alleged that Israel had deployed nuclear mines in the Golan Heights, that the Soviet Union was a principal target of the Israeli weapons, and that Israel went on a nuclear alert in 1991. Reviewers were harshly critical and unbelieving, charging that Hersh's informant was a man who was in fact a pathological liar.[3] Later, Hersh wrote a book on President Kennedy, *The Dark Side of Camelot*, that contained so many obvious untruths and outright lies that even more doubts were raised about the allegations Hersh had made in the earlier book about Israel.

But even though both Hersh and his book have been discredited, a great deal of other evidence leaves no doubt that Israel does have a considerable stockpile of nuclear warheads and the missiles and airplanes to deliver them to almost any target in the Middle East.

IRAN

In July 1998, Iran tested an MRBM with a range of 800 miles. This made it capable of reaching all of Israel, Afghanistan, and Pakistan, most of Saudi Arabia and Turkey, and part of Russia. The missile blew up in the latter stages of its flight, but it may well have been detonated deliberately.

Iran had bought a number of such missiles from North Korea, and named it the Shahab 3. Iran also bought the technology and equipment to make a warhead for such missiles from China, but Western intelligence believes it will be several years before it can be tested.

In December 1997, the Clinton administration certified that China was no longer helping Iran, Pakistan, or any other country build a nuclear bomb, and that China was ending its nuclear-power projects with Iran, which it said were not related to weapons. In March 1998, the United States also offered Russia an opportunity to expand its lucrative business launching American satellites if Moscow would clamp down on its sales of missile technology to Iran.

ALGERIA

Concern about Algeria's nuclear potential also burgeoned. It was well known in the West that the Chinese had supplied Algeria with a nuclear reactor some three years earlier. Many U.S. and other officials suspected that it was intended not for peaceful purposes but for research on nuclear weapons and eventually their production.

THE IRAQI NUCLEAR PROGRAM

In 1981, Israeli intelligence became convinced that Iraq was secretly attempting to develop an atomic bomb, and Israel bombed the installation at Twaitha where the work was going on. Although this bombing probably set back the Iraqi attempt to build nuclear weapons, Iraq must have immediately started a new, more tightly guarded, and much more extensive program.

As part of the agreement that ended the Gulf War, Iraq was forced to allow teams of U.N. inspectors to investigate suspected nuclear weapons plants and facilities. A cat and mouse game ensued, with Iraq attempting to hide materials and equipment related to its nuclear program and the U.N. teams trying to sniff them out. Gradually, however, the U.N. teams built up a picture of an Iraqi nuclear program that was both larger and more sophisticated than anyone in the West had suspected.

To make sure that at least one method worked, Iraq had sought to make the enriched uranium needed for a bomb by three completely different methods. One method was based on chemical separation, another on centrifuges to separate the uranium isotopes, and the third by a technique known as electromagnetic separation. U.N. officials suspect that a fourth method was also being used—the so-called "nozzle" technique developed by two German companies and used in South Africa in two uranium enrichment plants operating there. The nozzle technique separates out lighter isotopes by forcing uranium gas through a jet. This kind of plant would be relatively easy to conceal. However, U.N. officials indicated that if such a plant was found in Iraq, they would then look into the possibility that South Africa had aided Iraq with the knowledge and equipment. Iraq's main effort was apparently on the electromagnetic process of enrichment and the centrifuge process.

The Iraqi nuclear program employed over 10 thousand scientists and technical workers and cost at least $10 billion. American and allied bombing had destroyed a lot of the brick-and-mortar installations, but many key materials and much equipment survived. More important, Iraq's formidable corps of scientists, technicians, and weapons experts were unharmed and could be put back to work as soon as inspections and sanctions ended. Iraq, in fact, has the largest technical base in the Middle East—although Israel's is qualitatively better, Iraq's is larger.

Ominously, the program had received substantial help from foreign companies and governments. Although the United Nations did not make the names of these companies and governments public, U.N. authorities did say that they included a number in Western Europe. The help included highly sensitive and restricted technologies, such as carbon-fiber rotors that are used in high-speed uranium gas centrifuges and extremely hard maraging steel of the type that is used both in centrifuges and in an actual bomb.

Asked about American and European firms, a U.N. representative told the press that European firms were certainly involved, but he was unsure about American firms. The press reported that West German firms supplied centrifuge technology, Finnish firms supplied copper coil, British firms supplied precision machine tools, and Swiss firms supplied metal castings and special high-strength steel. The reports admitted that all of this equipment could be used for other purposes than developing a nuclear capacity, but they argued that imports of this kind should have raised suspicions. In fact, some foreign companies supplying the equipment were owned by their governments, and in those cases the governments certainly should have had some inkling of Iraq's nuclear program.

Some of the technology in the centrifuge machines resembled what had been developed by Britain, Germany, and the Netherlands in their joint, Dutch-based Urenco commercial reactor. It had been widely reported that Pakistan acquired Urenco know-how for its own nuclear program from a Pakistani scientist who had worked in the plant, so the suspicion also arose that Iraq may have acquired some of the information through Pakistan.

An Iraqi H-Bomb?

The evidence gathered by the U.N. teams not only suggested that Iraq could have tested a crude fission bomb within a year, but that it was also trying to develop the capacity for an H-bomb. Iraq had a stock of deuterium oxide, so-called heavy water, that it had purchased some years earlier. Hans Blix, head of the International Atomic Energy Agency, said that his inspectors had found documentary evidence that Iraq was planning to produce lithium 6, whose only known use is in H-bombs. When deuterium oxide and lithium 6 are combined, the product is lithium 6 deuteride, the main component of an H-bomb. The bottom line is that if Iraq finally succeeded in using these materials to make an atomic bomb that was not too crude and heavy, it might be able to transform it into a hydrogen warhead small enough to be delivered by an airplane or even by missile.

Nuclear Weapons Design

Iraq had apparently not made much progress in actually designing a weapon. It was frequently stymied in this because the complicated machinery needed was not available commercially. However, Iraq did have a weapons development program, and it was in the process of designing a device to detonate nuclear weapons.

U.N. officials also said that Iraq had tested a missile that would be able to carry a warhead of the size needed for a hydrogen warhead. Similar warheads carried by American missiles have the explosive power of 300 kilotons of TNT, as compared to the 14 kilotons of the Hiroshima bomb. Based on this information, experts estimated that if it had not been for the Gulf War, Iraq could have tested a reasonably sophisticated atomic device by 1993 or 1994, an atomic bomb some time later, and a H-bomb several years after that. However, it would still need to develop a delivery capability, which in some ways is a more difficult problem than building a bomb.

The Intelligence Failure

What is clear is that American and allied intelligence underestimated the size of the Iraqi nuclear program and overestimated the damage that the bombing during the Gulf War had done to it. On January 23, for example, President Bush said, "Our pinpoint attacks have put Saddam out of the nuclear bomb-building business for a long time." On different occasions in late January, General H.

Norman Schwarzkopf, the American commander of the Allied forces, said that the bombing attacks "had destroyed all their nuclear-reactor facilities" and "neutralized their nuclear manufacturing capability."

After the war, Pentagon officials admitted to the press that the intelligence failure about Iraq's nuclear program had been extensive and that the experience raised serious concerns about how much the United States could learn about the nuclear programs of other potentially hostile countries, such as Libya and North Korea.

In fact, the same could be said of Iraq in the future. Rolf Ekeus, head of the U.N. group charged with destroying Iraq's nuclear, biological, and chemical capabilities, presented a plan to carry out that mission, but Tariq Aziz, Iraq's deputy prime minister said that Iraq would not permit the United Nations to push it back to a preindustrial age. Ekeus predicted that Iraq would claim that everything the United Nations wanted to destroy could be used for peaceful purposes—that it had a "dual use" and as such was exempt from destruction. Other U.N. officials pointed out that what the U.N. inspectors had discovered in Iraq demonstrated that the treaties on nuclear nonproliferation contained both flaws and loopholes that tended to nullify their effectiveness.

But even though the Iraqi nuclear potential was greater than anyone had suspected, in late September General Colin Powell, chairman of the Joint Chiefs of Staff, told the press that Saddam Hussein's ability to develop nuclear weapons was not any real threat, either in the short term or even the medium term. In addition, he said that even if Iraq did succeed in developing the capacity to produce a few small nuclear weapons a year, for many years to come it would not be able to develop the means to deliver them anywhere except in its immediate neighborhood. Delivery capability was a much bigger problem in developing a nuclear capacity than the actual bombs and warheads.

Several Washington officials in background interviews about the same time said that all the storm and fury about Iraq's nuclear potential was not over either a batch of documents or Iraq developing the capability to threaten the great powers of the world with nuclear weapons. The real struggle was over who was calling the shots in the Persian Gulf's unstable peace, George Bush or Saddam Hussein.

Iraq's Motivation to Build Nuclear Weapons

Marshall Wiley, ambassador to Iraq during the Carter administration, pointed out on the "MacNeil/Lehrer Newshour" (September 23, 1991) that it was understandable that Iraq felt driven to try to build a nuclear capability. Iraq, with 18 million people, felt threatened from the East by Iran, with a population of 55 million controlled by a militant Shiite priesthood hostile to Sunni Muslims, and from the West by Israel, with a stockpile of some 200 nuclear warheads and the missiles to deliver them. Ambassador Wiley argued that whether it was Saddam Hussein who was the leader of Iraq or some military junta that succeeded him, the Iraqis would feel that it was essential for their national security that they have some kind of "high-tech weapons capability." Referring to President Bush's speech

before the United Nations on September 23, 1991, vowing that there would be
no compromise on eliminating Iraq's potential for building nuclear weapons,
Wiley said the Bush administration was making an open-end commitment that
would be extremely difficult to carry out unless it was approached on a regional
basis, rather than directed at a particular country, such as Iraq. No matter how
hard the United States pushed on this, as soon as it stopped pushing, Iraq—no
matter who was its head—would resume some kind of nuclear program.

Asked what in practical terms the United States or the United Nations could do to
back up Bush's very adamant stand, Wiley said that the only way the United States
could be sure that it had removed all the high-tech weapons from Iraq would be to
occupy the country with maybe a million men and keep them there for a period
of years, a cost that he did not believe the American people were willing to pay.
The Bush administration seemed to be focused on removing Saddam Hussein
and eradicating Iraq's high-tech weapons, and not really looking beyond the immediate future to what all this would mean to the long-term stability of the area.

One of the great ironies in these worries about Iraq's potential for nuclear
weapons, according to newspaper reports, was that *because* Iraq was being denuded of
its potential for building nuclear weapons, a number of Arab countries were considering acquiring their own. If Iraq had succeeded in building a few nuclear weapons
and the capacity to deliver them, the reasoning goes, it would have deterred Israel
from actually using its own nuclear weapons in some future crisis. With Iraq no
longer able to supply the deterrent, other Arab states are likely to feel it is necessary for them to fill the void. It is worth remembering that after the Israeli bombing of the Iraqi nuclear reactor in 1981, Saddam Hussein called on all "peace-loving
nations" to help not just Iraq but all the Arab world "in one way or another to
obtain the nuclear bomb in order to confront Israel's existing bombs."

It has been understood for some time that the long-range aircraft and missiles
to deliver nuclear weapons were in many ways more difficult for a country bent
on joining the nuclear club to build than nuclear warheads. But some additional
lessons were learned about dealing with rogue states that try to build nuclear
weapons from the Iraqi attempt to build nuclear weapons and the Israeli, U.S., and
U.N. attempts to stop them. The first lesson is that bombing does not solve the
problem. The Israeli attack on the Dimona reactor merely forced Iraq to make their
attempt more sophisticated and better concealed. Then the Gulf War demonstrated
that large-scale bombing in the midst of a full-scale war also fails to solve the
problem. The size and extent of the Iraqi attempt to build nuclear weapons—
and the locations of the nuclear installations—were not discovered until several
months of aggressive inspection by the United Nations after the war was over.

The trouble is that Iraq is not the only country to pose a nuclear threat. As we
saw, President Bush claimed after the fact that the American intervention in the
Gulf was justified because Iraq was building a nuclear capability. But if the United
States undertakes to remove all the potential nuclear threats unilaterally with
American military force, it will be very busy for a long time to come. In ancient
Rome, the Temple of Mars was closed only during time of peace, and for one

period it remained open for two hundred years. If the United States takes on the role of nuclear policeman to the world, the American equivalent of the Temple of Mars might be open for several times as long. It seems obvious that the only hope for a long-term solution to such threats is not unilateral action by the United States, but action by the United Nations or other international bodies.

NORTH KOREA

The debate about the Iraqi nuclear program quickly brought worries about other countries to the fore. First was North Korea. North Korea signed the nonproliferation treaty, but it refused access for U.N. inspectors. Then, in the fall of 1991, announcements from Washington, Tokyo, and Seoul asserted that there was a growing body of evidence that the North Korean nuclear complex at Yongbyon was intended to produce nuclear weapons.

At about the same time, in a move clearly designed to put pressure on North Korea to permit inspectors, President Bush announced that the United States would withdraw all of its nuclear weapons based in Korea. The president of South Korea also declared that the United States would no longer be allowed to keep nuclear weapons in South Korea.

The government of North Korea—and independent observers in other countries—immediately pointed out that both moves were hollow gestures, since American submarines armed with nuclear missiles continued to patrol Asian waters and American long-range bombers were based nearby in Okinawa.

In any case, five days after Bush's announcement, North Korea laid down two new conditions before it would permit inspection. First, South Korea must renounce protection of any kind by American nuclear weapons, including the protection of American long-range bombers based outside Korea and missiles launched by submarines. Second, American planes carrying nuclear weapons should be prohibited from flying over the Korean peninsula and ships carrying them prohibited from docking at Korean ports. At the same time, China succeeded in stalling the international effort to press North Korea to accept inspectors on the grounds that dialogue was more proper than pressure.

Over the preceding few years, the United States had reduced its troops stationed in South Korea to about 39 thousand men. Another reduction of 3 thousand had already been scheduled. But Richard Cheney, Bush's secretary of defense, announced during a visit to Korea that the next reduction of 6 thousand, which was to begin at the end of 1992, would be delayed as a result of North Korea's unwillingness to accept inspectors.

In December 1991, North and South Korea signed two agreements. One was a nonaggression treaty, which at least opened the way for travel and commerce between the two countries. The other called for the elimination of nuclear weapons throughout the Korean peninsula. In January 1992, North Korea also signed a nuclear safeguards agreement with the International Atomic Energy Agency in Vienna pledging to allow inspection of its nuclear plants.

Although North Korea denied that it had a nuclear weapons program, American intelligence sources said they had detected (apparently by the highly improved American satellite surveillance system) signs at North Korea's nuclear facility at Yongbyon of a reprocessing plant to make weapons-grade plutonium. The fear was that North Korea was stalling on permitting inspection in order to move the plutonium to secret locations or to sell it to Libya or Iran. North and South Korea held talks in February of 1992, but North Korea continued to stall on letting the inspectors actually see the plant.

However, by September 1992, North Korea had permitted three separate inspections. The inspections apparently confirmed that North Korea had been engaged in building a plutonium-reprocessing plant that could make weapons-grade fuel from the waste products of nuclear reactors and suggested that North Korea might have been able to produce enough weapons-grade plutonium for one or perhaps even two or three bombs.

But the information also suggested that the North Koreans were a long way from producing plutonium in larger quantities. At least one reason for this was that after the breakup of the Soviet Union, Russia had stopped supplying North Korea with nuclear technology and materials. However, the president of South Korea, Roh Tae Woo, made it clear that his government would not be satisfied until the North and South agreed to conduct mutual inspections that were both frequent and intensive.

In the meantime, the International Atomic Energy Agency had come to believe that North Korea might have succeeded in producing enough plutonium for at least one bomb and pressed for permission to inspect two sites that might contain the answer. The sites were ostensibly intended for nuclear wastes, but the satellite photographs suggested that one of them might in fact be a storage facility for weapons-grade plutonium.

North Korea objected strenuously to the pressure, and in March 1993, announced its intention to withdraw from the nuclear nonproliferation treaty. Various members of the United Nations immediately began to circulate the idea of economic sanctions against North Korea, but China killed the idea by threatening to use its veto in the U.N. Security Council—even though it was well known that China had consistently tried to dissuade North Korea from embarking on a nuclear weapons program. It was strongly suspected that both China and Russia were trying to persuade North Korea not to withdraw from the treaty.

On April 1, 1993, the International Atomic Energy Agency formally requested the United Nations take steps to force North Korean compliance. North Korea's withdrawal from the treaty would become effective on June 12. The United States and North Korea entered into direct negotiations, and the day before the deadline, North Korea agreed to "suspend" its withdrawal from the treaty and to permit a return to routine inspections. However, inspectors would still not be allowed at the two sites that were the subject of dispute, and intelligence officials said that North Korea was apparently continuing to move forward with its weapons project. An intelligence official explained what had happened by saying that the international community found that it had little leverage over North Korea because it could not further isolate a country that had already made itself one of the most isolated countries in the world.

In the meantime, on May 29 and 30, North Korea successfully tested a missile, the Roddong I, that had a range of 600 miles and was capable of carrying chemical weapons and even a small nuclear warhead. Israel, in particular, feared that Korea would sell the missiles to Iran.

In the fall of 1993, the Clinton administration offered a "package deal" that would, first, cancel a major military exercise that had been scheduled and, second, begin talks about economic aid and diplomatic recognition if North Korea would permit inspections and begin a dialogue with South Korea. The North Koreans rejected the offer, saying that there was "nothing new in it." They seemed particularly upset by the American statement that the next step would be to seek sanctions from the U.N. Security Council.

The Clinton administration's position came under considerable criticism for being too soft. Why not bomb the North Korean nuclear sites? The first objection to bombing was that the intelligence community estimated that North Korea already had a stockpile of at least two nuclear bombs but that it was not able to pinpoint their location. So the North Korean nuclear facilities could be destroyed but the bombs might well escape. The second objection was that the South Koreans had nine nuclear power plants within easy range of North Korean bombers. If North Korea's nuclear facilities were bombed, they would probably retaliate, and the fallout of radioactive material over South Korea would probably be substantial.

The alternative to a bombing attack on North Korean nuclear facilities would be a conventional attack on the ground. But in a briefing for the president and the secretary of defense, the new chairman of the Joint Chiefs of Staff, General John M. Shalikashvili, presented the Pentagon estimate that a conventional war with North Korea would require "up to four months of very high intensity combat" by a force comparable to the forces in the Gulf War.

Denying that it had backed down from its demand for continuous inspection, the United States announced that North Korea had agreed to permit inspections of the seven acknowledged nuclear sites, but not the two sites that the International Atomic Energy Agency suspected might also be nuclear sites. The administration met criticism by making two points. The first was that the North Koreans would soon be shutting down their biggest reactor to change fuel rods. If no inspectors were present, North Korea would have an opportunity to extract more fuel for bombs. The second point was that the question of the two additional sites would be the principal item on the agenda for the next phase of the talks.

In January 1994, the United States was reported to be planning to ship Patriot missiles to South Korea. North Korea denounced the plan. At the same time, a number of South Koreans said that the Gulf War had proved the Patriots to be ineffective, but at the same time they would be very provocative.

For its part, South Korea announced that in view of North Korea's decision to permit inspections, South Korea would reconsider whether it still wanted the United States to send it Patriot missiles.

Finally, North Korea agreed to abandon its nuclear program in exchange for shipments of oil and the construction of two light-water reactors, which are difficult to convert into the construction of nuclear weapons. Ground was broken for the reactors in August 1997. However, in July 1998 it was reported that North Korea was refusing to allow inspectors to its nuclear sites, raising concern that it had hidden away plutonium for bombs. At about the same time, North Korea suffered a major famine, the political results of which will not be known for some time.

Congress dragged its feet on appropriating the several million dollars to provide fuel oil for the North called for by the agreement. The North complained that the United States was going back on its promise, and there followed a string of provocations—missile sales to Pakistan, the incursion of a small submarine carrying nine commandos off the South Korean coast, and reports that North Korea was refusing to allow inspectors into its nuclear sites. Then, on August 17, 1998, the American intelligence agencies announced that spy satellites had detected a huge secret underground complex twenty-five miles north of Yongbyon, the nuclear center where it was believed the North has created enough plutonium for six or more bombs.

On August 31, North Korea fired a two-stage ballistic missile that flew over Japan and landed in the Pacific Ocean, demonstrating a range of about 1,250 miles and a capability to deliver warheads on American military bases in Japan as well as Japanese cities. Experts said that a two-stage missile was too costly to use to deliver conventional weapons and that the North must be planning for it to carry a nuclear warhead. Some observers thought North Korea was bluffing to hasten the aid they had been promised; others felt that Kim Jong Il had decided not to abide by his father's agreement with the West and had embarked on a program of building both nuclear warheads and the missiles to carry them.

On September 5, 1998, Kim Jong Il assumed the various titles held by his father— "Great Leader," Chairman of the National Defense Commission, and so on.

NOTES

1. The enriched uranium taken from warheads can easily be made useless for warheads while remaining usable in power plants. Plutonium, however, is different. Even the plutonium taken from the spent fuel of civilian reactors can be used in warheads. So plutonium needs careful procedures for storage and disposal. There have been three confirmed thefts of nuclear material in Russia, and two of them came from civilian installations. Also, some material was left by accident in Vietnam when the United States withdrew. The Energy Department said that the amount left behind was only three ounces and that it was not weapons grade. See *The New York Times*, 16 January 1997, p. A12.

2. Seymour Hersh, *The Samson Option: Israel's Nuclear Arsenal and American Foreign Policy* (New York: Random House, 1991).

3. See Michael Rubner, *Middle East Policy* 1, no. 1 (1992): 136; Gerald M. Steinberg, *Technology Review* 95, no. 2 (1992): 74; and Steven Emerson, *Commentary* 93, no. 1 (1992): 55.

Chapter 13

Soviet, Chinese, and European Nuclear Strategy

SOVIET STRATEGY

As soon as Stalin learned from Soviet secret agents that the United States was building an atomic bomb, he ordered Soviet scientists to do the same.[1] But at the same time he downplayed the importance of nuclear weapons, partly for the benefit of the United States but perhaps more to reassure the Soviet people and especially the Soviet military.

Stalin's argument was that World War II had demonstrated that the key to victory was the Soviet ground forces—infantry, tanks, and artillery backed by support from the air. In a war with the West, Soviet armies would attack and occupy Western Europe. The United States would, of course, attack Soviet cities with atomic bombs. But, Stalin argued, this would not bring defeat. The damage would be great, but not unacceptable, and bombing could not push the Soviet armies out of Western Europe. In effect, Stalin's policy was to deter the United States by the threat of retaliation—the retaliation not of striking back with nuclear weapons, but of attacking and occupying Western Europe with Soviet ground forces.

As dogma to guide the Soviet military, Stalin laid down the so-called five "permanently operating factors" that would determine victory in war:

1. The stability of the rear.
2. The morale of the troops.
3. The quality and quantity of the combat divisions.
4. The armaments of the forces.
5. The organizational ability of the command personnel.

What is notable in this list of the principles of war is the absence of the element of surprise. In the West, surprise has always been given a prominent place in any list of the principles of war, and with the advent of nuclear weapons it was given an even more prominent place. While Stalin lived, however, Soviet military writings stayed within the bounds set out in the permanently operating factors, including the neglect of surprise.

Stalin also spoke of the "fatal inevitability of wars." The implication was that sooner or later war would come, even though a particular aggressor could be deterred—presumably as the threat of occupying Western Europe would deter the United States from starting a war even in the period when it had a nuclear monopoly. So the Soviet Union should be prepared to fight and win a war, even a nuclear war.

The Soviet "Revolution in Military Affairs," 1953–1955

In September 1953, several months after Stalin's death, an article was published in *Military Thought* by General Nikolai A. Talenskii questioning the five permanently operating factors, including neglect of the element of surprise. There followed a debate in Soviet military journals that Soviet writers have characterized as the "revolution in military affairs." The debate focused on whether Stalin's permanently operating factors were valid and gave particular attention to the question of surprise. The culmination of the debate came in March 1955, when Marshal Rotmistrov argued that in a nuclear age surprise was essential. Merely repulsing an enemy attack would not do; it was necessary to launch a "preemptive" or "forestalling" strike.

The thrust of the writings by Soviet military officers, as by military officers in the West, was on integrating nuclear weapons into military arsenals—on fighting and winning nuclear wars. On the other hand, Malenkov, Stalin's immediate successor, said in March 1954, that nuclear war would be "the end of world civilization," much to the distress of the Soviet military, who apparently thought that Malenkov would use the idea as an excuse to cut the military budget. Molotov and others sharply criticized Malenkov for this statement, and Malenkov seems to have been forced to acknowledge that he had made a mistake.

Meanwhile, as the debate progressed, Soviet scientists and engineers continued to work on developing nuclear weapons. The SS-3, a battlefield missile, became operational some time in the middle of the 1950s. So did a medium-range bomber capable of carrying nuclear weapons, nicknamed the "Badger" by Western intelligence, and two long-range, intercontinental bombers, nicknamed by the West, the "Bison" and the "Bear."

The Khrushchev Era, 1955–1964

In 1956, shortly after he ousted Malenkov, Khrushchev as part of his denunciation of Stalin rejected the notion that war with the West was inevitable and also, by implication, Malenkov's idea that nuclear war would be the end of world civilization. Khrushchev had come to power with the help of the military, and at least at first he adopted their ideas on military questions, which was that nuclear war with the West was not inevitable, but the way to prevent it was by being prepared to fight and win it. With Khrushchev's encouragement the Soviet military set about to develop an appropriate strategic doctrine.

As one result of this effort, the Soviet military were reorganized in 1959, and the Strategic Rocket Forces created. Early in 1960, Khrushchev announced a new doctrine that was also a result of this effort. A future war would begin, he said, with missile attacks deep in Soviet territory. But Soviet retaliatory forces would survive and strike back. Because the Soviet Union was so large and its population so dispersed, he argued, the Soviet Union would suffer less than the West. A nuclear war, furthermore, would be short. Because of this and because of the power of nuclear weapons, the Soviet Union did not need to have as many men under arms as in the past. Khrushchev then announced that Soviet forces (mainly ground forces) would be cut by one-third, from 3.6 million to 2.4 million. However, the Berlin crisis of 1961 led Khrushchev to cancel some of the cuts.

The Soviet military did not all support Khrushchev's policies, especially the implication that traditional forces would play a less important role in future wars. But by 1963, a compromise was apparently reached that although nuclear weapons would play a key role in future wars conventional forces would also have a major part. A number of points were left fuzzy, but there seemed to be agreement that any future war would inevitably escalate to an intercontinental exchange of nuclear missiles and that any such war would be short.

Soviet strategy in this period, in effect, was a modification of the Stalin strategy of holding Europe hostage to deter the United States from a nuclear attack on the Soviet homeland. Whereas the Stalin strategy was to deter the United States by threatening to retaliate by conquering and occupying Western Europe with Soviet ground forces, the threat was now to retaliate against Europe with medium-range ballistic missiles and intermediate-range ballistic missiles. As mentioned earlier, the Soviets had built a huge stockpile of both.

Again, Soviet scientists and engineers continued to progress in developing weapons. The Soviet Sputnik was launched into orbit in 1957 by an SS-6 missile. As already described, the Soviets began to deploy this missile, but found it was too big and bulky, and instead of a missile gap in favor of the Soviets the gap that developed was in favor of the United States. As we saw, the Soviets deployed MRBMs and IRBMs to Cuba at least in part to try to close this gap. After the decision to withdraw the missiles from Cuba, the Soviets signed the Limited Test Ban agreement of 1963.

From Brezhnev to Gorbachev, 1964–1985

In 1964, Khrushchev was ousted and Brezhnev took over. Soviet policy became that of "ensuring" that the military would be given "all it needed to defend the homeland." For the next decade, the Soviet Union modernized and increased its armed forces all across the board—missile, air, ground, and sea.

Soviet military writings of this first decade of the Brezhnev years saw war as consisting of two phases. The first phase would be a nuclear exchange, and destruction would be widespread. The second phase would be an attempt by both sides to achieve victory with conventional forces "in the ruins," a concept that was rather similar to the earlier Western idea of "broken-back" war.

There was also speculation that wars might occur in which only conventional weapons were used and that even limited nuclear warfare might be possible. In any case, the arguments concluded that nuclear war was not only possible but that it could be won if the Soviet Union continued to build toward nuclear as well as conventional superiority.

Some time in the early 1970s, the Soviet Union perceived that it had achieved "nuclear parity" with the United States. Shortly thereafter, around 1977, economic growth in the Soviet Union slowed down, and a decision was made to cut defense spending by pegging it to the economy.

At about the same time, Brezhnev began to challenge the view that a nuclear war could be won. In a famous speech at Tula in January 1977, he said that no one could win a nuclear war and denied that the Soviet Union was trying to achieve nuclear superiority. He followed this with an announcement in a message to the United Nations in 1982 that the Soviet Union was willing to sign with the West a pledge of no first use. The West assumed that the offer was no more than a propaganda ploy and did not reply.

Over the next few years tensions between the military and the Party leadership were high. The chief of the General Staff, Marshal Nikolai Ogarkov, argued publicly that a nuclear war *could* be won. Then, in 1983, he abruptly changed his tune, rejecting both the idea that a nuclear war could be won and the possibility of a limited nuclear war. Some sort of deal was probably made, with the Party leaders agreeing to a policy that emphasized high-tech conventional forces.

However, Ogarkov continued to press for more money for defense, and this was apparently the reason he was suddenly dismissed in 1984.

Changes in the Early Gorbachev Years

Gorbachev came to power in 1985. Until 1978, he had been a provincial party leader with little opportunity to work with the military. It was only during the latter part of his time in Moscow before becoming general secretary that he had any official dealings with the military, since during the first part of his time in Moscow he apparently dealt mainly with agricultural matters. However, as F. Stephen Larrabee argues, Gorbachev's attitude toward the military was probably influenced by events in the period before he came to power that generally exacerbated relations between the Party and the military.[2]

The first such event in that earlier period was the deployment of the SS-20 intermediate-range missile beginning in 1977. The difficulty was that the decision seems to have been made at the urging of the military for "military–technical" reasons without full consideration of the political and strategic implications. The West was alarmed and responded by deploying the Pershing II and cruise missiles, so Soviet security was, if anything, diminished. In addition, the Soviet Union's relations with the West went sharply downhill.

A second such event was the Soviet invasion of Afghanistan in 1979, in the last years of the Brezhnev regime. Nine years later, in 1988 as the Soviets prepared to withdraw from Afghanistan, Soviet officials let it be known to the world that the decision to intervene had been made hastily by a very small group of top officials— Brezhnev, Ustinov, Andropov, and Gromyko—and not on the basis of recommendations by the military. Gorbachev saw this decision by his predecessor as a serious blunder, damaging relations with both the West and the Third World and costing lives and treasure out of proportion to any possible gains. Afghanistan, in the newspaper reporters' phrase, became the Soviet Union's Vietnam.

A third event was when the Soviets shot down a Korean Air Lines plane, KL 007, in September 1983. The incident not only demonstrated flaws in the Soviet air defense system and hurt the Soviet image throughout the world, but it came at a time when relations with the United States were beginning to improve. The fact that the incident was followed by a shakeup in the Far Eastern air defense command indicates that the Party was dissatisfied with the way the military handled the affair.

In any case, Gorbachev made a number of changes in the top military leadership in the months immediately after he came to power. Then, on May 28, 1987, a West German youth, Mathias Rust, flew a light plane right through Soviet air defenses without triggering an alert and landed very close to Red Square, making the Soviet military look not only incompetent but silly. It seems clear that Gorbachev used the incident as an excuse to carry out still more changes among the top military.

On defense spending, the Party changed the way it formulated its promise to the military. Instead of promising the military "all it needed to defend the homeland," as in Brezhnev's time, the Party promised to ensure that the military would "remain at a level that rules out the strategic superiority of the forces of imperialism." Soviet spokesmen also began to distinguish between "parity," implying absolute equality with the West in every aspect of defense, and "reasonable sufficiency," defined, to repeat, as a force level that "rules out superiority by the forces of imperialism." At the same time, Soviet spokesmen stressed the "defensive nature" of the Soviet military posture and argued that its goal was to prevent or deter war.

Military doctrine during the first years of Gorbachev's regime apparently anticipated a long war conducted mainly with conventional weapons. The doctrine conceded that nuclear weapons might be used, especially by the NATO forces on the battlefield. But the argument was that because of fear of escalation the NATO forces would not use nuclear weapons against the Soviet homeland even if they did use them on the battlefield. And the argument also was that the NATO powers would put limits on how they used battlefield nuclear weapons as well.

All this is at the level of the political leadership of the Soviet Union. The military, on the other hand, seemed to be reluctant to make changes in the Soviet force posture and to insist that Warsaw Pact forces must have the capability for counteroffensive operations.

CHINESE NUCLEAR STRATEGY

Understanding the Chinese attitude toward nuclear warfare requires a brief look at the history of their strategic thinking. Following the failure of their attempt at a coup in 1927, the Chinese Communists first fled to the nearby mountains and then made the "Long March" to Yenan. Once there, they had no alternative but to base themselves on the peasants and the countryside rather than on the workers and the cities, and so "to turn Marx and Lenin upside down."

In World War II, the only practical way the Chinese could fight the Japanese was by using the tactics of guerrilla warfare. After the war, the fighting between Chiang Kai Shek's Kuomintang troops and the Communists were traditional battles of battalion versus battalion and division versus division, and the Communists won. In the Korean War, however, traditional warfare brought the Chinese enormous casualties. Out of these experiences, Mao Zedong developed the doctrine and strategy of "people's" or "revolutionary" warfare.

Revolutionary warfare is, in the words of a familiar comment, guerrilla tactics plus political action. "Guerrillas are fish," Mao said, "and the people are the water in which they swim. If the temperature of the water is right, the fish will thrive and multiply." Mao then went on to describe revolutionary war as consisting of three stages. The first stage is purely political, with activist cadres building support among the people. The second stage is actual guerrilla warfare, with bands of guerrillas ambushing and harassing to make the government suspicious of the people and the people distrustful of the government. The third stage is to establish "liberated" areas and from these to turn the guerrilla war into a civil war in which government troops can be engaged in conventional combat and destroyed.

Applied to wars between states, these principles in effect described the Chinese Communists' strategy in fighting the Japanese. They conceded the cities to the Japanese, based themselves in the mountains and rural areas, ambushed Japanese convoys, and raided the Japanese lines of communication.

In 1965, when the Chinese feared that U.S. intervention in the Vietnam War might be a prelude to an attack on China itself, the defense minister at the time, Lin Piao, laid out a similar doctrine to deal with an American invasion of the Chinese mainland. The Chinese would not attempt to defend at the point of attack, but would fall back into the mountains and rural areas, harassing and ambushing along the lines of communication throughout a long war in which the Chinese people would eventually prevail.

Consistent with these ideas, Mao declared that the atomic bomb was a "paper tiger," bragging to Khrushchev that he, Mao, was the only world leader who could lose 300 million of his people in a nuclear war and still have 300 million left. Khrushchev responded by saying that this particular paper tiger had nuclear teeth. Mao in turn retreated only a little bit, arguing that the imperialists were to be despised strategically but respected tactically. At the same time, the Chinese Communists asked the Soviets for help in developing nuclear weapons of their own, and the Soviet refusal was an important factor in the Sino–Soviet rift. At one stage the rift led to actual fighting between Chinese and Soviet forces along the Ussuri River.

However, in 1964, the Chinese tested a fission weapon of their own, following it by a test of a hydrogen weapon in 1967. They also succeeded in developing missiles of at least medium to intermediate ranges of about 1,500 miles.

After Mao's death, the Chinese line was that China was a developing nation whose power and influence could be projected no further than the area of Asia and so posed no threat to the rest of the world. At the same time, the line continued, China's enormous manpower combined with even a very small nuclear and missile capacity would ensure that an aggressor invading China would suffer disastrous defeat.

WESTERN EUROPEAN STRATEGIC DOCTRINE

When North Korea attacked South Korea in 1950, both the Europeans and the Americans concluded, as we saw, that the Soviet Union was behind the decision and that Western Europe might be next. NATO was formed, and in 1952 the Allies, meeting in Lisbon, set a force goal of ninety-six divisions. The economic cost was formidable. The Eisenhower administration adopted the policy of massive retaliation and the new look in military posture of cutting ground and naval forces and increasing air forces armed with nuclear weapons, and NATO followed suit. It cut the force goals to thirty divisions and backed them with battlefield nuclear weapons.

Almost all Europeans writing about strategy criticized the Eisenhower administration's concept of massive retaliation on the grounds that it was simply not credible. As described earlier, after *Exercise Carte Blanche* simulating the use of battlefield nuclear weapons, they also worried about the dreadful consequences that NATO's dependence on nuclear weapons would bring to Europe and its peoples if war actually came. But also hanging over their heads was the Soviet bloc's overwhelming preponderance in conventional forces, and the thought of being conquered and occupied seemed just as horrendous.

The West Germans, for their part, had agreed to rearm on the condition that NATO would adopt a "forward strategy" to halt the Soviet bloc forces at the German border. A number of different strategies to accomplish this goal were argued. A wall of fortresses at the border was too reminiscent of the Maginot Line. The possibility of using militia to delay the attacking forces until a counteroffensive could be launched was also explored and rejected. Building strong enough conventional forces to bring about a "pause" if war came or to provide a "firebreak" between conventional and nuclear weapons were also discussed and rejected.

When McNamara began to push hard for a buildup of conventional forces by NATO and at the same time argued that the Europeans should not build their own nuclear forces but depend on those of the United States, Europeans were outraged. To many Europeans, McNamara seemed on the one hand to be suggesting that Europe should be the battlefield in the struggle against the Soviet Union, and on the other that the United States was preparing to abandon Europe in case of war. And what was perhaps worse, McNamara did all this, according to the Europeans, with overpowering self-confidence, even arrogance, and with little regard for the sensitivities and dignity of the Europeans.

The Europeans did not really see the need for a massive conventional buildup that would match the Soviet bloc man for man, and lacking evidence that the Soviets were readying themselves for an assault on Europe they were certainly not willing to pay for such a buildup. They were also unhappy at the notion of the NATO forces being so dependent on battlefield nuclear weapons. The compromise was to try to do both with the policy of flexible response. Informally this became the policy when the Allies approved McNamara's proposal for deploying a huge number of battlefield nuclear weapons to Europe immediately, in time of not only peace, but low East–West tensions. Flexible response was adopted formally in 1967.

In the European context, what flexible response meant was that in case of a small-scale conventional attack on Europe, NATO would not automatically go to a full-scale nuclear war including the exchange of ICBMs between the Soviet and American homelands, but would respond with a conventional defense, at least at first, and that it would go up the ladder of escalation only as additional steps were needed.

In the end, most Europeans put their hopes in strengthening deterrence, and tried not to think about the problem they would face if deterrence failed. They objected to any talk in the United States of cutting down the American ground forces stationed in Europe—and such talk occurred often in Congress. Few Europeans thought that the American forces would be able to halt a Soviet invasion, but they saw the American forces as a "plate-glass window" or "trip wire" that promised to trigger a nuclear retaliation. In truth, what they hoped was that the Soviets would see it this way and be deterred. Also in truth, if the Soviets were not deterred and launched an attack, many Europeans secretly hoped that the United States would not retaliate, since this would bring on a Soviet nuclear response that would include Europe as well as the United States.

The key word for most Europeans was coupling, as described earlier. In European minds, the fact that American ground forces were stationed in West Germany tended to couple a Soviet attack on Europe with an American nuclear retaliation against the Soviet homeland. When the Soviets deployed the intermediate-range SS-20s so that they threatened Western Europe, the European governments pressed the United States to deploy its intermediate-range Pershing II to Europe as well, on the grounds that the deployment of the Pershings would tend to couple with the Soviet SS-20 threat.

The British View

The British shared these conflicting fears and hopes, but they had built a nuclear weapon of their own. For a delivery system, they arranged to buy the air-to-surface Skybolt missile from the United States. But McNamara, in a fight with the U.S. Air Force, canceled Skybolt, and this precipitated a crisis in British–American relations that was calmed only by a summit meeting between Prime Minister Macmillan and President Kennedy at Nassau. There they agreed that the United States would sell the United Kingdom the Polaris missile, which was launched from submarines. For the British it proved an ideal solution. It gave them an independent nuclear retaliatory force, and it was comparatively very cheap.

A number of "good" reasons why the British should have an independent nuclear force were offered at various times, but the "real" reason was what was bothering the other Allies: When a crisis came, would the United States stand firm in its threat to retaliate against the Soviet homeland with nuclear weapons if the Soviets attacked one of the European Allies? The United Kingdom stayed in the NATO alliance, but it provided what the British called "a second decision-centre," in case the first decision-center, the United States, backed down.

The French View

The French reached the same conclusion—to build their own independent nuclear deterrent, the *force de frappe*. But France decided not to remain as a full member of NATO and forced NATO to move its headquarters to Belgium. De Gaulle admitted that France could not defeat the Soviet Union by itself. His argument was that the enemy would be deterred by the certainty that France had the power "to tear off an arm as he goes by."

NOTES

1. This chapter draws on the following works: Raymond L. Garthoff, *Soviet Strategy in the Nuclear Age* (New York: Praeger, 1958); Lawrence Freedman, *The Evolution of Nuclear Strategy* (New York: St. Martin's Press, 1983); John Van Oudenaren, *Deterrence, War-Fighting and Soviet Military Doctrine*, Adelphi Papers 210 (London: International Institute for Strategic Studies, 1986); James M. McConnell, "Shifts in Soviet Views on the Proper Focus of Military Developments," *World Politics* (April 1985); F. Stephen Larrabee, "Gorbachev and the Soviet Military," *Foreign Affairs* (Summer 1988); Robin Laird, *The Soviet Union, the West and the Nuclear Arms Race* (New York: New York University Press, 1986).

2. See Larrabee, "Gorbachev and the Soviet Military."

Chapter 14

Armageddon:
Six Scenarios of Nuclear War

Earlier chapters suggested again and again that nuclear war would be a horror beyond imagining. But it still might be instructive to look in more detail at how a nuclear war might come about and what the consequences might be.

One possibility is nuclear terrorism. A terrorist organization, for example, might smuggle a small, suitcase nuclear bomb into the United States, Russia, or some other major power, and set it off to dramatize whatever its demands might be.

A second possibility is nuclear terrorism by a state, as opposed to an organization. Suppose an outlaw state acquires or manufactures a few nuclear weapons. Suppose that it then tries to provoke a war between the United States and Russia or the United States and China by sending agents on a suicidal mission to plant suitcase nuclear weapons in, say, Washington and New York on the one hand, and Moscow and Leningrad or Peking and Shanghai on the other.

A third possibility is nuclear war between third and fourth countries, such as between India and Pakistan. Both India and Pakistan have tested nuclear weapons, and in case of war are very likely to use them.

A fourth possibility would be a war between Israel and one of the Muslim states of the Middle East. Israel has built a stockpile of nuclear weapons, but no one knows for certain just how large it is.[1] In the aftermath of the Gulf War, it became clear that Iraq had a very large program to develop nuclear weapons, and suspicion was widespread that Iran was also engaged in a nuclear weapons program. If one or another Muslim state acquired nuclear weapons and a war broke out with Israel, it could easily escalate, with both sides using nuclear weapons.

A fifth possibility is a war between the United States and another major nuclear power that is started purely by accident. In the immediate future, only Russia would qualify as a major nuclear power. But in a decade or two, China and one or two other countries might have to be included. Unless a way is found to establish a worldwide control of nuclear arms, it is likely that in a decade or two several dozen countries will have both nuclear weapons and the missiles to deliver them and so qualify as major nuclear powers. In any case, a war between two major nuclear powers could occur by accident—a missile in one or the other country accidentally goes off and hits Detroit or Gorki or Shanghai and the victim retaliates.

A sixth possibility is a so-called "bolt from the blue"—a bolt of lightning out of a cloudless sky. This is a war that starts when one side or the other attacks without warning at a time of low international tension and succeeds in achieving surprise. It could be the United States under a presumably psychotic leadership or a belligerent successor state to Russia or a more desperate China after it develops its missiles further.

The seventh possibility is probably the most likely of all, a crisis between the United States and an embittered successor state to Russia—a crisis, like the Cuban missile crisis, that was intended not as a Pearl Harbor but to right an imbalance or to deter the other side. As we have seen, anyone who looks carefully at the history of the Cuban missile crisis will realize how easy it would be for such a crisis to spiral out of control into nuclear war.

As we said, it should be instructive to look more closely at each of these seven scenarios to see what casualties and destruction they would be likely to bring. To make these calculations, we must first review what was mentioned here and there about nuclear weapons and missiles in earlier chapters and lay out more systematically the different types of nuclear weapons and missiles and their effects.

TYPES OF NUCLEAR WEAPONS

Nuclear weapons are of three types: fission, fusion, and fission–fusion–fission. The fission bomb, which was the type used on Hiroshima and Nagasaki, utilizes a natural isotope of uranium, U-235, or man-made plutonium 239. The latter is a byproduct of nuclear reactors, produced when U-238, the more plentiful natural isotope, absorbs neutrons.

U-235 and plutonium are unstable, spontaneously breaking down and releasing neutrons in the process. If one of these neutrons strikes the nucleus of another atom of U-235 or plutonium, it, too, splits, releasing still more neutrons. If a certain amount of U-235 or plutonium is assembled in one mass—the so-called critical mass—a chain reaction occurs, releasing enormous amounts of energy.

The Fission Bomb

A fission warhead or bomb is simply a device to bring together this critical mass very quickly and to hold it together for a fraction of a millisecond. The

Hiroshima bomb used a sort of cannon to fire one less-than-critical mass of U-235 into another, thus creating a mass that was critical.

This critical mass was held together for the necessary instant by sheer momentum. A later fission bomb used chemical explosives arranged around the outside of a spongy form of the necessary amount of U-235 or plutonium to create an implosion when they were triggered that drove the fissionable material together into a critical mass and held it for an instant or two.

A fission bomb or warhead has enormous blast, which not only kills, but knocks down buildings. It also has fallout, the radioactive byproducts of fission. Fallout kills living things that receive a large dose within two or three days, even though they escape the blast. Fallout kills those that receive a smaller dose more slowly, over a period of months and years. In Japan, forty years after the Hiroshima bomb was dropped, almost one-hundred people a year were still dying from the effects of the radiation they received from it.

The Fusion Bomb

A fusion bomb or warhead works on an entirely different principle. Although fission occurs when a very heavy atom splits, releasing energy. Fusion occurs when the nuclei of two very light atoms are brought together and they fuse, making a heavier element and releasing even more enormous quantities of energy. In the fusion bombs and warheads so far tested, the light element used has been hydrogen, hence the more common name for a fusion bomb is hydrogen bomb or H-bomb.

To accomplish fusion, very high temperatures are required, hence the alternative term for a fusion bomb is to call it a thermonuclear bomb. So far these temperatures have been obtainable only by exploding a U-235 or plutonium device as the first step of a two-step process.

Hydrogen is much cheaper than U-235 or plutonium. But of even greater practical consequence is that there is no theoretical limit to the size of a fusion bomb, while there are very definite limits to the size of a fission bomb. In a fission bomb, once a critical mass of U-235 or plutonium is brought together, it explodes. Practical engineering difficulties set a top limit on the amount of fissionable material that can be safely and effectively brought together, and this amount is only slightly larger than the critical mass itself. If any more than the critical mass is used the excess over the critical mass would simply be blown away unexploded. There is no such limit to the amount of hydrogen that can be brought together and exploded.

A fusion bomb kills mainly by its enormous blast and heat. It has relatively little fallout compared to a fission bomb. If a fusion bomb is exploded at altitude the only fallout comes from the fission trigger. However, if a fusion bomb is exploded at the surface it will in the process of exploding make radioactive a certain amount of material that it sucks up from the surface.

The Fission–Fusion–Fission Bomb

The third kind of nuclear warhead presently available is fission–fusion–fission. The U-238 present in a U-235 warhead does not split. But in the environment of an H-bomb, with its higher temperatures and faster-moving neutrons, it does, releasing still more energy. Thus, the comparatively cheap U-238 can be used as a jacket for the H-bomb. A tamper is needed in any case, and the U-238 first does the job of tamping and then itself contributes to the total energy released. Quite apart from the fact that the fission–fusion–fission warhead is economical, it is also compact, which is an important military consideration. A fission–fusion–fission bomb has enormous blast and heat, and it is also very, very "dirty"—that is, it produces a very large amount of radioactive fallout because of the U-238 tamper.

Fission warheads, bombs, and shells for nuclear artillery have been made as small as 1 kiloton—that is, having the energy equivalent of 1 thousand tons of TNT. The Hiroshima bomb was about 14 kilotons. Fusion and fission–fusion–fission warheads have been tested that range from about one-third of a megaton (a megaton being the equivalent of 1 million tons of TNT) up to 57 megatons, which was the size of a test bomb fired by the Soviet Union in 1961.

Both the Russian and American arsenals include a wide variety of so-called tactical or battlefield nuclear weapons in the kiloton range. The MX missile was designed to carry ten warheads, each of which is the equivalent of about 300 kilotons of TNT or twenty times the power of the Hiroshima bomb. The warheads are highly accurate: Half will hit within 400 feet of the programmed target at a range of 6 thousand miles.

Submarines of the Trident class were designed to carry twenty-four D-5 missiles, each of which carried eight warheads. The force of a D-5 warhead can be adjusted for different targets from 150 kilotons to 600 kilotons. Accuracy is 400 feet at a range of 4 thousand miles.

Land-based cruise missiles carry a single warhead of about 200 kilotons. The manned bombers in both the Russian and American fleets can carry a bomb of any size up to ten to twenty megatons—from 600 to 1,200 times the power of the Hiroshima bomb. U.S. B-52s usually carry two 4-megaton bombs, and the Russian bombers can probably carry bombs of similar size. Manned bombers can also carry cruise missiles with warheads in the kiloton range.

THE EFFECTS OF NUCLEAR WEAPONS

The effects of nuclear weapons when exploded on or near the surface of the earth are achieved through blast, heat, and nuclear radiation.

A fission bomb or warhead has enormous blast, which not only kills, but knocks down buildings. It takes 5 PSI of overpressure to knock down a building, and the blast at Nagasaki knocked down buildings at a distance of 7,500 feet or 1.4 miles from ground zero (the bomb was exploded at an altitude of 1,850 feet). A 3-

megaton warhead exploded on the surface will topple brick structures at a radius of 4 miles from ground zero, giving a total area of destruction of 50 square miles. For a 10-megaton bomb, the radius is 6.5 miles, and the area is 133 square miles. Doubling the size of the bomb, as described in the principles of physics, does not double the distance of blast. Thus, two well-placed 3-megaton bombs will destroy a much larger area than one 10-megaton bomb.

The urban area of greater Moscow is something over 1 thousand square miles; the urban area of greater New York, including Nassau, Rockland, Suffolk, and Westchester counties, is over 2 thousand square miles. Thus, greater Moscow can be totally destroyed by twenty-one missiles with 3-megaton warheads, if they are well targeted, and greater New York by forty-three. Nine 10-megaton missiles or bombs could wreak the same damage on Moscow and sixteen on New York.

These figures are for blast alone. The thermal effects of nuclear weapons can be even more destructive. Nuclear explosions will start fires at considerable distances, depending on the weather. As a rule of thumb, however, the distance can be assumed to be three times that of the blast effect and nine times the area. With a large number of fires starting simultaneously at many different points in a city under attack, firestorms will develop. The great heat rising from so many fires draws air in from surrounding areas at increasing speeds that fan the flames higher and higher into one great conflagration. Such a firestorm developed at Hiroshima, but not at Nagasaki, which nestles among hills. But most cities hit with nuclear weapons will develop firestorms, and the casualties and destruction from burning and suffocation beyond the blast zone will be as great as the casualties inside it due to blast alone. Because of firestorms, only three 3-megaton warheads or one 10-megaton warhead would probably be all that was needed to destroy Moscow and five 3-megaton warheads or two 10-megaton warheads to destroy New York.

Nuclear radiation can vary widely, depending on how the warhead is made and whether it is exploded at the surface or high in the air. A fission bomb exploded high in the air deposits only the radioactive products of the splitting. The area covered and the level of dangerous radioactivity will depend on wind and weather conditions at the particular altitude. A fission bomb exploded at the surface also sucks up other material and makes it radioactive, depositing both fission products and radioactive surface material downwind in a cigar-shaped pattern.

Although an H-bomb exploded high in the air produces radioactive tritium, carbon 14, and certain other radioactive products, it is no more dirty with dangerous radioactivity than its fission trigger. An H-bomb exploded at the surface, however, like an ordinary fission bomb or warhead, will suck up surface material and make it radioactive. The H-bomb exploded on the surface in a test by the United States on March 1, 1954, with a yield of between 10 and 20 megatons, deposited radioactive fallout in an elliptical pattern downwind that covered 7 thousand square miles. According to the official report, inside this area "survival might have depended upon prompt evacuation of the area or upon taking shelter and other protective measures."

The dirtiest bomb of all, however, is the fission–fusion–fission type. Many fission products have more intense radioactivity than surface materials made radioactive by a nuclear explosion. Also, surface materials lose their radioactivity much more rapidly than some of the more dangerous fission products. Many surface materials will lose half their radioactivity in a matter of hours (i.e., they have a half-life, the measure of how long radioactivity lasts, of several hours). By way of comparison, one major radioactive byproduct of fission, Strontium 90, which enters the food chain and is incorporated into the flesh of animals, has a half-life of 27.7 years. Areas dusted with radioactive fallout will be highly dangerous to all forms of life. Many people in such areas will die within a matter of several days. Others will develop cancers that kill them more slowly. Still others will survive, but with genetic damage that will affect future generations.

As described in Chapter 10, in 1992 the Bush–Yeltsin agreement specified that each side reduce their stockpiles of long-range missile warheads from the 1992 levels of about 12 thousand each to 3,500 each in the final stage. But again it should be repeated that the combination of blast, radiation, and probable firestorms means that it would probably take only about 200 warheads to destroy the seventy largest metropolitan areas in the United States, where over 50 percent of the American people live, and about 300 warheads to destroy the somewhat larger number of urban areas that are home to 50 percent of the Russian people.

THE DESTRUCTIVENESS OF PAST WARS

Wars in the past have sometimes been enormously destructive. In the Thirty Years' War, for example, the population of what is now the united Germany was reduced by three-fourths, the countryside laid waste, the farmhouses burned, and the fields untended. In World War I, the total killed in battle is estimated as 8,020,780, with another 6,642,633 dying of disease and other causes related to the war. In World War II, casualties, as estimated by the military historians, R. Ernest Dupuy and Trevor Dupuy, were some 15 million killed and 26 to 34 million dead of indirect causes.[2] However, these figures are probably much too low. Official Soviet figures are that the Soviets alone lost 20 million killed in action, missing, or died of wounds or in prison camps. Gerhard L. Weinberg, in his *A Global History of World War II*, puts Soviet casualties at 25 million, and total casualties worldwide at 60 million. In addition to the 25 million Soviet casualties, his estimates are China, 15 million; Poland, 6 million; Germany, 4 million; Japan, 2 million; Yugoslavia, between 1.5 and 2 million; United Kingdom, 400 thousand; and the United States, 300 thousand.[3]

In World War I, the physical destruction was small, mainly because most of the fighting was confined geographically, mostly to the stalemated trench warfare in France. In World War II, the fighting ranged more widely, and the bomber spread destruction farther still. What was devastated was not the countryside, as in the Thirty Years' War, but the cities. Hiroshima and Nagasaki were each hit with an atomic bomb, and the destruction was awesome. But cities that became battlegrounds between infantry and artillery, such as Stalingrad and Manila, suffered just as much.

The Hiroshima bomb, with the force equivalent of about 14 kilotons of TNT, started a firestorm that caused almost as much destruction as the bomb itself.

Nonnuclear incendiary bombs started firestorms in Tokyo, Hamburg, Dresden, and Darmstadt, and the damage and loss of life was almost as great as in Hiroshima. Moscow, Leningrad, Warsaw, Berlin, Köln, Frankfurt, Rotterdam, London, Coventry, Chungking, and many other cities all felt the hammer blows of the bomber, but with somewhat less destruction. But neither the Thirty Years' War nor World War II caused as much destruction as is likely in a war fought with nuclear weapons.

POSSIBLE NUCLEAR WARS

Terrorists and a Suitcase Bomb

With this background on the effects of nuclear weapons, let us look at the several possible scenarios that a nuclear war might follow. The first possibility, that of a terrorist organization getting hold of a small, suitcase bomb, seems remote, but it is not inconceivable. A terrorist organization might be given a weapon by a pariah state sympathetic to its views, it might bribe its way into possessing one, or it might conceivably steal one.

What does seem extremely unlikely is that a terrorist organization could get its hands on more than one or two nuclear devices. It may be cold comfort, but this means that casualties would be in the range of tens of thousands, rather than millions. As McGeorge Bundy pointed out, even a very successful terrorist attack with nuclear weapons would probably be no worse than the Chernobyl accident.[4]

Many both inside and outside the American government believe that the more immediately dangerous threat from terrorists is that they will acquire not nuclear weapons but chemical and biological ones.[5] In May 1994, the judge in the World Trade Center bombing trial announced that the defendants had put sodium cyanide in their explosive package. If so, it must have burned up in the explosion; otherwise, it could have created a cyanide gas cloud that could have poisoned thousands. In March 1995, two members of the Minnesota Patriots Council, a militia-type organization, were convicted of planning to use ricin to assassinate federal agents. A tiny bit of ricin can kill in a matter of minutes if ingested, inhaled, or absorbed through the skin. Also in March 1995, the Japanese doomsday cult, *Aum Shinrikyo*, released sarin nerve gas in a Tokyo subway at the height of the rush hour, killing twelve people and hospitalizing more than 5 thousand. In May 1995, a former member of Aryan Nation, a white supremacist group, was arrested in Ohio after ordering freeze-dried bubonic plague bacteria for what he claimed was "research purposes." In December 1995, a man with alleged ties to survivalist groups was charged with attempting to smuggle 130 grams of ricin into the United States.

The only way to prevent terrorists from getting any of these weapons of mass destruction, whether nuclear, chemical, or biological, is tight security and effective intelligence work.[6] Again, it is cold comfort, but Bundy's comment about a terrorist attack with nuclear weapons also applies to a terrorist attack with chemical and biological weapons. The result of even a very successful attack would be more like Chernobyl than Armageddon. Even so, a secret meeting in the White House in March 1998 concluded that the United States was unable to handle a germ warfare attack, and on May 22, President Clinton announced a program against what he called "biological, computer, and other twenty-first century threats."

A Terrorist State with Nuclear Bombs

The second possibility is a terrorist state as opposed to a terrorist organization. Suppose such a country acquired half a dozen nuclear weapons and went to war with one of its neighbors. Using either aircraft or agents with suitcase bombs, it could destroy the larger cities of its enemy neighbor and this might well make the difference between defeat and victory. The long and bloody war between Saddam Hussein's Iraq and the Ayatollah Khomeini's Iran ended in a stalemate, but if one side or the other had had half a dozen nuclear weapons it could have won.

In January 1999, Clinton proposed revising the Anti-Ballistic Missile Treaty to permit a system that could shoot down a few missiles launched by a rogue state such as North Korea, Iran, or Iraq. The idea was to spend $4 billion on research and testing over the next six years and to set aside $6.6 billion for future construction if a system was feasible.

Clinton's tone was tentative and reassuring, but Secretary of Defence Cohen said that the United States would not rule out withdrawing from the treaty if an agreement could not be reached. Russia regards the ABM Treaty as central to its security, and a defense ministry spokesman said that any "military expert understands that these countries do not have and will hardly acquire guaranteed means of reaching U.S. territory." Russian legislators also said that approval of START 2 would be contingent on keeping the missile agreement intact.

Madeleine Albright was then sent to Moscow to explain that the propsed system would not be deployed until 2005 and even then only if the threat from rogue nations turned out to be as great as expected and the system to be developed turned out to be effective.

From the perspective of this book, such a multibillion-dollar program seems most unwise. First, the United States must maintain an intelligence system, as described in the following chapters, capable of detecting the development of a missile delivery system by any country, not just North Korea, Iran, or Iraq. Second, the United States must maintain both nuclear forces and conventional, rapid-deployment forces, also as described later, capable of dealing with a wide varity of even worse contingencies. If so, the United States will have the means of detecting and eliminating the threat of a missile attack by a rogue state long before the missiles are actually launched.

Going forward with any kind of missile defense system, no matter how limited, would be vastly expensive. But much worse, it would put at risk the entire range of arms agreements already in place and alarm both the Russains and the Chinese. The idea should be quickly, publicly, and emphatically abandoned.

Nuclear War between Third and Fourth Countries

The third possibility of nuclear war is one between third and fourth countries, such as between India and Pakistan. Both sides would probably pick as first-priority targets the other side's nuclear facilities, airports, and major military installations. Both sides would also probably try to hold back a portion of their nuclear arsenals to be used to force a surrender or a stalemate by threatening the other side's cities.

The first thing that can be said is that a lot of people would be killed, even if cities were not attacked directly. The second thing that can be said is that if one side or the other had a monopoly of nuclear weapons, that side would undoubtedly win. But if both had nuclear weapons, the result is no more predictable than if the war was fought with conventional weapons alone.

Since the stockpiles on both sides are likely to be small, the effects on the rest of the world in terms of fallout would be about the same level as it was before the limited test ban treaty banned testing in the atmosphere.

As for the war escalating to the point where other countries, such as the United States and Russia, were drawn into the struggle, it seems unlikely. The United States and Russia would be much too concerned about the dangers of nuclear war between their two countries to let it happen in this roundabout way. However, the same thing can probably not be said about a nuclear war between Israel and one of the Arab states. The United States and the other great powers would have a large stake in trying to prevent such a war from coming about, but if such a war did come, keeping it localized would be difficult.

Accidental War

The fourth possibility is a war that begins purely by accident between the United States and Russia or, in the longer run, between the United States and China or some other power that achieves a stockpile of nuclear warheads and missiles. Suppose, for example, an American missile accidentally goes off and hits Gorki, or a Chinese missile accidentally goes off and hits Detroit.

The first thing to be said here is that all nuclear powers have taken elaborate precautions to prevent such an accident—the consequences are just too grave. One of the several reasons that the United States and the Soviet Union agreed immediately after the Cuban missile crisis to establish the hot line—a twenty-four-hour-a-day, 365-days-a-year open communications channel between the White House and the Kremlin—was to help avoid not only accidents but miscalculations as well.

Early speculation about just how the hot line would help if a missile was actually fired by accident led to nothing but a gallows-humor joke. If an American missile went off accidentally and headed for Gorki, the joke went, the American president would phone the Soviet chairman and say, "We're sorry. We didn't mean it. It was an accident. Use one of your missiles and take Detroit." Conceivably, however, an accident could happen, and a missile could be fired by mistake. It was because of the possibility of such accidents—as well as to protect against a terrorist missile—that Senator Sam Nunn proposed his accidental launch protection system designed to protect American cities.

More recently, during Clinton's January 1994 visit to Russia, he and Yeltsin agreed to target each side's missiles on empty ocean rather than each other. When Clinton visited China in 1998, the same agreement to target their missiles on empty ocean was made. This lessens the possibility of an accident, which is an important consideration. But it does little else, since changing them back again would take only fifteen minutes or so.

Nuclear Pearl Harbor I

The fifth possibility is a nuclear war that begins at a time of low international tension with an attack, like the Japanese attack on Pearl Harbor, that achieves surprise. Given the risks, it seems unlikely that either side would ever launch such an attack "out of the blue." But the purpose here is to examine, if only for the sake of argument, the worst case—the case in which a surprise first strike achieves the maximum possible success.

As already described, the Bush–Yeltsin agreements limited the final stockpiles for the United States and Russia to 3,500 warheads each, and this goal could be reached as early as the year 2000. The agreement did not deal with battlefield nuclear weapons, and each side has about 15 thousand of these. The agreement required Russia to give up its land-based SS-18 and SS-24 missiles, and the United States to give up its MX missiles and to replace the three independently targeted warheads on the Minuteman missiles with only one warhead each. The treaty let the United States keep its Trident submarines, provided that the total number of warheads carried by the submarine force was reduced to 1,750. Chapter 10 describes how the International Institute of Strategic Studies speculated that the United States would allocate its warheads. That earlier chapter also included an IISS chart speculating on Russian forces after the Bush–Yeltsin agreements are implemented. These estimates assume that the Russians would continue to produce ICBMs to match the Minuteman numbers, but this still leaves the Russians with only 2,968 of the 3,500 warheads permitted. Prudence dictates that the United States should assume that the Russians would try to achieve parity and that they would build two more submarines, giving them a total of 1,600 SLBMs, and make up the remaining difference by building a total of 632 ICBMs armed with 632 warheads, making a grand total the same as the United States. However, since this is a worst-case scenario for the Russians, let us accept the IISS speculation, even though it assumes a smaller Russian force.

Both the Russian and American ICBMs have a range of well over 5 thousand miles, which they could travel in about thirty minutes. Warning time at best would be fifteen minutes. The Americans have no missile defenses that would be effective against Russian ICBMs or SLBMs. Although the Russians have a number of anti-ballistic missile launchers around Moscow, there is reason to believe that the system is primitive and ineffective. So even though the reliability of both the American and Russian missiles is not 100 percent, it must be assumed that if one side or the other strikes first in a coordinated surprise attack, a rather high percentage of its ICBMs will be successfully delivered on target. Let us assume that the figure is 90 percent. Again let us also assume that each side would be able to deliver 90 percent of its submarine-launched ballistic missiles on target.

Both sides have air defense systems against bombers. We will assume that the United States will attempt to blast a corridor through Soviet air defenses that the twenty Stealth bombers can use to go through. The 950 B-52 bombers would stand off outside of Russia and launch 950 cruise missiles, and the 95 B-1 bombers would be the follow-up. Some of the B-1 bombers would carry one bomb each and the rest two bombs each for a total of ninety-five bombs. The B-2 Stealth bombers would carry two bombs each.

Russian air defenses might well knock out half or more of the attacking bombers, but we are deliberately looking at a scenario that is the worst case for Russia and the best case for the United States. So let us assume that 75 percent of the American bombers get through to drop their bombs on Russia, for a total of 800 bombs. Using these assumptions, the results are as follows:

U.S. Vehicles	Launched	Shot Down or Misfired	Warheads on Target
ICBMs (1 warhead each):	500	50	450
SLBMs (4 warheads each):	432	43	1,556
Bombers:	1,065	264	800
Total	1,997	357	2,806

SIOP-62 was for the year 1962. Later versions are still classified, but we can assume that the figures in SIOP-62 are close enough for our purposes. The U.S. National Strategic Target List for 1962 contained 3,729 targets in the Soviet Union and among its allies. All NSTL targets were not in the strike plan. Also, a significant number were in parts of the Soviet Union, like Ukraine, that are now independent. The total of NSTL targets not in the strike plan or in parts of the Soviet Union that are now independent comes to about one-third. So the SIOP list today for Russia alone probably totals something like 2,500 targets.

In SIOP-62, Soviet nuclear capabilities in this list had top priority, fixed targets that were essential to support Soviet ground forces facing NATO had second priority, and urban–industrial complexes had third priority. We can safely assume that the priorities of the current SIOP are much the same.

The number of warheads assigned to each DGZ depends on probability factors related to type and effectiveness of defenses. As outlined in SIOP-62, the 3,729 targets listed in 1962 would all be hit at least once if only 1,060 DGZs were targeted. If the same ratio held, the 2,500 targets we have assumed in Russia today would all be hit at least once if 675 DGZs were targeted. However, the proportion of targets in Russia is likely to be different, so let us assume that the number of DGZs to be targeted is 1 thousand.

So if the United States struck first, two warheads could be aimed at each of the 1 thousand DGZs and 806 of them could be targeted with a third warhead. Thus, there seems to be a very high probability that all but a fraction of the targets on the National Strategic Target List would be destroyed.

The Russian Retaliatory Strike

The loss of life in Russia would be horrendous, at least as much as 50 percent of the Russian population. But the question here is what the Russians would have left for a second, retaliatory strike.

Although the accuracy of both the Russian and American missiles is excellent, we cannot assume 100-percent success. So some of the missiles of the victim of a surprise strike might well have survived to strike back. However, the purpose of this scenario is to examine the case in which a surprise first strike by the United States achieved the maximum possible success. So let us assume that surprise was complete and accuracy perfect, so that none of Russia's ICBMs would survive.

The SALT II agreement banned mobile ICBMs. The treaty was never ratified, but both sides said they would honor it. So we assume that the Russians would not have any mobile missiles capable of reaching the American homeland. There is no evidence that the Russians maintain either an airborne or ground alert at this time. In any case, the purpose of this exercise is to try to estimate the maximum damage that an American first-strike blow would inflict, and the minimum damage that a Russian retaliatory second strike would inflict, so let us assume that this situation remains the same, that no Russian bombers are on either airborne or ground alert and that none survive the American first strike.

As for the submarine-launched ballistic missiles, submarines have the great advantage of mobility over the vast areas of the oceans. They also have the advantage of being able to maintain a high level of secrecy in their movements. Radar is not effective underwater, and the only method of detection with present technology is by sonar. Submarines, however, can operate at great depths, and this permits them to hide under temperature inversion layers that reflect sonar waves or under schools of fish.

Let us assume that, like the United States, Russia would have 50 percent of its submarines on patrol at any given time:

Type	Number on station	Missiles	Warheads
SS-N 18	7	112	112
SS-N 23	3	56	112
SS-N 30	3	80	800
Total	13	248	1,024

American intelligence might be able to pinpoint some of the Russian submarines on patrol. Any submarines so pinpointed could probably be destroyed by

American killer submarines, missiles, and bombers. But a number of the Russian submarines would undoubtedly escape detection and survive to launch their missiles. A success rate of 50 percent for American intelligence and subsequent attack would be extraordinarily high—almost impossibly high—but let us assume that a 50-percent success is in fact achieved. If so, the surviving Russian submarines would still be able to launch in a retaliatory strike a total of 124 missiles carrying 512 warheads to strike back at targets in the United States. Since the Americans had struck first, there would be no missile installations to attack, and the attack would have to be against cities. What is more, the Americans would not have evacuated their cities, since to do so would have destroyed the element of surprise.

As mentioned in Chapter 10, it would take only about 200 warheads to kill most of the inhabitants of the seventy metropolitan areas containing over 50 percent of the American population, while the Russian retaliatory strike would be with 512 warheads, about two-and-a-half times that amount.

The few survivors of such a blow could not by any stretch of the imagination achieve victory in the World War II sense of invading, occupying, and enforcing the American will on what was left of the Russian people. Merely finding food and water in the midst of the radioactive devastation would be a Herculean task.

Nuclear Pearl Harbor II

Suppose Russia struck first "out of the blue." Let us again assume the worst case for the Russians, even though they strike first, and the best case for the United States, even though it is the victim. First, let us assume that they consider the NORAD (North American Air Defense Command) air defense system so effective that they decide to use none of their bomber force in the attack, but only missiles. Assume that, like the United States, 90 percent of their ICBM and SLBM missiles get through to their targets. Assume also that the Russians have made no attempt to achieve parity and have only the 2,968 missiles of the IISS estimate. A summary of their attack is as follows:

Russian Vehicles	Launched	Shot Down or Misfired	Warheads on Target
ICBM SS-25		50	450
SLBM			
SS-N-18 (14)	224	23	201
SS-N-23 (7)	112	12	88
SS-N 20 (6)	120	12	1,080
Bombers			
Bear (ALCM)	0	None launched	
Bear	0	None launched	
Blackjack	0	None launched	
Totals	—	97	1,819

Again assuming the worst case for the Russians, let us assume that their SIOP equivalent of the United States SIOP contains no more than 750 DGZs, including American military bases in Europe and Asia. If so, the Russians could hit each DGZ with two warheads and 319 of them with three warheads.

The casualties would be almost unimaginable, with as many as 50 percent of the American population being killed immediately and many more dying in the days and weeks that followed. But again the question is what the United States would have left for a second, retaliatory strike.

It seems very unlikely that any of the American ICBMs in fixed silos would survive, even though hardened. The United States has no mobile ICBMs. As for bombers, any that were on air alert would probably survive. Since any bombers on ground alert could be airborne in fifteen minutes, it is conceivable that all could survive. However, let us assume that none of the American bombers would survive.

As for submarines, Russian intelligence might have been able to pinpoint some of the American submarines on patrol, although Russian antisubmarine technology is not as advanced as the American. Still, for our purposes, let us assume that it is as effective as we assumed for the American antisubmarine warfare. So we assume that the Russians sink half of the American submarines on patrol in their first strike. Half of the American submarine fleet is on patrol at any given time, carrying 216 missiles with four warheads each for a total of 864. If half of those survive, they could launch a retaliatory blow of 432 warheads. Assuming 10 percent misfire, this means a total of warheads on target of about 390. Since the Russians had struck first, there would be no missile installations to attack and the American retaliation would have to be against cities. What is more, the Russians would not have evacuated their cities, since to do so would have destroyed the element of surprise. As we saw, it would take only about 300 warheads to kill most of the inhabitants of the metropolitan areas containing over 50 percent of the Russian population, while the American retaliatory strike would be with 390 warheads, a surplus of ninety warheads. The result would be the mirror image of a first strike by the United States against Russia. The few Russian survivors of the American retaliation could not by any stretch of the imagination achieve victory in the World War II sense of invading, occupying, and enforcing the Russian will on what was left of the American people. For the Russians, if they struck first, as for the Americans in the opposite case, merely finding food and water in the midst of the radioactive devastation would be a Herculean task.

Nuclear War as the Outcome of a Crisis

The sixth possibility is a nuclear war that came in the midst of a crisis like the Cuban missile crisis. Calculating the results for this possibility is considerably more complicated, except that we can be absolutely certain that the casualties and destruction on both sides would be much, much higher than if one side struck first.

The reasons are obvious. Both sides would have all their forces on very high alert. The ICBMs on both sides would have counted down to a point just prior to launching and would be holding. A significant percentage could be launched with something less than the fifteen-minute warning that they would get if the other side launched a preemptive strike. A much higher percentage of the submarine fleet than the usual 50 percent would be at sea, and intelligence on their precise location would be more difficult. And a much higher percentage of each side's bomber fleet would be on airborne and ground alert. It is probably no exaggeration to say that in a nuclear war that came in the midst of a crisis like the Cuban missile crisis the casualties would be half again as many in both Russia and the United States as in a war beginning in a surprise first strike. The military capability of both sides would be reduced to close to zero.

CONCLUSION

It seems obvious, then, that no conceivable gains from nuclear war would be worth the cost. If a nuclear war comes, the United States and Russia will find themselves in a situation that can be described only as one of mutual assured destruction—MAD.

But the fact that neither side could possibly gain from nuclear war does not mean that nuclear war could not come. It is, of course, inconceivable that sane leaders on either side would attempt a surprise attack. The counterargument is that humankind has no guarantee that the leaders of either country will always be sane, as Adolph Hitler demonstrated. However, one can be fairly certain that neither the Russian nor the American military would carry out an order for a surprise nuclear attack at a time when international tensions were low, especially if they had any reason to believe that the nation's leader was not sane.

In fact, there is an historical example that tends to confirm the point. Just before Richard M. Nixon resigned as president, when the Judiciary Committee of the House of Representatives voted to recommend impeachment to the full House, the secretary of defense and the members of the Joint Chiefs of Staff were apparently worried about the possibility of an American version of the incident in which Hitler staged the Reichstag fire as an excuse to arrest leaders of the opposition.

At that time, an American equivalent of the Reichstag fire might have been, for example, that either President Nixon himself or one of his aides would telephone lower-ranking officers commanding battalions and regiments in and around Washington and order them, say, to occupy the Capitol and arrest the president's opponents in Congress on the grounds that they were secret Communists.

To guard against some such incident the secretary of defense and the Joint Chiefs of Staff quietly issued instructions that no order from the president was to be obeyed unless it came through channels; that is, the order must come from the president to the secretary of defense, to the Joint Chiefs of Staff, to the chief of staff of the particular service, to the army, corp, division, and so on down to the commanding officer of the regiment or battalion that was to carry out the order.[7]

The American military would probably behave in much the same way if they received an order to launch a surprise nuclear attack "out of the blue," and especially if they had any reason at all to suspect that the president was not sane. And there is no reason to suppose that the Russian military is any different in this respect from the American.

But nuclear war can also come in a world in which destruction is both mutual and assured even if the leaders of both sides are perfectly sane. Consider a crisis that neither side sought but resulted from events that spiraled out of control—a Cuban missile crisis that got out of hand. A series of miscalculations might convince one side or the other that its choice was between being destroyed by the other's first strike or striking first in a preemptive blow, a choice that was seen as being between utter, total destruction on the one hand and, on the other, horrendous casualties but enough survivors to constitute a viable nation and society.

And nuclear war can even more easily come in the midst of a crisis because of a series of mistakes and miscalculations on one side and then the other, as the Cuban missile crisis so vividly demonstrated. One move can logically lead to another until both sides suddenly find themselves in the midst of a war. At the outbreak of World War I, the former German chancellor Prince Bernard Von Bülow is supposed to have said to his successor, "How did it all happen?" The reply was, "Ah, if we only knew!"

Mutual assured destruction is a powerful deterrent, in other words, but it is not a guarantee. In a MAD world, nuclear war may come later rather than sooner, but if humankind can do no better than mutual assured destruction to deter nuclear war then sooner or later nuclear war will surely come.

NOTES

1. The Israeli nuclear weapons program and the Iraqi program are discussed in Chapter 12.

2. R. Ernest Dupuy and Trevor Dupuy, *The Encyclopedia of Military History* (New York: Harper & Row, 1970), 990, 1,198.

3. Gerhard L. Weinberg, *A World at Arms: A Global History of World War II* (Cambridge University Press, 1994).

4. McGeorge Bundy, *Danger and Survival: Choices About the Bomb in the First Fifty Years* (New York: Random House, 1988), viii.

5. The following is drawn from John F. Sopko, "The Changing Proliferation Threat," *Foreign Policy* 105 (Winter 1996–1997): 3–20.

6. Richard K. Betts, in "The New Threat of Mass Destruction," *Foreign Affairs* (January–February 1998): 26 ff, argues that while the threat of nuclear war has receded that of chemical and biological weapons of mass destruction has increased. A vial of anthrax dispersed over Washington, D.C., he believes, could kill as many as 3 million people. Since traditional deterrence will not stop a disgruntled group from striking at America, he concludes that the United States must pull back from excessive foreign involvements and begin a program of civil defense to protect against such weapons.

7. Theodore H. White, *Breach of Faith: The Fall of Richard Nixon* (New York: Athenaeum, 1975), 22–23; personal interviews.

PART V

ARMS CONTROL
AND DISARMAMENT

Chapter 15

The History of Arms Control

In both the Soviet Union and the United States a number of people hoped that arms control and disarmament would offer a solution to the dilemma that nuclear weapons and missiles had posed for humankind.[1] Intermittently from the end of World War II, the two governments negotiated on the subject. The Soviet position in the 1940s and 1950s was that negotiations must begin with the elimination of weapons of all kinds; that is, "general and complete disarmament." The United States thought the proposal was a trick or at least that it was unfair to be asked to give up its advantage in nuclear weapons without some concrete concessions from the Soviet Union, which enjoyed such a vast superiority in manpower. The United States therefore regarded the Soviet proposal as nothing more than propaganda.

For its part, the United States insisted that any agreement must include procedures for on-site inspection within each of the two countries. But the Soviets felt that inspection by foreigners, even U.N. observers from neutral countries, would inevitably introduce outside influences into Soviet life that were unacceptable. They were suspicious that the American proposals had ulterior motives designed to undermine their political system.

As a result, the only movement in arms control that occurred in the years that followed were the treaties barring military installations in Antarctica and those concerning sea-bed technology and outer space.

THE KENNEDY PROPOSAL

But there was one very bold initiative from the United States that has been almost completely forgotten in the various histories of arms control. On September 25, 1961, the United States presented to the General Assembly of the United Nations the "United States Program for General and Complete Disarmament in a Peaceful World."

For the United States, a willingness even to discuss general and complete disarmament was a startling departure, since it had maintained that the whole idea of general and complete disarmament was nothing more than a Soviet propaganda ploy. But the document the United States tabled on April 18, 1962, at Geneva was even more startling. Entitled *Blueprint for the Peace Race, Outline of Basic Provisions of a Treaty on General and Complete Disarmament in a Peaceful World*, the document differed fundamentally and radically from all previous proposals the United States had made.

President Kennedy announced the action himself at a press conference that same day. Describing the document as "a blueprint of our position on general and complete disarmament as well as elaboration of the nature, sequence, and timing of specific disarmament measures," Kennedy then went on to say, "This outline of a treaty represents the most comprehensive and specific series of proposals the United States or any other country has ever made on disarmament. . . . I want to stress that with this plan the United States is making a major effort to achieve a breakthrough on disarmament negotiations." Disarmament would be progressive and balanced so that no state would have an advantage at any point. Compliance would be verified, and as national armaments were reduced the United Nations would be strengthened.

Disarmament would be accomplished in three stages, the first to be accomplished in three years, the second also in three years, and the third as promptly as possible thereafter. In Stage I both nuclear delivery vehicles and conventional arms would be reduced by 30 percent. Half of the remaining inventories would be eliminated during Stage II. At the end of Stage III, states would have in their arsenals only, as Kennedy said, "agreed types of non-nuclear armaments for forces required to maintain internal order and protect the personal security of citizens." Verification would be accomplished by a new organization to be established within the framework of the United Nations, the International Disarmament Organization. By the end of Stage III, all the territory of every state would have been inspected. In Stage I, a U.N. Peace Observation Corps would be established to verify the various stages of disarmament. In Stage II, a U.N. Peace Force would be established and equipped with "agreed types of armaments and would be supplied agreed manpower." This U.N. Peace Force would be "progressively strengthened until, in Stage III, it would be fully capable of insuring international security in a disarmed world."

In the administrations that followed Kennedy's, the American approach changed from disarmament, which was the goal of the Kennedy proposal, to arms control. Instead of trying to escape completely from the arms race by eliminating the weapons of war, subsequent administrations tried to manage the arms race by controlling the number and types of weapons.

THE LIMITED NUCLEAR TEST BAN TREATY

No one knows whether the Kennedy proposal for general and complete disarmament would have made any headway if the Cuban missile crisis had not intervened. But during that crisis both sides shrank back from what they saw would be a nuclear holocaust. Kennedy realized that the crisis had been a sobering experience for the Soviet Union as well as for the United States, so within a few months he opened negotiations for what became the limited nuclear test ban treaty outlawing testing in the atmosphere. It was signed in August 1963.

By banning all nuclear tests in the atmosphere the limited test ban treaty saved millions of people from exposure to radiation and unknown numbers from dying of cancer. But what Kennedy had proposed was not a limited test ban but a comprehensive ban outlawing all nuclear tests of any kind—in the atmosphere, in outer space, and underground.

Edward Teller, the "father of the H-bomb," and his allies opposed the treaty, as they had opposed a similar move toward a test ban by the Eisenhower administration. Their argument was, first, that a test ban would prevent the United States from developing important new weapons and, second, that the Soviet Union would cheat. To get around this opposition to a comprehensive test ban, Kennedy proposed that each side be permitted to inspect seven sites in the other country each year. To the surprise of many long-time Soviet watchers, the Soviets agreed to on-site inspection in principle, but wanted to limit the number to three. The Kennedy administration then proposed six. As Jerome Wiesner, Kennedy's science adviser, said, the obvious compromise was five. But neither side would budge.

Kennedy was afraid that if he agreed to less than six inspections the military and other hard liners would lobby Congress, and the treaty would not be ratified. But if he could get a limited test ban ratified he reasoned that he had a good chance of eventually persuading both the Soviets and Congress to agree to a comprehensive test ban with five inspections the following year. But the idea died with Kennedy.

After Kennedy's assassination, Khrushchev told the American writer Norman Cousins that he, Khrushchev, had had the same problem with the Soviet generals and their allies that Kennedy did with the American military and that the failure to achieve a comprehensive test ban was a "tragedy for humanity." Jerome Wiesner, for his part, later wrote that "the world would be quite different if the comprehensive ban had been achieved. Many new destabilizing weapons systems such as multiple-warhead technologies and the Strategic Defense Initiative ["Star Wars"] would have been avoided."[2]

THE NUCLEAR NONPROLIFERATION TREATY

In 1967, the Soviet Union and the United States agreed to ban the use of space satellites as platforms for nuclear weapons. In 1968, the U.N. General Assembly approved a treaty to prevent the spread of nuclear weapons to states that did not already have them, the nuclear nonproliferation treaty. Within a short time sixty countries had signed the treaty, the United States and the Soviet Union being among the first. However, France, China, India, Israel, Egypt, Argentina, Brazil, South Africa, and Japan refused to sign, although Japan later did sign. Not long afterward, China and India constructed and tested nuclear weapons. In September 1995, France conducted a series of nuclear tests, but promised to renounce nuclear testing when those were completed. In 1995, the nuclear nonproliferation was indefinitely extended. In subsequent years treaties were signed banning the use of the ocean floor as a site for nuclear weapons and the production of biological and toxic weapons.

All these were helpful steps, but none of them struck at the central problem of the huge stockpile of nuclear bombs and missiles that remained in the arsenals of the Soviet Union and the United States. The U.S. stockpile included about 13 thousand bombs and warheads intended for strategic use (i.e., to be delivered by long-range bombers and missiles), and the Soviet strategic stockpile probably included almost as many. Each side also had approximately 15 thousand additional warheads intended for battlefield use.

SALT

In late 1969 the Strategic Arms Limitation Talks (SALT) were begun in Helsinki, Finland. Almost two-and-a-half years later the so-called SALT I agreements were signed in Moscow by Richard Nixon and Leonid Brezhnev. The first agreement, the "Interim Agreement," was for five years, until 1977 (it was later extended). It placed ceilings on the number of ICBMs each side would be permitted to have and on the number of submarine-launched ballistic missiles they could build.

A separate agreement on anti-ballistic missiles specified that the Soviet Union and the United States would each limit their anti-ballistic missile sites to two, with no more than one-hundred missiles at each. Both agreements provided that both sides would have unimpeded use of "national technical means of verification"; that is, the use of spy satellites and other intelligence means.

It was widely agreed that the SALT I agreements were not only a technical achievement but a political one as well. Détente—good relations between the Soviet Union and the United States—was given a substantial boost.

WORRIES AND SORE POINTS

However, the agreements left both sides with significant worries and dissatisfaction. The Soviets had been allowed 1,608 ICBMs and 950 submarine-launched missiles while the United States had been allowed 1,054 ICBMs and 710 submarine-launched missiles. The disparity reflected the existing situation and was also intended to compensate the Soviets for the technological lead that the United States enjoyed as well as certain disadvantages the Soviets suffered because of "geography"—since they had a "two-front" problem of having a newly hostile Communist China on one border and capitalist Western Europe on the other.

However, the difference in ceilings bothered many Americans both inside and outside government, and Senator Henry M. "Scoop" Jackson successfully sponsored an amendment that ensured that both sides would have equal numbers in any future agreements. Another sore point for the American side was the fact that the treaties did not do much to keep the Soviets from continuing to develop their very heavy missiles, which had a first-strike potential against American retaliatory forces.

For their part, the Soviets were not happy with the failure of the agreements to do much about the American lead in technology. However, in the case of MIRVs the Soviets correctly foresaw that for two basic reasons they would be the long-term beneficiaries of unrestricted MIRV technological development. First, the Soviet missile force was dominated by heavy ICBMs, and when MIRVed they would be able to carry more warheads of larger yield. Second, spy satellites could count missiles, but they could not count the number of warheads sitting on top of a MIRVed missile.

Another sore point for the Soviets was the issue of so-called forward-based systems. The Soviets contended that American tactical aircraft based in Europe or on aircraft carriers were capable of delivering nuclear weapons to the Soviet homeland and therefore should be counted among the strategic forces of bombers and missiles.

VLADIVOSTOK

All this was regarded only as the first step in continuing negotiations that were intended to lead to SALT II. After two years of negotiations, President Gerald Ford and Secretary Leonid Brezhnev met at Vladivostok on November 24, 1974. They agreed to an outline or framework for an agreement that would require further negotiations—which actually took another four-and-a-half years.

THE CARTER PROPOSALS

President Jimmy Carter was inaugurated on January 20, 1977, and in March, Secretary of State Cyrus Vance went to Moscow with a set of very radical proposals that would have severely cut back the strategic forces of both sides and limited the amount of modernization that either side could make. This so-called "Comprehensive Proposal" offered to cancel the MX missile if the Soviets would cut their force of SS-18 heavy missiles in half. It also restricted the kind and number of adjustments that each side could make to suit its own peculiar situation.

This limitation alone opened the proposals to challenge in both the United States and the Soviet Union. But the proposals also contained so many other questionable points about such matters as verification that critics argued that they contributed not to stability but instability. In addition, the Soviets apparently believed that the manner in which the proposals were presented was designed more for propaganda advantage than for serious negotiations.

In any case, the result was a debacle, with the Soviets making it clear that they did not want to start from scratch every time the United States elected a new president. The Soviets were so outraged that they violated SALT protocol by denouncing the proposals publicly.

The Carter administration had anticipated rejection and so had gone to Moscow with a fallback position that preserved what had already been accomplished in the preceding negotiations concerning SALT II. The delegation then presented this fallback position, but the confusion caused by the first set of proposals delayed agreement.

THE SALT II AGREEMENT

Finally, an agreement was reached that Carter and Brezhnev signed in Vienna in 1979. The SALT II agreement provided for numerical ceilings on broad categories of weapons that were the same for both sides, as Senator Jackson had demanded. Each side was permitted 2,400 missiles. This was fewer than the Soviets actually had in their arsenal but more than the United States had. It permitted the Soviets to keep a monopoly of the heavy missiles as compensation for the American forward-based systems and British and French weapons.

The concessions by the Soviets were that, although the SS-19 continued to be counted as a medium rather than heavy missile, it would be the largest missile that could be counted as a non-heavy. In other words, there would be no loophole for a new missile to be built halfway between the SS-19 and the SS-18. The United States agreed not to build a heavy missile (in fact it had no plans for building a heavy in any case). The MX was about the size of the Soviet SS-19, but it would have ten warheads. So the MX was the counter to the SS-19 in size and the counter to the SS-18 in number of warheads. However, mobile, land-based, intercontinental missiles were not permitted under SALT II, so the MX could not be deployed in the railroad-course basing mode proposed by the Carter administration until after the treaty had expired. Moscow also accepted a ceiling on launchers for MIRVed missiles close to the number they already had (820) and a freeze on the number of warheads per type of ICBM.

The Carter administration was clearly going to have a hard time getting Congress to ratify SALT II. The opposition was substantial, since both liberals and conservatives had their own particular objections. Although the Joint Chiefs of Staff endorsed the treaty as a modest but useful step, the Pentagon representative in the SALT II negotiations, General Edward L. Rowny, resigned in protest shortly before the signing, saying that SALT II left the United States with a "window of vulnerability," a phrase later adopted by Ronald Reagan in his campaign for the presidency. Rowny then went to work for Senator Jesse Helms, an extremely conservative Southern Republican, to try to prevent ratification of the treaty.

However, it seems clear that the greatest liability the treaty suffered was that even though it had been crafted over three separate administrations, the name on the bottom line was Jimmy Carter's. President Carter's handling of foreign affairs had earned hostility from Democrats as well as Republicans, and it seemed doubtful that SALT II would win enough votes in the Senate to be ratified. When the Soviets invaded Afghanistan all doubt was removed, and Carter withdrew the treaty from consideration (although the Carter administration did adopt a policy of adhering to the provisions of SALT II as long as the Soviet Union did).

THEATER NUCLEAR FORCES

Separate negotiations on so-called theater nuclear forces (IRBMs and MRBMs with ranges below 5 thousand miles) had begun in October 1980. Following the adoption of SALT I, the Soviets developed the SS-20. Its fuel was solid, rather than liquid, and it was therefore a more reliable weapon. It was MIRVed, carrying three warheads, was highly accurate, and was transportable by truck. But since its range was just under 5 thousand miles it was not classified as an ICBM, which would have made it subject to the SALT I limitations on mobility, but as an IRBM and so exempt from that limitation.

The Soviet bomber that allied intelligence called the Backfire also seemed to have been designed to come just under the definition of an intercontinental bomber, but the American FB-111 was a counterpart. The SS-20, however, had no American counterpart, and so created an imbalance in theater nuclear forces.

Thus, Soviet deployment of the SS-20 reawakened the old fears in Europe about decoupling—the fear that the Americans might not be willing to use ICBMs against the Soviet Union in retaliation for an attack that was confined to Europe. Chancellor Helmut Schmidt of West Germany was particularly concerned, arguing that if SALT did not constrain the Soviets from deploying powerful weapons below the strategic level, such as the SS-20, then NATO must deploy theater nuclear weapons to offset them—the intermediate-range Pershing IIs and the cruise missiles.

However, feelings in Europe were ambivalent. Most Europeans wanted an arms control agreement, specifically SALT II. The dilemma was that delay in developing and deploying the Pershing IIs and the cruise missiles might mean that Europe would have neither a meaningful arms control agreement nor theater nuclear forces to offset the SS-20. The Europeans suggested a two-track policy, and the Carter administration agreed.

The first track was to continue to take the steps leading to deployment of the Pershing IIs and the cruise missiles. The second was at the same time to offer to negotiate an agreement that would eliminate the SS-20s and so make deployment of the Pershing IIs and the cruise missiles unnecessary. But no negotiations on theater nuclear weapons took place during the Carter administration.

THE REAGAN ADMINISTRATION

In the Reagan administration the dominant view on arms control was that it had not only failed to help slow down the arms race and thereby lessen the Soviet threat but that it had actually weakened the American strategic position. The Reagan administration was determined to change things, including the names— from SALT, for Strategic Arms Limitation Talks, to START, for Strategic Arms Reduction Talks, and from TNF for Theater Nuclear Forces, to INF, for Intermediate Nuclear Forces.

The first decision the Reagan administration had to make was whether to continue the two-track policy. Support for the arms control track was slight. Powerful right-wingers in Congress were hostile, and equally powerful left-wingers were disillusioned. Some members of Congress and others outside the government also criticized the deployment track. The total warheads for both cruise missiles and the Pershing IIs was 572, which is very close to the number carried by just three Trident submarines. What is more, the submarine-launched missiles would cover most of the same targets, so why raise such a political storm? In spite of the criticism, President Reagan endorsed the two-track approach on the occasion of Prime Minister Margaret Thatcher's visit in February 1981.

A second decision also concerned continuing a Carter administration policy. After SALT I expired in 1977, the Carter administration promised in a unilateral declaration that the United States would adhere to its provisions until a new agreement was reached, as long as the Soviets did the same. Many top Reagan officials, especially in the Pentagon, wanted to do the opposite—they wanted to declare that both SALT I and SALT II were dead. Debate inside the administration on this question of whether to abide by the treaties went on and on, and it was only in a Memorial Day speech a year later that Reagan said that the administration would refrain from actions that would undercut existing arms agreements.

THE ZERO OPTION

The first initiative debated by the Reagan administration concerned the Soviet SS-20s and the deployment of cruise missiles and Pershing IIs as a counter to them. The proposal was the so-called zero option: If the Soviets would agree to dismantle the SS-20s worldwide then the United States would not deploy the cruise missiles and the Pershing IIs.

Again there was a seemingly endless debate, with variations, such as a plan called zero plus, being pushed by one or another faction. Nine months later, however, both the State Department and the Pentagon finally agreed to the original, zero-option proposal, and on November 18, 1981, Reagan delivered a speech endorsing it: If the Soviets would remove their SS-4s, SS-5s, and SS-20s, the United States would not deploy the Pershing IIs and cruise missiles. It was also in this speech that the name changes were made, from SALT to START and from TNF to INF.

The Soviets were not interested in the zero option, and no further progress was made. At one stage Paul Nitze and Yuli Kvitsinsky, the chief negotiators for the INF talks, on their own initiative worked out the so-called "walk-in-the-woods" compromise, but neither Washington nor Moscow accepted it.

The West Germans then proposed an "interim solution." This proposal was that since the zero option was not acceptable the United States should begin to deploy the cruise and Pershing II missiles but toward a ceiling less than the full 572. Prime Minister Margaret Thatcher endorsed the proposal, and on March 30, 1983, Reagan announced the interim solution as a new proposal.

However, earlier that month Reagan had delivered three somewhat belligerent speeches. His March 8 speech called the Soviet Union an "evil empire," his March 11 speech concerned Soviet activities in Latin America, and his March 23 speech, the Star Wars speech, called for a defense against missiles based in space. As a result, the interim solution proposal was apparently either overshadowed, or judged to be insincere. In either case, the Soviets were not interested.

The Bundestag vote on the deployment of the Pershing IIs and cruise missiles was in November 1983, and on November 23, the Soviets walked out of the arms control talks, discontinuing them without setting a date for their resumption. The Pershing II and cruise missiles began to arrive in Europe in January 1984.

THE GENEVA MEETINGS AND RENEWED TALKS

Then, in January 1985, Secretary of State George Shultz and Foreign Minister Andrei Gromyko met in Geneva and quickly agreed on an agenda for a new set of talks to deal with strategic missiles: the Strategic Arms Reduction Talks, talks on intermediate-range missiles, and talks on weapons in space. No one knew why the Soviets decided to resume the talks and why agreement was so quickly reached on the procedures and agenda to be followed. Gorbachev became General Secretary in March 1985, and it is possible that his promotion was already set and that the shift in Soviet negotiating posture on arms control was part of his agenda.

There was also speculation that the breakthrough came because of Soviet fears about the Star Wars proposals. The Soviets were as disbelieving as most American experts that the Star Wars systems would actually work, but even a partial success in developing antimissile defenses would degrade the Soviet ability to deliver warheads on target. Even a partial success would also mean that to stay in relative balance the Soviets would have to spend a great deal of money on countermeasures and on increasing the size of their missile forces in order to deliver the same number of warheads on target.

In June 1985, President Reagan announced that the United States would continue to adhere to the provisions of the unratified SALT II but that it would match any violations by the Soviets.

SALT: AN EVALUATION

The United States entered the SALT negotiations in an attempt to slow down the arms race and to impose some sort of control over the rush of technology to which both powers had become slaves. Presumably the Soviet Union had a similar goal. The negotiations began to go hand in hand with the attempt at political accommodation—détente. As Thomas Wolfe, the author of a RAND study of SALT, pointed out, SALT also began subtly to become a way for each side to further its preferred strategy, a means for correcting weaknesses in its own strategy and force posture and overcoming strengths in the opponent's strategy and force posture.[3]

In trying to slow down the arms race and impose some order on the rush of technology, SALT I's achievement was to put ceilings on strategic missiles and to put a freeze on the deployment of ABM systems. As for the symbiotic relationship between SALT and détente, SALT undoubtedly encouraged both sides in their moves toward détente up to 1972. Thereafter, difficulties in SALT seem to have weakened détente, and difficulties in détente seem to have created obstacles for SALT. The fact that arms control talks subtly became a means for each side to correct weaknesses in its own strategy and force posture and overcome strengths in the other side's strategy and force posture was certainly inevitable. What is more, it might well have been even desirable. The more obvious it became that neither side could really hope to achieve a meaningful superiority in a nuclear age, the more likely it would be that both would benefit from meaningful arms agreements.

The United States hoped that SALT would help to counter the potential Soviet threat to the Minuteman missile force, which probably could not survive a strike by the heavier Soviet missiles. This uneasiness was increased by the Soviet advantage in "throw-weight"; that is, the greater thrust of the heavy Soviet missiles that permitted them to launch much larger payloads. Congress and others also felt increasingly uneasy about the higher ceilings on the number of Soviet missiles permitted to compensate for the technological lead enjoyed by the United States and the Soviet geographical disadvantages. The Americans feared that their technological lead was only temporary, while the higher ceilings might easily become permanent.

The Soviet Union, for its part, hoped that SALT would compensate for the American advantage in certain technologies, although they foresaw that they would be the long-range beneficiaries of MIRV. By the time of the SALT II negotiations, the Soviets had achieved a MIRV capacity and were determined not to give it up. The Soviets also continued to be uneasy about the issue of forward-based aircraft and continued to present their argument that since these could attack the Soviet homeland they should be counted among the strategic weapons.

SUMMIT MEETING AT REYKJAVIK

President Reagan and General Secretary Gorbachev and their top aides met for a summit meeting at Reykjavik, Iceland, in October 1987. In the words of an editorial in *The New York Times* on October 28, 1997 (p. A39), the meeting produced "a roller coaster, first of hope, then disappointment and now confusion." Apparently Reagan went to Iceland expecting that the talks would be specific and narrow. Somehow, he found himself talking with Gorbachev about banning *all* nuclear weapons within ten years.

After the talks, Moscow said that it was indeed the banning of all nuclear weapons that had been discussed with Reagan. At first, Washington said that the talks had been about banning ballistic missiles. Later, Washington admitted that banning all nuclear weapons had been discussed, but only as a "long-term goal." What struck the rest of the world was that someone was not telling the whole truth, since neither the Soviet Union nor the United States would seriously contemplate leaving China, Britain, and France with unopposed nuclear forces, not to mention the countries that were suspected of having developed some sort of nuclear weapons, such as India, Pakistan, Israel, and South Africa.

WASHINGTON IN DECEMBER 1987

Reagan and Gorbachev met again in Washington in December 1987, to sign the INF treaty and agree on the goals for future negotiations on long-range missiles. In the INF treaty that was signed, the United States agreed to withdraw their 108 Pershing IIs stationed in West Germany and their 256 ground-based cruise missiles stationed in several of the Western European countries. For their part, the Soviets agreed to withdraw their 243 SS-20 missiles based in Europe (although they would keep those based in Asia) and to dismantle their 112 SS-4 missiles (already scheduled to be phased out as obsolescent). Both sides agreed to complete the removal of these missiles within three years after the treaty went into effect. They also agreed to withdraw shorter-range missiles with ranges of 300-plus miles from Europe within eighteen months.

The treaty provided for elaborate verification, including on-site inspections, over a period of thirteen years. Monitors were to be stationed outside of one missile factory in each country to make sure no banned missiles were illegally produced. Inspectors from each side were also permitted to visit installations that manufactured launchers for ground-launched cruise missiles. However, the inspectors would not be allowed to go inside factories. There would also be inspections on short notice of the sites where missiles had been based, stored, and repaired. These inspections would continue during the three years allowed for the rockets to be dismantled and for ten years thereafter.

However, even after all these intermediate and 300-plus mile missiles were removed, both sides would still have an awesome array of nuclear weapons targeted on Europe. These included aircraft that could carry nuclear bombs, artillery with nuclear shells, battlefield nuclear missiles, and nuclear land mines, all based in Europe; second, submarines and naval surface ships stationed off the European coast capable of launching aircraft with nuclear bombs or cruise missiles with nuclear warheads; and third, the intercontinental missiles based in the Soviet and American homelands that could be aimed at targets in Europe. In fact, the cynical explanation of why the Soviet Union and the United States agreed to the INF treaty was that the banned weapons were those that were least important to both sides.

On the goals and terms for further negotiations on a strategic arms reduction treaty, Gorbachev and Reagan announced that their goal was to negotiate and sign such a treaty during the first half of 1988. The major obstacle in the past had been Reagan's insistence on going ahead with Star Wars and the Soviet demand that reducing strategic arms should be tied to restrictions on any such missile defense systems. In Washington, the two sides agreed to set a limit of 4,900 on the number of warheads permitted on land-based and sea-based ballistic missiles as a compromise between the American call for a limit of 4,800 and the Soviet call for a limit of 5,100.

To ease problems of verification, the United States agreed to reverse its earlier decision to develop twelve warhead missiles for the Trident submarines and to restrict them to the eight warhead missiles they carried at that time.

Both sides agreed to work out rules for counting the number of warheads on their missiles and the number of nuclear-armed cruise missiles on bombers. The Soviets also agreed not to encode any electronic signals during missile tests, since the United States had charged that such encoding had impeded its ability to monitor Soviet compliance with limits in past treaties.

Four important issues were left unresolved. One was whether mobile, land-based missiles would be permitted under a START agreement. Reagan administration officials said that since mobile missiles are hard to find, they should be banned unless reliable procedures for verification could be developed. Critics, on the other hand, pointed out that this was a contradiction in terms. The very fact that mobile missiles were hard to find was what made them a second-strike weapon; that mobiles made for a stable, mutual deterrent; and that banning them would bring instability. Also, the critics continued, the need to keep ground-based mobile missiles light enough to be mobile prevented them from carrying more than one warhead each, at least given existing technology. Mobiles were therefore "cost effective." An enemy bent on a first strike would have to aim two or more warheads at each mobile missile to destroy just one warhead. A second issue concerned cruise missiles: How do you tell if a cruise missile is carrying a nuclear warhead or a conventional warhead? These questions about both mobile missiles and cruise missiles were connected with the third issue, reliable verification. As for mobile missiles, some of the critics argued that reliable verification is wonderful if you can get it, but reliable verification would also destroy the very quality that makes mobile missiles an important element in an effective deterrent for both sides. Other critics felt that the solution was to allow mobile missiles, but to insist on intrusive verification.

The fourth unresolved question was the one that broke up the Reykjavik meetings: whether the 1972 anti-ballistic missile treaty banned the testing in space needed for Reagan's Star Wars. On this question the two sides agreed to disagree. In a vaguely worded paragraph about the 1972 ABM treaty, the communique said that each side could interpret the treaty as it wished.

START I came into force in December 1994. Presidents Yeltsin, Clinton, and Kravchuk of Ukraine, in January 1994, signed the Trilateral Agreement by which Russia would be the only state of the former Soviet Union to retain nuclear weapons. START II was signed in January 1993, and ratified by the U.S. Congress in

January 1996. The Russian Duma held back on ratification and an effort was made to link a planned Clinton–Yeltsin meeting in 1998 to ratification. At the Helsinki summit meeting in 1997, Clinton and Yeltsin agreed that START III would follow Duma ratification of START II.

In an effort to put pressure on the Duma, which was dominated by a coalition of nationalists and Communists, the Congress had forbidden unilateral Amercan cuts. The cost of not making the cuts mounted to the hundreds of millions, and the Pentagon submitted to Congress a set of propasals for reducing the arsenal unilaterally. By the end of 1998, Russia's economic troubles finally persuaded the Duma to take up the treaty. But if the Duma continued to stall, the Pentagon was determined to take action, if only to modernize its forces.

NOTES

1. On arms control and disarmament, see John Newhouse, *Cold Dawn: The Story of SALT* (New York: Holt, Rinehart and Winston, 1973); Ralph E. Lapp, *Arms Beyond Doubt: The Tyranny of Weapons Technology* (Chicago: Cowles, 1970); Thomas W. Wolfe, *The SALT Experience* (Cambridge, Mass.: Ballinger Publishing, for the RAND Corporation, 1979); Strobe Talbot, *Endgame* (New York: Harper & Row, 1979); Strobe Talbot, *Deadly Gambits* (New York: Knopf, 1984); Alan Platt, *The U.S. Senate and Strategic Arms Policy, 1969–1977* (Boulder, Colo.: Westview Press, 1978); Michael Krepon, *Strategic Stalemate: Nuclear Weapons and Arms Control in American Politics* (New York: St. Martin's Press, 1984); Paul Huth and Bruce Russett, "What Makes Deterrence Work? Cases from 1900 to 1980," *World Politics* (July 1984); and Chihiro Hosoya, "Miscalculations in Deterrence Policy: Japanese–U.S. Relations, 1938–41," *Journal of Peace Research* (1968).

2. Jerome B. Wiesner, "The Glory and the Tragedy of the Partial Test Ban," *The New York Times*, 11 April 1988.

3. This section draws especially on Wolfe, *SALT Experience*.

Chapter 16

The Prospects for Arms Control

The reason that the Soviet Union and the United States made such little progress in reaching meaningful arms control agreements was that both sides looked at any proposal in the context of its own overall military strategy. The Soviets would accept an agreement only if the particular agreement fit with Soviet military strategy in a way that would enhance Soviet security. The United States would accept an agreement only if the agreement fit with American military strategy in a way that would enhance American security.

What made it difficult to craft an agreement that satisfied both sides was that the Soviet and American strategic forces were as difficult to compare as apples and oranges. The Soviet Union relied mainly on heavy, fixed, land-based missiles while the United States relied on the so-called triad of (1) land-based ballistic and cruise missiles, (2) submarine-based ballistic and cruise missiles, and (3) manned bombers carrying both bombs and cruise missiles.

Because of these difficulties there was no easy or obvious solution. Clearly, however, Gorbachev was much more flexible than his predecessors. Hints out of Moscow in 1988 indicated that the Soviets might agree to a number of things that they would not accept in the past, including some of the testing in space that Reagan's Star Wars required. On the U.S. side, Reagan's successor, George Bush, seemed likely to be less rigidly ideological and more flexible than Reagan was. The fate of any particular arms control proposal depended on the political struggle inside each of the two countries.

THE POWER LINE-UP IN THE UNITED STATES

Consider the power line-up in the United States. The most significant point about the different contenders involved in the debate on strategy as opposed to arms control was that their differences stemmed mainly from their different ideological positions. People who supported President Reagan's Star Wars were essentially conservative in the true sense of the word: They were nostalgic for a past that permitted the United States to rely on defense rather than deterrence. They based their hopes on the possibility that technology could take us back to an age when war was at least a tolerable part of the ebb and flow of life. As we said earlier, they wanted to rehabilitate war.

The advocates of no first use were also conservative, and they too wanted to rehabilitate war. The difference was that the advocates of no first use were skeptical that technology could work the miracle of providing 100-percent protection from missiles, and they understood that anything less than 100-percent protection was worthless. But they saw themselves as realists, and as such they could not visualize a world without war of some kind; that is, they could not visualize a world in which the social and political functions of war were performed by some other institution, such as world government.

The advocates of a counterforce strategy were not only conservative, they were also pessimists. They assumed that the Soviets were essentially "evil" and "aggressive" and that there was no hope for either arms control or world government in either the short or the long run. No matter how formidable the problems were, they believed the only solution was to work toward a capability to fight and win nuclear wars.

Advocates of a MAD strategy had more confidence in humanity than most of the others. Some seemed to believe that the leaders of both sides would always be too rational to permit the use of nuclear weapons in any circumstances. Others, however, accepted the possibility that crises, such as the Cuban missile crisis, were bound to occur and that sooner or later one or another would get out of hand. So their hopes were based on the possibility that some combination of both arms control and strengthening of the United Nations would bring a more or less permanent peace.

On arms control as opposed to strategy, the differences between the different factions in the United States were also mainly ideological. Thomas Wolfe, in his analysis of SALT, pointed out that among the various people who held power in the United States a group at one pole believed that nuclear war was unthinkable but accepted the notion that a certain number of missiles were essential for deterrence.[1] They saw only two alternatives for avoiding war: meaningful arms control or MAD. Realistically, they argued, a combination of the two was the only hope. In their view, arms control negotiations should aim at entirely eliminating the destabilizing, first-strike weapons and limiting the numbers of second-strike weapons. Even if one or another unilateral strategy combined with national weapons programs could achieve a high measure of security, which they doubted, it would be accomplished only at the expense of sharply increasing tension in Soviet–American relations, unacceptably high defense expenditures, and a considerable risk of nuclear war. As a result of their analysis, this group would probably have been willing to make significant concessions to achieve even a partial arms control agreement.

At the other extreme were groups that regarded arms control negotiations as necessary for political reasons only. The realistic foundation for effective deterrence, in this view, was unilateral strategic planning and weapons programs. Concessions for the sake of an agreement, they believed, would actually destabilize the world balance of power, damage U.S. security, and increase the risk of nuclear war. They argued that since Soviet–American relations were basically a function of the relative strength of the two powers and not a function of good feelings generated by agreements for the sake of agreements, any failure to achieve an agreement would not fundamentally affect those relations. Similarly, they argued that failure would not generate an arms race since the agreements reached in the past had always been tailored to each side's strategic planning. Sound strategy and weapons programs, they maintained, would not only deter aggression but avoid an arms race as well.

In the middle were people who regarded arms control negotiations as useful for formalizing changes in the strategic balance brought about by each side's unilateral efforts and for laying down the boundaries for Soviet–American competition. In this view, arms control agreements should not be seen as an instrument for solving either strategic or political problems. The value of such agreements should be understood as merely formalizing the areas of both competition and cooperation.

THE "MILITARY–INDUSTRIAL COMPLEX"

Any analysis of the power line-up on arms control in this period must also consider what President Eisenhower warned against in his farewell address: the "military–industrial complex."

At the outset it should be noted that there was nothing sinister in this informal military–industrial alliance. The military had been given responsibility for the nation's security, and it was their duty to fight hard for strong defenses, large armies, navies, and air forces, and the latest, most powerful, and most sophisticated weapons.[2] They would be skeptical about arms control agreements and diligent in examining such agreements for loopholes and hidden advantages for the other side. Indeed, if they were not, most people would ask whether they were doing their job.

The individual military services rightly fought for their particular weapons. The Air Force fought for manned bombers like the B-1, the Navy fought for missile-carrying submarines like the Trident and for aircraft carriers, and the Army fought for tanks and battlefield nuclear weapons. On such questions the military was able to wield great power. The subject was the security of the nation, and they were the experts on the subject. To oppose them on the narrow field of weapons was difficult and politically dangerous.

The industrial side of the complex was equally predictable. Inevitably, aircraft and missile manufacturers would favor large air forces and missile arsenals. The people who made submarines and aircraft carriers would favor strong navies. Those who made tanks and artillery would favor large armies. And these industries would quarrel among themselves about the relative merits of the weapons they produced.

The military industries also exercised great power. They commanded all the national security and patriotic arguments that the military did, and they also had economic arguments. A large military budget not only meant high industrial profits, it meant jobs. The unions associated with those industries were powerful allies and so were the merchants and operators of business in regions in which the factories were located. The members of Congress from those districts were diligent lobbyists for the cause and powerful allies.

The point was made in down-to-earth terms by Representative Joseph P. Addabbo, a Democrat from Queens who was head of the appropriations subcommittee on defense. On a visit to the headquarters of the Rockwell International Corporation, he noticed a map of the United States with strings radiating from the plant to every subcontractor that made a part of the B-1 bomber. The strings covered the entire map. Later, when he was leading a fight to kill the B-1 bomber program, the consequences of all those strings came home to him: "One by one I was losing members," he recalled. "They said to me, 'Joe, they've built a plant in my district. I need the jobs.'"[3]

Both the military and the industries associated with it were likely to have strong views on arms control issues, and their views were likely to be on the hawk side. However, two final observations must be made. The first is that the leverage the military–industrial complex was able to exercise in support of their views varied with how directly the issue related to defense. On a question of foreign policy that concerned something like bases overseas or troops stationed in Germany or Korea, the military and their industrial allies exercised great influence. For years a number of powerful people favored drastically reducing American troops stationed in Germany and Korea; returning to Japan its sovereignty over Okinawa, where the United States had a huge base; and cutting down the use of bases in the Philippines, the Portuguese Azores, and elsewhere. Among these powerful people were Mike Mansfield, for many years majority leader of the Senate; J. William Fulbright, chairman of the Senate Foreign Relations Committee; other leaders in both the Senate and the House; presidents and others in the White House; top officials in the State Department; and prominent persons in the newspaper and academic worlds and among the attentive publics. But the military and their allies in industry and Congress fought all these reductions and succeeded in preventing many of them and delaying the rest. On the other hand, on foreign policy and national security issues less directly related to military defense, the leverage of the military–industrial complex was not so great. An example was détente. Thus, if the issue in arms control was a narrow one concerning a particular set of weapons, the influence of the military–industrial complex was likely to be high. But if the issue was set in a broader context, such as détente and overall relations with the Soviet Union, their influence was much less.

The second observation to be made is that it is a mistake to assume that the military was always hawkish on all issues. In 1965, when President Johnson decided to bomb North Vietnam and then to send in American ground combat forces, the military were decidedly unenthusiastic, and President Johnson engaged in elaborate political maneuvers to split the Joint Chiefs of Staff and so nullify their opposition.[4] Of course, once the United States was committed to the war in Vietnam, the military pressed hard for whatever forces were needed to win a victory. To give another example, in late 1984 and early 1985, Secretary of Defense Caspar W. "Cap" Weinberger and Secretary of State George P. Shultz engaged in a rather sharp public debate on the use of force. But it was the secretary of state who took the more hawkish position, and the secretary of defense who took the more dovish.

In general, the military–industrial complex has favored a high level of preparedness and "tough" foreign policies, but they have usually shied away from actions that seem to lead directly to war. Thus, there seemed to be no obvious reason that the United States would not be able to reach a meaningful arms control agreement with the Soviet Union sooner or later.

Consider, for example, the Reagan administration. President Reagan and his administration were more heavily influenced by ideology than any administration of recent memory. Reagan called the Soviet Union an "evil empire," and a large number of the top posts in the administration were held by people who were convinced that the Soviet Union was committed to extending Communist rule throughout the world and that it simply could not be trusted. Reagan also had an almost religious faith in the capacity of American science and technology to produce an effective Star Wars defense. Many in his administration shared his belief, and others who did not still supported it because they believed that even a partial defense against missiles would enhance the American deterrent. But in spite of all these hawkish views, the Reagan administration moved toward accommodation with the Soviets.

Future administrations are likely to be more flexible from the beginning, and even if they are not, they are likely to become more flexible with their years in office, as the Reagan administration did. The Bush administration is an example. There was little in Bush's background or in his presidential campaign of 1988 that indicated that Bush had some grand plan for arms control and détente. When Gorbachev made his series of proposals, the reaction of President Bush and most of the top members of his administration was one of reluctance. But as a practical political matter, they were forced to go along with most of the Gorbachev proposals.

THE SOVIET UNION

In the Soviet Union the power line-up on questions of arms control was very similar to that in the United States. Although it is much more difficult to pin-point the evidence, what is available suggests that different groups in the Soviet Union also supported different strategies. The debates were less open, but at different times various groups inside the Soviet Union argued about the same questions of strategy debated in the United States: whether nuclear weapons should be used at the outset of a war in Europe, whether the Soviet Union should build an antimissile defense, a shelter program, and so on. They also argued about the various proposals for arms control, and in much the same way as the rival factions did in the United States. As we say, the debates were not public, but the evidence that they took place is conclusive.

However, with the breakup of the Soviet Union the question of its power line-up becomes moot.

CONCLUSION

It seems obvious that a combination of fear and ambition made the members of the nuclear club unwilling to give up their weapons and has made many non-members anxious to join the nuclear club themselves, especially Third World states that feel threatened by traditional enemies. Given the situation, it seems obvious that arms control agreements by themselves will not solve the dilemma that nuclear weapons and ballistic missiles pose to humankind.

However, some progress in arms control is possible and worth pursuing. For example, it would be a mark of progress if an agreement could be reached not to work on weapons that are theoretically possible but that have not yet been developed. As a practical political matter, it is easier to ban work on such weapons that are possible but not yet developed than to abolish weapons that are either ready for production or already deployed.

Arms control agreements can also bring about reductions in numbers of weapons or even on occasion the dismantling of some kinds of weapons, as the INF agreement did. These agreements can also extend the time in which the situation of MAD (as opposed to a MAD strategy) postpones crises and mutes those that do come.

But even the very best arms control agreements would leave a world of sovereign nation-states, and even with arms control many of these states would still have the scientific and technical capability to build nuclear weapons rather quickly once a war started. Arms control agreements do not prevent rivalries between nation-states nor do they make any special contribution to solving crises when they occur. Even with the best of arms control agreements, crises will occur. And sooner or later one or another crisis will get out of hand.

The conclusion seems inescapable. Humankind must strive for effective arms control agreements, but arms control is not—and can never be—enough. What is really needed is an alternative to war.

NOTES

1. This section draws on Thomas W. Wolfe, *The SALT Experience* (Cambridge, Mass.: Ballinger Publishing, for the RAND Corporation, 1979).

2. In addition to the works cited in earlier chapters, see Adam Yarmolinsky, *The Military Establishment: Its Impact on American Society* (New York: Harper & Row, 1971); Henry L. Trewitt, *McNamara: His Ordeal in the Pentagon* (New York: Harper & Row, 1971); Bruce M. Russett, *What Price Vigilance? The Burden of National Defense* (New Haven: Yale University Press, 1970).

3. *The New York Times*, 17 May 1985, p. 1.

4. For a detailed description of Johnson's maneuvers, see Roger Hilsman, *The Politics of Policy Making in Defense and Foreign Affairs: Conceptual Models and Bureaucratic Politics*, 3d ed. (Englewood Cliffs, N.J.: Prentice Hall, 1993), 99–102.

PART VI

WHY WAR?

Chapter 17

The Social and Political Functions of War

Why war? Individuals in most species fight one on one for food or territory and males for access to a female. A number of the different ungulates that travel in herds will protect themselves and their young by facing a predator shoulder to shoulder. Some ants seem to fight as colonies against other colonies. And on at least one occasion scientists have seen a pack of chimpanzees attack another pack. But in the millions upon millions of years that life has existed on the planet earth and among the millions and millions of different species that have come and gone, our species, *Homo sapiens sapiens*, appears to be the only one that institutionalized violence as war. Why?

War is not just casual physical violence between individuals. War is not the use of violence by a sib of Cro-Magnons fighting a sib of Neanderthals over an animal carcass or the use of violence by a band of outlaws robbing a stagecoach. War is violence that is highly organized by whole societies and directed against other societies for political and social ends.

Civil war is much the same. Civil war is not a mob in the streets demonstrating for or against something, even though the mob may use violence. The campus riots in the late 1960s protesting the war in Vietnam did not add up to civil war, even though they were often violent and on at least one occasion resulted in people being killed. The American Civil War, for example, was more like an international war than riots or civil disobedience. A part of the nation, the Southern states, that controlled an expanse of territory, reorganized itself into a separate political entity, the Confederacy, and fought to make its independent existence permanent.

Perhaps the answer to the question, "Why war?" lies somewhere here, in the presence or absence of statehood and government. In the past, political thinkers, beginning with Socrates, Plato, and Aristotle, asked the question, "Why should people have a government (or political system) at all?" For many political thinkers the answer was, "to keep the peace" or, in the words of the American Constitution, to "insure domestic Tranquility." It is a commonsense observation that societies with a working government and political system do indeed keep the peace within their borders more effectively than those societies without a working government and political system.

It is also a commonsense observation that large-scale, organized violence between two or more established societies—war—is more frequent than large-scale, organized violence within one particular established society—civil war. The United States, for example, has fought only one civil war since it was founded. But it has fought a foreign war in almost every generation, and in recent decades even more frequently than that.

There are problems in defining war: Do you include a border clash in which people are killed? There are problems in defining civil war: Do you include riots in which people are killed? And there are problems in defining an "established society." For example, there is an independence movement in the French-speaking part of Canada. Does this mean that Canada is not an "established society?" But in spite of the problems of definition, a well-established society with a working government and political system keeps the peace with only rare exceptions.

Why is this? Why have societies with a working government and political system been able to avoid large-scale, organized violence within their borders for long periods of time while the international community has failed so miserably to avoid such violence between states? And what is the difference between "established" states that have been able to avoid large-scale, organized violence within their borders and those that have not?

THOMAS HOBBES'S ANSWER: GOVERNMENT

One answer to the first question is that established states are ruled by governments that control police and armies to enforce their will. This was the answer given by the English philosopher, Thomas Hobbes. In his book, *Leviathan*, Hobbes argued that human beings are selfish and are moved chiefly either by a desire for power or by fear. Without an all-powerful sovereign to rule, he argued, a stable society free of organized violence would be impossible. People's lives, he said, would be "poor, nasty, brutish, and short."

ANOTHER ANSWER: SHARED VALUES

Other political philosophers have denied that stable societies can be established only through fear of the great "Hobbesian fist." The police forces of a state are small compared to the total population, so it seems obvious that established societies function peaceably at least partly because all but a tiny fraction of the people are generally law abiding and reasonably honest. It seems clear that members of a stable society share a consensus that the political system itself is worth preserving. Except in rare times that lead to civil war, they do not push their differences so far as to threaten the society itself.

Some of the citizenry value the political system as an end in itself. Others value it as a means to other ends. Those who value the system as an end in itself believe that the overall political system is of more value than the particular goal they have been unsuccessfully seeking. They will pull back rather than try to overthrow the system itself. They are also usually willing to settle for half a loaf, at least for the time being.

Those who value the system as a means tend to believe that the political system is malleable enough that sooner or later they will be successful in getting what they want through that system, as opposed to getting what they want by destroying the system. For example, the decades-long disputes over the rights of labor and over civil rights for blacks were bitter and often violent, but even the most bitter advocates and opponents of trade unions and civil rights rarely went so far as to try to overthrow the government itself.

This second characteristic—that most members of a working political system share a desire to preserve it—implies that the citizenry share other values as well as valuing the system. It seems obvious that the members of stable, working societies share concepts of right and wrong, fairness, and similar values and goals. Thus, solutions to social problems that bring even profound social and political changes are more often than not consistent with traditional goals and traditional notions of legitimate authority. Communist China under Mao Zedong, for example, probably underwent the most radical revolution of any country in recent times. But it is clear that Communist China is as much the child of Confucius as it is of Karl Marx.

Each of these two answers—Hobbes's fist and shared values—suggests its own reason why there have been so many more international wars than civil wars. Hobbes's fist suggests that the reason for international wars is the absence of a world government with, in Max Weber's phrase, "a monopoly of the use of legitimate force." Shared values suggests that wars arise from the obvious fact that the whole of humankind does not share as many values as the citizenry of an established state.

Although the U.N. General Assembly and Security Council have certain legislative functions and the International Court of Justice has certain judicial functions, both are limited. As a consequence, the United Nations does not constitute a government in the usual sense of the word. The United Nations also lacks the means to make its decisions binding. The international community does not control either a police force or an army, navy, and air force. Similarly, although humankind as a whole undoubtedly shares many values and goals, these are only a fraction of those shared by the members of an established society.

THE HISTORICAL REASONS FOR WAR

Clausewitz argued that war is the continuation of state policy by other means. But the historical record suggests a larger role, that wars and civil wars have been used to bring about—or to prevent—political and social change. War was the instrument for creating nation-states by aggregating feudal principalities or by breaking up dynastic empires. An example of the first is the Franco–Prussian War, which created modern Germany. An example of the second is World War I, which created several nation-states out of the old Austro–Hungarian empire.

War has been an instrument for spreading religion. It has been an instrument for spreading ideology—using the word in the sense of a systematic set of beliefs, such as capitalism, Nazism, or communism. War was the major vehicle for extending the dominance of Western civilization and for spreading its high valuation of modernization, its technology, and its mode of life. War has been the means for adding to the power of one state at the expense of another. Hitler and the Japanese militarists used war to try to create a new kind of empire, a new political and ideological dominance, and a new distribution of power. The Allies responded with war to prevent them from succeeding. War and civil war have replaced kings and emperors with parliaments and presidents. War and civil war have also replaced parliaments and presidents with storm troopers and dictators. War and civil war have shifted the locus of power within societies as well as between them. Warfare, in a word, has been an instrument for national policy and the midwife of social and political change, for both good and evil.

NUCLEAR WAR AS THE MIDWIFE OF CHANGE

Yet to speak of nuclear war as being either an instrument of national policy or the midwife of social and political change is only to be macabre. The fact that nuclear war is too costly to serve the functions that war has served in the past settles nothing. The threat of nuclear war remains. What the costliness of nuclear war does eliminate is any *rational* motive for war. It is difficult to imagine a rational leader of a country risking 50-percent casualties for a possible gain in territory, economic advantage, national prestige, an increase in national power, or to proselytize for religion or ideology.

The only possibly rational motive for nuclear war that remains is fear. Circumstances are at least conceivable in which the leaders of a state could come to see the choice before them as either accepting the risk of 50-percent casualties on the one hand, or, on the other, the certainty of total annihilation, and reluctantly deciding to choose the risk of 50-percent casualties.

As we said earlier, it is doubtful that either the Soviet or American military commanders would have obeyed an order to strike "out of the blue," although what they would do naturally depends on the evidence they had that the enemy had launched a first strike or was counting down for one. And it is especially doubtful that they would have obeyed such an order if they thought their leader was a madman. So, barring only the rise to power in a major state of a madman whose madness the military did not recognize, even fear seems an inadequate motive for a decision to initiate a war with nuclear weapons. If so, nuclear war seems most likely to occur in the midst of a lesser war which was itself the result of a series of incremental decisions, each one of which seemed reasonable at the time to reasonable though very anxious men and women.

In wars, miscalculations are common and inevitable. In an earlier age a miscalculation in the midst of war could have gruesome consequences. But in a nuclear age a miscalculation in the midst of an ordinary, conventional war could escalate the war into a holocaust for at least one or the other hemisphere and conceivably for the entire planet.

And there is the rub: the likelihood that nuclear war will come in the midst of lesser wars. Nonnuclear, limited, conventional war still can serve as the instrument for social and political change, and the leaders of states, great and small, still can and do believe that nonnuclear war can be used to accomplish the social and political goals for which war has been used in the past. Their only concern is that the risks of nonnuclear war escalating into nuclear war be manageable. The trouble is twofold. The first is that such a judgment that cannot always be calculated with complete precision. The second is that the leaders of states will sometimes think it can.

WAR AND THE STATE SYSTEM

The existence of war as an institution is related to the way the world is organized politically. In any political system composed of sovereign states, war is endemic. This is true whether the states are cities, empires, or nations. If the world is organized as a system of states, then war and the threat of war are inevitable.

In the past, wars have been fought, as we said, for territory, for economic advantage, for prestige, to proselyte for both religion and ideology, for power, and out of fear. And in the course of making decisions to go to war, every conceivable human emotion has undoubtedly contributed: hate, revenge, greed, envy, pride, fear (and through fear, love), and, in all likelihood, deep primordial aggressiveness and a sadistic fascination with violence. But neither the motives for war nor humankind's instincts toward violence have much to do with the fact that war is endemic to state systems. Most of the motives for war and all of the emotions surrounding it work on humankind acting as individuals or as members of a vast variety of different groups and organizations: fraternal organizations, mutual protective societies, business firms, trade unions, political parties, special-interest groups like the National Rifle Association, neighborhood and community organizations, and even Boy Scout troops. As a result, violence also occurs, between individuals and between groups and organizations. On occasion, the violence is organized and sustained. And sometimes it takes place on so large a scale that it is hard to distinguish it from war. Examples are not only revolution, rebellion, and civil war, but even some other phenomena, such as the strikes and strikebreaking that marked the rise of the trade union movement. But even though large-scale, organized violence sometimes occurs between groups of men and women organized in other ways than as sovereign states, war is not endemic to those relations.

War in this sense of large-scale, organized violence is endemic to state systems for two fundamental reasons. One concerns the absurdly elementary but intensely practical problem of acquiring and maintaining the means for large-scale, organized violence. In any dispute between human beings, violence is the ultimate arbiter. But what makes the state unique among humankind's infinitely varied organizations is that the state alone possesses, to repeat Max Weber's phrase, the "monopoly of legal violence." The state is consequently the legal and political authority for developing the means, both the material means and the manpower means through compulsory military service, necessary for the large-scale, organized violence that is war.

As a practical matter it is extremely difficult for an insurgent movement to manufacture, buy, or steal even the hand weapons and ammunition needed for large-scale, sustained combat. And it is only in quite extraordinary circumstances that an insurgent movement can manage to acquire machine guns, artillery, tanks, military aircraft, missiles, or nuclear weapons. To do so, the insurgents would have to subvert a substantial portion of the armed services already possessing the weapons or to seize a territorial base large enough to provide the necessary resources and to hold it long enough to develop a rival arsenal of its own.

If the insurgents acquire the weapons from an outside power, the situation will increasingly resemble international war rather than intrastate or civil war. International law holds that if a state permits its territory to be used so as to harm another state, the aggrieved state may take such action to protect itself as is necessary. For example, if a factory in Canada just north of the border with the United States is belching smoke and ash that falls on fields south of the border on U.S. soil and if Canada refuses or is unable to do something about the factory, then the United States has the right under international law to use force across the border to shut the factory down.

In the last few years Canada has demonstrated that its fields, lakes, and forests are suffering from acid rain caused by the discharge from American factories. If the United States continues to do nothing, Canada has the legal right under international law to invade the United States and shut down the factories itself. The reason that Canada is unlikely to take such action is a question not of legality, but of Canadians' sense of what is fitting and of relative power. It is conceivable that the Canadian people could become so incensed that they would come to believe that only force could solve the problem. But it is *not* conceivable that they would not recognize their hopeless inferiority in military power.

This same principle of international law was the legal justification for U.S. punitive expedition against Mexico just prior to World War I. The bandit Pancho Villa had raided a Texas town across the border, and the Mexican government of the time was not able to guarantee that he would not do so again. So the United States acted, under the sanction of international law.

Another example is the U.S. intervention in Vietnam. It is of course arguable whether South Vietnam had become a sovereign state as a result of the Geneva Agreements of 1954. But if it is accepted that it had, then the fact that North

Vietnam permitted its territory to be used for training the Viet Cong and supplied them with weapons and equipment had two consequences under international law. The first was that South Vietnam had the legal right both to ask the
United States to bomb North Vietnam, even though North Vietnam had not yet
attacked South Vietnam with its own troops, and to invite the United States to
send troops to South Vietnam to help in its defense. And, given the premise, the
United States had a legal right to accede to the request, however unwise the
action was politically or questionable in moral terms.

The same argument could have been used by Cuba against the United States
at the time of the Bay of Pigs incident. The fact that the American CIA trained
and supplied the Cubans who landed at the Bay of Pigs gave Cuba the legal right
to retaliate against the United States or to try to persuade some other country—
the Soviet Union, for example—to retaliate on its behalf.

THE ROLE OF LAW AND POLITICS

If the first reason that war is not endemic between groups inside an established
state is the practical difficulty of acquiring the means for waging it, the second is
that the incentive for groups living within an established state to wage war on
each other is significantly reduced by the fact that for most disagreements or
grievances other arbiters exist that are more or less satisfactory alternatives to the
risk inherent in an attempt at large-scale violence. Principally, these alternatives
are law and politics.

All states—dictatorships as well as democracies—have legal systems that provide an opportunity to redress certain kinds of grievances and to settle certain
kinds of disputes. The law may cover a wider range of disputes in one country
than in another, and it may be more just and impartially enforced in one country
than in another. But in even the most authoritarian of states, law provides an
alternative arbiter to the use of force for certain kinds of disputes, depending on
the particular state.

All states also have political systems, and no matter whether it is authoritarian
or democratic, a political system serves as an alternative arbiter to war for most
groups in the society that have the potential for organized violence. The point is
that a political system provides the means by which one group or the other can
acquire the political power to achieve its goal without the use of large-scale, organized violence. In one state the political system may involve elections, in another
using connections to enable one to have access to a king or dictator, and in a
third, behind-the-scenes maneuvering for allies in the secret police and the army
in preparation for a coup d'état. But in all three the social function is the same. In
all three there may also be violence—whether campus riots, street fighting, or the
murder of a king in the palace corridor—but it is not the large-scale, organized
violence of war.

Law and politics, of course, are also present in the relations between states. A
wide variety of disputes are settled by appeals to international law, and certainly

there is politics between states in the sense that states maneuver for support from other states, bargain, make deals, and even attempt to affect public opinion in other states and so to go over the heads of the governments. But there is a difference. Only minor matters have so far been settled by the International Court of Justice, and politics among nations has not been so much the politics of persuasion as the politics of force and violence and of manipulating threats of force and violence.

Although war itself, the actual use of force, is comparatively infrequent, the threat of force is present behind most international political maneuvers and negotiations. The difference goes back to the fact that the state has the monopoly of legal violence. Law can be a successful arbiter on weighty questions within a state in those cases when force, held by the state, stands behind the law and above the disputants. In international politics, the force that is present stands not behind the law and above the disputants, but is held by the disputants themselves.

Politics can even be a successful arbiter within a state when the struggle is among groups whose dispute is about who shall control the state, including its monopoly of legal violence, even though none of the contenders has arms of its own. In international politics, on the other hand, the struggle is never between unarmed contestants, but always between groups that have not only the right to maintain armed forces, but the duty to do so.

If both the legal and political systems of a state fail to provide satisfaction for important, deeply held aspirations of a significant group within the population over a sufficiently long time, violence will eventually ensue. The form it takes may be individual acts of terrorism, assassination, arson, bombings, strikes, and riots. But, as suggested, for an insurgent movement to transform its actions into full-scale revolution and civil war it will need the weapons of war rather than those of terror: machine guns, tanks, artillery, and military aircraft. If these are acquired from an outside power, the situation will begin to resemble interstate war rather than civil war or revolution.

CONCLUSION

War is not just casual physical violence between individuals or groups of individuals. It is highly organized violence used to attain social and political ends and directed by whole societies against other societies or by large groups within a society against other large groups. As a result, war and the threat of war will continue to be the central dynamism of international politics—simply because it *is* politics, although it is politics between nations rather than between groups within a nation.

But if humankind continues to accept war as an inevitable fact of existence, as part of life no more susceptible to manipulation than gravity, then not just war but nuclear war will be a part of the future. As we saw, arms control is helpful. If the leaders of the United States, Russia, other nuclear powers recognize the dangers of nuclear war, they may succeed in avoiding particular wars. But neither arms control nor recognizing the dangers of nuclear war addresses the root causes of war, and these conditions could not by themselves eliminate war entirely.

It is no accident, in sum, that the large-scale, organized violence that is war is endemic to state systems. Nor is it an accident that the similar large-scale, organized violence of civil war and revolution is exceptional within a single state. It is reasonable and plausible to hope that levels of organized violence resembling war can be effectively abolished within a single state, no matter how turbulent and aggressive its people. Within a state *system*, it is not. A conspiracy of unfortunate events can on occasion bring violence at the level of war within a single state. Within a state system it takes a conspiracy of fortunate events to avoid it.

The conclusion is obvious: The only measure that humankind can take to rid itself of the threat of nuclear war in the long run is to establish a government and political system for the planet as a whole.

Chapter 18

Nationalism

If the most effective measure that humankind can take to rid itself of the threat of nuclear war is to establish a government and political system for the planet as a whole, what are the prospects for doing this? Obviously, the problems in achieving a world government are awesome. In the first place, the record of both the League of Nations and the United Nations in keeping the peace is not encouraging. When one reflects on the cultural, religious, and political differences among the countries of the world, the probability of unifying them all without the use of force seems small indeed. And if force had to be used, the cost would probably be destruction and death as widespread as in nuclear war itself.

Even if a single world government is established, what reason is there to hope that endless civil war would not follow? Established states have avoided civil war, but the words "established state" presume a relatively homogeneous citizenry and a working political system. The history of "new" states that came into being after World War II is an endless repetition of civil war and insurrection. Malaysia, the Philippines, Burma, Indonesia, India, Sri Lanka, Nigeria, the Sudan, the Congo, Angola, Ethiopia, Somalia, and so on down a long, long list—all had civil wars or rebellions. And this does not include the wars in Korea and Vietnam, since they were as much international as civil wars. If you add the civil wars among "older" states that do not fit our definition of "established states," such as China, Cuba, Nicaragua, El Salvador, and Yugoslavia, the list almost doubles.

But in spite of this dismal historical record, the consequences if humankind continues to fight wars as it has in the past are so horrifying that even the slimmest chance of unification through some sort of world government is worth pursuing. If we understood the obstacles better we might find a way around them.

NATIONALISM

Of all the obstacles to unifying humankind, the most formidable is undoubtedly nationalism.[1] In Chapter 10, we mentioned the role played by nationalism in the breakup of the Soviet Union, but to understand just how formidable an obstacle it is to world government requires a closer look at the history of nationalism, its connections to the process of modernization, and why it has such a firm and peculiar grip on the citizens of a nation-state.

Most humans throughout most of history have had few political loyalties beyond their immediate family and local community. Throughout most of history, the peasants of Europe, Asia, Africa, and the Western Hemisphere identified with and loved a village or locality and were unaware or indifferent to any larger government that may have ruled over them. But on occasion humans have given loyalty to something larger than the family and local community—at different times, to the tribe, city–state, feudal lord, church, king, or emperor. Sometimes the forces generating larger political loyalties have been economic, sometimes religious, sometimes ideological. But the force that has been the most potent of all in generating larger loyalties is nationalism.

Nationalism has made big states out of little ones. Germany and Italy, for example, were only geographic expressions like Asia, Europe, and the Americas until nationalism swept away the feudal principalities and forged states where none had existed before. And nationalism has made small states out of big ones. The Austro–Hungarian empire, for example, was divided into six nation-states just after World War I, and the breakup of Czechoslovakia and Yugoslavia is producing even more. The Ottoman empire, to give another example, was shrunk to Turkey, while various other parts became independent states.

The most striking thing about nationalism is how very recent a phenomenon it is. We think of it as old, but if a careful distinction is made between a sense of shared identity and the true phenomenon of nationalism, no shred of evidence can be found of nationalism anywhere in the world earlier than two centuries ago, and some nationalisms are no older than two or three decades. The Chinese, French, Japanese, and many other peoples have had a sense of common identity going back many centuries and in some cases perhaps even millennia. But their sense of common identity had no more operational political significance than today's shared sense of identity among Europeans, Asians, or Africans.

We think of nationalism as old partly because nationalists have a compelling need to foster myths about their nations. "We imagine the past," L. B. Namier once said, "and remember the future."[2] For nationalism and nationalists, at least the first part of the aphorism is supremely true. It suited De Gaulle's purpose, for example, to evoke Joan of Arc as a French patriot. But in truth, as the French historian Charles Seignobos testifies, Joan herself was loyal not to France, which was in her time not very much more than a geographical expression, but to the king of the Armagnac party, which was at war with the Burgundian party, who were allies of the English.[3] Seignobos maintains that the Hundred Years' War had no effect on the development of the French nation. "This war," he writes, "carried on by adventurers with no national character, was a war between two royal families rather than between two nations." The hostility toward the English, he argues, came from local patriotism, not national.

To give a more recent example, it suited Nkrumah's political purposes to change the name of the newly independent Gold Coast to Ghana, but the truth is that the medieval empire that was Ghana probably embraced little if any territory controlled by the present state.

In his monumental study of the origins of nationalism, Hans Kohn found in the history of France and England nothing at all, whether in song, poetry, or historical documents, suggesting the modern concept of nationalism before the middle of the eighteenth century. In America, the colonists had no sense of loyalty to America as a nation, but only to the individual colony. In 1760, the father of Gouverneur Morris provided in his will that his son, the signer of the Declaration of Independence, never be allowed to visit Connecticut so as to avoid the danger of his being infected with "that low craft and cunning so incident to the people of that country."

The historians of nationalism and the historians of the American revolution agree that nationalism had little role in the American struggle for independence.[4] Nationalism, as we know it, then, began in the latter half of the eighteenth century in Western Europe. As good a date as any is 1789.

THE NATURE OF NATIONALISM

Louis L. Snyder, in the introduction to his *The Dynamics of Nationalism*, defines nationalism as "a condition of mind, feeling or sentiment of a group of people in a well-defined geographic area, speaking a common language, possessing a literature in which the aspirations of the nation have been expressed, being attached to common traditions, and, in some cases, having a common religion," although he hastens to add that there are exceptions to every part of his definition.[5]

Carlton J. H. Hayes speaks of cultural and historical forces, by which he means language and historical traditions, including religious past, territorial past, political past, and economic and industrial past.[6]

Rupert Emerson speaks of an "ideal model" of a nation, "a single people, traditionally fixed on a well-defined territory, speaking the same language and preferably a language all its own, possessing a distinctive culture, and shaped to a common mold by many generations of shared historical experience."[7] Pointing out that no such nation ever existed in total purity, he goes on to identify four elements "which insistently recur as essential to the creation of a sense of common destiny": territory, language, a common historical tradition, and "the intricate interconnections of state and nation." Elements that have appeared with "less regularity and whose relevance for this purpose is more dubious are race, religion, and a common economic system."

The four elements that historians most frequently cite—common language and literature; common religion; shared history, culture, and traditions; and territory and statehood—are not, as Dankwart A. Rustow has pointed out, "among the defining characteristics of a nation," but they are "likely to promote feelings of nationality."[8]

LANGUAGE AND LITERATURE

Certainly, the birth of nationalism in Western Europe was vastly aided in most cases by a common language and literature. This was true in those cases in which a state already existed—such as France, the Netherlands, Spain, Portugal, and Great Britain (where English had already replaced Scottish, Welsh, and Cornish as a practical matter)—and also in those cases in which a single state did not yet exist, such as Poland, Germany, and Italy. It was aided even more if the language was spoken only in the one area and nowhere else. This was true in all these cases, and this provided dramatic evidence of a people's similarities to each other and differences from their neighbors.

But distinct nationalisms have also developed in neighboring states sharing the same language and literature, notably in Latin America. And, of course, nationalism has also triumphed where there was no common language at all. In Switzerland, four different languages are spoken—French, German, Italian, and Rhaeto-Romansh—each in different cantons, and yet a nationalism arose that is peculiarly Swiss. Similarly, in Belgium, where two different languages are spoken, a peculiarly Belgian nationalism arose.

In one or two cases, nationalism can be said to have facilitated the spread of language rather than the other way around. In Ireland, the revival of Irish was motivated solely by Irish nationalism and hatred of the English. Kohn also cites the case of Norway and Denmark, whose people were of "common racial stock" and who spoke almost the same language. "Nevertheless," as Kohn says, "they consider themselves as two nationalities, and the Norwegians set up their own language only as the result of having become a nationality."[9]

RELIGION

Although not nearly so influential as language, religion has clearly played a role in the development of nationalism and continues to do so. Kohn credits religion as being one of the major factors in giving the Catholic Croats and the Orthodox Serbs a different sense of national identity and also in the separate development of the Netherlands and Belgium.

Ireland and Israel are other examples where religion played a major role. It might also be noted that the sole reason for the formation of Pakistan as a state was a common adherence to Islam and fear of Hindu domination. It is too early to speak of Pakistani nationalism, even in the western remnant surviving the secession of Bangladesh, but if nationalism does develop, religion will have played a central role.

SHARED HISTORY, CULTURE, AND TRADITIONS

Shared history, culture, and traditions also facilitate the growth of nationalism. In a number of countries, such as Japan, Hungary, Thailand, and Ireland, a sense of common identity existed long before modern times and long before what we think of as nationalism arose in those countries. Shared history, culture, and traditions were important factors in creating that sense of identity. Usually, a distinct language was also present, but not always—as mentioned, Irish was revived in Ireland as a *result* of nationalism.

But none of these three factors seems to be particularly powerful. First, in many countries the mass of the people had no identification with history until nationalism gave it to them. To the extent that the Prussians and Bavarians or Bretons and Burgundians considered that they shared a history with anyone it was with fellow Prussians, Bavarians, Bretons, and Burgundians, not with fellow Germans and fellow Frenchmen. Boyd C. Shafer contends that for most contemporary European peoples a common group history is almost wholly fictional if it is pressed back much beyond the nineteenth century. "The belief is real," he writes, "the actuality never existed."[10]

Second, as we have seen, some so-called shared history as a nationality was manufactured and some of the myths of nationalism were created, consciously or unconsciously, by nationalists precisely to further nationalism.

An even more dramatic example than those given is Turkey. Kemal Ataturk offered a theory that the Turks were a white, Aryan people, originating in Central Asia, and that they migrated to various parts of Asia as the bearers of civilization. As Bernard Lewis says, Ataturk maintained that the Chinese, Indian, and Middle Eastern civilizations had all been founded in this way, with the Middle Eastern pioneers being the Sumerians and Hittites, who were, according to Ataturk, both Turkic peoples. Anatolia, in Ataturk's view, had thus been a Turkish land since antiquity. "This mixture of truth, half-truth, and error," Lewis writes, "was proclaimed as official doctrine, and teams of researchers set to work to 'prove' its various propositions."[11] With the same kind of ingenuity Ataturk also solved the dilemma posed by the need to adopt foreign words so that Turkish would have the necessary technical vocabulary and the countervailing need to extol all things Turkish. He put forth the theory that Turkish was in fact the mother of all languages, so any foreign term, properly "re-Turkified," was merely returning to its own.[12]

TERRITORY AND STATEHOOD

"The nation is not only a community of brethren imbued with a sense of common destiny," writes Rupert Emerson, "it is also a community which, in contrast to others such as a family, caste, or religious body, is characteristically associated with a particular territory to which it lays claim as the traditional homeland."[13] The Jewish people before the establishment of the state of Israel are often cited as an example of a nation without a territory, but Emerson does not agree. "Whatever the propriety of regarding the Jews as a nation at all times in their history rather than as a religious community," he writes, "they stand out as a people for their devoted attachment to the land of their fathers. Throughout the centuries of the Diaspora the Jews through their religious ceremonies and by other means fervently maintained the symbolism of identification with the country from which they had been driven in the far-off past; and no other corner of the earth's surface could meet the need they, or at least many among them, felt to return to their own."[14]

It seems entirely natural that human beings would develop an affection for their immediate surroundings, the village and the locality where they were born and grew up, whose people, hills, valleys, streams, fields, and woods they know so well. But even with modern methods of transportation, most citizens of a country will never get to know very much of the terrain of the whole country so intimately, much less the people. At the time that nationalism arose in Europe, the masses had little awareness of any ties with anyone beyond their immediate locality, whether of language, culture, or blood.

Indeed, there were fewer similarities before nationalism than after, for nationalism was the most powerful force of all in blurring the differences of dialect and in spreading a single, national culture. Like all the other characteristics of nationalism, territory is both an element contributing to feelings of group identity and something which nationalists use in trying to promote those feelings.

Statehood is much the same. Some states, like Austria–Hungary, have succumbed to disparate nationalisms within their borders. But in others a major factor in developing nationalism seems to have been the fact of the state. In Latin America, as in the United States, the independence movement occurred before the rise of nationalism. States were formed around the old colonial administrative units—presidencies, *audiencias*, and captaincies. All share Catholicism as the principal religion, and all but Brazil have Spanish as a common language (although many Latin Americans speak one or another of the indigenous languages either as a second language or as their sole language). Thus, to the extent that nationalism has developed in Latin America, it seems to be the existence of the state that has been the most influential factor of all.

Much the same can be said of the Arab states, whose boundaries, except in Palestine, generally follow the lines of the partition of the Ottoman empire between 1830 and 1920.[15] To the extent that some rudimentary Czechoslovak nationalism, as opposed to separate Czech and Slovak nationalisms, actually did develop before the recent breakup into separate Czech and Slovak states, it was the fact of the state that was responsible. And to the extent that a rudimentary Yugoslav nationalism developed before its breakup as opposed to the several separate nationalisms of the constituent peoples of Yugoslavia, it was again the fact of the state that was responsible.

To sum up, all these elements—language and literature; religion; shared history, culture, and traditions; and territory and statehood—can and do contribute to feelings of nationalism and facilitate its growth. But nationalism can also grow in the absence of them. Fundamentally, nationalism is the notion that a particular group of people are distinct and that such a distinct people have a natural right to be a state. "Nationality," says Kohn, "is therefore not only a group held together and animated by common consciousness; but it is also a group seeking to find its expression in what it regards as the highest form of organized activity, a sovereign state."[16]

SELF-DETERMINATION

To the question, "Who will be a state?" the answer offered is self-determination, in which Woodrow Wilson at the Versailles Peace Conference put so much faith. As Sir Ivor Jennings remarked, "On the surface, it seemed reasonable: let the people decide. It was in fact ridiculous because the people cannot decide until somebody decides who are the people."[17] The fact is that no one has come up with a definition of nationalism that will hold water except that it is a state of mind. Ernest Renan called it a "daily plebiscite."[18]

All this explains what some have found a puzzle—that nationalists are rarely imperialist. Usually they are the opposite, getting rid of both people and territories that are not of the same "nation." When nationalism hit the Ottoman Empire, for example, it became Turkey and launched on a program to divest itself of territories where few Turks lived, and those parts became separate countries. Non-Turkish peoples who lived in territories where the majority of the population were Turkish were forced to emigrate. The most notable example were the Greeks. These people had lived in Asia Minor since well before the days of Troy, but they were forced to return to Greece.

The Armenians posed a problem for the Turks that could not be solved by either granting independent statehood or forcing emigration. Armenians occupied territory on the Turkish side of a mountain range that the Turks considered an essential boundary for reasons of defense. Since there was really no country that would accept the Armenians as Greece accepted the displaced Greeks, the Turks set about to exterminate them, one of the first modern examples of not so much genocide, since Armenians lived both in the Soviet Union and Iran, as what came to be known in the Bosnian War as, "ethnic cleansing."

Nationalists are also isolationist. Consider Burma, to give an example that is only slightly extreme. Nationalism hit Burma just before and during World War II, and Burma became independent in the immediate aftermath of the war. A few years later, General Ne Win, head of a group of Burmese nationalists, seized power and proceeded to evict foreigners. These included the Indian money lenders and Sikh tradespeople who were the underpinning of Burma's economy; the American missionaries, including those who ran a hospital and an agricultural experimental station; representatives of the Ford and Rockefeller foundations, who were supervising grants made to Burma; and all other foreigners with one exception. The exception was the overseas Chinese, whom the Burmese nationalists allowed to remain only because they feared that China would not tolerate their being evicted. Ne Win said that he sometimes wished that he had an atomic bomb that could cut Burma off from the mainland so it could drift out to sea.

Not only is nationalism isolationist, it is also turned inward on itself. Unlike socialism, which at least in theory is concerned with the plight of workers and peasants everywhere, nationalism incites revolution to bring about social and political change within its own nation, but it discourages concern with social and political conditions in other countries.

PREREQUISITES FOR NATIONALISM

Of course, the seeds of a national consciousness existed in Europe before 1789, notably in France and England. In both countries, the monarchy, based on what Karl W. Deutsch calls "core areas," such as the Île de France, had broken the power of the feudal lords and created a larger political unit that could be the vehicle of nationalism.[19] Religion had been divorced from both politics and territory in the Reformation and the wars of religion. Before the printing press, knowledge and learning were carried by the universalist language, Latin, known only to a tiny elite. But when the printing press made it possible to reach the masses it was easier for learned men to write in the vernacular and the masses to learn to read the vernacular than for the masses to learn Latin. This availability of learning in the vernacular and the translation of the Bible into the vernacular— done for religious reasons—tended to erase regional and local differences within any particular language area and to make everyone aware of a kinship wider than just their own village and locality.

Finally, nationalism, as Hans Kohn said, is inconceivable without the ideas of popular sovereignty preceding it: "The traditionalism of economic life had to be broken by the rise of the third estate, which was to turn attention away from the royal courts and their civilization to the life, language, and arts of the people. This new class found itself less bound by tradition than the nobility or clergy. . . . In its rise, it claimed to represent not only a new class and its interests, but the whole people."[20]

NATIONALISM'S LINKS WITH EGALITARIANISM AND MODERNIZATION

Most of the historians and other students of nationalism have remarked upon its links with both modernization and egalitarianism. The term "modernization" describes a process by which humankind gains control over nature by individual men and women cooperating with each other in a division of labor, a process that also transforms society and the values of individuals and their attitudes, especially their attitude toward each other.

The beginnings of modernization came in the Renaissance, and the beginnings of nationalism only in the eighteenth century. But after that they proceeded hand in hand: "Since then, in Latin America, Asia, and Africa, nationhood and modernity have appeared as two facets of a single transformation—a dual revolution loudly proclaimed and often ardently desired but never accomplished quickly or with ease."[21]

Egalitarianism also had earlier beginnings than nationalism, and it, too, was linked with modernization. The traditionalism of economic life had to be broken, and to do so—to pave the way for an economic division of labor—the feudal notions of inequality also had to be broken. But when nationalism appeared, it gave egalitarianism a mighty push. Nationalism implied equality. Membership in the nation was the important thing, not one's class and social position. Before nationalism, a feudal lord from France felt more at home with feudal lords from, say, England. After nationalism he felt more at home with other Frenchmen of any class than he did with Englishmen. Thus, nationalism served the purposes of both egalitarianism and modernization, and egalitarianism and modernization served the purposes of nationalism.

THE FRENCH REVOLUTION

It was the French revolution that launched the modern idea of nationalism. Even though it is linked to modernization and egalitarianism, nationalism, as already mentioned, is fundamentally the idea that there is such a thing as a group of people who are "one nation" and that such a "nation" should by natural right be a state; that it is the "nation" and only the "nation" that legitimizes the state. "The French Revolution presented the challenge," in Rupert Emerson's words, "of a state which was no longer the king but the people, and thrust across the face of Europe the power of a nation in arms."[22] Even when Napoleon became the sovereign, Emerson goes on to say, he headed not the France of Louis XIV, but the French nation.

Nationalism did not sweep all before it following the French revolution, but grew only slowly against the active resistance of many of the aristocratic elites, who recognized its links with egalitarianism and hence with democracy, which they feared. As late as 1862, Lord Acton could say, "A state may in course of time produce a nationality; but that a nationality should constitute a state is contrary to the nature of modern civilization."[23] But nevertheless, the notion spread and grew stronger, unifying Germany and Italy in 1871 and achieving full recognition in the rest of Europe at the end of World War I in the Treaty of Versailles.

KARL W. DEUTSCH AND NATIONALISM
AS SOCIAL COMMUNICATION

The nature of nationalism is obviously a puzzle. Nationalism may be a state of mind, but how did that state of mind come about? Much of the confusion—and mystery—surrounding nationalism was cleared up by the work of Karl W. Deutsch, who studied the rise of nationalism as a communications process. Deutsch starts with the premise that nationalism is a process of social learning and habit forming, resulting from a marked increase in social communication. Typically, the increase came from changes in the pattern of life associated with the beginnings of modernization. In Europe, the process began around a core area, such as the Île de France, Prussia, Prague, or Piedmont. The core area developed both economic needs and capabilities and administrative needs and capabilities that were of benefit to the hinterlands. Communication developed along natural lines—valleys, rivers, and, in the case of Switzerland, the mountain passes.[24]

Language developed and culture and common customs spread along with increased social communication. Consider the development of the Czech language and Czech nationalism in Bohemia, which Deutsch used as one of his case studies. Deutsch speaks of the proportion of a population that is at any given time mobilized for increased communication by economic, social, and technological changes. These can be measured by various yardsticks: the number of people engaged in occupations other than agriculture and forestry, the number living in towns, literacy rates, and so on. At the beginning of the nineteenth century, somewhat less than a third of the population of Bohemia was mobilized for intense communication, and, of these, half spoke German—the language of the rulers—including not only ethnic Germans but ethnic Czechs. Of the underlying population, which took no significant part in intensive communication, considerably more than two-thirds were Czech. In the following century, industrialization and social mobilization were extensive. By 1900, the proportion of Czech speakers among the mobilized population was proportional to the number of ethnic Czechs in the whole population. National conflict was intense. Some Germans, principally those living in the Sudetenland, were never assimilated and after World War II were expelled. But a considerable proportion of Germans were assimilated and became Czech, including not only city dwellers but many who were originally in the underlying population living in wholly German villages. "In the political and social struggles of the modern age," Deutsch writes, "*nationality*, then, means an alignment of large numbers of individuals from the middle and lower classes linked to regional centers and leading social groups by channels of social communication and economic intercourse, both indirectly from link to link and directly with the center."[25]

As Deutsch points out, when the phenomenon of nationalism is approached in this way it becomes clear "why all the usual descriptions of a people in terms of a community of languages, or character, or memories, or past history, are open to exception. For what counts is not the presence or absence of any single factor, but merely the presence of sufficient communication facilities with enough complementarity to produce the overall result." Although the Swiss speak four different languages, they are still one nation, Deutsch argues, because "each of them has enough learned habits, preferences, symbols, memories, patterns of landholding and social stratification, events in history, and personal associations, all of which together permit him to communicate more effectively with other Swiss than with the speakers of his own language who belong to other peoples." To illustrate the point, Deutsch quotes the editor of a prominent German–Swiss newspaper. "I found that my German was more closely akin to the French of my [French–Swiss] friend than to the likewise German (*Ebenfallsdeutsch*) of the foreigner.

The French–Swiss and I were using different words for the same concepts, but we understood each other. The man from Vienna and I were using the same words for different concepts, and thus we did not understand each other in the least."[26]

The link between nationalism on the one hand and on the other hand the list of factors previously discussed—language and literature; religion; shared history, culture, and traditions; and statehood and territory—is simply that these things facilitate increased social communication and thus the process of social learning and habit forming. Nationalism in turn blurred the differences among dialects of language or elbowed out competing languages, gave a sense of identity with events in the past, spread culture, and thrust toward statehood.

The link between nationalism and modernization was similarly reciprocal: The technological and social changes that marked the beginnings of modernization increased social communication. Increased social communication led to nationalism, which permitted still greater social communication.

The link between egalitarianism and nationalism was also reciprocal. The middle and lower classes—the masses—derived the greatest benefits from modernization and were in the forefront in spreading the idea of nationalism. Nationalism implies that all the members of the nation are equal, and the carriers of the idea of nationalism were those who benefitted most from egalitarianism.

All these were the functions that nationalism performed in bringing about the nation-state. Once established, the nation-state takes over still other functions, especially in the modern, social-service state. Deutsch found "that the increase in the responsibility of national government for such matters as social welfare and the regulation of economic life has greatly increased the importance of the nation in the lives of its members."[27] Thus, nationalism has become both more popular than ever before and more intractable.

NATIONALISM AND PERSONALITY INTEGRATION

One further aspect of nationalism remains to be explained. "The nation is today," writes Rupert Emerson, "the largest community which, when the chips are down, effectively commands men's loyalties, overriding the claims both of the lesser communities within it and those which cut across it or potentially enfold it within a still greater society, reaching ultimately to mankind as a whole. In this sense the nation can be called a 'terminal community' with the implication that it is for present purposes the end point of working solidarity between men."[28] All those who write on the subject of nationalism speak in much the same way; of the emotion that nationalism evokes, of the passion, of the command that nationalism has over the individual's loyalties, of the fact that individuals die in the name of nationalism and that they seem to do so in modern times more willingly than for church, ideology, class, or any other claimant to their loyalty. What remains to be explained, then, is the emotion.

In exploring possible tests for nationalism, Deutsch speaks of a nationality as a community of people in which there is *predictability from introspection*:

We try to predict other people's behavior by "putting ourselves into their place," by comparing it with the results of our own introspection. We try to predict their overall performance by comparing it with our own. To the extent that we succeed, we say we understand them. Here is one of the most important bases for the notion of a people, for that "consciousness of kind," of familiarity and trust, which we have for people whom we understand.[29]

Such predictions from introspection, Deutsch warns, should not be confused with *prediction from familiarity*:

Prediction from introspection is based on analogy of structured habits, prediction from familiarity on remembered outside observations from the past. A white Southerner may think that he can predict what another white Southerner will probably think or do in a certain situation, because he is a man of "his own kind." The same white Southerner may also believe that he can predict what a Negro will think or do in a certain situation, because, he thinks, he "knows Negroes." Both types of prediction are very much subject to error, but the second type is merely based on outside familiarity with overt behavior, usually only in a very limited range of situations, even if these limited situations, perhaps such as those between master and servant, may have occurred for many years.[30]

Deutsch points out that the experience of "foreignness" as being unpredictability is related to the feeling of strangeness so often described by the historians of nationalism, and suggests that both are related to the psychological process of identification and to the concept of "basic personality structure."

Put another way, it could be argued that the emotional content of nationalism is related to the source of the reference points around which personality is integrated. The integration of personality—the development of "identity"—is a complex process of interaction among the individual and his or her family, peer group, school, and community. Many of the reference points—the values, attitudes, and ways of looking at things—come from a very broad culture. Some of the values and attitudes around which both the Frenchman's and the American's personality are integrated, for example, may be the same, deriving from Western culture broadly conceived. But beginning with the latter part of the eighteenth century, the principal value and attitudinal framework for personality integration has been increasingly supplied by nationality. Hence the emotion. Nationality becomes part of the self, part of the individual identity. It is the larger identity that permits a person to relate to other human beings effectively. A Welsh nationalist (it is typical that he was a secondary school teacher of his nation's literature) commenting on the steady submersion of things Welsh into the larger British culture and nation put it in bitter and poignant terms: "Soon," he said, "there will be no fellow human left who loves the things I love, or even hears sounds the way I hear them or sees the earth and sky the way I see them. As a Welshman, death will be more final for me."[31]

Nationalism, it seems clear, has far from run its course. What is more, nationalism is so rooted in the integration of personality that trying to shift the loyalties of humankind away from the nation to some sort of world government seems quixotic.

NOTES

1. This section is based on the analysis in Roger Hilsman, *The Crouching Future* (Garden City, N.Y.: Doubleday, 1975).

2. L. B. Namier, *Conflicts: Studies in Contemporary History* (London: 1942), 70.

3. Charles Seignobos, *The Evolution of the French People*, trans. Catherine Alison Philips (New York: 1932), 153.

4. Hans Kohn, *The Idea of Nationalism: A Study of Its Origins and Background* (New York: 1948); C. H. Van Tyne, *The War of Independence: American Phase* (Boston: 1929), 271.

5. Louis L. Snyder, *The Dynamics of Nationalism* (Princeton: 1964), 2.

6. Carlton J. H. Hayes, *Nationalism: A Religion* (New York: 1960), 3–4.

7. Rupert Emerson, *From Empire to Nation: The Rise and Self-Assertion of Asian and African Peoples* (Boston: 1960), 103.

8. Dankwart A. Rustow, *A World of Nations: Problems of Political Modernization* (Washington, D.C.: 1967), 23.

9. Kohn, *Idea of Nationalism*, 14.

10. Boyd C. Shafer, *Nationalism: Myth and Reality* (New York: 1955), 54.

11. Bernard Lewis, *The Emergence of Modern Turkey* (London: 1961), 353.

12. Emerson, *From Empire to Nation*, 138.

13. Ibid., 105.

14. Ibid., 106.

15. On this point, see Rustow, *World of Nations*, 67.

16. Kohn, *Idea of Nationalism*, 19.

17. Sir Ivor Jennings, *The Approach to Self-Government* (Cambridge: 1956), 56.

18. Ernest Renan, *Qu'est-ce qu'une nation?* trans. Ida Mae Snyder, in *The Dynamics of Nationalism* (Princeton: 1964).

19. Karl W. Deutsch, *Nationalism and Social Communication: An Inquiry into the Foundations of Nationality* (New York: 1953).

20. Kohn, *Idea of Nationalism*, 3.

21. Rustow, *World of Nations*, 2. See also Rustow on modernization, ibid., 3.

22. Emerson, *From Empire to Nation*, 190.

23. Lord Acton, "Nationality," in *The History of Freedom and Other Essays* (London: 1909), 292.

24. "The rise of Switzerland from the thirteenth century on," Deutsch writes, "was related to the changes in the technology of transport and bridge building which made the St. Gotthard Pass crucial in world trade and furnished the economic base for an independent 'pass state' in that region." Deutsch, *Nationalism and Social Communication*, 16.

25. Ibid., 75 (emphasis original).

26. Ibid., 71.

27. Karl Deutsch, et al., *Political Community and the North Atlantic Area: International Organization in the Light of Historical Experience* (Princeton: 1957), 23.

28. Emerson, *From Empire to Nation*, 96.

29. Deutsch, *Nationalism and Social Communication*, 85.

30. Ibid., 86.

31. Personal communication.

Chapter 19

A World Political Process without World Government?

World government, to repeat the conclusion of the last chapter, seems out of reach in the immediate future. But the reason war has been virtually abolished within well-established states is not only that a state has the legal monopoly on the use of violence but because a state provides alternative ways of accomplishing social and political change: through law and politics. Even though a world state seems an impossible goal in the short run, is it possible for humankind to develop legal and political processes for bringing about social and political change for the whole of humankind without the structure of a world state? If so, even if war cannot be abolished some of the causes of war might be eliminated and war made much, much less frequent. What humankind might work toward is a global political process similar to what exists in individual states today but without an actual government, a political process in which certain features are much more prominent and certain others are considerably less prominent.[1]

Presumably, law and legal processes would be among the less prominent. Law comes about as the result of formal legislation and through precedent set by the courts. Since the global political process we visualize would lack the structure of a state and hence lack the state's monopoly of legal force, it would presumably also lack not only the formal legislative institutions but also the more formal enforcement powers by which a state implements its laws. But this is not necessarily a fatal lack. In its essence, law is the outcome of the kind of political process that exists in the individual state, not a rival or a substitute for it.

Similarly, if states had to enforce all their laws, rules, regulations, and agreements with the formal institutions of police and armed forces, no state would be effectively governed. The reason states can successfully govern is that the great majority of people in a working state abide by the laws and regulations without being coerced. The point is that some considerable portion of the kind of political process that provides an alternative to violence within a single state may be possible in an interstate system as well as within a single world super-state.

POLITICS DEFINED

The question now is what we mean by the word "politics." The ancient Greek philosopher, Aristotle, writing three centuries before Christ, declared that human beings are political animals. He said that nature intended them to live in groups and that politics concerned the governance of such groups. Although today we find it incredible, Aristotle also said that politics was humankind's "noblest invention."

Eighteen centuries later, Niccoló Machiavelli, writing in the period of the Italian city–states, defined politics as seeking, maintaining, and exercising power. Most political thinkers since then have also felt it necessary to give power some place in their definitions of politics.

In later generations, the main emphasis of political thinkers such as Locke, Montesquieu, Rousseau, and Marx was on how humankind might achieve the best possible government. This was true even of Thomas Hobbes, to whom power was as central as it had been to Machiavelli. All these philosophers tried to discern the essential nature of humankind and society and to deduce from that essential nature the elements of a truly good society and government.

TWENTIETH-CENTURY CONCEPTS

Modern definitions of politics frequently cite Max Weber, a German scholar of the early 1900s. Weber's concept of politics rested on his definition of the state as a "human community that [successfully] claims the *monopoly of the legitimate use of physical force within a given territory.*"[2]

Since the state is the sole source of the "right" to use violence, politics for Weber "means striving to share power or striving to influence the distribution of power, either among states or among groups within a state." Thus, Weber, like Machiavelli and Hobbes, put power central: "He who is active in politics strives for power either as a means in serving other aims, ideal or egoistic, or as 'power for power's sake,' that is, in order to enjoy the prestige-feeling that power gives."[3] Thus, some people dominate and others are dominated, and it is important, Weber argues, to understand why people obey. The point Weber is making goes back to Aristotle: "Authority" or "rule" is power that people recognize as legitimate.

Weber saw three ways of making the domination of other people legitimate and therefore acceptable to them. The first is the authority of the "eternal yesterday," of ancient tradition and custom: "My father was the king (or caliph, khan, maharajah, or tribal chieftain). He is now dead. I am therefore king, and you must obey me." The second is "rational–legal" authority: "I was elected president by legal and constitutional procedures, and therefore you must obey me (or at least you must obey those of my commands that are legal and constitutional)." Third and last is the authority of an "extraordinary and personal *gift of grace*" to which Weber gave the name *charisma*, derived from the Greek word for spirit: "God (or "history" or the "spirit of the nation") has laid His Hand upon me to make me the leader and therefore you must obey." The Ayatollah Khomeini of Iran claimed that his authority to rule Iran after the Shah abdicated was legitimate for this reason. So did Hitler and so do most revolutionary leaders.

More recent analysts of politics have stressed different aspects of these major themes. Some have stressed the territorial base of political groups. Some talk about the purpose of politics: "Who gets what, when, and how?" Some have defined politics as a struggle for power, pure and simple. Others have restricted politics to the search for and exercise of power only with respect to the process of government. Some have restricted politics to the making and executing of authoritative or legally binding decisions. Still others have combined these ideas to say that politics is any persistent pattern of human relationships that involves power, rule, or authority.[4]

Most of these definitions are reasonably valid and useful for particular purposes, but none of them are completely satisfactory for all purposes. It is probably not necessary to strain for the perfect definition—most people have a commonsense definition that is good enough. People speak of "office politics," for example, and everyone knows what they mean. As a general rule, it is assumed that politics is concerned with power, that it is more likely than not to be concerned with matters of governance (although there are many exceptions), and that political decisions of the largest moment are concerned with the ordering and regulating of society itself. In its broadest meaning, politics concerns the activities and relationship of groups of people as groups.

For our purposes, it seems most useful to look at a political process as a device for making group decisions. Thus, a political process is a more or less peaceable and orderly set of procedures by which a group of people can decide what they should do as a group, the goals they should seek, and the means for achieving those goals. These decisions would concern how they should divide among themselves those benefits already available, how the necessary sacrifices should be allotted, what rules should govern competition of various kinds, and how disputes between different groups should be resolved. Politics is concerned both with the making of such decisions and the maneuvering to acquire the power and influence to affect them.

Politics is not the only device for making group decisions. Another device is the marketplace. By buying certain products and not others, the mass of the people in a market economy determine how the resources of a society will be allocated and how the economic pie will be divided.

Still another way to make group decisions is by judicial and administrative procedures. Decisions are made by the interpretation, guided by precedent, of sets of laws, policies, rules, and regulations, or perhaps by tribal custom.

Conceivably, group decisions could also be made in a purely hierarchical way, in which only the leader had a voice. At the other extreme, a pure type of democratic decision making is also conceivable, in which there is no leader at all and decisions are made unanimously or by the majority, with each person having only one vote and no influence other than that vote.

But the real world is more complex. It differs from the pure hierarchical model of decision making in that more than one person has power or influence, and from the pure democratic model in that the participants have differing amounts of power and influence. The active cooperation of some people may be required for a decision, while only the acquiescence of others may be needed. Some participants might have to give formal approval before some decisions can be made. On other decisions these same people might be safely ignored.

And in the real world nothing is very clear-cut—several different kinds of group decision making will undoubtedly exist at the same time. Within a single department of the U.S. government, for example, some decisions are made by hierarchical procedures, some by judicial, some by political, and some by a bewildering combination of all of these.[5]

CHARACTERISTICS OF A POLITICAL PROCESS

A political process of decision making can be distinguished from other ways of making group decisions by four characteristics:

1. The presence of disagreement or conflict.
2. The presence of competing groups identified with one or the other side of the disagreement or conflict.
3. The presence of shared values (especially the value of preserving the system itself).
4. The presence of power.

DISAGREEMENT OR CONFLICT

Politics implies a diversity of goals and values that must be reconciled before a decision can be reached. It is not just a question of whether this or that value should be pursued, but what mixture of values should be pursued.

Politics also implies alternative means for achieving values whose precise effects may be in dispute. Political debates, for example, never take place over the question of what tensile strength is required for the truss members of a bridge. That can be determined scientifically. But political debates frequently take place over where to locate the bridge. Sometimes this is because the social and economic consequences of locating the bridge in one place rather than another cannot be predicted with sufficient exactitude. For example, a proposal made some years ago to build a bridge from Long Island to Connecticut sharply divided opinion among Connecticut residents into those who thought the Connecticut economy would benefit more if the bridge went from the middle of Long Island to the middle of Connecticut at Bridgeport and those who thought the bridge would do more for the Connecticut economy if it went from the eastern end of Long Island to Old Saybrook at the mouth of the Connecticut River. Economic and social theory was not sufficient to give a decisive, completely "scientific" prediction about the consequences of either alternative, and the result was a hot political debate.

Sometimes, however, the question of where to locate a bridge causes political debate *because* a prediction can be made with exactitude. The people of Old Saybrook were against having the bridge terminate in Old Saybrook because they knew beyond any doubt that it would destroy the essentially rural atmosphere of that small, peaceful New England town, an atmosphere they ardently wanted to preserve. Politics also arises, in other words, when a decision is uneven in its effects or call to sacrifice, when it brings either untoward benefit to one segment of society or untoward hurt.

Frequently a political struggle over the probable effects of alternative means is really a mask for an unspoken disagreement about goals. But it is noteworthy how often the struggle is truly over means and rival predictions about what a particular means will or will not accomplish. On the question of intervening in Vietnam, for example, both the doves and the hawks wanted the same goal, a stable and lasting peace in Southeast Asia. The trouble was that the doves thought a stable peace could only be achieved by withdrawal and negotiations, and the hawks thought it could only be achieved by defeating the Communist side militarily and thereby deterring it from future actions.

Everyone wants to avoid both recession and inflation, to give an example from domestic policy. The arguments are over how effective different policies will be in reaching the goal, and whether the cost will fall more severely on workers or on business.

Politics, in other words, begins to come to the fore when there is disagreement. The disagreement can take any one of several forms:

1. It could be about the goals the group should seek as a group. Should the United States make the struggle in Vietnam an American war? Should it spend the money to try to put a human being on Mars?

2. It could be about the predicted effects of alternative means for achieving the goal. Will bombing North Vietnam cause the Communists to give up, or will they fight even harder? Will a tax cut stimulate business enough to end a recession or will government spending be needed?

3. The disagreement can be about the rules governing competition between individuals and subgroups. The antimonopoly laws, the regulation of interstate commerce, and the laws regulating the stock market are all examples. So is legislation protecting civil rights and legislation providing equal rights for women.

4. The disagreement could be about the allocation of benefits held or distributed by the group as a whole. Welfare payments, unemployment compensation, medical care, and farm subsidies are examples.

5. The disagreement can be about the sacrifices required by different segments of the group as a whole. Will a recession be ended by means that make for high unemployment so that workers bear the brunt of the sacrifice, or will the recession be ended by additional taxes that fall mainly on business?

The point is that it is not competition as such that produces politics. If there is substantial agreement, for example, that unrestrained economic enterprise should govern the distribution of material benefits, the competition will take place in other than political terms. It is when there is disagreement about the rules for economic competition that politics begin.

COMPETING GROUPS

The second characteristic of politics flows from the first: the presence of competing clusters of people who are identified with each of the alternative goals and policies. One thinks immediately of the traditional political parties, but this is only the beginning. Even inside the government itself there are competing groups of people identified with alternative goals and policies.

The principal departments and agencies such as Treasury, Commerce, Labor, Health and Human Services, Justice, Defense, and State are often in competition over policy. But much of the struggle is not between formal organizations but among highly informal coalitions and alliances. In the American policy-making arena, to continue to use the United States as an example, there are subgroups of many kinds within the Executive branch and even within a single department or the White House itself. More often than not, these are not only informal but also temporary alliances that cut across departmental or institutional lines, including the line between the Executive branch and Congress. Throughout the struggle over policy toward Vietnam, the group within the State Department that took a hawk view had friends and allies in the Pentagon, in the CIA, in Congress, in the press, and in the attentive public, while the rival group that took a dove view had an entirely different set of friends and allies in the same places.

Consider what happens on a trade bill, to take another example. The United States cannot sell abroad unless other countries earn the dollars to buy its goods by selling their goods in America. Those people in the Department of Agriculture who are concerned with wheat farmers are in favor of international trade. But those who are concerned with cattle raisers are less enthusiastic; they want to protect the beef industry from too much competition from Argentina.

Then there are the interest groups entirely outside the formal structure of government: farmers' organizations, trade unions, the National Association of Manufacturers, and a vast array of groups with more special interests, such as the National Rifle Association, which opposes gun control, antiabortion groups, and groups opposed to nuclear energy.

A foremost political scientist of a generation ago, David B. Truman, saw these interest groups as part of what he called an "intermediate structure" between government and the mass of citizens, and he argued that they performed a vital function in modern government:

This structure—which in its simplest terms includes at least the great array of interest or pressure groups, corporations, trade unions, churches and professional societies, the major media of communications, the political parties, and, in a sense, the principal state and local governments—this pluralistic structure is a central fact of the distribution of power in the society. It is a structure that is intervening between government at the national level and the rank and file of the population, intervening rather than subordinate or dominating.[6]

This intermediate structure performs two functions that are particularly significant for a mass society: aggregating interests and representing interests to the central government. Elements of the intermediate structure are composed of people who tend to share interests and attitudes. By various devices, formal and informal, democratic and autocratic, institutions in the intermediate structure build a consensus among the conflicting views within their membership and develop a common goal, priorities among goals, and the tactics and techniques for attaining their goals. Organizations from both business and labor, for example, may bargain together and reach a compromise that government and society as a whole merely accepts. This relieves government of the job of legislating a solution. Institutions of the intermediate structure also speak for individual members in dealing with the legislature and with the bureaucracies.

Thus, the intermediate structure makes it possible for a large society and its government to be responsive to particular needs. It provides an upward path for the mass of the people to participate in decisions, and at the same time it provides a downward path for government to explain its policies and decisions to people with special interests through organizations specializing in those interests.

These groups within the intermediate structure also make informal and temporary alliances in the process of aggregating interests, and sometimes they end up making very strange bedfellows indeed. During the struggle over the Reagan economic program in his first administration, for example, lobbyists for the dairy industry, which had supported Reagan in the election, approached the congressional subcommittee responsible for the food stamp program, whose beneficiaries were mainly the urban poor, to form an alliance to prevent Reagan's proposed cuts from hurting either constituency, the recipients of dairy subsidies or of food stamps.

On every major policy dispute, foreign or domestic, this same pattern is found of formal and informal groups struggling with each other over both the goals of policy decisions and the means to achieve those goals, forming temporary alliances, and making deals. From all accounts the same is true of the Soviet Union, China, and every other established state.

THE "STRAIN TOWARD AGREEMENT" AND SHARED VALUES

A third characteristic of politics is that along with disagreement, struggle, and conflict there is simultaneously and paradoxically a "strain toward agreement."[7] By this is meant an effort to build a consensus, and a push for accommodation, for compromise, or for some sort of agreement on the policy decision. There are independent participants in the process who may be able to block a policy, to sabotage it, or at least to snipe away at it from the sidelines. There may be other people whose active, imaginative support and dedicated efforts are required if the policy is to succeed. To enlist this kind of willing cooperation may take concessions aimed directly at these people and their interests.

Finally, there is among all the participants of a working political system an intuitive realization that prolonged intransigence, stalemate, and indecision on urgent and fundamental issues might become so intolerable as to threaten the very form and structure of the system of governance. Thus, successful—that is, working—political systems are characterized by a general consensus that the system itself is worth preserving.

Most of the citizenry hold one of two beliefs along these lines. Some believe that the overall political system is of more value than the particular goal they have been unsuccessfully seeking. Others believe that the political system is sufficiently malleable so that sooner or later they will be successful in getting what they want through the political system, as opposed to destroying the political system, even though they will get what they want only half a loaf or less at a time. Disputes over policy can be bitter—as it was, say, over Roosevelt's New Deal program—but even the most bitter opponents do not usually carry their opposition so far as to resort to violence.

This third characteristic of a working political system—that most members of the system share a desire to preserve it—implies that they share other values as well. As discussed in the preceding chapter, it seems obvious that the members of stable, working societies share concepts of right and wrong, fairness, and many other values and that solutions to social problems that bring even profound social change are more often than not consistent with traditional goals and traditional notions of legitimate authority. Communist China, as we said, is as much the child of Confucius as it is of Karl Marx.

POWER

The final characteristic of a political process is power. In a political process the relative power of the different people and groups involved is as important to the final outcome as the appeal of the goals they seek or the wisdom and cogency of their arguments. The case for workers' rights, decent wages, safe working conditions, unemployment benefits, and retirement were just as valid in the late nineteenth century as they are today. But it was not until the labor movement organized workers and made them a political power center that conditions began to change fast enough and fundamentally enough to make a real difference. For generations, farmers in the Midwest, Southwest, and West, to give another example, complained that they were being exploited by Eastern bankers, farm equipment manufacturers, and the railroads. But it was not until those complaints could be expressed through the levers of political power that conditions really changed.

The powerful, too, must sometimes bow to countervailing power. When Lyndon B. Johnson was majority leader of the Senate, his power was second only to that of the president. But he was the senator from Texas, and as such even he could not dare to vote against the oil-depletion allowance: "What Senator [Paul] Douglas needs," Johnson once said in weariness over one of Douglas's more sanctimonious speeches, "is a few oil wells in Illinois."[8] Only thus, Johnson felt, could Douglas learn true humility. What Johnson forgot for the moment was that if Johnson had oil producers in Texas, Douglas had corn growers in Illinois. John F. Kennedy, as senator from Massachusetts, had the textile industry to teach him humility. The liberal Frank Church of Idaho could never really vote for a gun-control law, no matter how persuasive the facts supporting one might be. In a political situation, the power of those who advocate or oppose a policy is just as important as what they advocate or oppose.

THE NATURE OF POLITICAL POWER

But just what is political power? All great social thinkers have devoted attention to this question. As Robert A. Dahl has pointed out, the existence of so much comment arouses two suspicions.[9] The first is that where there is so much smoke, there must be fire, and some "thing" that can be called power must exist. The second suspicion is that "a Thing to which people attach many labels with subtly or grossly different meanings in many different cultures and times is probably not a Thing at all but many Things." If Dahl is right, power need not necessarily be the motive force behind politics, nor the cause of politics, nor even a necessary condition for politics. What it may be is merely one of several instrumentalities of politics, along with persuasion, bargaining, and compromise. Certainly many observers have noted that although seeking power may be one of the motives of people involved in politics, it is certainly not the only motive, and sometimes it is not a part of their motivation at all. If all this is true, then the reason that philosophers have given such a central place to power is not that it is the only instrumentality of politics but that it is the single most pervasive and decisive of the several instrumentalities of politics.

THE SOURCES OF POLITICAL POWER

What are the sources of political power? Mao Zedong said that power grows out of the barrel of a gun. Clearly, at certain times and in certain places military power is indeed starkly central to politics. Civil war is the obvious example. But to the extent that military strength is a source of power in the day-by-day politics of policy making, the mechanics hardly seem so crude. In the making of foreign policy on such issues as arms control and Vietnam, the military–industrial complex has a large stake, and its members express a view and a position. On the question of the size of the defense budget and the kinds of weapons to be procured, their stake has been equally large. But even on these issues the military–industrial complex has been loosely organized, amorphous, and more potential than structured. On other issues outside of defense budgets, weapons procurement, and foreign policy issues bearing more or less directly on security, the military–industrial complex has been even more ambiguous in their exercise of power. On a broad range of issues from welfare to civil liberties they seem to exercise no discernible power at all.

Great inherited wealth is another obvious source of power, one typified by names like Rockefeller, Harriman, Du Pont, Morgan, and Vanderbilt. So are positions at the top of corporations like General Motors, American Telephone and Telegraph, and United States Steel. Social position is another obvious source of power. Members of the Cabot, Lodge, Lowell, and Adams families, for example, have exercised power in the city of Boston, in the state of Massachusetts, and in the nation at large to some extent simply because they belonged to the top social strata.

But power in the American political system clearly has more varied and subtle sources than either force and violence or wealth and social position. Power grows not only out of the barrel of a gun, as Mao would have it, or out of economic control, as Marx would have it. Power also comes from legitimacy, from legal authority, from expertise, and from the right to speak for a special interest that is accepted as legitimate, such as the interest of the farmer in agricultural policy or that of the banker in monetary policy. Power is so varied and subtle in its sources that one wonders whether the concept can be expressed in just one word.

Consider the power of presidents. One source of presidential power is obviously constitutional prerogatives. The Constitution makes the president the chief of state and the commander in chief of the armed forces. It gives the president the responsibility for administering the laws, and it also gives him the power of the veto, so the president helps make the laws as well as administer them. In addition to prerogative powers, the Supreme Court has held that the president has other powers that are implied in the Constitution. Congress also often delegates some of its powers to the president.

But all this may not mean as much as it seems to mean. As Richard E. Neustadt remarked, "In form all Presidents are leaders nowadays. In fact this guarantees no more than that they will be clerks." Neustadt argues that a modern president has to face demands for aid and service from the executive branch, from Congress, from the press, from his partisans, from citizens at large, and from abroad. In effect, these are constituency pressures, and the president's clerkship is expressive of these pressures. "*The same conditions that promote his leadership in form preclude a guarantee of his leadership in fact.*" What Neustadt is arguing is that all the various powers of presidents—prerogative, implied, and delegated—express only their *potential* power. If presidents are actually to exercise their potential power, Neustadt insists, they must consciously and deliberately seek to add to their *personal* power and influence: "The search for personal power is at the center of the job of being President."[10]

Almost all "president watchers" implicitly recognize what seems to be the principal source of the day-to-day power of presidents, but none really spell it out in any detail. They seem to regard it as crucial, and yet too obvious to name. The name it probably should be given is political brokering. Political brokering, in fact, is central to any political process, whether that process is totalitarian, authoritarian, monarchic, aristocratic, oligarchic, or democratic.

Politicians engage in three types of activities, all of which overlap and interweave. The first is working to attain office or some less formal position in which they will have political influence and power. The second, the true center of any political process, is the work of brokering: mediating, trying to work out compromises, bargaining, negotiating, pressuring, threatening, dangling tempting baits and prizes, and using both sticks and carrots. All this is done in trying to reach some kind of decision that will be acceptable to the different power centers in Congress, the members of the Cabinet, powerful bureaucrats, generals and admirals in the armed services, leaders of interest groups, governors and other state and local leaders—all the many and varied power centers that make up American society.

Only when politicians have succeeded to some degree in the activities of attaining office and brokering are they occasionally able to afford the luxury of the third activity. This is to exercise power for their own purposes, to tilt policy in the direction that they personally would like to see it go or that will benefit them in some way, to change the world toward their preferences, or to establish something entirely new in the world for which they can take the credit and to which their name will be attached.

Presidents are inevitably and inescapably involved in the second, most central role of the political process, brokering among the demands of the different individuals, groups, organizations, and regions having power and influence. Political brokering is as much a tactic as a role, a way to enable presidents to be more than clerks who carry out other people's desires and to impose on the policies and decisions of the government their own preferences and those of the people who support them. The job of political brokering comes to presidents because they are at the hub of all the many kinds of government decision making, legislative or executive. The White House is the only place where *all* issues cross and converge. Thus, the function and role of political brokering entails mediating among the conflicting demands of competing power centers. Many of these conflicts are simple disagreements. Others are more dramatic: strikes, riots over school desegregation and busing, and the fiscal collapse of cities. The role of political brokering is central to the entire political process, whether day by day or in a crisis. It is the essence of the job of president, and performing it occupies most of a president's time.

POLITICAL BROKERING AS A SOURCE OF POWER

Thus, the role of political broker is also the principal source of the president's power. It gives presidents the right to be involved in the major issues that are the object of political struggle. It gives their participation legitimacy. It allows presidents to take part in the debate even though they do not represent the power centers involved in the sense that the head of an interest group does. It makes presidents the central mediator among rival power centers. It makes presidents the point at which pressures are brought to bear. It is the main source of what has been called the president's only true power, the power to persuade.

THE SOVIET POLITICAL SYSTEM

What we are doing is attempting to understand the basics of a political system in the hope that some sort of global political system can be devised that would help to reduce the frequency of war in the absence of world government. The question now is whether the characteristics of the political system we have found in the United States are valid for other political systems. The United States is a two-party democracy with a president sharing power with a legislature that is divided into a House of Representatives and a Senate, both of which have power. Would the characteristics of the American democracy we have described be valid for a dictatorship? For example, would we find these same characteristics in the old Soviet Union, before its breakup?

The Soviet Union was an authoritarian, one-party state, where power was concentrated in the general secretary of the Party, the Politburo, and the Party's central committee. The number of people, formal organizations, and informal groups having power in the Soviet system was smaller than in the United States, and often different in nature. Among the power centers of the Soviet Union were the general secretary, the members of the Politburo and the central committee, the ministers of the various departments of the government, the top officers in the armed forces, the secret police, the managers of industry, and Party officials in the cities, provinces, and towns across the country. In addition, the mass electorate in the Soviet Union could not choose between rival parties, and so the voters could not reject a set of policies by changing the leadership directly.

But the Soviet system also clearly had an "intermediate structure." It was made up more of formal organizations sponsored by the government than informal ones organized by people with a shared interest. Still, the function of the intermediate structure seems to have been very much the same: a sort of transmission belt that articulated interests and sent them upward and carried information downward about costs and contrary interests. But since the masses in the Soviet Union lacked the ultimate sanction of the ballot and since such institutions as the secret police had so much power, the downward function of the intermediate structure in shaping and manipulating interests and demands got greater emphasis in the Soviet Union than in the United States.

The penalties for being on the losing side of a policy battle were also greater in the Soviet Union. Loss of influence and power were the first penalties in both countries. At times, as in Senator Joseph McCarthy's witch hunts, being on the losing side in the United States could carry other, more severe penalties as well, although nothing to compare with what happened to Stalin's opponents at the height of his power.

But the Soviet political system could still be described in the same basic terms as the political system in the United States. At the top levels in Soviet society were a number of organized power centers with particular, parochial interests: the top party leaders of the Politburo and the central committee; the *apparatchiki* of the Party; the leaders of the secret police and the armed forces; the managers and executives of industry and agriculture; the scientific and academic community; the cultural and literary community; and the leaders of certain regions, such as the Ukraine or the Leningrad area. Particular segments of the top leadership of the Communist Party and the Soviet state represented these power centers and drew their own individual power from them. The Party provided the arena for a process of conflict and consensus building by which these various interests were reconciled and policies were adopted, with the top leadership serving as the political brokers as well as being power centers themselves with their own parochial interests.

Although the masses were denied the kind of ballot that could change the country's top leaders as an expression of discontent with policy, they did in fact have influence on policy by expressing their attitude and interests through the intermediate structure. Partly the masses had influence because their cooperation was required on so many policies, and partly the masses had influence because the people at the top of organizations in the intermediate structure drew power themselves from their role as spokesmen of the masses. The top leadership in the Soviet Union also had a stake in representing and serving the interests of the intermediate structure associated with them. The people at the top of organizations in the intermediate structure, in turn, had a stake in representing and serving the masses with whom they were connected. Thus, people at all levels had some stake in seeing that particular interests were served, thereby blunting discontent and enlisting loyalty.

POLITICAL PROCESS ON THE INTERNATIONAL LEVEL

A rudimentary form of this same kind of political process, as suggested earlier, already exists in international affairs. International affairs, like domestic, is a process of conflict and consensus building. In international affairs, the principal mode of conflict is war, and people correctly assume that conflict between states is fundamentally different, because war is large-scale violence, organized and directed by whole societies.

Yet in even the "total" wars of recent times the use of force has always been limited. Humankind uses force against some natural enemies with the full intention of exterminating them, as the wolves were deliberately exterminated in England and the snakes in Ireland. But with one exception no modern state has deliberately set about to destroy another people. The Turks' policy toward the Armenians was more like the ethnic cleansing seen recently in Bosnia than genocide. The Turks did not want to destroy the Armenians, they wanted only to remove them from Turkey. The one exception, of course, was Hitler's maniacal policy toward the Jews.

Physical violence, in fact, is not really a very common state of affairs between states. In the history of most countries the years of peace far outnumber the years of war. Even when conflict is the dominating theme in a set of relationships, statecraft is not really concerned as much with actual physical violence as with threats of physical violence.

It is on the conflict in international affairs that a pure-power theory of world politics focuses. Yet for all its utility in explaining the maneuvering of states, a pure-power theory has limitations. Without a sizable list of inelegant qualifications, it cannot account for the long periods of peace in interstate relations, for the stability of certain friendships, and for the not uncommon occasions when states knowingly relinquish positions of power. For the practical purposes of estimating the consequences of different policies and so of choosing among them, at least, a pure-power theory of international politics is a cumbersome and uneconomic tool.

The difficulty comes from the multiplicity of values shared by people on both sides of state boundaries: peace, security, prosperity, self-determination, and the sanctity and freedom of the individual. Thus, one state's gain is not always another's loss, and accommodation and concerted action occur at least as frequently in interstate affairs as conflict. The obvious example of states acting in concert are alliances for security against a common enemy, but states also act in concert for a variety of lesser purposes: to regulate trade, to counter economic depressions, to conserve such natural resources as fisheries, to combat crime, and to provide international postal and other services.

There is also accommodation between adversaries. Rival states often agree, formally or tacitly, to respect spheres of exclusive influence, to act together in neutralizing a third country, or to refrain from bringing certain matters into the arena of competition. The bitterest rivals have a stake in restricting their competition to means that are appropriate to the goals at issue and in avoiding measures that will bring about the sacrifice of things more cherished than those to be won. Even states at war have reached agreements. Use of poison gas was outlawed in World War II, although not all the participants had signed the convention on the rules of war. In the Korean War there was a tacit agreement to respect sanctuaries. The U.N. forces refrained from bombing north of the Yalu River, and the Communist side conformed by avoiding the U.S. bases in Japan.

However, it would be a mistake to put too fine a point on either the example of poison gas in World War II or that of respecting sanctuaries in Korea. In World War II both sides recognized that if one side used gas the other would retaliate, and neither side saw any advantage to itself in such an exchange. In Korea, the United States feared that attacking north of the Yalu might bring the Soviet Union into the war, probably under the fiction used by the Communist Chinese that their troops were "volunteers." For its part, North Korea did not have the military capability of striking at American bases in Japan, and the Soviets probably refrained from supplying what was needed out of a general fear of what might happen if the war spread beyond the Korean peninsula.

Thus, interstate politics has a mixture of conflict and accommodation similar in many ways to that in domestic politics. As a consequence, the business between states, like the business of reaching decisions within a single state, requires techniques for persuasion, negotiation, and bargaining, as well as for manipulating power.

The practitioners of statecraft in foreign offices and embassies do not make a practice of generalizing about the "political process in international affairs" or about the "interstate decision-making system." Yet faced with the problem of doing something in international affairs—whether it is trying to bring about a Geneva conference on arms control or implementing a decision to blockade Cuba—any practitioner, from desk officer to foreign minister, would unerringly tick off the steps to be taken. "This great power would have to be consulted in advance; those lesser powers need only be informed; this line of argument should be taken in the United Nations; that line of argument with the press. Moscow should be told this at that stage; Paris should be handled in a different way." Practitioners may not generalize about the "international political system," but they intuitively know it exists, and they consciously know how to manipulate it.

All this adds up to what is only a rudimentary political process. Of the several functions that a political process serves, the present-day international political system provides an arena and techniques for resolving certain kinds of disputes, for allocating certain kinds of benefits, and for establishing rules for certain kinds of competition. But the present-day international system provides little else, and certainly not enough to be as effective as the political process within a stable, well-established state with a working political system of its own.

In international affairs, the actors are states. If humankind is to move toward a global political process that is something more than what we have just described, it must be possible for both groups of individuals and individuals themselves to work other than through their own particular state. If the present structure is inadequate and establishing a world state is unrealistic, what can be done?

NOTES

1. This chapter is a further development of some ideas from Roger Hilsman, *The Crouching Future*; Roger Hilsman, *The Politics of Policy Making in Defense and Foreign Affairs: Conceptual Models and Bureaucratic Politics* (Englewood Cliffs, N.J.: 1987).

2. Max Weber, *From Max Weber: Essays in Sociology*, trans. and ed. H. H. Gerth and C. Wright Mills (New York: 1946), 78 (emphasis original).

3. Ibid.

4. The first definition is that of Charles E. Merriam, *Political Power: Its Composition and Incidence* (New York: 1934). The second is that of Harold Lasswell, *Politics: Who Gets What, When, How* (New York: 1936). After Merriam, the author who is most noted for defining politics as a struggle for power is Hans J. Morgenthau, *Politics Among Nations*, 4th ed. (New York: 1970). V. O. Key is the one who restricts politics to the process of government, defining politics as the "human relationship of superordination and subordination, of dominance and submission, of the governors and the governed." V. O. Key, *Politics, Parties, and Pressure Groups*, 4th ed. (New York: 1964). The definition of politics as the making and executing of authoritative decisions is from David Easton,

The Political System (New York: 1953), and David Easton, "An Approach to the Analysis of Political Systems," *World Politics* (April 1957). The definition that combines power with authority or rule is from Robert A. Dahl, *Modern Political Analysis*, 2d ed. (Englewood Cliffs, N.J.: 1970). Another definition that might be added is a "system of interactions to be found in all independent societies by means of the employment, or threat of employment, of more or less legitimate physical violence." Gabriel A. Almond, *The Politics of Developing Areas* (Princeton: 1960).

5. On the overlapping of different forms of decision making, see Robert A. Dahl, "Hierarchy, Democracy, and Bargaining in Politics and Economics," in *Research Frontiers in Politics and Government* (Washington, D.C.: 1955).

6. David B. Truman, "The American System in Crisis," *Political Science Quarterly* (December 1959).

7. Warner R. Schilling, "The Politics of National Defense: Fiscal 1950," in Schilling, Hammond, and Snyder, *Strategy, Politics, and Defense Budgets* (New York: 1962), 23.

8. The incident is recounted in Harry T. McPherson, *A Political Education* (Boston: 1972).

9. Robert A. Dahl, "The Concept of Power," *Behavioral Science* (July 1957).

10. Richard E. Neustadt, *Presidential Power: The Politics of Leadership* (New York: 1960) (emphasis original).

Chapter 20

A Curious Creature

Since establishing a world state seems unrealistic at this time and since the present international political system is not adequate to the task of abolishing war, what can be done? Is it possible to build toward something between the present international political system and a world state that might make war less frequent?

A possible example is the recently established European Community. Created by fusing the European Atomic Energy Community, the European Coal and Steel Community, and the European Economic Community (Common Market) into one organization, the members of the European Community are Belgium, Denmark, France, Germany, Greece, Ireland, Italy, Luxembourg, the Netherlands, Portugal, Spain, and the United Kingdom. The goal is to establish a completely integrated common market leading eventually to a federation of Europe.

Karl Deutsch's study of the Atlantic community provides some clues as to whether the European Community is a step toward what we have in mind. Following his study of nationalism, Deutsch and a number of associates tried to see if humankind might be moving toward something beyond nationalism by studying the Atlantic community. Specifically, they wanted to see if the countries bordering the North Atlantic—Western Europe, Canada, and the United States—contained the seeds of a new political entity, a super-state.[1] Among other things, they identified what they called a "pluralistic security community," a relationship between two or more states involving numerous contacts of all kinds coupled with the expectation that war between members of the community was unthinkable—a "no-war community." Examples are the relationship between the United States and Canada since the 1870s and among the United States, Canada, and Mexico since the 1930s.

Judged by the criteria of the Deutsch group, the European Community is far from being a super-state. But it has clearly become a no-war community. The formation of a common market was a landmark step in this, but even more dramatic is the fact that for the first time in history not one of these nations is making any preparations for war with any of the others. There are no Maginot lines under construction, much less any Schlieffen plans being concocted. For whatever reason, war among any of these nations is now unthinkable.

NATIONALISM IN THE EUROPEAN COMMUNITY

Of several curious developments, the most curious of all is that as all forms of regionalism have grown in Western Europe and integration rather dramatically increased, nationalism appears not to have weakened and may have grown stronger. Integration has proceeded in Western Europe, and it has had very specific and palpable consequences for the lives of Europeans in economic terms, in institutional terms, and in terms of the patterns of individual lives. But it has not meant the submergence of nationality into some transnational identity.

INTERNATIONAL INTEGRATION AND NATIONALISM

The significance of this coexistence of European integration and nationalism may be very great. It may be that integration can take place side by side with nationalism without either affecting nationalism or being affected by it. The possibility exists, in other words, that when nationalism has accomplished the functions of achieving and legitimizing statehood, and when it has substantially accomplished the function of modernization, it may under certain conditions not necessarily form a barrier to certain kinds of international integration. What we might end up with is neither a super-state nor a no-war community, but what is admittedly a curious creature: a pluralistic, no-war community in which the nation-states continue as individual entities for certain purposes, especially those related to culture and personality integration, but in which decision-making power in a wide range of other fields is transferred to international agencies, regional in some cases but perhaps worldwide in others.

Is some kind of curious creature, something between the present international political system and a world state, what we are looking for? Perhaps asking what functions this curious creature would serve can provide some sort of answer. If the functions it serves are necessary, beneficial, and unlikely to be served in any other way, it may be a feasible goal for humankind to work toward a similar arrangement on a larger scale.

In the economic sphere, some kind of curious creature is what we are looking for. A common market gives all the economies of scale. Large markets permit mass production, more and better goods, and better wages. There is a larger capital market. Labor is more mobile. Better transportation is possible. The opportunities for a wider, richer life are enhanced. In a preindustrial society, integration would not have served these functions. Even in an industrial age, it is only at the more advanced stages that a larger-size economy becomes crucial. But at that stage, it *is* crucial.

And size is even more crucial as these societies move toward a post-industrial stage. Advanced technologies and the advanced and continuous research they require cannot be sustained without large-scale enterprises. Even some individual satisfactions may depend on the existence of large-scale enterprises. For example, the so-called brain drain from Europe to the United States a few decades ago resulted more from the opportunity to work on interesting problems in these large-scale research efforts than from better salaries. Although it is too soon to be certain, the same thing seems to be at least partly true of the new brain drain of scientists moving from the former Soviet Union to the United States and the West.[2]

The interlocking of the economy, greater mobility of persons, and increased communications would also tend to serve a political function of putting pressure on the individual governments to even out social and welfare legislation. Conceivably, this might prove to be an incentive to segments of particular populations.

And there are other possible functions this combination of international regional authority with the nation-state would serve. Increasingly, as any newspaper reader knows, advanced technologies are bringing ecological and environmental problems. In meeting these problems, regions such as Europe will have to be treated as entities—in fact, for some ecological and environmental problems, the entity will have to be the entire globe. Increasingly, too, the measures to meet ecological problems will require uneven sacrifices, and hence increasingly they will become the subject of political struggle. If so, regional policy-making and decision-making agencies will come to be indispensable.

A curious creature, to sum up, does hold out the promise of providing a structure that could be used to deal with at least some of the problems that press so insistently on humankind. Problems in the economic sphere, problems of scarce resources, of pollution, of overpopulation, and many of those concerning the tensions between the developing and developed worlds would all seem less formidable and intractable if there were some such structure through which they could be approached. At the least, some such structure would be a step toward a no-war community that would encompass most of the world's greater powers.

But it would be a mistake to try to push this kind of speculation too far. It is not within the potentialities of forecasting to see more than the general outlines of something so new in the world. What we see now is weak and rudimentary. It could hardly provide the structure for an effective political process on a global scale. But what we can see is suggestive. What we can see does not constitute a trend, much less an inevitability, but it does provide the outlines of a goal toward which humankind might work as an interim substitute for something grander.

The need is both urgent and obvious for some such goal that is both realistic and yet holds the promise of serving at least a portion of the social function that war has served in the past. By its rivalries, envies, ambitions, and fears, humankind is driven toward collision with itself. In weapons and technology, humankind has created instruments that can spiral events beyond control. It may seem ironic that politics, so often despised, offers a hope that is also realistic. But perhaps it is not so strange. Politics, to repeat Max Weber's observation, is the striving for power and the using of power in the service of a cause. As he insisted, some kind of faith must always be present.

And politics does not always fail. In these crisis years since World War II, someone else remarked, the only thing that has stood between the world and disaster is a thin red line of people practicing politics.[3] What was true of politics in the past may also be true in the future.

NOTES

1. Karl W. Deutsch, *Political Community and the North Atlantic Area: International Organization in the Light of Historical Experience* (Princeton: 1957).

2. See, for example, the story about the outstanding Soviet physicist, Aleksei Abrikosov, who came from Russia to work at the Argonne National Laboratories near Chicago. Sergei Leskov, "America's Soviet Scientists," *The New York Times*, 15 July 1993, p. 25.

3. The remark was made by Warner S. Schilling. My thanks go to him not only for letting me use the quote, but for letting me tamper with it slightly. What he originally said was that all that has stood between the world and disaster is a thin red line of *politicians*.

PART VII

CONCLUSIONS

Chapter 21

A Long-Term Solution, a Medium-Term Compromise, and a Short-Term Stopgap

Our overall conclusion is that if humankind does not drastically alter course, sooner or later nuclear war will come. We looked at arms control as a way of avoiding nuclear war. Our conclusions were fairly optimistic. First, useful agreements on arms control have in fact been reached, especially since the dissolution of the Soviet Union. Second, the outlook over the next few years for reaching even more significant agreements seems good. Third, the sum of these developments should reduce the likelihood of nuclear war.

But we also concluded that arms control agreements will not by themselves solve the dilemma posed by nuclear weapons and ballistic missiles so long as war remains part of international politics. Even the best of arms control agreements would do nothing to preclude international crises and sooner or later one or another crisis will get out of hand. Arms control agreements may reduce the number of nuclear weapons the great powers have on hand at the beginning of a war and may even succeed in abolishing nuclear weapons from the world's arsenals, but the great powers can build new stockpiles in the midst of war. The United States, after all, created nuclear weapons from scratch in the midst of World War II, and the task will obviously be much easier now that everyone knows that it can be done and most nations have a corps of scientists who know exactly how to do it.

Next we looked at the possibility of establishing a world government. If war between sovereign states is frequent but civil war within established states is relatively rare, then the most obvious way to reduce the risk of nuclear war is to establish one government for the whole of the planet. However, the obstacles to establishing a world government are awesome, especially the obstacle posed by nationalism.

But even though a world government seems unattainable in the immediate future, it may be possible for humankind to build toward something short of world government but better than the present international political system. We looked at the European Community to see if it held any promise of becoming what might be a possible example. It seems to be on its way to becoming a curious creature, a pluralistic, no-war community in which nation-states continue as individual entities for certain purposes, especially those related to culture and personality integration, but in which decision-making power in a wide number of other fields is transferred to international agencies, regional in some cases but perhaps worldwide in others.

THE LONG-TERM SOLUTION

The long-term solution to the problem of nuclear weapons is world government. Only by establishing a single government for the whole planet can the chances of avoiding nuclear war be maximized.

A MEDIUM-TERM COMPROMISE

But since the obstacles to establishing a world government in the short run are so formidable, a compromise for the medium term may be the best that can be achieved. The first step in such a compromise would be to encourage the establishment of these curious creatures like the European Community that provide ways other than war of solving some kinds of international political and social problems. The second step would be to try to integrate these several curious creatures into one, unified, worldwide, pluralistic, no-war community. In this way world government might be brought about as the final stage in a step-by-step process.

Part of this kind of medium-term compromise would be an international treaty signed by all independent states that would provide for the following:

1. The destruction of all national stockpiles of nuclear weapons and the prohibition of building any more.

2. The continuous international inspection of all manufacturing and military facilities in all countries to see that no nuclear weapons were being produced secretly.

3. The establishment of an international military force reporting to the Security Council of the United Nations equipped with, say, fifty nuclear warheads and the missiles to deliver them anywhere in the world.

4. The prohibition of any use of this force except by order of the Security Council of the United Nations against a country found to be violating the treaty by building nuclear weapons.

A SHORT-TERM STOPGAP

Getting an international agreement on eliminating nuclear weapons, establishing an international nuclear deterrent force, and developing a worldwide, no-war community will take time. What can be done to make nuclear war less likely in the meantime?

Obviously, the effort to reach arms control agreements should be continued. Any agreement that reduces the number of nuclear weapons is bound to help. But, as we have seen, arms control does not promise any final answer. What is worse, it provides no answer at all to three immediate problems. The first of these is how to avoid nuclear war in the interim before a worldwide, no-war community is established. The second is how to deal with rogue countries that embark on programs to build nuclear weapons in spite of the nonproliferation treaty. And the third is what to do about nonnuclear, conventional wars that threaten to escalate into larger wars that have the potential for becoming nuclear.

What we need is a short-term stopgap, and the problem has two parts. One part is deterring nuclear war in the interim; that is, deterring nuclear war until an agreement is made to abolish national nuclear stockpiles, establish an international deterrent force, and create a worldwide, no-war community. The second part is dealing with nonnuclear, conventional wars in the interim—avoiding them if possible and containing those that cannot be avoided so that they remain limited and nonnuclear and do not escalate into very large wars that have the potential for becoming nuclear.

Nuclear Forces for the Interim

Given the inadequacies of arms control agreements and the difficulty of establishing a world government in the immediate future, the only answer to the problem of avoiding nuclear war in the interim is deterrence. The United States should have sufficient nuclear forces to deter any nuclear power or combination of nuclear powers from launching an attack. An effective deterrent would be a second-strike force that is capable of absorbing a surprise attack, whether by conventional or nuclear weapons, and striking back with devastating force against any country or combination of countries that launched the attack. The exact composition of this force will be discussed in Chapter 25.

The Rogue Country Problem

Another problem is that of a rogue country that refuses to sign the nuclear nonproliferation treaty or that signs it and then clandestinely attempts to build nuclear weapons in secret. As we saw earlier, North Korea is a possible example.

To repeat what was said before, it is important to remember that the capacity to build a few nuclear weapons is only the first step. The second, and more difficult, step is developing the means to deliver them. It is also important to remember that even if a rogue country succeeds in building a few nuclear warheads and the means to deliver them and ends up actually using them, the consequences are not even remotely as catastrophic as a nuclear war between two fully developed nuclear powers, such as the United States and Russia. The result of a nuclear attack by a rogue country would be a disaster, but a disaster more like Chernobyl than Armageddon.

Even so, a Chernobyl disaster is enough of a disaster to demand our full attention. The general principle for dealing with rogue countries is that the United States should aggressively lead the international community in monitoring potential violators and in dealing with any that are discovered.

First, the international community should pursue a full-scale intelligence effort to chart the offending country's progress. If any potential violations are found, it should demand permission for the United Nations or other international body to conduct the necessary inspections. If inspection is not permitted, the international community should isolate the country diplomatically and economically. If the offending country remains intransigent and if intelligence reveals that the country is persisting in building a nuclear arsenal in spite of the sanctions, the international community should take appropriate action to bring the effort to a halt, including military action.

So one part of the short-term stopgap the United States needs in the interim before a worldwide, no-war community can take over responsibility is a force that can remove the threat posed by a rogue country that tries to build a nuclear arsenal. If the intelligence work is diligent and adequate and the will and determination are sufficient to reach a decision promptly, the force required need not be nuclear. A well-designed nonnuclear, conventional force would be adequate.

The question here is what kind of nonnuclear, conventional forces will be needed. It will not be enough merely to destroy the rogue country's nuclear facilities. Israel destroyed Iraq's Dimona nuclear reactor, but Iraq then proceeded to build even bigger and better nuclear facilities. If preventive action is ever needed, it must remove not only the nuclear facilities, but the offending regime as well.

North Korea, as we say, is a possible example. The evidence leaking from the Pentagon in late 1993 and early 1994 was that North Korea had a well-equipped and well-trained army that would be a formidable fighting force. The Pentagon's conclusion was that if an invasion of North Korea became necessary, what would be needed are ground, naval, and air forces of just about the same size and strength as those deployed in the Gulf War.

Of course, as we saw, the intelligence judgment about the size and fighting capabilities of Saddam Hussein's armed forces painted a similar picture, yet the victory was easy. On the other hand, as we also saw, the easy victory in Iraq owed a great deal to Saddam Hussein's decision neither to fight nor surrender. Had he decided to fight, Iraq would have surely been defeated, but the Allied casualties would not have been nearly so light. In the case of North Korea, as in the case of

Iraq, an old aphorism of the German Army is applicable: If it will take ten divisions to win a battle, put in twenty, and you may not have to fight at all.

Nonnuclear, Conventional Forces for the Stopgap

If it will take substantial nonnuclear, conventional forces to deal with a rogue state, what about the forces to halt nonnuclear, conventional wars with the potential to escalate into larger wars that might go nuclear? How many and what type of "small wars" fought since World War II would have had this potential? It is to this subject that we now turn.

Chapter 22

The Lessons of the "Small Wars" since World War II

The period following World War II was marked by a staggering number of "small wars." Did any of these have the potential for escalating into much larger wars and thence to nuclear war itself, thus requiring American intervention?

THE LONG LIST OF CIVIL WARS

The period following World War II was marked by a long, long list of dismal civil wars: in the Congo, Nigeria, Angola, Laos, Sri Lanka, Kampuchea (Cambodia), and so on. But none were judged by the United States to have a significant potential for spiraling into World War III or threatening the United States itself.

THE SOVIET UNION'S SMALL WARS

The Soviet Union intervened with military force in Czechoslovakia and Hungary, it had border clashes with Communist China along the Ussuri River, and it fought a long and bloody conventional war in Afghanistan.

In the 1952 election campaign, the Republicans talked of "rolling back" the Soviets from Eastern Europe, but when the Soviet Union intervened with troops to put down the rebellions in Czechoslovakia and Hungary, the United States did nothing. It became obvious that an American intervention would be extremely costly, that it would have little hope of success, and that it might well lead to World War III.

When the Soviet Union and Communist China clashed along the Ussuri River, there was no talk of intervention. The reaction of most Americans seems to have been to wish for "a plague on both their houses," and among some a naïve hope that the two Communist giants would destroy each other.

The American attitude toward the Soviet intervention in Afghanistan was different. American sympathies were with the Afghan rebels, but the logistics of an American intervention were daunting. Not only was Afghanistan on the other side of the world, but the supply lines would have to cross Pakistan, at least, and both the Pakistanis and the Americans feared that the Soviet Union might use the presence of American troops in Pakistan as an excuse to invade. In the end, the United States contented itself with supplying the Afghanistan rebels with arms, including Stinger antiaircraft missiles, ammunition, supplies of many types, and money.

GREAT BRITAIN'S SMALL WARS

Great Britain fought the Suez War against Egypt, a war against Argentina when it occupied the Falkland Islands, and the long civil war in Northern Ireland.

The United States was not consulted before the invasion of Suez, probably because both the British and the French believed that the Americans would not approve. In any case, the Eisenhower administration mobilized world opinion against the war and succeeded in forcing the British and French to withdraw.

The United States regarded Argentina's invasion of the Falklands as a violation of international law and the British counterattack as fully justified. Britain could, of course, handle the problem on its own, and the United States confined itself to political and some minor logistical support.

As for the troubles in Northern Ireland, the United States did what it could to bring about negotiations but did not see the rebellion as being a threat to the United States or to world peace. The conclusion is that none of these three interventions is an example of a situation that would call for intervention by the United States in the future.

THE UNITED STATES AND ITS SMALL WARS

Since World War II, the United States has fought substantial wars in Korea during the Truman administration, in Vietnam during the Johnson and Nixon administrations, and in the Persian Gulf during the Bush administration. It also intervened with combat troops in one part of the world or another in every administration since World War II except those of Eisenhower and Kennedy, which both sent advisers to Vietnam and various other places but not troops. The Johnson administration sent American troops into combat in the Dominican Republic. The Ford administration sent troops into combat at the time of the *Mayaguez* incident, and the Carter administration sent them to Iran in the aborted attempt to rescue the hostages. President Reagan sent marines into Lebanon and 241 were killed in their barracks in Beirut by a fanatic driving a truck bomb. President Reagan also ordered the invasion of Grenada, and he ordered the bombing of Libya in retaliation for the terrorist attack that killed two American soldiers in a disco in Germany. President Bush invaded Panama to seize President Noriega, who was accused of drug dealing. President Clinton ordered air attacks on Iraq following a threat to former President Bush, air attacks in the former Yugoslavia, an intervention with troops in Bosnia on a peacekeeping mission, and a second series of air attacks on Iraq in 1998 and 1999.

As for the Korean War, a view from the broad sweep of history suggests that if the United States had not intervened, the same sort of attack might have been made on West Germany by East Germany. Thus, a persuasive argument can be made that the American intervention accomplished a useful purpose by deterring the Communist world from an attack in Europe.

As for the American intervention in Vietnam, a view from the broad sweep of history suggests it did not serve any useful purpose. The struggle in Vietnam was carried on by a nationalist, anticolonialist movement whose leaders, by an accident of history, were members of the Communist Party. It is obvious that the leaders of Vietnam were not the vanguard of some sort of worldwide Communist aggression. For a thousand years, the Vietnamese had been resisting Chinese imperialism, and they were determined to avoid giving China any excuse for intervening. So they accepted logistical support from both the Chinese and the Soviets but were determined not to allow the introduction of either Soviet or Chinese troops.

Although the so-called "domino theory" was popular in the American press at the time, the Communist Vietnamese had no imperialistic ambitions that would have threatened Thailand, Indonesia, or the Philippines. Some Vietnamese may well have dreamed of reestablishing French Indochina with the Vietnamese dominating, but, as events made clear, Vietnam was willing to settle for the neutrality of Laos and Cambodia so they would serve as buffers between Vietnam and the rest of Southeast Asia. Quite clearly the struggle in Vietnam had little potential for spreading beyond the former Indochina.[1] Of a war that cost so much as the war in Vietnam and achieved so little, the most charitable thing that can be said is that it was tragically misguided.

As for President Johnson's intervention in the Dominican Republic, the situation clearly had no wider implications. Even if Communists had succeeded in taking over the leadership of the coup, the result might have been unpleasant for the United States, as the Castro control of Cuba has been unpleasant, but no actual threat. Similar situations should be handled by diplomacy and the good offices of international organizations, not by military force.

The *Mayaguez* incident, in which thirty-eight Marines died forcing Cambodia to release an American ship, is another situation that should have been handled, at least initially, by diplomacy and the good offices of international organizations. The most charitable thing that can be said about President Ford's decision is that it was hasty, and made without considering the alternatives.

President Carter's decision to try to rescue the hostages held at the American embassy in Iran was undoubtedly inspired by the success the Israelis had had in rescuing the hostages who were held at Entebbe airport in Uganda in 1976 and who were being threatened with immediate execution. But the American hostages in Iran were not being threatened with death, and it was foolish to the point of absurdity to think that hostages held in the center of a large city could be rescued as easily as hostages held at an airport some distance outside a city. As with President Ford's decision about the *Mayaguez*, the most charitable thing to be said about Carter's decision to try to rescue the hostages by force is that it was hasty and ill-considered. It was diplomacy and the good offices of international organizations that eventually freed the hostages and not military force.

President Reagan's decision to station troops in Beirut was not an issue of the Cold War, which most of the other American interventions were at least perceived to be. The motive was mainly to try to head off a larger war between Israel and the Arabs. Concentrating the American marines in a barracks without adequate precautions to ensure their safety was silly, but the blame belongs not to President Reagan and the civilian leadership in Washington, but to the Pentagon and the local commander. So the actual decision to send the troops to Lebanon seems to fit the criterion of heading off what might be a spiral into a large war.

As for Grenada, it is extremely improbable that American security was threatened. Like President Johnson and the problem of the Dominican Republic, President Reagan would have done better to deal with the problem of Grenada—if it was indeed a problem—with diplomacy and the good offices of international organizations, rather than military force.

As for President Reagan's decision to bomb Libya, although it is impossible to prove, it is at least conceivable that the bombing led Qaddafi to curb the terrorists based in Libya at least temporarily. But the same result might well have been achieved by asking other Arab states to try to persuade Qaddafi to abandon his support of terrorists. The trouble with bombing is that in the eyes of much of the world, especially the Third World, killing civilians—dramatized by the fact that one of them was Qaddafi's three-year-old adopted daughter—put the United States in the same gutter as Libya. "Never wrestle with a pig," as the old saying goes, "you both get dirty, and the pig likes it."

President Bush's decision to invade Panama to seize Noriega was regarded by most Latin Americans as a violation of international law and of the Rio treaty. Again, the use of military force put the United States in the same gutter with Noriega. And also, if the longer-range consequences are considered, the situation would have been better handled by diplomacy and the good offices of international organizations rather than military force.

President Johnson's decision to invade the Dominican Republic, President Reagan's decision to invade Grenada, and President Bush's decision to invade Panama were also of questionable legality in terms of international law. What is more, all three decisions were made without adequate consultation with the governments of Latin America. Parenthetically, it is worth noting that during the Cuban missile crisis, in the face of nuclear missiles capable of destroying every city in the United States except Seattle, Kennedy still went to the trouble of obtaining the approval of the Latin American countries before he ordered the quarantine. If these invasions of the Dominican Republic, Grenada, and Panama were really necessary, they should have been done only after obtaining the proper international approvals and then only if key Latin American countries had participated with military forces of their own.

All three decisions were also made in haste, as was President Carter's decision to try to rescue the hostages in Iran. Clemenceau once said that war is too important to be left to generals. Looking at this record, it seems that war is also too important to be left to presidents.

THE GULF WAR

President Bush justified going to war against Iraq on four separate grounds. If these four arguments are valid, they set a precedent that would probably require fairly frequent American intervention with military force and the United States would have to maintain rather substantial forces for that purpose. Because of the possible precedent set by the Gulf War and the implications of that precedent, Bush's arguments demand close scrutiny.[2]

The first of Bush's arguments justifying intervention against Iraq was a general point: The world could not let stand an unprovoked aggression of one country against another, such as Iraq's invasion and annexation of Kuwait. Second, Bush compared Saddam Hussein to Hitler, arguing that World War II could have been avoided had the Allies dealt with Hitler from the outset, nipping Nazi aggression in the bud. In a speech on August 15, 1991, Bush said, "A half a century ago, our nation and the world paid dearly for appeasing an aggressor who should, and could, have been stopped. We are not going to make the same mistake again." Third, Bush argued that heroic measures were needed to prevent a dictator from controlling Middle Eastern oil, on which the industrialized world was so heavily dependent. In that same August 15 speech referring to a possible attack on Saudi Arabia by Saddam Hussein, Bush said, "Our jobs, our way of life, our own freedom and the freedom of friendly countries all around the world would suffer if control of the world's great oil reserves fell into the hands of Saddam Hussein." Finally, after it was over, Bush justified the Gulf War on the grounds that Iraq was secretly engaged in building not only chemical weapons but nuclear weapons as well—which, he argued, the world simply could not tolerate. President Bush cast all these arguments in terms of his vision of a "new world order" in which the great powers would assume responsibility for maintaining the peace against aggressors throughout the world.

On President Bush's first point, not tolerating aggression, the American decisions in past cases have turned not so much on the moral issue of tolerating or not tolerating aggression as on two other questions. One was whether the United States and its interests were in fact threatened. The second was the pragmatic question of whether an American intervention would succeed. The United States fought in Korea and Vietnam on the grounds that the ultimate enemy in both cases was the Soviet Union and world Communism. In both cases the chances for victory seemed good before the fact. But in the case of Czechoslovakia, Hungary, and Afghanistan, the aggressor was the Soviet Union itself, the chances for an American victory seemed very slim indeed, and the United States decided that the better part of wisdom was not to intervene.

When it comes to aggressions like that of Iraq against Kuwait, the United States has tolerated dozens in recent history: the Indian takeover of Goa, the most recent Vietnamese invasion of Kampuchea, the Israeli occupation of the Gaza Strip and the West Bank, Israel's attack on Lebanon and its occupation of the Golan Heights, the Indonesian attack on East Timor, and the Iraqi attack on Iran, to name but a few. What weakened the argument that Iraq's aggression against Kuwait should not be tolerated still more is that the United States was itself vulnerable to charges of aggression in the invasions of Cambodia, Grenada, and Panama.

Bush's argument that Saddam Hussein was a new Hitler is particularly ironic, the irony being that for years both the Reagan and Bush administrations had supported Hussein, preferring to see him win in the Iran–Iraq war rather than the Ayatollah Khomeini. It was only when Hussein attacked Kuwait that Bush began to liken him to Hitler and called upon the Iraqi people to overthrow him.

Bush's argument was not just that Hussein was evil. Hussein was and is evil, but that did not keep the United States from supporting him against Iran. Bush's argument was that Hussein was like Hitler in being a threat to world peace. No one has any doubt that Hussein is indeed a villain in the mold of Hitler, but in the sense of being a threat to the United States and the world, the comparison is ridiculous. Hitler commanded a highly industrialized nation with a population larger than any other in Western Europe. Germany had a long history of military excellence in terms both of its generals and its soldiers. Germany under Hitler conquered Europe, and threatened both the Soviet Union and the United Kingdom. For its part, Iraq had little industry except for its chemical, biological, and budding nuclear capacity, and it had only 18 million people. While Hitler was a threat to the entire world, it is very doubtful whether Hussein and Iraq—which is, after all, a comparative midget of a country—could ever be a threat to anyone except Iraq's immediate neighbors. In a word, Bush's comparison of Saddam Hussein to Hitler trivialized Hitler and inflated Saddam Hussein.

As for Bush's argument that the United States could not permit Saddam Hussein to control Kuwaiti oil and perhaps Saudi Arabian oil, the fact is that even if Saddam Hussein did come to control both, it would do him no good unless he could sell it. If he had continued to control Kuwaiti oil, he would undoubtedly have raised the price, but if he raised it too high, the United States and the other industrial nations had several alternatives. At a somewhat higher price, oil from Canada, Venezuela, Mexico, and Texas begins to be competitive. The United States could also have turned to other sources of energy, such as coal, solar power, and nuclear energy. What determines the price of oil is not what the oil producers desire but the "substitution price," the cost of the substitute forms of energy. In any case, the people of France and the United Kingdom have been paying three or four times what an American pays for a gallon of gasoline for many years, and the difference is hardly worth the lives lost in the Gulf War—over 400 American, British, and Arab allies and an estimated 200 thousand Iraqi, half military and half civilian.[3]

President Bush, finally, justified the war on the grounds that Iraq was attempting to build chemical, biological, and nuclear weapons and that this simply could not be tolerated. This last argument seems to be based on "good" reasons rather than real ones. In the first place, since Iraq lacked a long-range delivery capability, the chemical and biological warfare threat was mainly to Iraq's neighbors. Any threat to the larger world was minor and would be followed by a terrifying retaliation. In view of all this, the only way the threat could be handled without an Arab backlash against both the United States and Israel would be to have the Arabs themselves handle it.

As for the nuclear threat that Bush put so central, it was only after the war that the United States discovered that Iraq's nuclear program was more extensive and further along than the world had realized. But the United States also discovered at the same time that the program was still limited. Iraq might well have been able to build a few nuclear warheads similar to the 14-kiloton bomb dropped on Hiroshima, but as the director of the Defense Nuclear Agency, General Gerald G. Watson, said, if Iraq did succeed in building such a nuclear weapon "it would weigh five tons and have to be carried on a flatbed trailer." The point is that it is not warheads that are the crucial factor in a nuclear threat, but delivery capability. It would take many years for a country like Iraq with a small population and a limited industrial capacity to develop a delivery capability that could reach any farther than its next-door neighbors.

What weakens Bush's argument even more is that several other countries pose a similar threat. Humankind is going to have to do something to bring all nuclear weapons under some sort of international control, the known stockpiles held by the United States, Russia, France, Great Britain, China, and Israel, as well as the potential stockpiles that North Korea, India, Pakistan, Libya, and Iran have already built or may build in the near future. If instead of working for international control the United States tries to use war to solve the problem of small countries building nuclear weapons, it will be involved in more or less continuous warfare all over the world for years to come.

The conclusion seems inescapable that the American and allied decision to expel Iraq from Kuwait by war was not really justified by any of President Bush's four arguments. What is more, the political costs of the American intervention in the Gulf were both high and undoubtedly long-lasting. During the war the United States bombed Iraq's water purification, electrical generating, and sewage plants. Bombing these plants had almost no military effect, but it contributed significantly to the total of about 150 thousand deaths of Iraqi civilians, the majority of whom were children. Many people in both Arab and Third World countries will not forgive the United States for decades to come. Another political cost came when Bush encouraged the Shiites and Kurds to rebel, and then, when they did so, left them hanging, easy victims of Hussein's Republican Guard.

So the final result of the Gulf War was twofold. The first was successfully ousting Iraq from Kuwait and restoring the monarchy to its throne, although it must also be said that this is a corrupt and despotic monarchy for whom most Arabs have little affection. The second was to leave Saddam Hussein and the Baath party in power—and also to leave them controlling sufficient military force for Saddam Hussein to put down both the Shiite and the Kurdish rebellions, which he promptly did.

As for President Bush's notion of a new world order, it was not favorably received, especially by the Third World. To many developing nations, Bush's new world order suggested a "new American imperialism." It sounded especially ominous because of the turmoil in what had been the Soviet Union. When there were two superpowers, one restrained the other. When there is only one, the developing world speculated, what will happen to us?

The final criticism to be made of the Gulf War is that the diplomatic and international alternatives to war were never given more than cursory examination. Iraq had several legitimate complaints before the crisis began, including the fact that Kuwait was pirating oil from the Iraqi part of the Rumaila oilfield with slant wells and the fact that Kuwait was violating the OPEC oil quotas, which kept the price low and hampered Iraq in paying off its debts.[4] If the United States had joined the Arab states in offering their good offices, the Iraqi invasion of Kuwait might well have been avoided altogether. Given his ambition to be a leader of the Arab world, Hussein would not have lightly turned his back on a "brotherly" Arab solution.

After the invasion, one alternative was a boycott. A boycott would probably not have forced Iraq to withdraw from Kuwait. But if it had been coupled with a program to make the United States less dependent on Middle Eastern oil—which will be necessary in a very few years in any case—any gains that Iraq hoped to make by invading Kuwait would have been soon nullified.

If the situation had to come to war, it would have been infinitely better politically if the ground fighting to evict Iraq from Kuwait had been done by Arabs, with the Americans and other allies supplying the air and naval contingents. In the "worst case" scenario in which the Arabs refused to take responsibility, Hussein might have waited until the United States finally withdrew its forces from Saudi Arabia and proceeded to invade. Hussein would then have controlled 21.5 percent of global oil production and a somewhat higher percent of known reserves. Price increases, as mentioned, would have brought wells in Venezuela, Canada, Mexico, and Texas into production to make up the difference. If the United States then adopted an aggressive program to find oil substitutes, Hussein's leverage would not have lasted long.

Apart from oil, had Hussein been able to forge his conquests into a single, homogeneous nation—which is very doubtful—its population would still have been less than 50 million and its industrial capacity limited. Egypt and the rest of the Arab states would have been thoroughly alarmed and much more likely to take major responsibility for containing any future Iraqi expansion.

As with the war in Vietnam the most charitable thing that can be said about the Gulf War—which cost so much and achieved so little—is that it was tragically misguided. The conclusion seems to be inescapable, then, that the Gulf War holds few if any lessons about the nature and frequency of nonnuclear, conventional wars for which the United States must be prepared.

President Clinton's Bombing of Iraq

In 1993, former President Bush visited Kuwait to accept its thanks for his intervention and expelling Iraq from Kuwait. Intelligence reported that Iraq planned to try to assassinate Bush during the visit, and in response President Clinton ordered a guided missile attack on certain military installations in Iraq. The attack was undoubtedly the source of some psychological satisfaction to all Americans, regardless of party, demonstrated by the fact that Clinton's popularity rating went up eleven points in the following days. But even if the Iraqi government did indeed plot Bush's assassination, the trouble with a policy of tit for tat is that Iraq might feel compelled to try to retaliate for the retaliation—by attempting another assassination, by planting bombs on American airplanes, or by trying to find an American skyscraper, tunnel, or bridge to blow up.

Iraq and Its Chemical and Nuclear Weapons

Several months after the end of the Gulf War, President Bush authorized a $15 million CIA program to oust Saddam Hussein, and then expanded it to $40 million. In spite of the Congressional ban on assassinating foreign leaders, several members of Congress called for Hussein's assassination.

In the spring of 1993, the Clinton administration concluded that the Bush administration's covert CIA program to overthrow Saddam Hussein had failed even to weaken him. It said that much of the aid had been misdirected to groups with no popular following in Iraq and that too much money had been spent on propaganda efforts that had little impact. Senior officials of the Clinton administration said that the Bush administration's demonization of Hussein as worse than Hitler was foolish because it raised expectations that he would be overthrown in spite of the fact that there were no organized opposition groups in Iraq. The Clinton administration said that it would focus on Iraq's compliance with U.N. sanctions. However, it did plan to maintain a scaled-down version of the covert program with only half the funds.

In 1998 a news story on a new set of CIA plans to overthrow Saddam Hussein was followed the next day with an editorial in *The New York Times* arguing two points.[5] The first was that the idea that covert operations mounted by the United States can overthrow someone like Saddam Hussein is fantasy. The second was that covert operations make matters worse because they do not remain covert for long. The White House, the *Times* argued, should consider supporting an opposition group to form a provisional government on Iraqi territory protected by

American air power. This seems impractical for now, it said, although there may be other ways to help build an opposition front that could someday be a credible alternative to Saddam Hussein. But Washington ought to recognize that the CIA is not the answer. The *Times* was undoubtedly right—except that the idea that the United States could build an opposition outside of Iraq that could someday be a credible alternative to Saddam Hussein is also fantasy.

Subsequent Events

As a condition of the cease fire after the Gulf War, the United Nations demanded and Saddam Hussein agreed that Iraq would within fifteen days declare the number and location of its nuclear, chemical, and biological weapons and the missiles to deliver them. The United Nations set up a special commission of experts (UNSCOM) to inspect Iraqi installations to ensure compliance.

As President Clinton charged in a speech on February 17, 1998, Iraq tried to prevent UNSCOM from doing its work. It repeatedly made false declarations about the weapons it still had in its possession. When UNSCOM uncovered evidence that gave the lie to these declarations, Iraq simply amended its reports. Iraq, President Clinton went on to say, revised its nuclear declarations four times within just fourteen months, and it submitted six different biological warfare declarations, each of which was rejected by UNSCOM.

Lt. General Hussein Kamal, Saddam's son-in-law, was the overlord of Iraq's biological warfare effort. In 1995, he defected to Jordan, and he then revealed that Iraq was continuing to conceal such weapons and their missiles. Iraq then admitted having an offensive biological capability: 5 thousand gallons of botulinum, 2 thousand gallons of anthrax, twenty-five biological-filled Scud warheads, and 157 aerial bombs. Earlier in 1995, two Iraqi generals had admitted to U.N. inspectors that Iraq had produced enough deadly microbes to kill everyone in the world. However, the location of 150 bombs and warheads built by Iraq to dispense germs remain a mystery. So do a dozen special nozzles to spray germs from aircraft and helicopters. Inspectors have found undeclared "dual use" nutrients that have legitimate uses but also could be used to make deadly pathogens. Inspectors have been told of thousands of gallons of biological agents, but they have not been able to find them. The government of Iraq says they were destroyed, but there are no records of this. The U.N. inspectors can account for only twenty-five germ bombs of the 157 Iraq has admitted making. Also, the inspectors have no idea what happened to some twenty-five germ warheads that Iraq made for missiles with a range of 400 miles. Iraq says they were destroyed, but no proof has been found.

Many nations experimented with germ warfare agents in the 1950s and 1960s, but quit after they concluded that such weapons were too difficult to handle. Iraqi officials confessed that they had produced, at the factory at Al Hakam, thousands of gallons of deadly anthrax and botulism toxin, enough to wipe out whole cities and nations. But they denied having made the weapons to deliver these agents.

The defection of Hussein Kamal, Saddam's son-in-law, occurred after a quarrel at a family dinner that left six bodyguards dead. Shortly after Kamal revealed Iraq's biological warfare program, Iraq produced documents on the production of biological weapons "that the traitor Kamal had hidden from the Iraqi government." The documents showed that Iraq had done research on germ warfare agents; field tested germs in sprayers, rockets, bombs, and so on; and begun a crash program to speed germ development. They also showed that when Iraq invaded Kuwait, it had built and loaded twenty-five germ warheads for missiles with a range of 400 miles and a number of bombs with germ warfare agents, deployed these weapons at four locations, and kept them at the ready throughout the war. After the war, Iraq claimed that it had destroyed all these at the end of the war, although doing so was a violation of the cease fire. Inspectors doubted that the weapons had been destroyed. As for Kamal, he returned to Iraq, repentant over his defection. However, he was almost immediately killed in circumstances not yet known in the West. As a result of all this, the Pentagon announced it would give anthrax vaccinations to all active duty and reserve troops.

Then, in the fall of 1997, Iraq began interfering with the U.N. inspectors, and by January 1998, it had blocked inspectors from eight particularly suspicious sites. One, for example, was the site of a presidential palace comprising 40 thousand acres, the size of Washington, D.C. These sites are not likely to contain weapons, but they probably contain records that would permit the inspectors to reconstruct the Iraqi program. In his speech on February 17, 1998, Clinton went on to say that "throughout this entire process, Iraqi agents have undermined and undercut UNSCOM. They've harassed the inspectors, lied to them, disabled monitoring cameras, literally spirited evidence out of the back doors of suspected facilities as inspectors walked through the front door. Our people were there observing it and have the pictures to prove it."

The U.S. response was to build up its military forces in the region. As of February 1998, there were two American and one British aircraft carrier battle groups in the Persian Gulf with another British one on the way. The United States also had a squadron of Tornado bombers in the area, and Navy warships equipped with Tomahawk cruise missiles. The most advanced Air Force bombers and weaponry were stationed ashore in Kuwait, Saudi Arabia, and Bahrain. Both B-52 bombers on the island of Diego Garcia in the Indian Ocean and B-2 Stealth bombers in the United States could make round trips to Iraq. Although Saudi Arabia refused to allow attack planes on its soil as it did during the Gulf War, it did allow AWACS (airborne warning and control system) aircraft and airborne fuel tankers to be based there.

The planned air strike on Iraq, codenamed Desert Thunder, would involve up to 300 daily bombing raids against a wide range of targets and go on for four days, twenty-four hours a day. All the important targets would be hit nearly simultaneously in a night attack with Tomahawk missiles and precision bombs from carrier and land-based aircraft. The attack would include B-1 bombers with heavy bomb loads and B-52s with missiles that can be launched from well outside the target area. The B-2 Stealth bombers would go after air defenses and other particularly valuable targets, such as the Iraqi air force. Targets buried underground would be attacked with deep penetration bombs, which had been vastly improved since the Gulf War. Other preferred targets included the Republican Guard, supply depots, and communications systems. However, in response to calls to make Saddam Hussein a principal target, the American military said that lack of intelligence and Hussein's practice of sleeping each night in a different location makes the idea a will-o'-the-wisp.

The United States made a crucial decision to exclude targets that had a high risk of civilian casualties. It took chemical and biological factories off the list for fear of unleashing a toxic plume over Baghdad, but about 1,500 civilian casualties were still expected. The planners did not expect Iraq to launch a chemical or biological attack in retaliation because Iraq is too vulnerable to a devastating response by the United States.

However, American officials admitted that bombing is a poor substitute for oversight by inspectors on the ground, but they insisted it is the best alternative. The first idea was a long bombing campaign with pauses. But the feeling was that a drawn-out campaign created too great an opportunity for world opinion to object.

After a tour of the Middle East in which he met with the leaders of a number of Gulf states, Secretary of Defense William Cohen reported that they were hostile to military action against Iraq. Also, the press reported that senior American military men believed an air campaign would neither destroy Iraq's weapon stockpile nor drive Hussein from power.[6] A bombing campaign, one general said, would just put holes in the desert. Air power using conventional bombs has never forced an enemy to give up by itself. In the 1991 Gulf War, a month-long, round-the-clock bombing campaign failed to make Hussein withdraw from Kuwait. To drive him out took half a million ground forces. Also, it seemed likely that pressure from Russia, France, China, and the Arab countries would persuade Clinton to limit targets to known and suspected sites of chemical and biological weapons to minimize civilian casualties. Most military men felt that an air campaign alone will just be an annoyance to Hussein.

President Clinton declared that the United States preferred to find a diplomatic way to do what had to be done if at all possible. But a diplomatic solution must not gloss over the remaining problem, he said. Iraq must promptly agree to free, unfettered access to sites anywhere in the country. The United States, he said, had spent several weeks building up our forces in the Gulf and forging a coalition of like-minded nations. If Saddam Hussein rejects peace and we have to use force, our purpose is clear. We want to reduce the threat posed by Iraq's weapons of mass destruction. A military operation cannot destroy all his weapons of mass destruction, the president continued. But it can and will leave him significantly worse off than he is now in his ability to threaten the world. The president also made it clear that the economic sanctions would remain in place until Saddam Hussein complied fully with all U.N. resolutions.

Almost everyone with military and foreign policy experience agreed that bombing alone would not succeed in eliminating Iraq's weapons of mass destruction. To accomplish that task, bombing would have to be accompanied by an invasion of ground forces.[7] Yet both the Republican and Democratic leaders in Congress, none of whom have had military experience, not only repeatedly called for bombing Iraq but also insisted that no ground forces should be involved.

In what was apparently an attempt to build public support for the idea of bombing Iraq, President Clinton directed Secretary of State Madeleine Albright, Secretary of Defense William Cohen, and National Security Adviser Samuel R. Berger to conduct a public meeting on the subject at Columbus, Ohio, on February 18, 1998. The result was ninety minutes of public angst and opposition. The three were needled with skeptical and hostile questions from hawks who wanted to see Saddam Hussein destroyed even if it required an invasion by American troops, and from doves who opposed any use of military force.[8]

Secretary Cohen replied to a question about our moral right to bomb Iraq by asking rhetorically if Saddam Hussein had the right to use weapons of mass destruction against his own people. *The New York Times*, February 19, 1998, reported that the answer to a veteran's nearly tearful concern that bombing would fall short of ending Hussein's rule failed to describe a coherent end-game strategy. A history teacher asked Secretary Albright about our apparently inconsistent stance toward rogue states other than Iraq, and Albright "patronizingly" instructed the teacher to "study carefully what American foreign policy is." In the view of one commentator, it was not the screaming protestors so much as the secretary of state's self-righteous condescension that most recalled the Vietnam era in which the best and the brightest of Ivy League trained policy makers were impaled on their own arrogance. The arrogance also showed during one of Albright's appearances on the NBC "Today" show only a few days later. "If we have to use force," she said, "it is because we are America. We are the indispensable nation. We stand tall. We see further into the future."

One theory of why Albright, Cohen, and Berger were sent to Ohio was that Clinton did not dare go himself because he would be asked questions about Monica Lewinsky, the White House intern who had a sexual relationship with him. Clinton himself would have handled the questions with skill, flattering the questioners rather than putting them down. The veteran's pain would have been felt by the president. The teacher would have been flattered rather than insulted.[9]

Also on February 17, the same day that Clinton was speaking, the U.N. Security Council gave its blessing for Secretary General Kofi Annan to go to Baghdad to try to resolve the crisis. Hussein agreed to permit unrestricted inspection of eight previously closed presidential sites, to let the regular U.N. inspectors do the inspecting, and to drop the sixty-day time limit. In return, Annan agreed that diplomats could accompany the inspectors. Annam duly submitted the question of lifting the sanctions to the Security Council, and on February 20 it adopted a resolution that increased the amount of oil Iraq could sell to finance its relief needs from $2 billion every six months to $5.2 billion every six months.

President Clinton welcomed the agreement, saying that if fully implemented, the commitment would allow UNSCOM to fulfill its mission. He went on to say that if Iraq reneges this time everyone will understand that the United States and its allies would have "the right to respond at a time, place and manner of our own choosing." The U.N. Security Council unanimously endorsed Annan's agreement with Saddam Hussein, but it did not authorize an automatic air attack by the United States if Iraq did not honor the agreement. A White House statement in reply said that the warning by the United Nations that "severest consequences" would follow if Iraq broke the pact meant the use of military force.

In late July 1998, the International Atomic Energy Agency reported that it had found no evidence that Iraq had any nuclear weapons in its possession. But it went on to say that Iraq's failure to account for key nuclear equipment left open the possibility that it had been hidden for future use. Also, the inspectors had not been able to confirm that Iraq had destroyed, as it claimed, a furnace to melt uranium into spheres to form the core of a nuclear bomb. On August 5, Iraq stopped on-site inspections by the U.N. arms monitors. Richard Butler, the chief U.N. inspector, met with Iraq's deputy prime minister, Tariq Aziz, and offered him a five-week schedule of inspections to resolve the problem, but Aziz refused. Even so, in the U.N. Security Council, both Russia and France were eager to ease sanctions; Kofi Annan, the U.N. Secretary General, seemed uncertain of what to do; and so did the United States. In response to further attempts at mediation, Iraq said they would not permit inspectors to work until they declared the nation free of nuclear, chemical, and biological arms and the U.N. Security Council lifted the trade embargo.

In response, the United States began a buildup of military forces in the Persian Gulf. Unlike the earlier crisis, there was no opposition from Russia, France, or the U.N. secretary general. Egypt, Syria, and six other Arab states warned Iraq that it alone would take the blame for defying the United Nations and that failing to allow the arms inspectors to resume their work "will expose the Iraqi people to more misery."

On November 13, after a five-hour meeting with the Security Council, Kofi Annan sent an appeal to Saddam Hussein. In his reply, Hussein agreed to permit the U.N. inspectors to resume their work, under certain conditions, such as the completion in seven days of the U.N.'s comprehensive review of Iraq–U.N. relations, changes in the structure of UNSCOM and its practices, and other conditions that had already been rejected by the United States, Britain, and other council members. Samuel R. Berger, the national security adviser, said that the conditions were unacceptable and that the offer had "more holes than a Swiss cheese."

The attack was scheduled to begin on Saturday at 9 A.M. EST. Berger was awakened by a phone call shortly after 8 A.M. saying that CNN was reporting from Baghdad that the Iraqis had sent a letter to the United Nations agreeing to allow the inspectors to resume their work. Seven B-52 bombers, fully loaded, were actually nearing Iraq on a bombing mission and fourteen U.S. warships in the Persian Gulf were counting down to fire nearly 300 cruise missiles. Berger rushed to the White House and after consultations advised the president to postpone the attack. According to newspaper reports, White House officials felt that you could not order an attack that would kill thousands of people if the adversary was giving in to your demands. President Clinton picked up the phone and aborted the attack. But he rescheduled it for Sunday.

President Clinton canceled a scheduled trip to Asia, deciding to send the vice president in his place. A copy of Hussein's letter to Kofi Annan arrived at the

White House in the middle of the morning. After studying the letter, the president and his advisers decided that it was unacceptable. Saturday evening copies of two more letters to the U.N. Security Council arrived at the White House. In these letters, Iraq eliminated the unacceptable conditions, promised to provide two sensitive documents on its chemical and biological weapons programs that had earlier been refused, and promised to permit the inspectors full and unfettered access to all sites, including those that had been most in dispute. By telephone, British Prime Minister Tony Blair said that Iraq should specifically renounce its August 5 and October 31 refusals to comply with the weapons inspectors. Another letter from the Iraqis arrived at 9:06 P.M. that met Blair's demand. The discussions continued throughout the night, and included conversations with the secretary of defense, the director of the CIA, the chairman of the JCS, Tony Blair, French President Jacques Chirac, and long telephone conversations with the vice president on his way to Malaysia and with Secretary Albright, who was already there.

In the early hours on Sunday, a consensus was reached that the United States could not attack Iraq if the Iraqis had already acceded to Washington's demands. At 3 A.M., Berger talked to Kofi Annan to make sure that they agreed on what the Iraqis' statements meant and what they had promised. A few minutes later a call to General Shelton at the Pentagon canceled the attack. Later that day, the president reported to the American people.

In his report, President Clinton said that since Saddam Hussein had unconditionally retreated and had vowed complete cooperation with the U.N. inspectors, he had called off the planned air strikes. However, he went on to say, "Iraq has backed down, but that is not enough." He said that Iraq must live up to its obligations and that the American and British forces assembled for the attack will remain poised to act. The president then went on to call more openly than ever before for the overthrow of Saddam Hussein, calling him "an impediment to the well-being of his people and a threat to the peace of his region and the security of the world."

Iraq continued obstructing the inspectors. For example, a document indicating that Iraq had stockpiled chemical and biological munitions was literally snatched from their hands. Iraq hoped to have the sanctions lifted, but the U.N. Security Council refused until there was full cooperation with the inspectors.

Inspections were allowed again in early December, but within days inspectors were barred from the Baghdad headquarters of the ruling Baath Party. Richard Butler, the chief U.N. inspector, protested and removed his people. Twenty-four hours later, President Clinton ordered the "strong sustained series of air strikes" that he had earlier threatened.

In Washington, the Republicans postponed the scheduled vote on impeaching President Clinton, but they were bitter about the timing of the bombing. Tradition calls for unity when American troops are engaged, but Senator Trent Lott, the Republican majority leader, said that he could not support military action at this time: "Both the timing and the policy are subject to question."

The air strikes by American and British forces lasted four nights, ending just before the start of the Moslem holy month of Ramadan. The targets included command posts, missile factories, airfields, an oil refinery, intelligence installations, military communications sites, the headquarters and barracks of four divisions of the Republican Guard, the headquarters of the Baath Party, and seven of Saddam Hussein's presidential palaces. Biological and chemical warfare sites were avoided for fear that bombing would disperse lethal agents. One hundred targets were hit by 450 sea and air launched cruise missiles and 650 sorties of manned aircraft. Forty-three targets were severly damaged, thirty received moderate damage, twelve only light damage, and at least thirteen were not damaged at all.

Initial assessment was that the attack may have set back Iraq's goal of building the means to deliver weapons of mass destruction by a year. Some observers thought it would take Saddam two or three years to build missiles that would threaten his neighbors, less time if he could obtain enriched uranium from Russia. Others said he could rebuild his biological and chemical programs by June.

In the period following the attack, Iraqi antiaircraft batteries occasionally fired on allied aircraft patrolling the no-flight zones over Iraq. The goal of such attacks was not clear, but there was speculation that the Iraqis wanted to capture a pilot to use as a bargaining chip.

Sanctions hurt more than bombing. They are estimated to have cost Iraq $120 billion in oil revenues. Denis J. Halliday, head of the U.N. humanitarian workers in Iraq until his resignation in 1998, said that sanctions "are starving to death 6,000 Iraqi infants every month, ignoring the human rights of ordinary Iraqis and turning a whole generation against the West." An earlier U.N. report said that 40,000 more children and 50,000 more adults die each year in Iraqi hospitals than died before the sanctions were imposed. Although only a handful of the Arab governments condemned the bombing, most are opposed to continuing the sanctions. So are a growing number of members of the U.N. Security Council.

However, there is evidence that Iraq has put off buying or distributing vital food and medicines it can import through authorized oil sales. For example, almost $25 million has been budgeted for high-protein biscuits and fortified milk for children under five and nursing mothers, but Iraq has placed no orders despite repeated urging by U.N. officials.

Analysis

In view of all this, it seems clear that short of another full-scale invasion of Iraq, followed this time by a long-term occupation, no American unilateral action will change the situation in Iraq very much. A combination of time, an effort to enlist world opinion, steps to involve the United Nations, and patience seems to be the wisest course. The only thing that a bombing attack on Iraq accomplishes is to increase the Third World's sympathy for Iraq and its hostility toward the United States.

BOSNIA-HERZEGOVINA

If the major purpose for intervening in local struggles in the years ahead is to head off a spiral into wider and bigger international wars, then the policy the Europeans followed for so long of blocking an intervention in Bosnia-Herzegovina was more sensible than many Americans thought. Civilians, women, and children were slaughtered in the name of ethnic cleansing, which is simply another form of Hitler's Holocaust. But the struggle was not likely to spread beyond the Balkans.

The reasons are fairly obvious. The fundamental cause of the breakup of Yugoslavia was nationalism. Each nationality wanted a state of its own, and each wanted either to seize enough territory from one of the other former members of Yugoslavia to make a viable state or to protect its own territory from an aggressive rival. The second motive was to take revenge for outrages perpetrated in the past. Revenge against the Muslims for what the Turks had done to the Christians was one motive. Another, at least for the Serbs, was revenge for what the Croatian allies of the Nazis had done during World War II. None of the contenders had any designs on the territory of any state that was not a member of the former Yugoslavia. Nor did any of the other Balkan countries have designs on any territory of the former Yugoslavia.[10]

The Muslim countries were sympathetic to the plight of their coreligionists, but it became very clear very quickly that although they might protest bitterly about what was happening, they were not about to do anything more than protest and send a few volunteers as advisers. The Muslim powers had too many more serious problems much closer to home. Second, the number of their coreligionists was too small and Bosnia was too far away for them to intervene on their own.

As for the great powers, none had any political, strategic, or power stake in the struggle except to keep it from becoming a wider war, which, as already mentioned, was not considered very likely.[11] The grounds for intervention by any of the great powers would have to be solely humanitarian, to reduce the killing. Even so, there were doubts that intervention would reduce the killing in the long run. If intervention included ground troops, it might impose a peace by sheer force of arms. But the likelihood is that no matter how long the peacekeepers stayed, whether ten, twenty, or even one-hundred years, once they were withdrawn the contenders would be back at each other's throats. If the intervention was limited to air power, the result was likely to do no more than increase the killing by escalating and prolonging the fighting. What the British foreign minister, Douglas Hurd, said about sending arms to Bosnia also applied to intervention limited to air power—the most it could hope to do was to "level the killing fields," escalating the losses but solving nothing. As it happened, President Clinton did decide to intervene on humanitarian grounds, which will be examined in Chapter 23.

SUMMARY

Neither the host of civil wars nor the Soviet intervention in Afghanistan meets the criterion of heading off a larger war. Neither does the Vietnam War, the Nixon incursion into Cambodia, the Johnson intervention in the Dominican Republic, the Carter attempted *coup de main* in Iran, the Reagan invasion of Grenada, the Reagan bombing of Libya, the Bush invasion of Panama, the Bush intervention in the Gulf, nor the two Clinton bombings of Iraq. None of them were intended to halt wars that might spiral into a wider war.

President Bush's decision to send troops to Somalia was purely humanitarian, not an attempt to head off a wider war. No one even suggested any possibility that the fighting would escalate beyond Somalia. Neither ethnic nor religious rivalries were at issue. The purpose was to see that food and medical supplies were protected from rival warlords and safely delivered to starving people. As such, the motive was not antiescalation, but humanitarian, and accordingly it will be dealt with in Chapter 23.

In the case of Bosnia-Herzegovina, the first point to note is that the motives behind most of the proposals were peacekeeping. The goal in these instances was to stop the fighting by getting a political agreement on how to divide the territory under dispute. An example was the original Vance–Owen plan, which proposed to pressure the contenders to agree to divide the territory of the former Yugoslavia among the major ethnic, religious, and nationalist contenders— Bosnians, Serbs, and Muslims—and then to use military force under U.N. auspices to enforce the agreement. Another example was the Dayton agreement.

Some of the other proposals, such as President Clinton's original idea of bombing the Serbian troops attacking Muslim or Croatian towns and villages, were to use military power to try to force the contenders to work out their own compromise, as long as it would stop the killing. Other proposals were to arrange a peace and let the borders be wherever the troops were at the time—simply to stop the killing. Still other proposals were not really peacekeeping or aimed at establishing a peace but were intended merely to level the killing fields. An example was the proposal to lift the embargo on arms to Bosnia. It is also true that some of the advocates of the idea of bombing the Serbs who were attacking Muslim and Croatian towns and villages wanted more to level the killing fields than to force a compromise.

To sum up, if the principle is that the United States should be prepared to intervene to halt wars that might spiral into much bigger wars with a potential for becoming nuclear, the only wars in recent years in which an American intervention was justified were the intervention in Korea during the Truman administration and the intervention in Lebanon during the Reagan administration. Failure to respond to the attack on South Korea would have encouraged East Germany to attack West Germany in an attempt to unify the country on Communist terms. And an attack by East Germany on West Germany would most certainly have run the risk of spiraling into World War III. As for the intervention in Lebanon, the purpose of sending the Marines to Beirut was to try to head off a larger war between Israel and the Arabs that might escalate even further.

CONCLUSION

What lessons can be drawn from these two examples of intervention to head off a larger war? As for Korea, it does not necessarily follow that the United States must maintain forces in peace time to deal with something similar in the future.

The Korean War occurred in the midst of the Cold War struggle between the United States and the Soviet Union, a struggle that we assume will not be revived. No similar threat is on the horizon and there is no reason to maintain forces to meet that kind of attack. If a rivalry like that of the Cold War does arise in the future with a newly belligerent Russia, a newly hostile China, or with some unforeseen power there should be time to build the necessary forces.

However, the same cannot be said about the intervention in Lebanon. The possibility remains of a minor war erupting in the Middle East that could spiral into a major war with the potential of becoming nuclear. And this alone is justification enough for the United States to maintain a standing force that could intervene and stop such an escalation.

The conclusion, then, is that the United States should maintain the capacity to intervene to stop a war that has the potential for escalating into a wider struggle that could become nuclear. The nature and structure of such a force will be examined in Chapter 24.

In the meantime, a quite different problem needs to be examined: where to lodge responsibility for purely humanitarian interventions and for peacekeeping operations. An example of the first is the original mission in Somalia of protecting the distribution of food and medical supplies. As for intervening with military force in an ongoing war or civil war to stop the killing when the war in question has little potential for escalating, the most vivid recent example is President Clinton's decision to commit troops to separate the warring sides in Bosnia in 1995.

NOTES

1. For an analysis of the struggle in Vietnam, see Roger Hilsman, *To Move a Nation: The Politics of Foreign Policy in the Administration of John F. Kennedy* (Garden City, N.Y.: Doubleday, 1967); and Roger Hilsman, "Two American Counterstrategies to Guerrilla Warfare: The Case of Vietnam," in *China in Crisis*, vol. 2, ed. Tang Tsou (Chicago: University of Chicago Press, 1968).

2. This analysis is drawn from Roger Hilsman, *George Bush vs. Saddam Hussein: Military Success! Political Failure?* (Novato, Calif.: Presidio Press, 1992).

3. Ibid., 161, 209.

4. For a detailed examination of the events leading up to the Gulf War, see ibid.

5. Tim Weiner, "C.I.A. Drafts Covert Plan to Topple Hussein," *The New York Times*, 26 February 1998, p. A11, and "James Bond vs. Saddam Hussein," *The New York Times*, 27 February 1998, p. A24.

6. Bernard E. Trainor, "American Arms vs. Iraq," *The New York Times*, 13 February 1998, pp. 1, 8.

7. See, for example, Richard Perle, "Time to Get Saddam Hussein Out: Halfway Measures Won't Work—Here's What We Should Do in Iraq," *The Washington Post National Weekly Edition*, 16 February 1998, p. 21. Perle has the reputation of being very much a hard liner, and in this piece he argues that Saddam Hussein must be ousted, but that bombing alone will not work and an invasion by ground forces is essential. Apparently recognizing that few Americans would support invading Iraq, he wistfully argues that the Iraqi political opposition in exile can create the forces necessary among the Iraqi people.

8. *The New York Times*, 19 February 1998, p. A9.

9. I have a personal theory about why Clinton sent the team to Columbus that is somewhat different. In 1972, when Joseph Duffy ran for the Senate in Connecticut on a campaign directed solely against the war in Vietnam, young people came from all over the United States to work for him. My oldest son, Hoyt, was one of these, and he ended up being a paid worker in charge of New Haven. His boss was a Yale Law School student named Bill Clinton who was in charge of New Haven, Bridgeport, and one other town. The two of them spent a lot of time together, and long before Clinton became a candidate for the presidency Hoyt reported that Clinton had a psychological compulsion to be liked by everyone. He would begin every session by asking who was on the right, who was on the left, and how might they find a middle ground that would please both. Hoyt said that about half the time Clinton would succeed in finding such a middle ground, but half the time he would not and on those occasions he would look like the epitome of a waffler.

It seems to me that three other comments might be added to these insights. The first is that Clinton is exceptionally bright and very clever in dealing with people. The second is that these qualities have given him a supreme self-confidence, a feeling that he could talk his way out of any jam. The third is he is exhilarated by taking risks, that he gets a gambler's thrill out of challenging the odds.

In any case, Hoyt's observations seem to explain a lot about the way Clinton has operated. Take, for example, the Medicare fiasco. Hillary was in charge but Clinton himself was clearly calling the tune. The Clintons tried to please the doctors and the insurance companies as well as the recipients of health care. In the end, the doctors and insurance companies turned on them, and the American people ended up with nothing. But, as Hoyt said, Clinton often does find a formula that pleases everyone. Looking at Bosnia a few years ago, it seemed as if the best the United States and its allies could do would be to draw a ring around the country and let the inhabitants fight it out among themselves. The hatreds of the peoples of the former Yugoslavia go back 2 thousand years. But the pressure on Clinton to intervene to stop the killing was enormous. Clinton had obviously been burned by the experience in Somalia. As the casualties mounted, pressure to withdraw was overwhelming. Clinton withdrew the American forces, and Somalia ended up being worse off than if the United States had never intervened at all. Clearly, Clinton was determined not to repeat that mistake. He resisted the pressure to intervene in Bosnia for some time. But he was caught in a dilemma.

To the amazement of most observers, Clinton finally crafted an intervention in Bosnia that avoided the problem. He put in a force *between* the contending factions to keep them apart. He made that force so strong that the contending Yugoslav factions did not dare attack it. And he then laid down rules of engagement forbidding the American troops to go outside their zone to chase war criminals or anyone else. The result was that in over fourteen months no Americans were killed in combat. A tiny handful were killed in automobile accidents and one accidentally stepped on a mine, but that was all.

Then comes Iraq. In Congress, members on both sides of the aisle screamed for the United States to bomb Iraq and to oust Saddam Hussein. But when a number of retired generals and military experts took the position that it would be impossible to remove Hussein with bombs alone and that an invasion by ground troops would be needed, Congress rejected the advice, at times somewhat emotionally. They wanted to use force, but they wanted the force to be immaculate. Madeleine Albright was just as innocent of military expertise as Congress and just as hawkish. As one commentator remarked, if she had lived at the time of the French revolution, she would have been knitting at the guillotine. And neither Cohen nor Berger had either the know-how or stomach to stand up to her.

But Clinton understood both that he would never get the support needed to send ground troops into Iraq and that bombing would not work. He directed Albright, Cohen, and Berger to go to Columbus, Ohio, to build support for intervention. As some commentators have remarked, given the fact that Columbus, Ohio, is in the center of the isolationist Middle West, it might be more accurate to say that Clinton suckered them into going. In any case, the three of them went to Ohio and got clobbered between screaming hawks and screaming doves.

One suspects that Clinton figured that the result was likely to make it clear to everyone both that bombing would not work, that the opposition to sending ground troops was overwhelming, and that the United States should go back to diplomacy. If things did not work out that way, Clinton might have calculated, and he had to bomb after all, he could use unmanned, guided missiles, and so avoid incurring any American casualties at all. The United States had used such weapons when it thought Saddam Hussein was going to try to assassinate former President Bush on his visit to Kuwait. There were no American casualties, and since only two or three of the missiles went astray, the civilian casualties were kept to a handful. Those weapons are even better today, so the chances are that the civilian casualties would be even less.

And Clinton may also have thought that, just incidentally, the possibility of a war in the Middle East will distract attention from Kenneth Starr and Monica Lewinsky.

10. Some Greeks looked longingly at the part of Yugoslavia called Macedonia and some feared that the former Yugoslav Macedonia had designs on Greek Macedonia. But neither Greece nor Macedonia was party to the fighting.

11. At least one Cassandra did predict a wider war—George Kenny, who resigned from the State Department and as acting desk officer for Yugoslavia during the Bush administration in protest for the failure of the United States to intervene. In September 1992, he prophesied that there was a greater than 50-percent chance of a general European war within six months. He predicted that Serbia would conquer Bosnia by the spring of 1993, that Albania would feel threatened and intervene, that Macedonia would come in, then Greece to annex Macedonia, and then Turkey to contain Greece. At that stage, he argued, Iran, Libya, and other Muslim countries would join in. All this, Kenny argued, would drag the great powers into what would rapidly become World War III.

Former colleagues described Denny's problem as a bad case of an affliction well known to the State Department: "localitis." This is the tendency of desk officers and ambassadors to take up as their own the attitudes of the country for which they are responsible more zealously than the country's actual officials and citizens do. In addition, Kenny was obviously mesmerized by the events of 1914. But, as Fareed Zakaria dryly remarked after describing Kenny's nightmare, "In 1914, conflict in the Balkans led to a general European war because the Great Powers cared too much about instability in the Balkans; today they care too little. This may cause many problems, but it cannot cause general war." See Fareed Zakaria, "Bosnia Explodes 3 Myths," *The New York Times*, 26 September 1993, p. 15.

Chapter 23

Humanitarian and Peacekeeping Forces

Our conclusion so far is that the United States should maintain two kinds of military forces. The first is a nuclear force sufficient to deter any country or combination of countries from launching an attack with nuclear weapons, to be dealt with in Chapter 25. The second is an antiescalation force armed with conventional weapons that can intervene to stop a rogue country from building nuclear forces and that can bring to a halt any wars that have the potential of spiraling into much bigger wars and thus into nuclear war itself. The nature of this second force will be addressed in Chapter 24.

The question in this chapter is where to lodge responsibility for two other kinds of interventions, if and when they are needed. The first is a purely humanitarian intervention. An example is the original mission in Somalia to protect the distribution of food and medical supplies. The second is a slightly different kind of humanitarian intervention, a peacekeeping intervention with military force to stop the killing and bring about peace in an ongoing conflict that has little or no potential for spiraling into a bigger war. The most recent example is the intervention in Bosnia in late 1995 and early 1996 by the United States, its NATO Allies, and Russia, in which Clinton sent a force with severely circumscribed rules of engagement.

The vast majority of interventions with military force in history had their roots in rivalries between states. Most of the recent military interventions by the United States have such roots. For interventions that are either humanitarian or peacekeeping, the best place to look is in the history of the United Nations.[1]

The first thing one notices about the list of U.N. humanitarian and peacekeeping operations is how extensive they have become. U.N. forces are engaged in almost every corner of the globe. What is more, one of the first responses to trouble anywhere seems to be to propose a U.N. peacekeeping or observer force. So far, there have been forty-six U.N. interventions.[2] Of these, those in Somalia, Cambodia, and Bosnia-Herzegovina illustrate the range of situations with which such interventions have tried to deal, and an examination of these three should provide a base from which to consider how to deal with such problems.

SOMALIA

On November 25, 1992, in the last few weeks of his administration, President Bush sent 28,150 American troops to Somalia to join the U.N. forces already there on the humanitarian mission of protecting the distribution of food and medical supplies from pillaging by rival warlords. In accordance with previous American policy, the troops were not placed under the U.N. command, but operated independently.

By early 1993, the bulk of the troops were withdrawn, leaving behind a force of 3,100 soldiers. Partly because their mission was to provide logistic support for the other U.N. troops, the Americans were made part of the U.N. force. This was the first time that an American force was put under U.N. command, a political decision that was made easier by the fact that the U.N. troops were commanded by a retired American admiral, Jonathan Howe.

The original mission of the U.N. force was humanitarian—to secure the distribution of food. But the U.N. Security Council then expanded the mission to include both restoring order and rebuilding the country's political structure. Inevitably, of course, rebuilding the country's political structure meant that some of the warlords—indeed, perhaps all but one of them—would lose their power. In February 1993, the United Nations sponsored a meeting in Ethiopia of the representatives of fifteen of the warlords and prodded them into agreeing to disarm and to form regional and countrywide councils as a step toward rebuilding Somalia politically. General Mohammed Farah Aidid, a warlord based in the south of the city of Mogadishu, saw this as a threat to his own power and shortly afterward began to attack the U.N. forces precisely to shock everyone into withdrawing them. On June 5, 1993, Aidid's troops ambushed a Pakistani U.N. unit, killing twenty-four. The U.N. Security Council passed a resolution calling for the "arrest and detention for prosecution, trial and punishment" of those responsible, meaning General Aidid. The U.N. forces put a price on Aidid's head and ordered his arrest, and on June 12, U.N. planes bombed Aidid's headquarters.

On July 12, after an attack by a U.N. helicopter killed several dozen Somalis, an angry mob stoned four foreign journalists to death. The U.N. force included 2,900 Italians, and Italy objected strenuously to the decision to enlarge the mission's responsibilities. Shortly afterward, two Italian soldiers out jogging were ambushed and killed. A joint force of Americans and Pakistanis was also attacked by one of Aidid's units. Aidid had mixed women and children in with his troops, and when the U.N. soldiers fired back over one hundred Somalis were killed, mainly the women and children.

In late August 1993, the United States sent to Somalia another 16 thousand soldiers, but kept them under American command separate from the 3,100 under U.N. command. A special force of 410 American Rangers was also added, including an elite counterterrorist team whose task was to find and seize Aidid.

On September 21, the counterterrorist team succeeded in capturing a chief aide to Aidid, but Aidid himself continued to elude them. That same day, three more Pakistani soldiers were killed and several wounded. A few days later an American helicopter was shot down, and three American soldiers were killed, bringing the total of American dead to eleven. Angered by the escalation of events and the killing of American soldiers, the Senate passed a nonbinding resolution calling on the Clinton administration to withdraw American troops by November 15, 1993, or to consult Congress on just what their mission should be.

In the meantime, the U.N. commander, Admiral Howe, said that as many as 5 thousand more troops were needed to effect "the rebirth of Somalia in the hands of Somalis." In response, President Clinton ruled out any increase of the forces in Somalia, but defended the continued presence of the American troops already there, pointing out that "over 300 thousand people have lost their lives there." He went on to argue that the U.N. forces should not leave until a government was established and stabilized so that it would not collapse when the U.N. forces left.

However, on September 27, administration officials said that the United States had decided to move away from the goal of capturing Aidid, which had turned out to be extraordinarily difficult, to that of isolating him and creating a political structure in Somalia without him.

On September 28, by which time the American dead totaled fifteen, the House passed the same resolution the Senate had passed calling for the withdrawal of American troops by November 15, 1993, or consultations with Congress on just what their mission should be.

On October 3, a small group of American Rangers was sent on a raid in the hope of capturing Aidid. They did seize several of his aides, but as they departed one of their supporting helicopters was shot down. The Rangers moved to protect the downed helicopter and were then surrounded. Shortly thereafter, another helicopter was shot down, but the Rangers were pinned down and unable to reach it. The Quick Reaction Force was dispatched to their aid, but it took nine hours to reach them. Later, American and U.N. military officials said that the Quick Reaction Force did not have the proper equipment and that the Pakistani and Malaysian troops dispatched to help them did not have the proper training. The Rangers, these officials said, had been trapped because of bad luck, faulty intelligence, and poor planning. The result was a fifteen-hour battle before they were relieved. A third helicopter was hit, but wobbled away to a safe spot for a crash landing. About 300 Somalis were killed and 700 wounded, of whom one-third were women and children. The American casualties were eighteen killed, seventy-five wounded, and one captured, Michael J. Durant, a helicopter pilot. What particularly outraged both Congress and public opinion were pictures of a dead American soldier with a rope tied around his feet being dragged through the streets by a mob of Somalis.

At the same time, it transpired that the American commander in Somalia had some time before requested additional firepower, including tanks, that his request had been backed by General Colin Powell, but that Secretary of Defense Les Aspin had refused the request because he thought it would run into opposition in Congress.

In both Congress and the press, criticism of continuing an American presence in Somalia was intense. *The New York Times* described events there as "the clan politics of a chaotic country that poses no international threat." In response, on October 5 President Clinton instructed Secretary of Defense Aspin and Secretary of State Warren Christopher to meet with members of Congress to explain the situation. Over 300 attended the meeting, complaining bitterly that the policy goals were vague and demanding a clear "exit strategy." The White House also conducted a review of the whole Somalia enterprise. The U.N. casualties up to this point in the Somalia operation totaled sixty-nine dead and more than 200 wounded. The cost in dollars was $1.55 billion for twelve months.

The 4,700 Americans at this point were the backbone of the 27-thousand-man U.N. force, which was drawn from thirty-three different countries. The 3,100 Americans under U.N. command provided the logistics—water, food, and transport—for all the other U.N. forces. A total of 1,300 other Americans bolstered by 420 Rangers made up the Quick Reaction Force. This force had the dual burden of trying to locate and seize Aidid and to provide rapid support for any of the U.N. forces that came under attack.

The fact that at least one American was being held prisoner by Aidid's forces made an immediate withdrawal of the American forces from Somalia impossible. But administration assertions that the United States should not "cut and run" brought much criticism from members of Congress and others who found such talk all too reminiscent of Vietnam.

On October 7, President Clinton announced his decision to send to Somalia 1,700 more soldiers and 104 more armored vehicles, an aircraft carrier with its support ships, and two amphibious groups with 3,600 combat Marines to stand offshore. At the same time, he set March 31, 1994, as a date certain for the withdrawal of all American troops. He also said that General Aidid would not be the "principal focus" of the American efforts and suggested that Aidid could be included in any negotiations to end the fighting. At the same time, President Clinton sent Robert B. Oakley, a retired foreign service officer, to Somalia to seek a diplomatic solution. Oakley had served as the Bush administration's envoy to Somalia and had a reputation for blunt honesty. In keeping with that reputation, he made no secret of the fact that he thought the U.N. decision to target General Aidid had been a bad mistake.

On October 10, Boutrous Boutrous-Ghali, the U.N. secretary general, announced plans for a meeting of African, Arab, and Muslim leaders to try to map out a strategy to keep Somalia from collapsing into anarchy when the American troops withdrew in March. Unless something was done, he warned, "the gangs will just be waiting to start fighting again when we have gone."

On October 14, Aidid released Michael Durant, the helicopter pilot, and a Nigerian peacekeeper who had been captured on September 5. Aidid expressed the hope that some seventy-five of his people held by the United Nations would also be released. He also announced a unilateral cease fire and removed the barriers on the main roads in Mogadishu.

On October 15, the administration blamed the United Nations and Secretary Boutrous-Ghali for letting policy in Somalia get off the track. But the press quickly pointed out that after the Pakistani soldiers were killed the administration had helped draft the resolution calling for capturing and punishing Aidid and then lobbied other members of the Security Council to get it passed. The administration could not disavow the U.N. resolution, but it indicated that the appropriate course was to have an "African commission" look into the deaths of the Pakistani soldiers. Conveniently, such a report would not come out until long after the March 31 deadline that President Clinton set for an American withdrawal.

Administration officials called the new policy in Somalia "constructive ambiguity." When peace finally did come to Somalia, they said, the United States would have nothing to say if Aidid ended up not just as one of the people who ruled Somalia but as the actual president of the country.

On October 19, the U.S. commander in Somalia, General Thomas M. Montgomery, said that American soldiers would no longer join U.N. forces in patrolling or in seeking to disarm any of the warring factions. Their main role would be to defend U.N. soldiers and their military compounds and to protect the peace-keeping operations and food deliveries carried out by the other U.N. forces. A secondary task would be to help open supply routes in the city of Mogadishu. Montgomery also announced that the marines on the ships standing by would be brought ashore to augment the nearly 10 thousand Americans already there. However, 705 Army Rangers, the ones whose mission was to hunt down Aidid, were withdrawn. The withdrawal reflected the decision to pursue a political rather than military course.

However, one of Aidid's rivals, Mohammed Ali Mahdi, said that if the United Nations did not disarm Aidid, Mahdi's forces would have to resume fighting. A few days later troops of the two factions engaged in a two-hour skirmish along the so-called Green Line, between the southern part of the city, controlled by Aidid's clan, and the northern, controlled by Mahdi's. The casualties were three people killed and forty-five wounded.

On November 29, a conference of the fifteen rival Somalia factions convened in Addis Ababa, Ethiopia. Some of Aidid's representatives were present, but Aidid himself, who was still on the United Nation's wanted list, was not. Instead, Aidid held a news conference in a Mogadishu hideout and demanded that the United Nations get out of Somalia entirely so it could be replaced by an independent body. He also announced that he would hold his own "Somalis for Somalia" conference in January. Later, Aidid indicated that his representatives would participate in the Addis Ababa conference if the United Nations would release eight of his high-ranking aides that it held prisoner.

Then, on December 3, in an ironic twist, the United States provided an American military airplane to fly Aidid to Ethiopia and American bodyguards when he got there. Explaining the decision, State Department and White House spokespersons said that since the U.N. order for his arrest was still in force, Aidid refused to fly in a U.N. plane, and that it was in the interests of both the United States and the United Nations to try to move matters forward. The argument was that the only way that peace could be brought to Somalia was by an agreement among the rival factions.

Queried at a news conference on December 6, President Clinton said that the decision to ferry Aidid to the conference on an American plane had been made on the spur of the moment by the American special envoy, Robert B. Oakley, but that he, Clinton, supported the decision. Asked how he would explain the decision to the families of the eighteen American soldiers killed by Aidid's troops only two months earlier, Clinton said that he would remind them that their sons "went over there fighting ultimately for a peace to take place." He said that Oakley's decision reflected his own determination to find a political solution in Somalia, rather than pursue a manhunt for General Aidid.

However, the goal of this particular conference was only to set a date and place for an "official" reconciliation conference. Some observers were optimistic, arguing that all the different factions were tired of the killing. Exact figures are impossible to discover, but it was estimated that there had been 6 thousand to 10 thousand Somalia casualties in the preceding few months. During the same period, eighty-three U.N. peacekeepers were killed and 302 wounded, of which twenty-six of the killed and 170 of the wounded were Americans.

But many outside observers were not optimistic. The remaining Western countries and Turkey announced that they, too, would withdraw their troops by March 31, 1994, leaving only the Pakistani and Indian contingents. Anticipating the March 31 deadline, various factions began attacks on relief agencies and U.N. units in early February. It seemed obvious that sooner or later the United Nations would have to withdraw, and when it did the fighting between the factions would resume, to end, if ever, only when one of the factions had triumphed over all the others.

CAMBODIA

The U.N. intervention in Cambodia was to supervise an election and protect the polling places, so it was clearly an example of using military force in a peacekeeping role. What made it distinctive was that it was not only successful in its mission but was also successful in avoiding actual combat except for a few scattered incidents.

Prince Norodom Sihanouk was installed as king of Cambodia as a young man by the French, but after independence he transformed himself from king to president and built widespread support among the peasantry. During the Vietnam War, the Communist Vietnamese used the Cambodian border areas as sanctuaries, and Sihanouk, desperate to stay neutral, turned a blind eye. The Cambodian military were opposed to this policy, and they ousted Sihanouk by a coup while he was on a trip abroad. Communist China and North Korea gave Sihanouk sanctuary.

The Communist Khmer Rouge, with the help of the Vietnamese, then drove out the military junta. The Khmer Rouge had spent many years isolated in a camp in Communist China, and they had spent the time developing a bizarre theory of an "agrarian" Communism based on the peasants and the countryside, rather than on city dwellers. While Marx saw the bourgeoisie as evil and city-dwelling workers as the wave of the future, the Khmer Rouge saw both as decadent and evil. When the Khmer Rouge came to power under the fanatical Pol Pot, they launched a genocidal program of eliminating the cities, city-dwellers, and educated people entirely. Of a population of 6 million, about 2 million were killed or died of starvation and disease.

When fighting broke out between Communist Vietnam and Communist China along their common border, the Khmer Rouge began to talk of reclaiming parts of Southern Vietnam that had been Khmer in ancient times. Finally losing patience, the Vietnamese invaded Cambodia and installed a pro-Vietnamese, Communist government in Phnom Penh. The Khmer Rouge were driven back into areas along the Thai border, where they maintained themselves with Thai and Chinese help.

The result was that three factions contended for power in Cambodia: the pro-Vietnamese Communist government in Phnom Penh headed by Hun Sen, the "revisionist" Communist Khmer Rouge, headed by Pol Pot, and a small force loyal to Sihanouk that he managed to maintain with some help from China and North Korea. Over the years these three factions struggled to a standstill and finally signed an agreement in 1992 to hold countrywide elections supervised by the United Nations.

The U.N. mission was headed by an international civil servant from Japan, Yasushi Akashi. The military forces consisted of about 19 thousand soldiers from several different countries headed by General John Sanderson from Australia. After the preparations for the election were well along, the Khmer Rouge became convinced that they would be the big losers. They withdrew from the agreement and started a series of guerrilla raids on their two rivals, the People's Party fielded by the Vietnamese-sponsored government in Phnom Penh that was headed by Hun Sen, and Sihanouk's Royalist Party. Hun Sen's People's Party adopted the same tactics as the Khmer Rouge, intimidating and murdering their political opponents in both of the other groups.

But Akashi and Sanderson were determined to avoid being dragged into the fighting. The U.N. forces made no attempt to disarm the Khmer Rouge or to fight off the attacks on the others by Hun Sen's People's Party. Instead, they relied on diplomatic pressure to try to curb abuses of human rights. However, the civilian observers at the polling places, fearing for their lives, began to flee to Phnom Penh. Akashi and Sanderson were forced to disperse their forces to hundreds of polling places. The whole U.N. intervention hung by a thread.

In what seemed a miracle that no one has yet been able to explain, no large-scale intervention materialized. The elections were held with relatively few military clashes. Nearly 90 percent of the electorate voted, and Sihanouk and his faction won in a landslide. Sihanouk became king, one of his sons became prime minister, and his party controlled the legislature. Hun Sen and the People's Party threatened to fight rather than give up power. But Sihanouk, true to his personal tradition of trying to unite the Cambodian people, persuaded both his own party and the People's Party to form a coalition. As for the Khmer Rouge, some 2 thousand of their 10 thousand troops defected.

The lessons of the U.N. intervention in Cambodia are fourfold. The first lesson is that under certain very special conditions peacekeeping can work. In Cambodia, the warring factions had reached a true stalemate, with none able to dominate. In addition, the peacekeeping force was extremely strict and self-disciplined in not taking sides and in avoiding any military action except that of defending themselves when attacked. The second lesson is that situations where these conditions prevail are likely to be the exception rather than the rule. The third lesson is that even when all the conditions are met, if the intervention is to succeed it still needs a very large measure of pure luck. The fourth lesson is that even if the intervention succeeds in accomplishing what it set out to do, the final result may overturn everything the intervention achieved. In the years following all that has just been described, the Communist faction lead by Hun Sen seized power in a coup d'état.

BOSNIA-HERZEGOVINA

The U.N. intervention in Bosnia-Herzegovina began as humanitarian. The original mandate in March 1992, deployed U.N. forces to Croatia to establish three "United Nations Protected Areas." In June 1992, it was enlarged to ensure the security of the Sarajevo airport and delivery of humanitarian assistance, and the U.N. forces entered Bosnia and Herzegovina. In November 1992, authorization was given to monitor the ban on military flights. In December 1992, the United Nations sent a small force to Macedonia to monitor its border areas, and in June 1993, the U.N. forces were authorized to use force to defend "safe areas" for Muslims.

The U.N. forces escorted convoys delivering food and medicine, but when the convoys were stopped by the troops of the warring factions, they did not attempt to use force to break through, but withdrew.

In the fall of 1992, the U.N. Security Council banned flights over Bosnia-Herzegovina and called upon NATO to monitor the ban by regular air patrolling. Then, in March 1993, it authorized the NATO planes to shoot down any violators. But since violations were few and there were no interceptions, the authorization had little practical significance. For several months NATO planes flew over Serbian artillery positions at low levels, but they neither fired nor were fired upon.

The decision to authorize U.N. troops to establish safe areas for Muslim refugees could easily have turned the U.N. mission into one of peacekeeping by the use of military force. But the enclaves were not actually attacked except by sporadic shelling, and the U.N. forces did not respond.

President Clinton's early proposal to bomb the Serbian forces attacking the Muslim forces would have been an example of using military force in a peace-keeping role, but the NATO Allies blocked any such bombing.

If the various factions had agreed on a peace settlement, rather than merely acquiescing in "no war, no peace," then the proposed intervention by NATO would have been another example of a peacekeeping mission using military force. But so long as the no war, no peace situation prevailed, so long as the U.N. forces continued their policy of neither forcing their way through roadblocks nor replying to the occasional artillery shelling, and so long as none of the contenders launched full-scale ground attacks against the U.N. forces protecting Muslim enclaves, the intervention continued to be humanitarian rather than peacekeeping.

Under the label of "ethnic cleansing," the Serbs embarked on what was really a policy of genocide. A U.N. war crimes commission later reported that several thousand Muslim women were raped by Serbs as a deliberate part of their policy of ethnic cleansing to drive Muslims out of the country. The Serbs began to intensify their siege of Gorazde, Maglaj, and Tuzla, reinforcing the forces at the latter two towns with tanks that had been concealed in the exclusion zone around Sarajevo. Elsewhere in Bosnia, the Serbs also intensified their so-called ethnic cleansing.

Gorazde, with a mainly Muslim population of 25 thousand swollen by some 40 thousand Muslim refugees, had been declared a safe area by the United Nations. The question of whether or not to try to relieve Gorazde with NATO air strikes was hotly debated within the Clinton administration. The debate became public when the secretary of defense, William J. Perry, and the chairman of the Joint Chiefs of Staff, John M. Shalikashvili, made a public statement ruling out air strikes on the grounds that the terrain around Gorazde would make the strikes ineffective. However, the administration quickly made it clear that air strikes had not been ruled out.

Faced with opposition both at home and abroad, the Clinton administration announced in early May 1993, that it was putting its policy toward Bosnia on hold. Later that same month, President Clinton said that so long as the fighting continued, he was opposed to sending ground forces even as peacekeepers. For the moment, the only measure he was willing to take was to use American air power to protect the U.N. troops.

Shortly after President Clinton's statement, the third-ranking officer of the State Department, Undersecretary Peter Tarnoff, gave a private talk on Bosnia to reporters that seemed to lay down the principles behind Clinton's announcement. Although his remarks were off the record, the substance of them quickly leaked.[3] Tarnoff said that the administration's decision to follow European advice on intervening in Bosnia was a considered choice based on a new approach to the post–Cold War era. Since the superpower rivalry that characterized the Cold War had ended with the breakup of the Soviet Union, the United States should pursue a less interventionist, more multilateral foreign policy, acting independently only when vital interests close to home were threatened. At the same time, Tarnoff said, Washington should keep the expenditure of American resources in line with the interests at stake.

To the surprise of most observers, Secretary of State Warren Christopher seemed to go out of his way to disavow Tarnoff's position. Christopher said that he had had no idea in advance of what Tarnoff was going to say, but that his own view was that "our need to lead, our determination to lead is not constrained by our resources. I think that where we need to lead, where our vital interests are threatened, we will find the resources to accomplish that." In what was interpreted by the press as a rebuke to Tarnoff, Christopher then added, "The President makes foreign policy, and I make foreign policy, and it is not made by other officers of the department no matter how valuable and effective they are."[4] But in a seeming inconsistency Christopher then added that the war in Bosnia was a "quagmire" and a "morass" and said that the United States would not act there unilaterally.

To many observers, what Tarnoff had to say made good sense. It seemed doubtful that the ancient hatreds and rivalries of the Balkans could be solved by an American intervention. What was worse, an intervention might well turn into the same kind of quagmire that Vietnam had become. It also seemed unlikely that the troubles in Bosnia-Herzegovina would spill over to the wider world. If such an escalation was unlikely, the only American responsibility would be humanitarian, to stop the fighting and bring a permanent peace. If the United Nations called for NATO to intervene, if NATO decided to do so, and if a NATO intervention seemed likely to bring a permanent peace without NATO itself getting embroiled in a lot of fighting, then the argument for American participation would indeed be persuasive, but only as NATO's junior partner in a problem that lay not on America's doorstep but on Europe's. So if NATO did decide to intervene, American participation, the argument continued, should be limited to those forces that were already assigned to NATO and the American role should be that of follower, not leader.

But one caveat was immediately raised: Would an intervention motivated by humanitarian concerns end up being humanitarian? Or would it end up in even more killing? For a concrete example, consider the British and French forces protecting the Muslim minorities. Suppose that no consensus emerged among the Croatian, Muslim, and Serbian peoples about a settlement. The people of Britain and France would hardly welcome either staying on forever in a repetition of Northern Ireland or abandoning the Muslims to their fate. The only alternative would be to offer to evacuate the Muslims to any country that would accept them and then set a date certain when the British and French forces would be withdrawn, irrespective of whether any Muslims still insisted on staying.

In early September 1993, in response to a plea for help from the president of Bosnia, President Clinton seemed to side with Tarnoff. He said flatly that the United States was willing to use diplomacy and economic sanctions to put pressure on the Serbs to negotiate, but that there was no support in the United States for an American military intervention. He said that he was committed "in principle" to send American troops to monitor a peace settlement to which the parties had agreed, if Congress approved, but not to bring a peace settlement about.

The only exception to the use of force that President Clinton made was a situation in which U.N. personnel were threatened. In such circumstances, the United States would be willing to use air power to help support them. Almost a year later, on April 10, 1994, General Sir Michael Rose of Britain, the U.N. commander in Bosnia, requested an air attack on the Serb forces besieging Gorazde on the grounds that U.N. personnel were in danger, although only fifteen of Gorazde's 65 thousand inhabitants were from the United Nations. By doing so, his request came under a U.N. resolution providing protection for U.N. personnel and so did not require prior approval of the United States or the other NATO powers involved. Russia was also excluded and after the bombing protested vigorously.

In February 1994, a mortar shell exploded in the crowded marketplace in Sarajevo, killing sixty-eight. NATO demanded that Serbian heavy artillery pieces be turned over to them. Shortly afterward, Boris Yeltsin, president of Russia, announced that Russian troops would be deployed in Sarajevo to ensure that Bosnian government forces did not exploit the absence of the Serbian artillery by launching an infantry offensive against the city. On August 28, 1995, another mortar smashed into the marketplace in Sarajevo, and this triggered a NATO air and cruise missile strike on Bosnian Serb positions.

Shortly afterward, Richard Holbrooke was dispatched on a diplomatic mission to try to bring about a negotiated settlement. The result was a prolonged set of negotiations between the contending parties conducted in Dayton, Ohio. An agreement was reached on November 21, 1995, and signed in Paris on December 14, 1995, by the presidents of Bosnia, Serbia, and Croatia. Most observers concluded that the ultimate consequence of the agreement was a partition of Bosnia. For his part, Holbrooke adamantly denied this on the grounds that the two contending forces would eventually come under a single command and be amalgamated. Skeptics replied that Holbrooke was being hopelessly optimistic.

In any case, the agreement at least temporarily partitioned Bosnia-Herzegovina. It also established a military Implementation Force (IFOR) of 60 thousand under NATO command. President Clinton insisted on very specific rules of engagement for the American contingent of this force. Its mission was to occupy a strip of territory separating the contending forces. It was not authorized to go outside of this territory. Neither was it authorized to pursue war criminals or to impose restrictions on the contending parties except to keep them apart. Finally, a deadline of June 1998 was put on its involvement. In effect, the American force was so strong that the contending factions would be effectively deterred from attacking it and, at the same time, the force was forbidden from doing anything at all except to separate the warring factions. The result was that the only casualties the Americans suffered were less than half a dozen in vehicle accidents and one man killed when he accidentally stepped on a mine.

On November 15, 1996, President Clinton announced that the American forces would remain in Bosnia until June 1998. A year later, in December 1997, he announced that the June 1998 deadline had also been abandoned.

KOSOVO

Kosovo was an autonomous province of Serbia until 1989 when its autonomy was revoked by Slobodan Milosevic, at the time president of Serbia and now president of the rump state of Yugoslavia that includes Serbia, Kosovo, and Montenegro. Kosovo has a population of 2 million, of which 90 percent are Albanian.

In early 1998, Serbian police cracked down on demonstrations for independence from Serbia inspired by the Kosovo Liberation Army, leaving eighty dead and scores missing. In response, the United States reissued a diplomatic warning first issued by President Bush in December 1992. In a letter to Milosevic, Bush had said that the United States was prepared to use force against the Serbs if they tried to drive ethnic Albanians out of Kosovo. Describing the American response, a Clinton administration official said that while the United States had not drawn up any contingency plans for an attack on the Serbs, the American "view remains what it was in December 1992—that we are not going to sit back and accept a major Serb military operation in Kosovo."

In early summer of 1998, the Serbs launched an offensive against the rebel enclaves, but discovered that the rebels had acquired arsenals of antiaircraft and antitank weapons and substantial reinforcements including dozens of former professional soldiers. What was a ragtag band had been turned into a viable military force. A cease-fire was finally arranged and the Organization for Security and Cooperation in Europe undertook to send 2 thousand unarmed observers, the Kosovo Verification Mission, to verify Serbian compliance with U.N. resolutions, in particular the withdrawal of Serbian troops from Kosovo and return of ethnic Albanian refugees. NATO has plans to create a 1,700-member "rapid reaction" force to defend the monitors safety. Some observers feared that if fighting breaks out again and the international missions fell apart, the resulting battles could lead to Western intervention similar to the case in Bosnia.

"PEACE-FORCING"

Some observers have said that "peacekeeping" hardly seems the proper word for the U.N. interventions described in this chapter, since the U.N. forces often ended up doing at least some fighting. However, even though none of the interventions succeeded in totally preventing military clashes, the fighting would probably have been much heavier if there had been no U.N. forces present. Still, the peacekeepers often ended up fighting against one or another of the warring factions that had violated a cease fire or that tried to seize more territory. Because of this, a more accurate term than peacekeeping for this kind of intervention would probably be "peace-forcing."

It can also be said that because peacekeeping is so often peace-forcing, the great powers are increasingly reluctant to expose their soldiers to the dangers that are inevitably involved. For some time Great Britain, France, and the other European countries effectively vetoed the first American proposals for intervening in Bosnia, and within the United States, both Congress and the public were not only reluctant to become involved in Bosnia, especially with ground forces, but were anxious to get out of Somalia. It was no accident that in his speech to the U.N. General Assembly in September 1993, President Clinton said that if the American people are to say yes to peacekeeping, the United Nations must learn when to say no.

In Somalia, the dangers of peacekeeping were vividly demonstrated. In Cambodia peacekeeping was successful, but all concerned understood that the success was dicey. And in the end the accomplishment was reversed by a coup, and Hun Sen seized power. In Bosnia the dangers were ever-present—and continue to be, especially in Kosovo. In view of this record, it is understandable that the great powers have come to believe that the dangers of peacekeeping to the peacekeepers are substantial, and if things go wrong the political consequences among their own people are so explosive that they are going to be very reluctant to become involved in future peacekeeping. It was obviously these concerns that led Clinton, when he finally did decide to intervene in Bosnia, to send a force that was much, much more formidable than had ever been used for such purposes before, that its mission was limited to keeping the local factions separated, and that it was expressly forbidden to undertake such tasks as arresting war criminals or supervising elections.

This reluctance of the great powers to become involved in the kind of peacekeeping that is really peace-forcing is not cowardice. The truth is that the chances of a peace-forcing mission being successful are not great. Such a mission is very likely to impose a settlement that creates long-lasting, smoldering resentments. In many cases one faction or another will be left believing that the intervention prevented them from getting what they otherwise would have gotten and what their ethnicity, religion, or nationalism entitled them to get. So the result is not likely to be a permanent peace, but rather a seething discontent on one side or another that will sooner or later explode into renewed fighting. The ultimate argument will be that imposing a settlement may run the risk of making the eventual outbreak even more bloody than if the rival factions are allowed to fight it out among themselves.

But in spite of the poor chances of success, it seems likely that horror at the killing in such situations will lead many people in the future to advocate intervention on one or another occasion. In the future as in the past the advocates of intervention will most often urge bombing as the means to intervene, persisting in believing against all the evidence that intervention by air power is clean, effective, and relatively cost free. Both points, that many people will advocate intervention and that the means they will advocate using will be bombing, are illustrated by the large number of American newspaper columnists and public figures who advocated intervening in both Bosnia and Iraq by bombing.

A Hypothetical Somalia Example

Even if it is understood that bombing will rarely solve the problem and that intervention will lead to casualties among the intervening forces, there will be many who will still want to intervene. Consider what might have happened in Somalia. Somalia did not have the potential of escalating into an international war, and the motive for the original U.N. intervention was purely humanitarian. But suppose all the members of the U.N. Security Council understood from the very beginning that it would be almost impossible to confine the U.N. mission to protecting food supplies and that the U.N. forces would inevitably have to take sides in the struggles among the warlords. Is it likely that the members of the Security Council would have agreed to intervene on the grounds that a peace-forcing intervention was justified?

Suppose that the Security Council recognized that the U.N. forces would have to do some actual fighting, that the U.N. forces, the soldiers of the warlords, and innocent civilians would all suffer losses. Even if everyone understood this, a convincing argument could still be made that the total of these losses would be much smaller than the losses that would be suffered by the forces of the warlords and innocent civilians if the United Nations did not intervene. After all, in the years before the U.N. intervention in Somalia the casualties in the struggles between the warlords were about 300 thousand dead and an untold number of wounded.

It seems obvious that situations will arise in the future in which the U.N. Security Council will decide that intervening will cost fewer lives than not intervening. If this is true, then on one occasion or another the U.N. Security Council is going to vote to intervene in what we have called a peace-forcing mission. If this is so, then something surely must be done to change the system of using national forces on loan to the United Nations to do the job.

The drawbacks to using national forces are considerable. The first has already been mentioned: The people of the country contributing the forces will inevitably ask if the country's interests and those of the United Nations coincide. This will lead to efforts to change the mission in some cases and in others to precipitous and ill-timed withdrawals.

The second drawback is that the structure, equipment, and training of regular national forces do not fit the needs of peacekeeping. Regular national forces are organized, equipped, and trained not just for defense but for offense, and rightly so. If attacked, the commanders of such forces will find it difficult to resist the temptation to do what their forces were designed to do, especially when attacked by what will probably be a force inferior in both training and equipment. What national forces are trained and equipped to do when attacked is to take the offensive as soon as possible—to seek out and destroy the enemy.

But as the experience in Cambodia, Somalia, and Bosnia shows, a peacekeeping force should not go on the offensive, even when it is attacked. If it does go on the offensive, one of two results are likely to follow. Either it will fail in its offensive, as the forces in Somalia failed to capture Aidid, or it will suffer enough casualties to give its own people and government second thoughts about the intervention, which is also what happened in Somalia.

What a peacekeeping force should do is to defend itself, the convoys it is protecting (as in the case of the early days in Bosnia and the early days in Somalia), and the polling places (as in the case of Cambodia), and keep the contending forces apart (as in the later days in Bosnia).

In Cambodia the peacekeeping forces did exactly what they should do: They defended themselves and the polling places and they refrained from trying to take the weapons away from the Khmer Rouge or to intervene in the fighting between the three factions. The U.N. forces in Cambodia did the right thing because both the civilian and military commanders understood the problem and because they had the courage and determination to reject proposals to take the offensive.

President Clinton's intervention with troops in Bosnia is another example. He made sure that the force was strong enough so that neither side dared attack it. He then laid down rules of engagement that confined the force to a small area, forbidding forays against the contending forces. The result was to limit American casualties, as we saw.

But it is too much to expect that the civilian and military leaders of national forces in future U.N. operations will always have the qualities and luck that the U.N. commanders of the force intervening in Cambodia had, or even that they will have them very often. Even if the circumstances are right, subsequent events may reverse the outcome, as happened in Cambodia. It is also too much to expect that the situation on the ground will permit the highly circumscribed intervention that Clinton ordered in Bosnia.

There is, however, a simple alternative to lending national forces to the United Nations, forces that must exercise unusual self-discipline to refrain from using their offensive equipment and training and whose people and government will inevitably cause problems when the going gets difficult. The alternative is to provide forces that are trained and equipped only for the kind of defensive operations such forces will be called upon to perform.

What this suggests is that if the United Nations is to engage in peacekeeping operations it should be authorized and financed to recruit its own forces and train and equip them accordingly. The historical parallel is the French Foreign Legion. The United Nations should be authorized and financed to recruit individual soldiers from all over the world to serve as peacekeepers under the command of the United Nations itself.[5]

President Clinton seems to have at least begun to think in general terms along these lines. In his September 1993 speech to the United Nations, in addition to warning that the United Nations must learn to say no upon occasion, he said, "The United Nations must also have the technical means to run a modern world-class peacekeeping operation. We support the creation of a genuine U.N. peacekeeping headquarters with a planning staff, with access to timely intelligence, with a logistics unit that can be deployed on a moment's notice, and a modern operations center with global communications."

If it makes sense for the United Nations to have a headquarters and planning staff for peacekeeping, it also makes sense for it to have troops who are specially trained and equipped for peacekeeping and who are free from the domestic political pressures that are inevitable with forces contributed by member states.

Unlike national forces, these U.N. forces could be trained and equipped only for defensive operations, thus removing the temptation of commanders to preempt a threat by attacking first. There undoubtedly will be situations in which offensive forces are needed, but that need can be met by having one or two of the U.N. units equipped and trained for offensive operations. These can be held as a sort of reserve to be introduced into a particular situation when it becomes clear that the U.N. forces trained and equipped for defense only are in trouble.

In any case, a U.N. force specially trained for the peculiar needs of peacekeeping will be much better suited for the task than national forces. National forces intervening on behalf of the United Nations are under constant political pressures both to serve national goals and to be withdrawn entirely when casualties mount. A U.N. foreign legion of professionals would undoubtedly experience some political pressures from the U.N. Security Council and the General Assembly, but it would be free from these particular ones.

NOTES

1. A useful rundown of the U.N. experience and problems with peacekeeping is Mats R. Berdal, *Whither UN Peacekeeping?* (London: Brassey's, for the International Institute for Strategic Studies, 1993). See also John Hillen, *Blue Helmets: The Strategy of U.N. Military Operations* (Arlington, Va.: Brassey's, 1997).

2. The following list of the forty-six interventions was drawn from the official U.N. account, *The Blue Helmets: A Review of United Nations Peacekeeping*, 3d ed. (U.N. Department of Public Information, 1996).

U.N. Truce Supervision Organization (UNTSO), 1948 to present. Established to help in supervising the truce in Palestine, it also supervises the General Armistice Agreements of 1949.

U.N. Emergency Force (UNEF I), November 1956–June 1967. Established following the 1956 invasion of Suez by France, Great Britain, and Israel to serve as a buffer between Egyptian and Israeli forces and to supervise cessation of hostilities and withdrawal of French, Israeli, and British troops from Egyptian territory.

U.N. Emergency Force II (UNEF II), October 1973–July 1979. Established in 1973 following the attack by Egypt across the Suez and by Syria on the Golan Heights to supervise the cease-fire between Egypt and Israel.

U.N. Disengagement Observer Force (UNDOF), June 1974 to present. Established to supervise the cease-fire in the Golan Heights and the disengagement of the Israeli and Syrian forces.

U.N. Interim Force in Lebanon (UNIFIL), March 1978 to present. Following a commando raid that killed thirty-seven Israelis, Israel invaded Lebanon and occupied a large region. UNIFIL was established to confirm the withdrawal of Israeli forces and monitor the cease fire. In 1983, the situation worsened and the United States sent a force of Marines to help. As described in Chapter 22, an Arab fanatic drove a truck loaded with explosives into their barracks, and 241 were killed. The purpose of both the original U.N. intervention and the American participation in 1983 was to forestall a war between Israel and Syria that seemed to have the potential for escalating to engulf the whole of the Middle East. A U.N. force of over 5 thousand men is still there.

U.N. Observation Group in Lebanon (UNOGIL), June 1958–December 1958. In 1958 the Lebanese government complained that the United Arab Republic, the temporary union of Egypt and Syria, was intervening in Lebanon's internal affairs. The mission of UNOGIL was to ensure that there was no illegal infiltration of personnel or arms into Lebanon.

U.N. Yemen Observation Mission (UNYOM), July 1963–September 1964. Established to observe and certify implementation of the disengagement agreement between Saudi Arabia and the United Arab Republic.

U.N. Military Observer Group in India and Pakistan (UNMOGIP), 1949 to present. Established to monitor the frontier between India and Pakistan in Kashmir and later assigned the task of observing developments pertaining to the strict observance of the December 1971 cease-fire.

U.N. India–Pakistan Observation Mission (UNIPOM), September 1965–March 1966. Established to observe and report on breaches of the cease-fire after hostilities erupted all along the cease-fire line in Kashmir.

U.N. Peace-Keeping Force in Cyprus (UNFICYP), 1964 to the present. Established with troops from a number of countries to patrol the 180-kilometer border between Turks and Greeks. After many years, the cost of the continuing operation led Finland, Sweden, Denmark, Austria, and Canada to withdraw. The cost to Canada alone over the years had been over $566 million.

U.N. Operation in the Congo (ONUC), July 1960–June 1964. Established to verify the withdrawal of Belgian forces, secure law and order, and prevent civil war.

U.N. Transition Assistance Group (UNTAG), April 1989–March 1990. Established to monitor the cease-fire in Namibia and the withdrawal of South African troops.

U.N. Angola Verification Mission (UNAVEM I), January 1989–May 1991; (UNAVEM II), May 1991–February 1995; (UNAVEM III), March 1995–July 1997. U.N. Observer Mission in Angola (MONUA), July 1997 to present. The first mission was to verify the withdrawal of the Cuban troops from Angola. The second mission was to monitor the so-called Peace Accords signed in 1991. The third mission was established in 1994 to monitor a cease-fire. MONUA succeeded UNAVEM III to continue the demobilization process.

U.N. Mission for the Referendum in Western Sahara (MINURSO), April 1991 to present. Established to monitor the cease-fire, the reduction of Moroccan troops, and so on.

U.N. Operations in Somalia (UNOSOM I), April 1992–March 1993; (UNOSOM II), March 1993–March 1995. Described in the text of this chapter.

U.N. Operation in Mozambique (ONUMOZ), December 1992–December 1994. Established to monitor and verify the cease-fire, withdrawal of foreign troops, and other matters.

U.N. Observer Mission Uganda–Rwanda (UNOMUR), June 1993–September 1994. Established to see that no military supplies reached Rwanda, to restrain Rwanda's army, and so on. On April 6, 1994, a plane returning the president of Rwanda and the president of Burundi was shot down, killing all on board and setting off a wave of violence between the rival Hutu and Tutsi tribes. Over the next few days in Rwanda, tens of thousands were butchered. The U.N. force in Rwanda sought authorization and reinforcements to stop the killing, but the Clinton administration, still reeling from the experience in Somalia, defined U.S. interest in a faraway place like Rwanda very narrowly. At the same time, administration spokespersons were instructed not to use the word "genocide" when discussing Rwanda. In 1998, during his tour of Africa, Clinton said, "We did not immediately call these crimes by their right name: genocide." He confessed that "people like me" had failed to see the storm of mass killings.

U.N. Assistance Mission to Rwanda (UNAMIR), October 1993–March 1996. Established to act as intermediary between Rwandan factions, and to observe and facilitate the cease-fire.

U.N. Observer Mission in Liberia (UNOMIL), September 1993 to present. Established to observe and monitor the cease-fire.

U.N. Aouzon Strip Observer Group (UNASOG), May 1994–June 1994. Established to verify withdrawal of Libyan troops from Aouzon strip.

U.N. Observer Group in Central America (ONUCA), November 1989–January 1992. Established to verify compliance of the agreement not to aid insurrection forces in the region (observers included Guatemala, El Salvador, Costa Rica, Honduras, and Nicaragua).

U.N. Observer Mission in El Salvador (ONUSAL), July 1991–April 1995. Established to verify implementation of the 1991 agreements between the government and the *Frente Farabkundo Marti para la Liberacion Nacional* (FMLN)—maintaining the cease-fire, reforming the armed forces, creating a new police force, and so on.

U.N. Advance Mission in Cambodia (UNAMIC), October 1991–March 1992. Established to ensure observation of the cease-fire.

U.N. Transitional Authority in Cambodia (UNTAC), March 1992–September 1993. As described in ths chapter, established to set up free elections, implement cease-fire, and maintain peace and stability.

U.N. Protection Force (UNPROFOR), March 1992–December 1995. Established to deal with the situation in Bosnia as described in Chapters 22 and 23.

U.N. Confidence Restoration Organization in Croatia (UNCRO), March 1995–January 1996. Established to observe the cease-fire and monitor border crossing, especially of arms equipment.

U.N. Preventative Deployment Force (UNPREDEP), March 1995 to present. As events in the former Yugoslavia threatened to spill over into Macedonia, the UNPREDEP was established to monitor and report any developments in the border areas.

U.N. Mission in Bosnia and Herzegovina (UNMIBH), December 1995 to present. Establishment of temporary international police task force to observe judicial institutions.

U.N. Transitional Administration for Eastern Slavonia, Baranja, and West Sirmium (UNTAES), January 1996–January 1998. Established to ensure peaceful transition of this region to Croatia.

U.N. Mission of Observers in Prevlaka (UNMOP), January 1996 to present. Established to monitor the demilitarization of the Prevlaka peninsula (in Croatia).

U.N. Observer Mission in Georgia (UNOMIG), August 1993 to present. Established to monitor and verify the implementation of the cease-fire between Georgian and Abkhaz forces.

U.N. Mission of Observers in Tajikistan (UNMOT), December 1994 to present. Established to monitor the implementation of the cease-fire on the Tajik–Afghan border and assist in reintegrating ex-combatants.

U.N. Mission in Haiti (UNMIH), September 1993–June 1996. Established to help modernize armed forces, establish new police forces, and ensure free and fair elections.

U.N. Temporary Executive Authority (UNTEA), and U.N. Security Force in West New Guinea (West Irian) (UNSF), October 1962–April 1963. Established to have full authority in West New Guinea (West Irian) from October 1, 1962, until May 1, 1963, at which time administration of the territory would be transferred to Indonesia. The agreement also stipulated that the secretary-general would provide a United Nations Security Force (UNSF) to assist UNTEA with as many troops as the U.N. administrator deemed necessary.

Mission of the Representative of the Secretary General in the Dominican Republic (DOMREP), May 1965–October 1966. Established to observe the installation of a newly elected government.

U.N. Good Offices Mission in Afghanistan and Pakistan (UNGOMAP), May 1988–March 1990. The secretary-general appointed a personal representative on the situation relating to Afghanistan to act as an intermediary between the governments of Afghanistan and Pakistan providing for the withdrawal of Soviet troops from Afghanistan.

U.N. Iran–Iraq Military Observer Group (UNIIMOG), August 1988–February 1991. Established following eight years of war between Iraq and Iran to verify, confirm, and supervise the cessation of hostilities and the withdrawal of forces.

U.N. Iraq–Kuwait Observation Mission (UNIKOM), April 1991 to present. Established to monitor the demilitarized zone between the two countries. After Iraqi forces crossed the border to seize abandoned military equipment, it was transformed into an armed force of 3,600.

U.N. Support Mission in Haiti (UNSMIH), June 1996–June 1997. Established to assist in professionalization of police force and maintain secure environment to establish national police force.

U.N. Verification Mission in Guatemala (MINUGA), January 1997–May 1997. Established to observe cease-fire between government and revolutionaries and the demobilization of forces.

U.N. Transition Mission in Haiti (UNTMIH), August 1997–November 1997. Established to help with further training of police in crowd control, rapid reaction, and palace security.

U.N. Civilian Police Mission in Haiti (MINPONUH), December 1997 to present. Established to assist the government of Haiti in supporting and contributing to professionalization of the Haitian National Police.

U.N. Police Support Group (UNPSG), January 1998 to present. Established to monitor the Croatian police in the Danube region.

3. *The New York Times*, 28 May 1998, p. A28.
4. *The New York Times*, 1 June 1998, A3, A6.
5. For a discussion of peacekeeping and the many proposals that have been made about it, see Paul F. Diehl, *International Peacekeeping* (Baltimore and London: Johns Hopkins University Press, 1993). See also Joseph T. Jockel, *Canada and International Peacekeeping* (Toronto: Canadian Institute of Strategic Studies; Washington, D.C.: Center For Strategic and International Studies, 1994); Michael Pugh, "Peacekeeping and Humanitarian Intervention," in Brian White, Richard Little, and Michael Smith, *Issues in World Politics* (London: Macmillan Press, 1997); A. B. Fetherston, *Towards a Theory of United Nations Peacekeeping* (New York: St. Martin's Press, 1994).

Chapter 24

Conventional Forces for the Medium-Term Compromise

In the interim before a worldwide, no-war community is able to take responsibility, the United States will need conventional forces that can intervene anywhere in the world to accomplish two different missions. The first mission is to halt conflicts that might spiral into nuclear war. The second is to prevent some rogue state from building a nuclear capability that threatens world peace. In addition, for the immediate future at least, a certain number of American forces should continue to be stationed in the NATO area and in South Korea as deterrents.

NATO

Consider NATO's role first. After its establishment in the wake of the attack by North Korea on South Korea in 1950, NATO built up and maintained conventional and tactical nuclear forces in Germany large enough to discourage anyone in the Soviet Union who might entertain the notion that a surprise attack on Europe could win a quick and easy victory. But the breakup of the Soviet Union removed any such threat. Russia is the only one of the successor states that has the military might to be a threat to the West, and it has clearly rid itself of any such ambitions. Even if one or the other individual Russian leader occasionally dreams of recreating the old Soviet empire, Russia has its hands full with its own internal troubles and with the instabilities in the other successor states.

Nevertheless, the NATO Allies were opposed to dismantling NATO, in spite of the breakup of the Soviet Union and the dissolution of the Warsaw Pact, and the Clinton administration came to agree. Almost immediately, the Czech Republic, Slovakia, Poland, and Hungary made bids to become NATO members. Obviously, they saw membership in NATO as a protection against potential future threats from Russia or from a revived Soviet Union. They undoubtedly also saw membership in NATO as providing better access to the European markets. Russia was alarmed. The biggest worry was that an expansion of NATO would isolate Russia from its allies and become an obstacle to Russia's own access to the European markets. Some Russians also worried that an expanded NATO might some day itself become aggressive.

The rationale for the Clinton administration's decisions both to continue NATO and to expand it were given by the undersecretary of state, Strobe Talbot.[1] The Clinton administration was concerned, first, about "regional conflict or instability, stemming from ethnic and other tensions arising inside or between European states." Another worry was an "external threat from the South or from the East," by which Talbot presumably meant from some country in the Middle East, such as Iran, and from China. If an alliance continued to be needed, the administration concluded, it is better to keep NATO than forge a new one.

Not only has NATO performed an essential military function in the past, Talbot argued, it has also performed a useful political function. It helped Italy and Germany become part of the trans-Atlantic community. It spurred reconciliation between France and Germany and laid the groundwork for the European Union. Its unified command removed the incentive for military competition among West European powers, and it helped keep the peace between Greece and Turkey. NATO could perform a similar political function, Talbot argued, with the former members of the Warsaw Pact—the Czech Republic, Slovakia, Poland, and Hungary. Membership in NATO will help these "post–Communist lands continue to evolve toward civil society, market economies and harmonious relations with their neighbors."

Arguing that an enlarged NATO is not a threat to Russia, Talbot recognized that Russian reformers and democrats genuinely fear that NATO "enlargement will inflame nationalistic, anti-Western and militaristic forces in Russia." But instead of seeing enlargement as a blow to Russian pride and a "Western vote of no confidence in Russia's future," Talbot argued, they should see it as part of an evolution from which Russia will benefit.

NATO forces today do not spend their time preparing to fight Russia but in training for peacekeeping missions with NATO allies and others, "including sometimes with the Russians themselves." Talbot pointed out that there is a Russian liaison office at NATO headquarters in Brussels, and he says that the United States has suggested "expanding these exchanges and including Russian officers at all the top levels of the Alliance command structure."

It is true that the expansion of NATO has some appeal as an interim solution to the instabilities in Eastern Europe. In the long run, however, the best course might be to disband NATO gradually with the goal of eventually replacing it with Europe-wide economic and political institutions that would include both Russia and the Eastern European states.

Whichever course is chosen, the highest priority should be to eliminate nuclear weapons. As per the agreement between Russia and the United States, the SS-20s, the Pershing IIs, cruise missiles, and the short-range missiles with ranges of

300 miles have been removed. The nuclear weapons that were not covered by the agreement, which include nuclear bombs, nuclear artillery, and battlefield nuclear missiles, should also be removed, and a public announcement of the removal should be made in dramatic terms. Part of the benefit would come precisely because the decision was publicized as still another step in putting the Cold War behind us.

As for the nonnuclear forces, in 1998 the United States still had 121,600 men and women assigned to the European Command. Of these, 60,500 were Army, including one armored and one mechanized infantry division, each of which had two rather than three brigades, and assorted artillery and other forces. Equipment for four armored/mechanized brigades had also been pre-positioned in the NATO area. The Air Force had 25,400 men and women assigned to NATO, organized in one fighter wing and one airlift wing.

The two American divisions could be reduced immediately to one brigade each with corresponding reductions in support troops with no significant risk. In a few years all that should be needed is a "trip-wire" or "plate-glass–window" deterrent to any sudden attempt to seize either West Germany or Western Europe, and removing these two brigades would be a good first step toward that goal.

KOREA

In East Asia, North Korea has presented an immediate and very real problem. It clearly was attempting to build nuclear warheads, and it succeeded in developing missiles with a range of several hundred miles. Obviously, it was toying with the idea of using both as a means of annexing South Korea. In early November 1993, North Korea massed troops along the cease-fire line, causing at least one high American official to speculate that it was contemplating an attack. The move was more likely to have been mere bluster or a paranoid fear that South Korea might seize the opportunity to take advantage of North Korea's manifold economic troubles. As discussed earlier, relations between the United States and North Korea later improved. On the one hand, there are indications that North Korea is at least in the process of giving up its efforts to develop nuclear weapons. On the other hand, as late as July 1998, North Korea was refusing to allow international inspectors full access to its nuclear sites. When and if all doubts are removed about North Korea having abandoned both its nuclear program and its ambitions to reunify Korea by military force, the United States should withdraw the 2nd Infantry Division stationed in Korea and disband it.

POTENTIAL TROUBLE SPOTS

As for trouble spots where the United States might feel compelled to intervene to halt conflicts that might spiral into nuclear war, at the moment there are only a few.

In Latin America, nothing very threatening looms. Although there are conflicts aplenty, none has a significant potential for spiraling into what might become a nuclear war. The only Latin American countries with the economic potential to become nuclear powers are Argentina and Brazil. It is conceivable that an aggressive totalitarian regime could arise in either of these two countries in the far future, but there are no present signs of any such development.

In Africa, south of the Sahara, there are some bitter and potentially bloody conflicts, but since South Africa took itself out of the nuclear business with such dramatic finality, there are none that threaten to spiral into nuclear war.

In Europe, Ukraine agreed during Clinton's visit in January 1994 to dismantle the nuclear weapons remaining on its soil, and that process has been successfully concluded. Although a problem might develop in the future, Russia can be counted on to deal with it.

In Asia, there continues to be tension between Japan and Russia over the Kurile islands annexed by the Soviet Union following World War II, but it is not a tension that is likely to lead to war. The long-simmering dispute between China and Russia along the Ussuri River boundary is another tension that is not likely to lead to war. Russia, as we said, has its hands full.

China, of course, has long had both a stockpile of nuclear weapons and the missiles to deliver them to ranges of several hundred miles and perhaps more. But with its surge of economic growth and new prosperity, China has little incentive for adventurism of any kind, much less nuclear adventurism. China is in turmoil, but the turmoil is social, political, and economic, which is not likely to lead to war with its neighbors.

In Southeast Asia, there are tensions between Vietnam and China and between Cambodia and Vietnam, but neither are likely to result in a war that might spread.

In South Asia, the tension between India and Pakistan remains high. Both sides recently tested nuclear weapons, and a war between them might escalate. But it is also clear that even if India and Pakistan came to war and even if that war became nuclear, it would have little potential for escalating into a wider war that threatens world peace or draws in either Russia or the United States.

In the Middle East, Israel has a stockpile of both nuclear warheads and the missiles to deliver them anywhere in the immediate vicinity. The danger is a war between Israel and the Arab world that goes so badly that Israel begins to believe it will be engulfed. In such circumstances, Israel might well exercise the "Samson option" and bring the whole of the Middle East tumbling down. However, the handshake between the Arab and Israeli leaders on the White House lawn and subsequent negotiations between Israel and the Palestinians, although disappointing, have helped to quiet such fears and so has the fact that both sides clearly understand just how horrendous the consequences would be if events spiral out of control. But these and other tensions in the Middle East can easily turn into small wars that have the potential for escalating into something that is much, much more serious, including nuclear war itself.

ROGUE STATES AND NUCLEAR WEAPONS

Another kind of problem is a rogue state building a nuclear capability that threatens world peace. Both Libya and Iran have been at work trying to develop the capacity to build nuclear warheads and both may have succeeded in acquiring missiles from China that are capable of delivering them at ranges of several hundred miles. But even if Qaddafi is the madman that some people think he is, his delivery capability would not extend any farther than Libya's immediate neighbors, and it is difficult to see how Qaddafi could believe there was any gain in using nuclear weapons against them.

Iran

In the case of Iran such comforting thoughts are more difficult to come by. The most dangerous people in the world have always been "true believers," in either a religion or an ideology. The word that best describes Iran, at least for the time being, is "unpredictable." However, better relations between Iran and the United States would have benefits for both parties. Nevertheless, if the United States is to assume responsibility for dealing with situations that could develop into nuclear war until a worldwide, no-war community is able to take over, it must have the capacity to intervene if Iran becomes a nuclear threat to the world.

THE SPECIAL PROBLEM OF BIOLOGICAL AND CHEMICAL TERRORISM

Chapter 14 suggested that tight security and effective intelligence will greatly reduce the threat of terrorists armed with weapons of mass destruction, even though they cannot be 100 percent effective. Recently the United States stepped up its efforts in both areas. In his 1998 State of the Union message, Clinto vowed to confront the hazard of germ warfare by "outlaw states, terrorists, and organized criminals." In May he unveiled a plan to stockpile vaccines at strategic sites around the country to fight germ warfare. He also appointed Richard A. Clarke to be the national coordinator for antiterrorist programs. In 1992, Clarke had moved to the NSC Staff from the State Department, where he had served in both the Reagan and Bush administrations. He was one of the few NSC officers Clinton held over.

Then, on August 7, 1998, bombs exploded at the American embassies in Nairobi, Kenya, and Dar es Salaam, Tanzania, killing 12 Americans and 253 citizens of the the two countries. American intelligence agencies gathered what officials described as overwhelming evidence that the attacks were masterminded by Osama bin Laden, an exiled Saudi Arabian millionaire based in Afghanistan and a suspect in two earlier bombings.

In retaliation, on August 20, the United States fired eighty Tomahawk cruise missiles from ships in the Red Sea and the Arabian Sea at two installations. One was a complex of six sites at the bin Laden base in Khost, Afghanistan, where as many as 600 of his people were meeting to plan more attacks. The second, also linked to bin Laden, was the Shifa Pharmaceutical plant in Khartoum, Sudan, which was engaged in manufacturing VX nerve gas.

Prior to the attack, the United States closed down several embassies that had been specifically threatened. However, senior American officials warned that this was the start of "a real war against terrorism," that it was "not a one-shot deal," and that "the prospect of retaliation against Americans is very, very high."

In December 1998, the United States announced that in the upcoming NATO meetings in April it would propose a new NATO Center for Weapons of Mass Destruction to be a clearing house for sharing intelligence on such weapons.

In January 1999, President Clinton said it was likely that a terrorist group will launch or threaten a germ or chemical attack on American soil within the next few years. "I want to raise public awareness of this," he said, "without throwing people into unnecessary panic." The president was also weighing a proposal to establish a military commander-in-chief for the defense of the continetal United States with special responsibility for biological and chemical warfare. A new budget was also unveiled that earmarked $8.5 billion for efforts to defend American embassies and $2.8 billion to be divided among both old and new programs to counter biological, chemical, and the threat of "cyberwar," invisible attacks on the nation's computers.

All these efforts are well justified, but from the perspective of this book, one additional measure seems imperative. The United States should immediately call an international conference to reach and publicize an agreement that the great powers will joinly invade and destroy any state that attacks another state with nuclear, biological, or chemical weapons or that supports a terrorist organization that does so.

FORCES NEEDED

For a job like this, three kinds of forces are needed. The first is a Rapid Deployment Force of infantry, artillery, and armor. The second is the air and sea transport to take these forces and their supplies to where they are needed. And the third is the air and sea power to protect and support them when they get there.

As its name suggests, a Rapid Deployment Force must be highly mobile. But it must also be as little dependent upon bases overseas as it is possible to make it, for several reasons. The first reason is that if trouble can break out almost anywhere with rather short notice, this force must be able to deploy rapidly, not just to the obvious trouble spots in the Middle East and East Asia, but to unforeseeable trouble spots in Latin America, Africa south of the Sahara, South Asia, or the rest of Asia outside of Korea. No single base or set of bases would provide the flexibility that is needed. The only solution is mobility.

A second reason is that if the United States is dependent on a base in a particular country it may become hostage to that country's parochial ambitions. This is what happened in the early years of NATO when the American need for bases in the Azores made it hostage to Portugal's desire to keep its colonies in Africa.

A third reason is that if nationalism continues to be the powerful force it has been this past century, the countries in which the bases are located might quite suddenly demand that the United States give them up. French nationalism, for example, was what motivated De Gaulle to force NATO to move SHAPE (Supreme Headquarters, Allied Powers of Europe) headquarters to Belgium. Spanish nationalism was the ultimate cause of Spain's 1988 decision to withdraw permission for the American F-16 bases. And Filipino nationalism was not going to permit the Philippine government to tolerate very much longer the American Air Force base at Clark Field or the naval base at Subic Bay, no matter how much rent the United States was willing to pay. The eruption of Mount Pinatubo hastened the process, but the end result was inevitable even without the eruption.[2] Even in West Germany, opposition to American bases is clearly growing. As we have seen, some of these attitudes result from the demise of the Soviet Union and the fact that Europe is less fearful of an attack from the East than it was, but much of the opposition is a direct consequence of nationalistic feelings.

What all this means is that whatever forces the United States needs, whether to halt conflicts that might spiral into nuclear war or to prevent some rogue state from building a nuclear capability, those forces must be structured to be as little dependent on bases overseas as it is possible to make them.

Current U.S. Forces

The most authoritative nonclassified summary of the world's armed force is *The Military Balance*.[3] The 1997–1998 edition says, "The United States is the only country in the world with the weapons, mobility, logistics, intelligence and communications capabilities to conduct effective, large-scale military operations with a global reach." This scale of military capability, it continues, has been maintained despite cuts in both spending and personnel of about one-third since 1990. The Clinton administration has announced that it intends to maintain American forces at the current level. Indications are that these levels are not likely to be changed very much by successor administrations.

Both the Bush and Clinton administrations conducted what was called a bottom-up review of the armed services, and this was institutionalized as the "Quadrennial Defense Review." In presenting the results of this review in May 1997, Secretary of Defense William Cohen said that a balance was being struck between exploiting advanced technologies and maintaining a sufficient number of active forces and logistic support to be, in the words of the 1998 budget statement, "capable of prevailing in two nearly simultaneous regional conflicts."

Active military personnel will be reduced to 1,422,000 by the end of fiscal year 1999 and reserve personnel to 889,000. The Army will maintain ten active divisions and eight reserve divisions, plus a number of enhanced brigades. The reserve combat units will be reassigned to combat-service support roles. Navy surface ships will be reduced from 126 to 116, and attack submarines to fifty. Procurement of the F/A-18 E/F aircraft (Hornet) will be cut back on the assumption that the Joint Strike Fighter will enter production for the Navy in 2008. The Navy will retain twelve carrier battle groups (eleven active and one training) and twelve amphibious groups. The Air Force will shift one air wing from active list to reserve, for a total of thirteen active fighter wings and seven reserve. Bombers will total 184. The number of F-22 aircraft to be procured will be reduced. It should be noted that the F-22, unlike the F-15 C/D which it replaces, will be able to conduct air-to-ground tasks as well as air defense. It should also be noted that the first B-2 bomber wing became operational in April 1997, and became engaged in active duty missions in the Middle East. The Marine Corps will remain about the same, with three Marine active Expeditionary forces and one reserve.

The following list summarizes these developments, but differs from the way in which the Bush and Clinton reviews were actually implemented in the following particulars.[4] First, the reviews specified thirteen fighter wings and *The Military Balance* specifies only twelve. Second, the reviews specified fourteen Ohio class submarines each carrying twenty-four Trident II (D-5) missiles with multiple warheads, while *The Military Balance* specifies eighteen submarines, type not specified. The nuclear forces numbers become effective upon entry into force of START II, and the number of bombers does not include ninety-five B-1 bombers assigned to conventional missions.

	1990	1998	Target
Active Forces			
Army Divisions	18	10	10
Navy Aircraft Carriers	15	11	11
Navy Air Wings	13	10	10
Navy Surface Combatants and Attack Submarines	287	192	192
Marine Divisions and Air Wings	3	3	3
Air Force Tactical Wings	24	12	12
Reserve Forces			
National Guard Divisions	10	8	8
Navy Air Wings	2	1	1
Navy Aircraft Carriers (training)	1	1	1
Marine Divisions and Air Wings	1	1	1
Air Force Tactical Wings	12	8	8
Strategic Nuclear Forces			
ICBM	1,000	550	500
Warheads	2,450	2,000	500
SSBNs	31	18	18
SLBMs	568	432	336
SLBM Warheads	4,864	3,456	<1,750
Bombers	324	87	92
Military Personnel			
Active Forces	2,069,000	1,431,000	1,360,000
National Guard and Reserve Forces	1,128,000	892,000	835,000

The Military Balance goes on to make the following comment:

The planned force structure outlined above would enable the US to participate in a major regional conflict, while also being engaged in one or more lesser peacekeeping operations, such as the NATO-led Stabilisation Force (SFOR) in Bosnia and Herzegovina. Whether it could conduct two major regional conflicts simultaneously, or, in the words of the 1998 budget statement, nearly simultaneously, is questionable; much would depend on the quantity and quality of allied support. Nevertheless, the budgetary objective of maintaining such a capability enables the US to sustain a powerful, broad spectrum of forces with the command, control, surveillance and intelligence systems essential for the US to remain the world's dominant military power.[5]

Is the Planned Force Really Needed?

The two tasks for which the United States will need nonnuclear forces are halting conflicts that might spiral into nuclear war and preventing some rogue state from building a nuclear capability. The question is, with the breakup of the Soviet Union, is the rather large defense array remaining after the Bush–Clinton reductions really necessary?

Earlier we argued that the Gulf War was unwise, that it would have been better to have dealt with the problem of Iraqi aggression by diplomatic and political means. But suppose for the sake of argument that military intervention *was* required. If so, it seems very obvious that the amount of force assembled to oust Iraq from Kuwait was a gigantic case of overkill. The Gulf War lasted one-hundred hours. American casualties were 148 killed, of whom 35 were actually killed by friendly fire, and 467 wounded, of whom 72 were the result of friendly fire. Another 156 were killed in accidents of various kinds. The British suffered 24 soldiers killed in combat, of whom 11 were by friendly fire and 23 in accidents. Among the Arab Allies, 44 Saudis were killed in combat. Detailed figures on casualties among the other Allies are not available, although the numbers were undoubtedly small, since fewer of their troops were involved. The total Allied confirmed killed was 216, and if the figures for Arab Allies are added it may be as high as 300. The Iraqi military casualties were between 100 thousand and 150 thousand killed and an unknown number wounded. In addition, about 150 thousand civilians were killed or died as a direct result of the war, most of whom were children.[6]

The American and Allied divisions deployed against Iraq consisted of a ground force equivalent to about thirteen divisions, nine American, one British, and three from the other Allies, mainly French and Arab. And these ground forces were supported by a large array of air and naval forces. As we said, the first question about the Gulf War is why it could not have been handled politically and diplomatically rather than by military force. The second question is whether it could have been handled by a force considerably smaller than was actually used.

As already mentioned, the counterargument to the second question is the German Army aphorism that if it will take ten divisions to win a battle, put in twenty and you may not have to fight at all. Putting such overwhelming force in the field against Iraq undoubtedly was a large factor in making the victory so cheap. The other factors were, as we saw, that the Iraqi army was vastly overrated and that Saddam Hussein chose neither to surrender nor to fight.

But the question for us here is whether the fact that overwhelming force made the victory in the Gulf War cheaper justifies keeping such a large standing army in the absence of any immediate threat. It seems obvious that there are no threats that would justify such a large standing Army, Navy, and Air Force. For the immediate future only a war with China or Russia would require such large forces, and given the present state of the world, neither one is likely to start a war that could escalate. And if the situation changes and either Russia or China does become aggressive, the resulting war could not be dealt with by a standing force in one-hundred hours or one-hundred days. A war with China or Russia would require full mobilization at the outset.

As for ground forces, the Army has on active duty a total of ten divisions and a variety of independent brigades and regiments. The divisions include two armored divisions, four mechanized divisions, one air assault division, one airborne division, and two light infantry divisions. Considering the reduction in potential threats, these forces could be substantially smaller. Rather than two armored divisions, one should suffice. Rather than four mechanized divisions, two should do. On the other hand, both the air assault division and airborne division are well suited to the two tasks that we foresee. They should be part of any standing force. The Army now has two light infantry divisions, and the Marine Corps has three divisions that are roughly the equivalent of an Army light division while being even more mobile. With three of these divisions, the Marines should be able to meet any foreseeable challenge to which such forces are appropriate. The Army should disband its two light divisions. It also is possible that similar reductions could be made in the independent brigades and regiments. Thus, the total divisions would be eight, five Army and three of the specialized Marine divisions to perform the tasks of light divisions.

It should be said that although the purpose in reducing standing military forces is not to save money but to move the world toward a situation in which war can be effectively abolished, in the process money would be saved. According to estimates by the U.S. Army Cost and Economic Analysis Center the annual operations of an armored division for 1998 is $1.019 billion. The cost of annual operations for a mechanized division for 1998 is $1.016 billion, so eliminating two mechanized divisions would save $2.032 billion per year. The cost of annual operations for a light division for 1998 is $638.85 million, so eliminating two light divisions would save $1.278 billion per year. The total savings per year would be $4.33 billion.[7]

Air Force

The needs for a nuclear deterrent will be discussed in the next and final chapter. Here we need to look only at the Air Force contribution to a Rapid Deployment Force. The number of aircraft the United States has on active duty at the present time should be about right for the Rapid Deployment Force as well. However, the principle is to rely as little as possible on bases overseas, so both air and sea lift should be increased.

From the concern in this book that the United States have a Rapid Deployment Force capable of dealing with events in remote parts of the world, the most acute problem is posed by the troubles of the C-17. The C-17 four-engine transport aircraft was designed to deliver 102 paratroopers or 110 thousand pounds of cargo over intercontinental distances to land at small, austere landing fields near the battle zone. The requirement has been reduced from 210 to 120 planes, but there have been significant delays due to technical and cost problems, and it is possible that the program might be abandoned.

Quite obviously, dealing with a rogue state or intervening in a war that threatens to escalate requires a substantial number of aircraft to perform the mission the C-17 was designed to fill. If the problems of the C-17 are too large to be fixed, a completely new intercontinental cargo plane that will meet this requirement must be designed and built. If a new aircraft must be developed to perform the mission of the C-17, the total savings in ground, naval, and strategic forces would be somewhat reduced.

Navy

For the needs foreseen here, it seems excessive to maintain a force of eleven active aircraft carriers and one in reserve. First, as the repercussions of the end of the Cold War settle down, it would not be necessary to have the carrier groups permanently stationed overseas. The two carrier groups earmarked to meet crises in the Mediterranean and the Persian Gulf could be based on the Atlantic coast and the one carrier group earmarked for a crisis in the far Pacific could be based on Hawaii. In this way, instead of four carriers to maintain each battle group, only three would be needed. One would be ready to sail and the other two would either be in overhaul or in training. Thus, the total carriers needed on active duty would be nine rather than eleven.

Again, the basic purpose of reducing standing forces is not to save money, but money would be saved. Since the operating and support costs for a battle group are about $1 billion per year, the savings would be considerable—on the order of $2 billion.

As discussed in Chapter 12, the decision to build another carrier and another Seawolf submarine were made for two reasons. The first was to keep the shipyards in Groton and Newport News going. The argument was that shutting them down and starting them up again would be more expensive than keeping them going with the additional carrier and Seawolf, even though neither was really necessary. The second argument had nothing to do with defense, but was merely to build the two ships as a form of welfare through defense employment.

The first argument blithely ignores the possibility that a concerted political and diplomatic effort to reduce the likelihood of war might well remove the need for more carriers and submarines in the future. If that effort fails, the shipyards can be started up again in plenty of time, even if the cost does turn out to be somewhat greater, which is far from certain.

The second argument is simply wrongheaded. If welfare employment is needed, it would be much better to subsidize something that benefits people more than armaments, such as a better transportation system, better housing, and so on down a long, long list. The plans to build an additional carrier and Seawolf submarine should be canceled.

Again, even though savings is not the purpose, savings would be accomplished. Canceling the new carrier would save $5 billion in fiscal year 1999. Canceling the Seawolf would save $225 million immediately and $70.2 million in fiscal year 1999.

However, given the needs of the Rapid Deployment Force contemplated here, another look at the number of roll-on, roll-off fast sealift ships seems to be called for. More may well be needed. Building more roll-on, roll-off fast sealift ships would reduce the savings achieved by reducing the number of carrier battle groups and canceling the new carrier and the new Seawolf, but only slightly.

CRUISE MISSILES

Both the Air Force and the Navy are equipped with cruise missiles, and they should be an important element in the conventional forces needed for the medium-term compromise. No reduction in the planned number of missiles should be made.

It might be noted that it was unmanned cruise missiles that were used in both Clinton administration attacks on Iraq. These missiles carry 1 thousand pounds of high explosive. Matching a television image to a map, they can follow terrain features on a flight path that avoids antiaircraft installations. Considering the distances they travel, these missiles are remarkably accurate, especially compared to ordinary bombs (as distinguished from the so-called "smart" bombs). Forty-four cruise missiles were fired in the attack on the Iraqi intelligence installations in the first attack, for example, and only three missed their target. The consequences of the three misses were tragic, but that has to do with the decision to fire in this particular case not the utility of the weapon.

What is more, a guidance system for cruise missiles is also under development that would make them even more accurate—to within a few inches according to some of the more hyperbolic accounts. But the point is that while an accuracy of even several hundred feet is redundant for a cruise missile armed with a nuclear warhead, a very high degree of accuracy makes a cruise missile with a conventional warhead a formidable weapon for limited, conventional warfare.

CONCLUSION

For the two tasks of intervening to halt a war that threatens to escalate and to disarm a rogue state that is building nuclear weapons, the United States needs a Rapid Deployment Force of infantry, artillery, and armor, the air and sea transport to take these forces to where they are needed, and the air and sea power to support them when they get there.

The ground forces needed are a total of eight divisions: one armored, two mechanized, one air assault, and one airborne division in the Army, and three Marine divisions to perform the tasks of light divisions. For the Air Force the current force structure seems right, except that there is a very real need for an intercontinental cargo plane, like the C-17, that can land on small, austere airfields near the battle zone. If the problems of the C-17s are too great to be fixed, a completely new long-range cargo plane must be designed and built. For the Navy the total number carrier groups, each consisting of an aircraft carrier and its supporting ships, can be reduced from eleven to nine. However, to support the Rapid Deployment Force properly, the Navy may well have to add more roll-on, roll-off fast sealift squadrons. Finally, both the Air Force and the Navy should be equipped, as current planning provides, with an ample supply of the newer cruise missiles with highly accurate guidance systems.[8]

NOTES

1. *The New York Times*, 18 February 1997, p. A19.

2. For an expansion of this argument, see Roger Hilsman, "The U.S. Base Agreement with the Philippines," *ADA Today* 44, no. 3 (1989).

3. *The Military Balance* (London: International Institute for Strategic Studies, 1997–1998).

4. Ibid., 13.

5. Ibid.

6. For a rundown on the estimates of Iraqi military and civilian casualties, see Roger Hilsman, *George Bush vs. Saddam Hussein: Military Success! Political Failure?* (Novato, Calif.: Presidio Press, 1992), 205–209, 219, 223–225.

7. U.S. Army Cost and Economic Analysis Center, in response to a specific request.

8. In response to complaints about military readiness, Clinton proposed to increase the military budget by $12 billion in the coming fiscal year and more than $100 billion over the next six years. Of this $12 billion, $2.5 billion would go for raises and retirement benefits, $2 billion would go for the force in Bosnia, and $7 billion would go for maintenance, spare parts, and so on. The $100 billion would pay for "modernization." However, it is anyone's guess how much of this the Congress will actually appropriate.

Chapter 25

Nuclear Forces for the
Short-Term Stopgap

The long-term solution to the problem of nuclear weapons is world government, but it is doubtful that world government can be achieved quickly or easily. Ethnic, religious, and cultural differences are great, and too fast a pace might result not in world government but in worldwide civil war. Civil wars are often as bloody as wars between states and sometimes even more bloody, and a worldwide civil war might be the bloodiest of all. Can something be done in the interim before a world government can be established that would facilitate movement toward world government and at the same time reduce the chances of nuclear war?

One possibility is an international treaty signed by all states providing for the destruction of all national nuclear stockpiles; the establishment of an international inspection procedure to see that no nuclear weapons are produced secretly; and the establishment of an international force equipped with, say, fifty nuclear weapons to be used only by order of the U.N. Security Council against any country found to be violating the treaty by building nuclear weapons. This U.N. nuclear force would be used only as a last resort, after diplomatic and political efforts had failed, and then only if circumstances were such that a conventional force would not be able to accomplish the task of disarming the rogue country. As a practical matter, the U.N. force would probably serve solely as a deterrent and an earnest of U.N. intentions.

In the meantime, the United States must maintain a second-strike force capable of absorbing a surprise attack and striking back with devastating force against the country or combination of countries that launched the attack. What should be the composition of this deterrent force?

THE INTELLIGENCE REQUIREMENT

The first requirement is an effective intelligence effort that can detect any attempt to build a nuclear arsenal before it has progressed too far. Old-fashioned espionage and the cloak-and-dagger methods of traditional spying have not been very successful in the past, and they are not likely to be adequate to the needs of the future.[1] However, better means are available.

The U-2 discovered that the Soviet Union had secretly deployed nuclear missiles to Cuba. Its replacement, the SR-71 Blackbird, flies at Mach 3.2, 2,200 miles per hour with bursts to 2,600. The plane's skin is made entirely of Titanium no thicker than a soda can. Its two jets produce as much thrust as the engines on the Queen Mary, and it can outrun both the fastest fighters and the best antiaircraft missiles. It flies at altitudes of 85 thousand to 100 thousand feet, higher than any other airplane. It takes pictures of such high resolution that it can read the numbers on a license plate when it is flying fifteen miles up. At the same time it records electronic emissions of all kinds. Since it flies higher than fighter planes and since it can outrun both fighters and antiaircraft missiles, it needs no armaments. It does its work with almost total impunity.

But the SR-71 costs $400 million a year to maintain, as much as ninety fighter jets, and it guzzles fuel so fast that it requires six refueling planes when it goes on a long mission. When the SR-71 was retired in 1990 the speculation was that a faster, higher-flying airplane had been developed, but the reason was apparently that satellites can do almost as well with less risk and at less cost. Later the decision was reversed and three SR-71 aircraft are operational today.

However, satellites, at least in peacetime, are also protected by an international agreement that makes the space in which they operate the same as international waters. If a rogue state shot down a satellite that act itself would be treated as equivalent to violating the treaty on nuclear weapons and justifying a retaliatory strike massive enough to destroy any facilities devoted to building nuclear weapons.

A new generation of smaller satellites is planned for the year 2003 that will give almost constant coverage of any place on the globe at fifteen-minute intervals. They may also have Stealth qualities and the capacity to change orbit.

The U-2 took pictures with traditional cameras and film. The film had to be brought back to earth, flown to the special laboratories that developed it, and the pictures then flown to the photographic interpreters—a time-consuming process. The pictures that satellites take are electronic images that can be relayed almost instantly to the photo interpreters on the ground. It may take a little longer to program a satellite to take pictures at a particular spot than it did to fly a SR-71 there, but the time lag is minimal.

The drawback to all overhead reconnaissance, whether by plane or satellite, is that it cannot look inside buildings or caves. But in a variety of ways it can monitor what is going into the building or cave and what is coming out. The suspicious activity in North Korea is an example. Although a ground inspection would be needed to be absolutely sure, overhead reconnaissance determined that something suspicious was going on that might be related to the storage of weapons-grade plutonium.

Electronic intelligence can also be gathered by ordinary aircraft, by ships, and by ground installations. In these days of computers few codes are broken soon enough to be timely, but electronic intelligence can provide a great deal of useful information even when codes are not broken. To give just one example, in the days before the introduction of North Vietnamese troops into South Vietnam, it was important to know whether the Viet Cong guerrillas were independent or controlled by North Vietnam. The United States was not successful in breaking the radio codes. But the question was settled when radio direction finders showed that radio traffic to and from areas where Viet Cong battalions were operating was not from some hidden headquarters in South Vietnam, but from Hanoi in the North.

Another enormously successful source of a special kind of information is the network of listening devices the U.S. Navy maintains to monitor the oceans. It can detect even a very quiet submarine and identify it by the characteristic pattern of the sound waves it produces.

A SHORT-TERM STOPGAP

Beyond the intelligence effort, the forces needed for an effective deterrent should fulfill three requirements. The first is that the deterrent force must avoid as much as possible posing the threat of a first strike. The second is that it must provide a deterrent at least as effective as MAD. The third is that it must provide both sides with several incentives: incentives to adopt a stabilizing strategy and force structure, incentives to negotiate still more arms control agreements, and incentives to build toward some sort of world community. If a name for such a strategy is needed, it might be called a deterrent/incentive strategy.

The first requirement, that of not posing the threat of a first strike, can be tricky. A second-strike force is one designed to absorb a blow and still be able to strike back. But such a force can obviously be used first, before it is attacked. To make matters even worse, almost every weapons system can make some contribution to a first-strike strategy. Take as an example a purely passive civil defense system. If a passive civil defense system is combined with a highly accurate missile force, and if the passive defense system is effective enough to significantly reduce the effects of a retaliatory strike, the passive defense system becomes an essential element of a first-strike strategy. At the same time, the first priority of a second-strike force is to destroy the remaining enemy offensive forces. So a second-strike force that avoids posing a threat that it could be used to disarm the other side in a surprise attack is something of a contradiction.

Improvements in accuracy have made hardened missile silos almost useless in providing a second-strike capability. This means that a deterrent/incentive strategy requires weapons systems that are mobile and preferably that can also be concealed. In addition, all the reasons for keeping the Rapid Deployment Force independent of bases overseas apply even more categorically to the nuclear deterrent force.

In addition to these requirements for mobility, concealment, and freedom from overseas bases, the second-strike force should as much as possible operate in areas far removed from population centers. Thus, if deterrence fails and one side or the other launches a preemptive attack, civilian casualties—although they would undoubtedly be awesome—would be somewhat less than they would otherwise.

For example, missiles mounted on all-terrain trucks that could roam the desert in the Southwestern United States would be better than missiles mounted on trucks that traveled on the American highway system or mounted on railroad cars that traveled on the American rail system. And missiles that were launched from submarines roaming remote ocean areas would be better still. In other words, if deterrence fails, the second-strike force should by its basing system or by its inherent nature draw fire away from populated areas.

However, no one should have any illusions that if deterrence failed and nuclear war came that these measures would reduce civilian casualties to a figure that would be comparable to civilian casualties in, say, World War I or even to the much greater number in World War II. Even if both sides had only second-strike forces based on submarines and confined their attacks on the other to its submarine-based forces, the civilian casualties from fallout alone would probably be much, much greater than the millions of civilian casualties in World War II—depending on where the submarines were and the direction of the wind.

An effective second-strike force should also be able to maintain a high percentage of its weapons on alert for long periods of time. If the percentage of the force on alert is small, one side or the other would be tempted in a time of crisis to launch a preemptive attack against the forces not on alert to prevent them from being used in a second-strike retaliation. Although bombers on continuous airborne alert fulfill all the other conditions, it is obvious that it is much, much easier to maintain submarines at sea for long periods than bombers in the air.

In addition to these characteristics of the second-strike force itself, the threat to launch a retaliatory attack with the second-strike force must also seem logical. It should be reasonable, that is, for each side to believe that even after receiving a blow the other side would still have an incentive to launch its second-strike force. The threat to retaliate should be credible.

It is hard to visualize a nuclear force that did not have the capacity to attack both the enemy's forces and his cities. But suppose one could be designed that could only attack cities. Suppose the United States had such a force and suppose a belligerent successor to the present Russia considered using its inherited nuclear weapons to launch a surprise attack on all the Minuteman missiles that the present agreements permit the United States to have and on all the American bomber bases and submarine bases, and at the same time to attack as many of the U.S. bombers on airborne alert and submarines on patrol at sea as it could locate. But suppose that it considered a strategy of refraining from an attack on American cities, and it considered leaving some military installations untouched precisely because they were near cities. Suppose, also, that it considered holding back from its first strike enough missiles to threaten the one-hundred largest American cities with the idea that such a threat would lead the Americans to surrender. If the American forces had been designed to destroy the enemy's forces they would threaten these follow-on forces. So they would have some deterrent value. But if the American forces were designed to destroy cities alone, and posed no threat to the enemy's follow-on forces, the only incentive they would offer would be for the enemy to use his entire stockpile in the original attack.

The credibility problem for a second-strike force is similar to the European worries about coupling, which were also related to the kind of targets chosen. Before the breakup of the Soviet Union, a major European worry was as follows. If the Soviet Union attacked Europe but refrained from attacking the American homeland, would the United States actually attack Soviet cities, knowing that doing so would inevitably bring down an attack on American cities? At the same time, if the only choice open to the NATO forces in response to a Soviet attack limited to Europe was either to surrender or to use battlefield nuclear weapons with all the attendant civilian casualties, many Europeans might well have chosen to surrender.

Quite clearly, if a deterrent/incentive strategy is to be credible, each side should take whatever steps it can to make the other side feel comfortable that the second-strike force is not designed to attack urban–industrial targets. Given the power of nuclear weapons, it would be difficult to convince an opponent of this, but if anything can be done, it should be done.

The final aspect of what constitutes an effective second-strike force is the question of how much destruction would be "devastating." The problem is really one of perception. Consider again our hypothetical example of a belligerent successor state to Russia attacking the American nuclear forces but holding back enough missiles to attack the one-hundred largest American cities in a follow-on strike. Would the leaders of this belligerent successor state regard as devastating the loss of its military capability either to "win" the war or to continue the attack? Or would it take substantial civilian casualties to bring them to this conclusion? If the answer is that it would require civilian casualties, then the question is, "How many civilian casualties?" Would the leaders of this belligerent successor state regard the loss of 10 percent of the state's population as devastating, or would it have to be as high as 50 percent?

The question of how much destruction is devastating is similar to the question of credibility. If a second-strike force is designed to destroy the military capability of this belligerent successor state to continue to attack either by missiles against American and Western European cities or by its ground forces against NATO defenses—*and if that second-strike force is clearly capable of carrying out the design*—then no sane leader of such a belligerent successor state could believe that the successor state could "win" a war. Devastation of the successor state's military capability to continue to attack, in other words, would be devastation enough.

But even if military installations are the targets of a second strike and not cities, if the deployment of the strategic forces of both sides remains the same as it is today a huge number of civilians would still be killed—probably not as many as 50 percent of each side's population, but very likely much more than 10 percent. On the American side, both the Minuteman missiles and the strategic bomber bases would attract nuclear strikes, and civilian casualties would be inevitable and very large. Whether the casualties are in the millions or tens of millions would again depend on which way the wind was blowing. On the Russian side, both the strategic bomber bases and the SS-25 ICBMs would attract nuclear strikes, although significantly more of the SS-25s would be likely to survive than the Minuteman missiles since the SS-25s are road mobile and the Minuteman missiles are in fixed silos.

WEAPONS

In light of these requirements, which of the weapons either now available or planned would contribute to a deterrent/incentive strategy and which would not?

Milstar System

Milstar—an acronym for "military, strategic, tactical, and relay system"—was initiated in the early 1980s as part of the Reagan administration's nuclear buildup. Its goal was to provide a military command and control system that could continue to operate after both the Pentagon and Washington had been destroyed. The design goal of Milstar was to permit the military to fight a nuclear war lasting at least six months. The project was so highly classified that no inkling of it reached Congress and the public until 1990. But when it did, the assumption that a nuclear war would last six months was regarded as absurd by most critics. Even more appalling was the idea of making preparations to keep on fighting after both Washington and the Pentagon—and presumably much of the rest of the country—had been destroyed.

It should be said that Russia also has a "doomsday" system that provides for nuclear retaliation if Russia's top military and civilian leadership is wiped out. An underground radio station was built that will transmit coded messages ordering the missiles to be launched if three conditions are met. First, the station must have received preliminary sanction from the Russian general staff. Second, there must be a total loss of communications with the top military commanders. Third, there must be evidence of nuclear explosions.

The cost of Milstar made it the most expensive single project in military history. The research and development costs alone appear to have been on the order of $8 billion. Each of the six Milstar communications satellites would cost $1.4 billion, for a total of $8.4 billion, and the rockets to launch them would cost a total of $10 billion. The various supporting equipment—several thousand portable data links and computer terminals, mobile command units in tractor trailers, and so on—would cost several billions more. A number of government officials said that the total cost over a twenty-year period will be at least $30 billion. Even the Air Force was sufficiently appalled by the cost to try to kill Milstar, but to no avail.

The only change in Milstar sparked by the breakup of the Soviet Union was to scale it back slightly and to make it appropriate for nonnuclear wars as well as nuclear. The first Congressional reaction to Milstar was a statement by the Senate Armed Services Committee that "the Department of Defense has not justified the extraordinary expense of this overdesigned system." The system was then somewhat scaled down in design but not in cost, with the final four satellites being adapted to meet the needs of nonnuclear wars such as the Gulf War and to make them less complicated and more practical. Nevertheless, the House Government Operations Committee announced that it would begin a new set of hearings shortly after the first of the satellites was launched in February 1994.

Since satellites, exposed as they are in space, are extraordinarily vulnerable, Milstar was designed with the capability of retreating when necessary from an orbit of 23,300 miles to an orbit of 110 thousand miles. Milstar also includes devices intended to shield it from nuclear explosions and electromagnetic pulses. But critics remain skeptical. They argue that there are a number of much cheaper ways of achieving the same communications goals. Lou Rodriguez, the official in Congress's General Accounting Office (GAO) who has studied Milstar for several years, says that redesigning the system could save $18 billion and still accomplish the basic mission. Other critics argue that commercial satellites without Milstar's elaborate and as yet unproven defenses could do the same job for $200 million. Pentagon officials admit that it will take years—and probably a large-scale war—before they can be sure that Milstar will work as intended.

One month after the first of Milstar's six satellites was launched, the primary power unit failed. The Pentagon said that the satellite would be able to operate on its backup power system, but critics said that the backup system was the same as the primary system and was no more reliable. The report of the House Government Operations Committee, which had been promised to follow the launching of the first of the satellites, was published on October 20, 1994.[2] It called on the secretary of defense to reevaluate requirements for the military satellite system and see if these could be met by buying or leasing commercial satellites, and called for the Department of Defense to "underscore a clear policy that encourages full and open discussion of alternatives." It also noted that the GAO had concluded that canceling the acquisition of Milstar satellites five and six would save $2 billion and that this potential saving was especially important in view of the fact that another GAO study reported a shortfall of $150 billion in available defense funds over the next five years.

Minuteman Missile

The Minuteman is obviously less destabilizing when it is armed with only one warhead than when it was armed with three. However, the Minuteman in fixed bases is vulnerable and has little if any value as a second-strike weapon. So it also has little value as a deterrent. On the contrary, since the principal value of Minuteman missiles would be in either a first strike or in a retaliatory strike on cities, they would be a serious worry to an enemy. Inevitably, in a crisis the enemy would be sorely tempted to take the Minuteman missiles out in a preemptive attack. Even if the Minuteman is equipped with only one warhead, in other words, it is still destabilizing. The Minuteman should not be part of a deterrent/incentive strategy. The Minuteman should be scrapped.

If the Russians decide to follow the American lead and reshape their nuclear forces to serve a deterrent/incentive strategy, they will have to consider whether or not their SS-25 should be a part of their forces. Since the SS-25 is road mobile it is better as an element of a second-strike force than the American Minuteman. However, roads go between population centers, which means that the SS-25s will draw fire that is bound to kill civilians—again, just how many depends on which way the wind is blowing. Also, the fact that the SS-25s would share the road with other vehicles means that mistakes would be made and innocent vehicles would also be attacked. The conclusion is obvious that, although the SS-25 is better for a second-strike force than the Minuteman, it is also destabilizing and should not be part of a Russian deterrent/incentive strategy. It, too, should be scrapped.

Bombers

The scenarios for nuclear war in Chapter 14 assumed that all of the bombers the United States keeps on air alert would survive a first strike and that half of those on ground alert would survive. However, the criteria for a deterrent/incentive strategy rules out including any bombers at all in the deterrent/incentive force. Since the location of bomber bases can be pinpointed and since they are very vulnerable, the mere existence of a bomber force offers an incentive for an enemy to preempt. So even if it is possible that a significant number of bombers on air and ground alert could survive a preemptive attack, they defeat the purpose of a deterrent/incentive strategy. All the B-52s earmarked for strategic bombing should be mothballed, leaving ninety-five B-52s assigned to conventional tasks on duty. The B-1 has no role in the deterrent/incentive force and no significant conventional role. It should be scrapped.

Stealth Bomber

The Stealth Bomber (B-2) may possibly be an exception to this general conclusion that bombers should not be part of a deterrent/incentive force, at least for the time being. The Stealth bomber has a very small radar profile, and its mission was intended to be to penetrate Soviet air defenses via a path cleared principally by cruise missiles and then to hunt down and destroy Soviet command posts and mobile Soviet missiles mounted on trucks and trains. As long as Russia maintains the mobile SS-25s as part of their nuclear forces, the United States has a good reason to keep the B-2.

But notice the reason to keep the B-2 is not because it is a good vehicle for nuclear weapons in a deterrent/incentive strategy, but only because of its hunter/killer capabilities against a mobile, ground-based missile system such as the SS-25. The Stealth bomber is costly—$500 million per plane without armaments—and its "stealthiness" is probably not going to last very long. Stealth technology is designed to scatter the radar waves rather than bounce them back to the transmitter. So one method to foil Stealth technology is to put the radar transmitter in one place and the receiver in another so the receiver can pick up the scattered waves. In addition, Stealth technology is designed to foil ground-based radar, so it is vulnerable to very high-flying airborne radar looking down on it. The Soviets should be persuaded to scrap the SS-25, and then the United States should scrap the B-2.

As for Russian bombers—the Bear ACLM, the Bear, and the Blackjack—the conclusion is the same as it was for the B-52 and B-1: None of the three should be part of a Russian deterrent/incentive force. They should be scrapped.

Cruise Missiles Armed with Nuclear Warheads

Cruise missiles can be launched from a land-based platform, from aircraft, from ships, and from trucks. As already described, both the United States and Russia have agreed to forbid land-based cruise missiles in Europe and both sides have withdrawn cruise missiles from their surface ships. As for cruise missiles with nuclear warheads launched from aircraft, we concluded that neither the American B-52 H bombers carrying cruise missiles nor the sixty Russian Bear bombers carrying cruise missiles should be part of the American and Russian deterrent/incentive forces. They should be scrapped.

As for cruise missiles armed with nuclear warheads and mounted on trucks ranging through uninhabited areas, since cruise missiles are slow flying and vulnerable they do not pose a serious threat of being used in a first-strike force. Also, because cruise missiles carry only one warhead, they are not simultaneously provocative and tempting as MIRVed missiles on fixed bases are.

A considerable amount of work has been done on cruise missiles that have ranges of 3 thousand miles and 6 thousand miles and that have Stealth technology providing low radar profiles. Mounted on trucks, such missiles would be candidates for a second-strike, deterrent/incentive force.

However, cruise missiles, being air-breathing unmanned aircraft, can be shot down by an improved version of traditional air defense systems. So making them a part of a deterrent/incentive force would violate the incentive criterion. The other side would be forced to build a very extensive and very expensive traditional air defense system. As a consequence, cruise missiles have no place in a deterrent/incentive force.[3] They should be scrapped.

Submarine-Based Missiles

Of all the systems so far developed, the least vulnerable is the Trident submarine. This means that it provides little incentive for an enemy to preempt.

This discussion so far has been focused on the incentive side of a deterrent/incentive strategy. Before the breakup of the Soviet Union, its heavy ICBM forces in their fixed silos, like the American Minuteman and M-X systems, were vulnerable to a preemptive strike. In time of crisis, both weapons systems would generate a "use-them-or-lose-them" psychology. Since the U.S. principal weapon was the submarine-based D-5 missile that had the accuracy and power to take out the heavy ICBMs with relative ease, Yeltsin had little incentive to try to hold on to them. A similar pressure was at work on the American leadership in its decision to give up the MX. As already discussed, the same arguments apply to the Minuteman missile, even when its warheads are reduced from three to one.

In addition to providing exactly the kind of incentive desired in a deterrent/incentive strategy, the Trident D-5 system has other advantages. Trident submarines are not only mobile, but can be concealed under schools of fish and temperature inversion layers. And they can also maintain a high state of alert for long periods of time, with at least half of the fleet on routine patrol.

However, Trident presents two serious problems. First, it places upon Russia the choice of accepting second-level status or building a Trident of its own, which it can ill afford. The decision, according to news reports in December 1998 and January 1999 has been to build an entirely new missile, the Topol-M. A generation ahead of any planned by the United States, it has a range of 6,200 miles, utilizes solid fuel, carries a single warhead, and weighs so little it can be based on trucks. It is also remarkably accurate. In a test firing in December 1998, it hit within a few dozen meters of a target at a range of several thousand kilometers. What is really remarkable, however, is that the Topol-M has a unique zig-zag flight trajectory. Russian TV showed it streaking through the night sky in an absolutely eccentric manner. This will make it invulnerable to any antimissile system yet conceived. A thousand such relatively cheap missiles would give Russia an effective alternative to either accepting second-level status or building a Triden system of its own. So far ten Topol-M missiles have been deployed in the Saratov region 750 kilometers southwest of Moscow.

Command and Control

The second problem that Trident poses is command and control. For fixed, land-based missiles, command and control can be made very secure indeed. The missiles can be hard wired so that the following steps must be taken before they can be fired:

1. The president must in effect throw a switch by electronic means using a code that is changed daily.

2. This order must then be confirmed by the secretary of defense and the Joint Chiefs of Staff, who must in effect throw a second switch.

3. The same procedure is required right on down the line, from army commander to corps commander and so on down to the people in the command silo of each missile to be fired.

4. In the command silo itself two officers are routinely stationed inside bulletproof glass cages, protected from each other and from anyone else in the command silo. Each of these two officers is armed with handguns, but no one else in the silo is allowed to carry arms of any kind. Both officers have to unlock the missile before it can be fired.

Because the system is hard wired, it inspires a high degree of confidence: Switches do in fact have to be closed.

Unfortunately, a hard-wired system is not possible for a submarine on patrol. But the system used in missile submarines is still very good. Before a missile can be fired from a Trident, the president must send a coded message through channels and that message must be authenticated by at least two officers on the submarine who are equipped with special codes to which only they are privy. The message must then be further authenticated by the executive officer of the submarine and the captain, both of whom have their own special codes. After the captain orders the crew to begin preparing the missiles for firing, he must obtain launching keys from a safe to which he does not have the combination. Two more officers must open the safe, one the outside door and the other the inside door.

For the launch itself, four more keys are needed, turned by four different officers. Two of these officers are in the missile control room, a third is two decks below at the gas generator that provides the gas to propel a missile out of the launching tube, and the fourth is the captain in the command center. Although the Trident is not as foolproof as a hard-wired system, it is about as close to being foolproof as human ingenuity can make it.

HOW BIG A TRIDENT FORCE?

For all the reasons outlined, the obvious conclusion is that missile-carrying submarines—the Tridents—should be the main weapon in a deterrent/incentive strategy. The next question is how many. As described, the United States plans a fleet of eighteen Trident submarines. The plan is to keep twelve submarines at sea at all times. Each submarine will have two crews, one at sea and one on shore at any given time. Each submarine will carry twenty-four D-5 missiles with four warheads each, rather than the eight which the D-5 is capable of carrying. This fully alert force can deliver a total of 1,152 warheads on target.

In 1993, the Congressional Budget Office published a study asserting that even if none of the eighteen submarines in the current fleet are replaced, the Navy plan would cost $46.6 billion. The study had two major suggestions. The first was to retire the six oldest submarines instead of refitting them with new missiles. The second suggestion was to keep only six submarines at sea at all times, thereby reducing the crews needed from two to one per vessel. The study argued that these changes would not significantly lower the level of security provided, but would save $17.5 billion.

Each of the six Trident submarines on full alert suggested by the Congressional Budget Office would carry twenty-four missiles and each missile would carry four warheads—a total of ninety-six warheads per submarine. With six submarines on full alert, the total warheads would be 576, and this, too, seems excessive for the needs of a deterrent/incentive force. SIOP-62, after all, listed only 1,062 DGZs, and these included urban–industrial complexes throughout the Soviet Union and targets among Soviet allies, neither of which would be included in a deterrent/incentive strategy. If only military installations are targeted, the total number is no more than 300.

As already mentioned, a worldwide network of listening devices on the ocean floor can locate submarines when their engines are running. Submarines drifting with their engines off can escape detection by such listening devices. And they can also escape detection by sonar if they have positioned themselves properly. Also, locating the submarines is only the first part of the problem. Once located, they still have to be destroyed. This can be done by mines, but that is a happenstance—the mines have to have been fortuitously placed in the submarine's path. Presumably, a submarine could also be taken out by long-range missiles, but a submarine on the move can be elusive, and the collateral damage is likely to be very great. Finally, the submarine can be taken out by an attack submarine, but the attack submarine has to be lucky enough to be nearby, and it still has the problem of interception.

So even with the very best intelligence and the very best of the antisubmarine equipment and techniques that are available today, an enemy could not be confident of taking out more than one or two Trident submarines on patrol before they launched their missiles. If four Tridents survived, they could deliver warheads on 384 separate targets. This would give a built-in surplus of 22 percent. As Winston Churchill said, beyond a certain point firing any more warheads would only "make the rubble bounce." Even if some unforeseen technical breakthroughs occur in the next few years, there would be time enough to deploy a larger Trident force. And in the highly unlikely event that a breakthrough went undetected, an enemy could still not hope to take out more than three or four of the Tridents at sea no matter how good his forces were, how lucky they were, or how inept the American submarine commanders were. So even in a worst case scenario occurring some years from now, two Tridents would survive, and two Tridents could launch nuclear warheads on 192 targets.

For the purposes of a deterrent/incentive strategy there is even more reason to argue that the United States should start with the smaller force. Starting with the smaller force would demonstrate the United States's good intentions—and so constitute an incentive for the Russians from the beginning. The United States could then offer a further incentive by declaring that it would reduce the Trident force further as Russia eliminates its land-based missiles. In other words, by starting with six Tridents on patrol and announcing its intention to reduce the number of Tridents as Russia eliminates its land-based missiles, the United States would emphasize the incentive side of the equation in the strongest possible terms.

CONCLUSION

A deterrent/incentive strategy would redesign the Milstar system, eliminate the Minuteman and the B-52 and B-1 bombers, and would keep the Stealth bomber only as long as Russia kept the SS-25. The nuclear deterrent would be a force of twelve Trident submarines, with six on alert at all times.

Again, the purpose here is not to save money, but in the process money would be saved. The savings would be $18 billion on the Milstar system, $3.1 billion on the Minuteman III missile and $5 billion on its planned upgrade, $5 billion on the B-52 bomber, $4.1 billion on the B-1 bomber, and $17.5 billion on the Trident submarine, for a total of $52.7 billion. The cost of keeping the Stealth production lines open is $1.8 billion and the cost of continued development is $1.6 billion, so if Russia eliminated the SS-25 and the United States eliminated the Stealth bomber, the savings for the United States would total $3.4 billion. The total saved from missiles and bombers would be $56.1 billion.[4]

The savings listed earlier for the Army were $4,329 million. For the Air Force, no savings were envisioned, but a possible increase if a new aircraft is needed to replace the C-17. For the Navy, the savings resulting from a reduction in carriers would be $2 billion per year, and a one-time savings of $5 billion if the plans for a new carrier are canceled and $295 million if the plans for a new Seawolf submarine are canceled. Thus, the total savings are $11.6 billion, although they would be offset somewhat if it becomes necessary to design and build a replacement for the C-17 and it if it becomes necessary to build more roll-on, roll-off ships.

So the grand total of savings would be $62.3 billion if the Russians did not eliminate the SS-25 and the United States kept the Stealth bomber to deal with it, and $67.7 billion if they did and the United States eliminated the Stealth. Notice also that this $67.7 billion savings is for one year only. Savings from many of the programs eliminated would continue each year for several years.

A Unilateral Decision

One of the greatest attractions of a deterrent/incentive strategy is that adopting it can be a unilateral decision. Once the United States adopted a deterrent/incentive strategy, Russia would have no incentive to maintain its present ICBM force. In fact, Russia has decided on the Topol-M, as we have seen, and this will provide an incentive to scrap the SS-25 and its fixed ICBMs. Both sides will have a large incentive to agree to reduce all their forces to the barest minimum.

What is probably even more important is that the stage would be set for more rapid movement toward some sort of government and political system for the entire planet and for humankind as a whole. The alternative is a world in which war continues to be accepted as part of life, as it has been accepted in the past. In such a world, individual wars may be avoided but war as such will be inevitable and a war fought with nuclear weapons will also be inevitable—sooner or later. When the inevitable nuclear war does occur, the loss of life and the devastation will be beyond human comprehension.

NOTES

1. For an analysis of espionage in the past, see Roger Hilsman, *Strategic Intelligence and National Decisions* (Glencoe, Ill.: Free Press, 1956; reprint, Westport, Conn.: Greenwood Press, 1981). See also Roger Hilsman, "Does the CIA Still Have a Role?" *Foreign Affairs* (September–October 1995): 104ff.

2. House Committee on Government Operations, *The Milstar Communications System: Comprehensive Reevaluation Needed*, 103rd Cong., 2d sess., 1994, H. Rep. 103-864. The second Milstar satellite was launched in November 1995.

3. As noted earlier, a guidance system for cruise missiles is also under development that would make them accurate to within a few feet. This makes a cruise missile armed with a conventional warhead a formidable weapon for certain kinds of nonnuclear, conventional warfare, but it is redundant for a cruise missile armed with a nuclear warhead.

4. For more detailed costs of these weapons, see the publications of the U.S. Nuclear Weapons Cost Study Project of the Brookings Institution: Stephen I. Schwartz, *Atomic Audit: What the U.S. Nuclear Arsenal Really Cost*. The study showed that the United States has spent $5.48 trillion on nuclear weapons programs, as compared to $13.2 trillion on other defense programs and $7.9 trillion on Social Security, the only other programs more expensive than nuclear weapons.

Index

ABOUT THE AUTHOR

ROGER HILSMAN has been Professor of Government and International Politics at Columbia University since 1964. Before that he was President Kennedy's Assistant Secretary of State for Intelligence and Research, then Assistant Secretary of State for Far Eastern Affairs. He is author of more than a dozen books on world politics and military strategy, including *The Cuban Missile Crisis: The Struggle over Policy* (Praeger, 1996).